Human Trafficking and
Slavery Law and Practice

Philippa Southwell
Solicitor Advocate, Birds Solicitors

Michelle Brewer
Barrister, Garden Court Chambers

Ben Douglas-Jones QC
5 Paper Buildings

Contributors

Paramjit Ahluwalia, *Barrister, Garden Court Chambers*
Christine Beddoe, *Independent Advisor on Human Trafficking*
Steven Bird, *Director, Birds Solicitors*
Lindsay Cundall, *Solicitor, Wilsons Solicitors*
Felicity Gerry QC, *Carmelite Chambers*
Bernie Gravett, *Director, Specialist Policing Consultancy Ltd*
Steve Harvey, *Independent Law Enforcement Advisor and Human Trafficking Expert*
Louise Hooper, *Barrister, Garden Court Chambers*
Gemma Loughran, *Barrister, Garden Court Chambers*
Shu Shin Lui, *Barrister, Garden Court Chambers*
Maya Sikand, *Barrister, Garden Court Chambers*
Eileen Walsh, *Helen Bamber Foundation*
Mary Westcott, *Barrister, Doughty Street Chambers*
Rachel Witkin, *Helen Bamber Foundation*

Bloomsbury Professional

Bloomsbury Professional

An imprint of Bloomsbury Publishing Plc

Bloomsbury Professional Ltd
41–43 Boltro Road
Haywards Heath
RH16 1BJ
UK

Bloomsbury Publishing Plc
50 Bedford Square
London
WC1B 3DP
UK

www.bloomsbury.com

BLOOMSBURY and the Diana logo are trademarks of

Bloomsbury Publishing Plc

British Library Cataloguing-in-Publication Data

A catalogue record for this book is available from the British Library.

ISBN:	PB:	978 1 78451 933 9
	Epdf:	978 1 78451 932 2
	Epub:	978 1 78451 934 6

Typeset by Phoenix Photosetting, Chatham, Kent
Printed and bound by CPI Group (UK) Ltd, Croydon, CRO 4YY

To find out more about our authors and books visit
www.bloomsburyprofessional.com. Here you will find extracts, author
information, details of forthcoming events and the option to sign up for our
newsletters

Foreword

Until recently, most would have thought that, even though it had taken well into the twentieth century to abolish slavery, it was a scourge and heinous crime that no longer afflicted us. However, slavery had gone underground. As was said in the introduction to the Report of the Review Panel (Frank Field MP, Baroness Butler-Sloss and Sir John Randall MP) in 2013:

> 'Slavery flourishes to this day, although unlike two hundred years ago, it is now invisible. It continues behind front doors, in factories and on farms, in brothels and on the streets of our towns and cities. To give just a few examples, across the country today there are Vietnamese boys forced to work on cannabis farms, Nigerian women held in domestic servitude, Polish and British men controlled by criminals as forced labourers, and British and Eastern European girls trafficked into prostitution. This, however, is by no means a comprehensive list of either the forms of modern slavery taking place in Britain or of the primary nationalities that are being exploited. Victims of modern slavery are hidden in plain sight, often trapped by forces more subtle than lock and key.'

From 2000 International Conventions were agreed to deal with this scourge. Although in 2009 the UK government established a National Referral Mechanism to determine whether those who claimed to have been trafficked had in fact been trafficked, it was left to the judiciary (utilising the flexible nature of the common law in a series of decisions in 2011–2013) and to the Crown Prosecution Service (through the exercise of their independent prosecutorial discretion) to develop a legal regime for England and Wales in which the international obligations as they successively developed were given effect in the domestic law of England and Wales. In 2015 the Modern Slavery Act was passed, putting the law on a statutory footing with the additional benefits of strengthening the protection given to the victims of modern slavery and of making it easier to prosecute those who engage in trafficking. The Act generally came into effect on 31 July 2015, but was not retrospective.

Thus, in a relatively short period of time, a non-statutory and then a statutory regime were created to deal with the complex issues to which modern slavery gives rise. What was plainly needed was a practitioner's book that clearly described and explained the legal regimes and gave practical guidance to lawyers which would enable them to identify whether a person was a victim of modern slavery and how best to protect that person.

This book gives a very comprehensive guide to the legal regimes and much practical assistance. For example Chapter 6 gives a very comprehensive account about what should happen on arrest at the police station and the matters that the lawyer should consider; this is reinforced by clear guidance on ethics in Chapter 16. Another example of the practical guidance given, drawn from the experience of the authors, is Chapter 15, which provides a clear summary of ways in which victims are trafficked and exploited.

I therefore warmly welcome this book and very much hope it will make a real contribution to the protection of victims of trafficking and modern slavery and to the prosecution of those who perpetrate this most heinous of crime.

John Thomas
Lord Thomas of Cwmgiedd
January 2018

Preface

Our intention with this book was to provide an accessible distillation of the law and issues relevant to practice surrounding human trafficking and modern slavery. We have worked together and against one another in many of the significant human trafficking cases of the last decade. Over the years, we have delivered training together. As such, our objective has been to draw on the different perspectives from which we look at the multifarious issues involved in human trafficking and modern slavery to create a balanced practitioner's text.

We hope the book will appeal to legal practitioners and other professionals who deal or might deal directly or indirectly with those affected by modern slavery and trafficking, including criminal, public, immigration, commercial and civil lawyers and accountants who may encounter people through dealing with supply chains, contract and employment issues, those who work in law enforcement, the judiciary, academics and students.

Law and practice involving modern slavery and human trafficking comprise a fast developing, wide range of topics traversing many different disciplines.

The book is intended to be a manageable guide and introduction to this field, drawing on the expertise and experience of various professionals in different disciplines. We hope that it will fill the current void in available texts for practitioners working in this arena.

We express our great thanks to all those who have contributed to this book, all of whom we have worked closely with in this field.

Philippa Southwell
Michelle Brewer
Ben Douglas-Jones QC
February 2018

Contents

Editors' biographies

Philippa Southwell is a consultant Solicitor Advocate and head of the human trafficking and modern slavery department at Birds Solicitors. She has been highly commended by The Law Society for her human trafficking and modern slavery work, who have described her as 'a fierce criminal defence solicitor, who specialises in defending and representing victims of human trafficking who have been prosecuted for criminal offences. She is the leading criminal solicitor in this field. She is passionate about this area and helping raise awareness of human trafficking.' Philippa drafted the Law Society practice note on human trafficking and modern slavery. She regularly delivers training to law enforcement and legal professionals on many areas of modern slavery law, including modern slavery regulatory compliance, both in the UK and internationally. Philippa has been involved in many of the significant and leading cases relating to victims of modern slavery and forced criminality, including representing five of the six applicants in the specially convened victims of trafficking court before the Lord Chief Justice.

Michelle Brewer specialises in judicial review, human rights and civil claims against public authorities. Michelle advises and acts for claimants, NGOs and other organisations. She has acted for victims of human trafficking at all levels including at the Supreme Court and the European Court of Human Rights. In Chambers Bar UK Guide, Michelle is described as, 'very highly regarded for her expertise on immigration detention and trafficking cases. With an established track record of being at the forefront of trafficking case law, she is renowned for her handling of cases where children and vulnerable witnesses are involved'. Michelle has been instructed as counsel in a series of test cases before the Lord Chief Justice to determine the scope and application of the non-punishment provisions in the regional and international instruments on trafficking as applied to victims exploited for the purpose of criminality.

Ben Douglas-Jones QC is a barrister at 5 Paper Buildings in London. He is also an attorney-at-law in Grenada, with rights of audience in the Eastern Caribbean Court of Appeal. He specialises in human rights, appeals, complex fraud, serious crime and regulatory law, including consumer and intellectual property. His human rights and appellate practice has seen him appear in all recent leading cases concerning victims of human trafficking and refugees who commit offences, including special court cases before the Lord Chief Justice. The Legal 500 describes him as having 'a fabulous acumen for seeing the point and exposing deficiencies in the other side's case.' Chambers and Partners describes him as 'a great barrister'. Ben co-wrote the Crown Prosecution

Service Guidance on charging and prosecuting victims of human trafficking and the Law Society Guidance on refugee defences. He provides domestic and international training on human trafficking and modern slavery in the context of practitioner and regulatory compliance training.

Contributors' biographies

Paramjit Ahluwalia is a criminal defence barrister (called 2002, BA Oxon) based at Garden Court Chambers, with particular expertise in immigration crime, trafficking and exploitation offences and a specialism in first instance and appellate work concerning section 45 Modern Slavery Act 2015 defences. Paramjit is sole and lead junior in first instance cases concerning human trafficking and immigration crime. In 2016, she was selected for OSCE simulation in Vincenza Italy, assisted ATMG in 'Class Acts' publication and was a speaker at ECPAT conference on defences available to children.

Christine Beddoe has spent 25 years working against the trafficking and the sexual abuse of children. Christine has worked in UK, Australia, Thailand, Cambodia, India, Vietnam, Kenya, Sri Lanka, Nepal and more. Christine is now a freelance consultant and adviser, but was Chief Executive of ECPAT UK for eight years until 2012, and prior to that worked with ECPAT (End Child Prostitution, Pornography and Trafficking) in South East Asia and Australia since 1994. Christine has made many media appearances, has written dozens of reports, book chapters and articles and continues to do research on child trafficking and child exploitation. Her post-graduate research was conducted in Sri Lanka in 1993 on the sexual exploitation of boys and in 2004 she was awarded a Winston Churchill Fellowship for applied research on advocacy campaigns for the protection of children.

Steven Bird founded Birds Solicitors in October 2000. He has been involved in criminal defence work since 1988 and qualified as a solicitor in 1990. He specialises in serious criminal cases including serious fraud, murder and other serious offences of violence, serious sexual offences, large drug cases and confiscation proceedings. Steven is the current Chairman of the Criminal Appeal Lawyers Association and has a busy appellate practice both in the Court of Appeal and by way of applications to the Criminal Cases Review Commission. He represents previous victims of miscarriages of justice in claiming compensation from the Home Office. He is rated as a star individual in the Chambers and Partners directory and a leading individual in the Legal 500. Steven is the co-author of the 'Police Station Advisers Index', first published in September 1995, and contributed chapters to the second edition of *Taylor on Criminal Appeals* dealing with the funding regime for appellate work. He has also contributed the chapter on Restraint and Confiscation to the *Drugs Offences Handbook*, also published by Bloomsbury. He co-wrote the article 'Does the new Slavery Defence Offer Victims any Greater Protection' in *Archbold Review* (9 November 2015, issue 9).

Lindsay Cundall has worked as an Immigration and Asylum Accredited caseworker for the last eight years. She regularly attends Immigration Removal Centres to advise and assist detainees. Her practice is focused on assisting detained clients through legal aid representation, although she also assists many non-detained clients. She has conduct of a complex caseload of claims involving asylum, human rights, criminal deportation, detention and bail, victims of human trafficking/modern slavery, nationality law, claims based on EU treaty rights and judicial reviews. She has worked with Wilson Solicitors LLP since June 2013 and her training was based in the immigration and public law departments. Lindsay previously worked at the Refugee and Migrant Justice, Brighton Housing Trust and the UNHCR, Ecuador. Lindsay studied Hispanic Studies and Politics at the University of Sheffield, before completing her LLB in Law alongside her work commitments.

Felicity Gerry QC works internationally. She is admitted in England and Wales and Australia and has had ad hoc admission in Hong Kong and Gibraltar. She specialises in cases involving vulnerable people. She assisted in the reprieve from execution of Mary Jane Veloso, who was sentenced to death for drug trafficking in Indonesia, but was reprieved when she raised her status as a human trafficking victim. Felicity is also a senior lecturer and member of the parameterise research group at Charles Darwin University where her research specialises in using technology to combat human trafficking. As an Adjunct Fellow at the University of Western Sydney Felicity has lectured on sexual offending, terrorism and cybercrime and has provided training to judges from Bangladesh on similar topics. She is widely published on issues relating to women and the law, including sexual offending, human trafficking, vulnerability in justice systems and women in prison. She gave evidence to the Parliamentary Inquiry into whether Australia should have a Modern Slavery Act and provided training on Modern Slavery at Westminster for the Commonwealth Parliamentary Group.

Bernie Gravett is a retired Police Superintendent from the Metropolitan Police. He completed 31 years in the police service in April 2011. He is a Senior EU Expert in combating transnational organised crime, child sexual exploitation and trafficking in human beings. Bernie is an expert on the Europol AWF Intelligence system and an accredited Eurojust expert on Joint Investigation Teams and Mutual Legal Assistance in criminal investigations. Bernie created and led 'Operation Golf', an investigation into Romanian Roma Organised Crime Networks. This investigation targeted one of the largest human trafficking rings in Europe. The investigation was a Joint Investigation Team under EU law and is the first such operation in Europe. The investigation achieved the first conviction in the UK for the trafficking of a child for criminal exploitation and also for 'internal' trafficking within the UK for criminal exploitation. He has developed training for law enforcement that has been delivered around the world.

Steve Harvey served as a UK police officer for 25 years, including five years with the National Criminal Intelligence Service, supporting the UK's first investigations into the trafficking of human beings and smuggling of migrants. In 2003 Steve joined EUROPOL in The Hague, coordinating EU cross border THB investigations and was Head of Unit for Organised Crime in South East Europe. He was the Europol lead in the EU's first THB Joint Investigation Team, involving Romania and the UK, and between 2007 and 2011 was one of the European Commission's Group of Experts on THB. Since 2013 Steve has worked for ICMPD in Albania, Azerbaijan, Bosnia Herzegovina, Moldova, Pakistan and Turkey, with IOM in the Pacific region and in Africa and Mongolia with the US State Department. In December 2017 Steve was selected as the Lead Expert in an initiative to implement regional law enforcement cooperation (RELEC) in Afghanistan, Bangladesh, Iran, Iraq, Pakistan and Turkey.

Louise Hooper is a barrister at Garden Court Chambers and a founder member of the Anti-Trafficking Legal Project. She has extensive experience of challenging NRM decisions and bringing damages claims resulting from detention and breaches of Article 4 ECHR. She is a recognised expert in gender and violence against women. She frequently provides training on trafficking and gender based violence to judges, prosecutors, police, immigration officers, NGOs and lawyers, both in the UK and internationally on behalf of professional organisations including the Council of Europe and UNHCR. She co-authored the International Commission of Jurists' Practitioner Guide No 11 'Refugee Claims Based on Sexual Orientation and Gender Identity' and is a regular contributor to *Macdonald's Immigration Law and Practice*, most recently contributing to the 'Trafficking in Human Beings' chapter of the 9th edition.

Gemma Loughran was called to the Bar in 2008 and practises in immigration, asylum, human rights, trafficking and public law at Garden Court Chambers. She regularly represents victims of trafficking in the Asylum and Immigration Chamber of both the First and Upper-tier Tribunal. Gemma also appears in the High Court in a broad range of judicial review matters, including challenges to trafficking decisions under the National Referral Mechanism and other immigration-related public law challenges. Gemma is recommended in the Legal 500 at tier 4 and ranked in Chambers and Partners as 'Band 4'. She was the senior contributing author of the 'Trafficking in Human Beings' chapter in *Macdonald's Immigration Law and Practice*, First Supplement to the 9th edition and is one of the joint co-ordinators of the Anti-Trafficking Legal Project (AtLep).

Shu Shin Luh is a barrister at Garden Court Chambers. Her practice has a strong human rights and anti-discrimination focus and spans both the public and private law areas. She is well known for her expertise in the area of anti-trafficking and modern slavery at both the domestic and international level. She regularly acts for individuals in public law challenges to the decisions relating to the identification and provision of support to victims of trafficking and modern slavery as well as in private law claims for compensation against public authorities, companies and traffickers. She has represented NGOs in public interest litigation including in respect of the nature and scope of the state's obligation to protect victims of trafficking (*Chowdury v Greece* [2017] ECHR 300), and access to legal aid (*ATLEU v Lord Chancellor*). She has given written and oral evidence before the All-Party Parliamentary Group on Human Trafficking and regularly provides legal policy advice relating to modern slavery by leading NGOs in the UK, at the EU level and in Asia. Shu Shin is part of the lawyers' network run by the EU's Group of Experts against Trafficking in Human Beings.

Maya Sikand is a civil liberties and human rights barrister at Garden Court Chambers specialising in public law as well as private law damages claims against public bodies. Her specialist areas include inquests, public inquiries, criminal justice related judicial reviews; prisoners' rights; human rights and tortious damages claims against the police and prisons; statutory compensation claims via the Criminal Injuries Compensation Authority and the Miscarriage of Justice Application Scheme. She also has an appellate only criminal practice which focuses on trafficked victims and the sentencing of women, and children and young people. She is a contributing editor of the seminal criminal textbook *Archbold Criminal Pleading, Evidence & Practice* (Sweet & Maxwell); a previous contributing editor of *Blackstone's Criminal Practice* (OUP); General Editor of the *Blackstone's Guide to the Criminal Justice and Immigration Act 2008* (OUP, 2009) and author of *ASBOs: A Practitioner's Guide to Defending Anti-social Behaviour Orders* (LAG, 2006).

Dr Eileen Walsh is a clinical psychologist. She is currently Head of Therapy Services at the Helen Bamber Foundation. She has specialised in working with people with a history of chronic trauma, including victims of trafficking and modern slavery. She has over 10 years' experience of providing psychological treatment, working at specialist PTSD clinics in the NHS. She has extensive experience of preparing independent psychological medico-legal reports for the court, and has a strong interest in the contribution of psychological research to legal processes.

Mary Westcott (called 2007) is a respected extradition specialist with a background in criminal and public international law. She now works almost exclusively defending extradition requests as part of Doughty Street's extradition team. She has successfully represented many particularly vulnerable clients, such as victims of trafficking, domestic violence and/or those suffering from post-traumatic stress disorder. She has acted alone in numerous Divisional Court test cases (eg *Tyza v Poland* [2015] 1017 (Admin) and *A v Hungary* [2013] EWHC 3132 (Admin)) and been Junior Counsel in the Supreme Court both for the individual defending extradition (*Poland v Zakrzewski* [2013] 1 WLR 324) and for the Issuing Judicial Authority (*Goluchowski & Sas v Poland* [2016] 1 WLR 2665). Mary also advises on related issues such as 'import' extradition from other jurisdictions and the preparation of extradition requests to countries without a functioning bi-lateral extradition treaty (eg Iraq and Pakistan).

Rachel Witkin is the Head of Counter-Trafficking at the Helen Bamber Foundation, which provides a long-term model of integrated care for survivors of human rights violations including modern slavery. She has worked in a front-line capacity with victims of trafficking who are facing legal procedures for organisations including the Helen Bamber Foundation, Amnesty International UK, the British Refugee Council and human rights law firm Winstanley-Burgess. Publications include: 'Get it Right: How Home Office Decision Making Fails Refugees' (AIUK, 2004), 'Trafficking in Human Beings amounting to Torture and other forms of Ill-Treatment' (OSCE/HBF 2013) and Healthcare as a Human Rights Issue (Transcript Verlag 2017). She is a contributing author for the UK Trafficking Survivor Care Standards (Human Trafficking Foundation 2015) and has a keen interest in promoting best practice methods for professionals from all fields who come into contact with modern slavery.

Table of Statutes

Table of Statutory Instruments

Table of European Legislation

[All references are to paragraph number]

Table of Cases

1 Legal policy and framework on trafficking

Introduction

1.1

Lord Judge CJ said of trafficking:

> 'this vile trade in people has different manifestations. Women and children, usually girls, are trafficked into prostitution: others, usually teenage boys, but sometimes young adults, are trafficked into cannabis farming: yet others are trafficked to commit a wide range of further offences. Sometimes they are trafficked into this country from the other side of the world: sometimes they enter into this country unlawfully and are trafficked after their arrival: sometimes they are trafficked within the towns or cities in this country where they live. Whether trafficked from home or overseas, they are all victims of crime. That is how they must be treated'[1].

It is a common misconception that to be a victim of trafficking there must be a crossing of national borders. A person may be trafficked within his or her own country; there need be no border crossing. On the other hand, smuggling migrants across borders is not trafficking unless the purpose of doing so is exploitation rather than just obtaining a financial or other benefit[2].

The definition of human trafficking

General

1.2

When determining whether someone is a victim of human trafficking, the UK government has mandated through policy that the regional and international definition of a victim of trafficking is to be applied. This definition has been applied by the Criminal Court of Appeal in the key cases concerning victims

---

1   *R v L* [2013] EWCA Crim 991, [2014] 1 All ER 113.
2   *R (on the application of AA (Iraq)) v Secretary of State for the Home Department* [2012] EWCA Civ 23, (2012) Times, 5 March.

of trafficking[3]. The definition distinguishes between adult and child victims of trafficking, in recognition of the particular vulnerability of children to the crime of human trafficking[4].

1.3

The two key regional instruments are:

(i)   the Council of Europe Convention on Action against Trafficking in Human Beings (referred to throughout this work as 'ECAT'), which was signed on 23 March 2008 and ratified on 17 December 2008 by the UK; and

(ii)   Directive 2011/36/EU of the European Parliament and of the Council of 5 April 2011 on preventing and combating trafficking in human beings and protecting its victims, replacing Council Framework Decision 2002/629/JHA ('the EU Trafficking Directive')[5].

ECAT, Article 4, provides the following definitions:

'Article 4 Definitions

For the purposes of this Convention:

a   "Trafficking in human beings" shall mean the recruitment, transportation, transfer, harbouring or receipt of persons, by means of the threat or use of force or other forms of coercion, of abduction, of fraud, of deception, of the abuse of power or of a position of vulnerability or of the giving or receiving of payments or benefits to achieve the consent of a person having control over another person, for the purpose of exploitation. Exploitation shall include, at a minimum, the exploitation of the prostitution of others or other forms of sexual exploitation, forced labour or services, slavery or practices similar to slavery, servitude or the removal of organs;

---

3   *R v L* [2013] EWCA Crim 991, [2014] 1 All ER 113; *R v Josepth* [2017] EWCA Crim 36, [2017] 1 WLR 3153.

4   Children are defined as those under the age of 18 years' old: Palermo Protocol, Art 3(d); ECAT, Art 4(d); EU Trafficking Directive, Art 2(6). The EU Trafficking Directive refers in the preamble at [8], [12], [19], [22], [23], [24], [25] and in Arts 2, 13, 14, 15 and 16 to the special status of child victims, in particular where the children are separated children. As noted by Anne T Gallagher in *The International Law of Human Trafficking* (Cambridge University Press, 2010) p 324: 'An important source of vulnerability for children lies in their lack of full agency – in fact and under law. A lack of agency is often made worse by the absence of a parent or legal guardian who is able to act in the child's best interests. Such absence is typical: child victims of trafficking are generally "unaccompanied", with deliberate separation from parents or guardians being a strategy to facilitate exploitation. In some cases, parents or other authority figures are complicit in the trafficking.'

5   The UK opted in to the Directive in July 2011. This was accepted by the European Commission in October 2011. The transposition date was 6 April 2013. The Directive is stated 'to build on the existing international instruments designed to combat human trafficking, in particular the Council of Europe Convention on Action against Trafficking in Human Beings to which the UK is a signatory'.

b   The consent of a victim of "trafficking in human beings" to the intended exploitation set forth in subparagraph (a) of this article shall be irrelevant where any of the means set forth in subparagraph (a) have been used;

c   The recruitment, transportation, transfer, harbouring or receipt of a child for the purpose of exploitation shall be considered "trafficking in human beings" even if this does not involve any of the means set forth in subparagraph (a) of this article;

d   "Child" shall mean any person under eighteen years of age;

e   "Victim" shall mean any natural person who is subject to trafficking in human beings as defined in this article'.

The three elements of trafficking

1.4

The definition of trafficking has three constituent elements:

(i)   the act (what is done): recruitment, transportation, transfer, harbouring or receipt of persons;

(ii)   the means (how it is done): threat or use of force, coercion, abduction, fraud, deception, abuse of power or vulnerability, or giving or receiving payments or benefits to a person to achieve the consent of another person with control of the victim;

(iii)   the purpose (why it is done): for the purpose of exploitation, which includes exploiting the prostitution of others, sexual exploitation, forced labour or services, including slavery or practices similar to slavery, the exploitation of criminal activities, or the removal of organs.

1.5

When applying the terms of the definition to a particular case, a gender sensitive[6], human rights, child rights and labour rights perspective is to be adopted[7]. An adult would need to establish that all three components of the definition are present together, but for a child it is sufficient to establish that an act was undertaken for the purpose of exploitation, in order to meet the requirements of the definition: a child does not need to satisfy the 'means' element of the definition[8]. The consent of a victim to exploitation is always irrelevant where any of the means have been established[9]. An important principle in the trafficking definition is

---

6   See EU Trafficking Directive, Art 1 and *Joint UN Commentary on the EU Directive – A Human Rights-Based Approach* (2011) p 30.

7   *Joint UN Commentary on the EU Directive – A Human Rights-Based Approach* (2011).

8   EU Trafficking Directive, Art 2(5); ECAT, Art 4(c).

9   ECAT, Art 4(b); EU Trafficking Directive, Art 2(4).

that a child can never consent to his own exploitation[10]. A person who is or has been the subject of trafficking, as defined, has the status of being a victim of trafficking. There is no further requirement that the person should continue to be in a situation of trafficking, or subject to the influence of traffickers, or in need of assistance or protection under the trafficking convention in order to retain that status. Home Office policy that had distinguished between 'victims of trafficking' and 'historical victims' has been held to be unlawful[11].

First element of the trafficking definition: the act

1.6

The acts provided for in the definition are intended to bring within the definition of human trafficking the conduct not just of recruiters, brokers and transporters but also owners and managers, supervisors, and controllers of any place of exploitation such as a brothel, farm, boat, factory, medical facility, or household.

1.7

Recruitment is to be understood in a broad sense, meaning any activity leading from the commitment or engagement of another individual to his or her exploitation. It is not confined to the use of certain means. The definition's reference to recruitment covers recruitment by whatever method (oral, through the press or via the internet). It would include recruitment through a recruitment agency or an intermediary[12].

1.8

Transportation is also a general term; no particular means or kinds of transportation are specified. The act of transporting someone from one place to another is sufficient to constitute this element[13]. It is not necessary for the victim to have crossed any borders[14], nor is it necessary for the victim to be present illegally in a state's territory[15].

---

10 EU Trafficking Directive, Art 2(4) and 2(5); ECAT, Art 4(b) and (c).

11 *R (on the application of Atamewan) v Secretary of State for the Home Department* [2013] EWHC 2727 (Admin), [2014] 1 WLR 1959.

12 CETS, *Explanatory Report to the Council of Europe Convention on Action against Trafficking in Human Beings*, para 79; Council of Europe and United Nations, *Trafficking in Organs, Tissues and Cells and Trafficking in Human Beings for the Purpose of the Removal of Organs* (2009). The Office of the Special Representative and Co-ordinator for Combating Trafficking in Human Beings, in its report *Unprotected Work, Invisible Exploitation: Trafficking for the Purpose of Domestic Servitude* at p 17 recognised in its typology of domestic servitude cases that most of the trafficked migrant workers were recruited via placement agencies.

13 Council of Europe and United Nations, *Trafficking in Organs, Tissues and Cells and Trafficking in Human Beings for the Purpose of the Removal of Organs* (2009); ECAT, Art 2; *Explanatory Report to the Council of Europe Convention on Action against Trafficking in Human Beings*, para 80.

14 ECAT, Art 2: 'This convention shall apply to all forms of trafficking in human beings, whether national or transnational'.

15 *Explanatory Report to the Council of Europe Convention on Action against Trafficking in Human Beings*, para 80.

1.9

Transfer includes any kind of handing over or transmission of one person to another. This is particularly important in certain cultural environments where control over individuals (usually family members) may be handed over to other persons. As the term and scope of this element is broad, the explicit or implied offering of a person for transfer is sufficient; the offer does not have to be accepted for this component of the definition to be satisfied[16].

1.10

Harbouring means accommodating or housing persons in whatever way, whether during their journey to their final destination or at the place of exploitation[17].

1.11

Receipt of persons is not limited to receiving the persons at the place of exploitation, but includes meeting victims at agreed places on their journey to give them further information or instructions as to where to go or what to do[18].

Second element of the trafficking definition: the means

1.12

Use this.

Where any of the means referred to in the definition have been used to secure the consent of a victim, this consent is deemed irrelevant[19]. The definition may be satisfied if the 'means' element is used to accomplish the 'act' or the exploitation[20]. Children (ie those under the age of 18 years old at the time of trafficking) do not have to meet this 'means' requirement.

1.13

Coercion can be physical or psychological. The Home Office guidance notes that physical coercion refers to the threat or use of force against the victims of trafficking or against their family members, but it may also entail more subtle measures of control such as withholding travel or immigration documents[21]. The Home Office guidance lists the following as examples of psychological coercion: blackmail; ritual oaths; forcing someone to pay an excessive amount of money for substandard accommodation; making significant deductions from an individual's 'salary'; threats of rejection from, or disapproval by a peer group

---

16 Council of Europe and United Nations, *Trafficking in Organs, Tissues and Cells and Trafficking in Human Beings for the Purpose of the Removal of Organs* (2009); AT Gallagher, *The International Law of Human Trafficking* (Cambridge University Press, 2010) p 30.

17 Ibid.

18 Ibid.

19 ECAT, Art 4(b); EU Trafficking Directive, Art 1(4).

20 AT Gallagher, *The International Law of Human Trafficking* (Cambridge University Press, 2010) p 45.

21 Home Office, *Victims of modern slavery – Competent Authority guidance* (21 March 2016) p 32.

or family or anger or displeasure from the person considered by the victim to be his or her partner; grooming and 'Stockholm syndrome where, due to unequal power, victims create a false emotional or psychological attachment to their controller'[22]. It has been argued that severe economic pressures may constitute psychological coercion[23]. In the context of domestic servitude, the European Court of Human Rights has emphasised that 'a complex set of dynamics, involving both overt and more subtle forms of coercion, to force compliance' may be in play and that investigating such conduct 'requires an understanding of the many subtle ways an individual can fall under the control of another'[24]. These can include retention of the victim's passport and wages, manipulation of his or her fears arising from unlawful or insecure immigration status, and implicit or explicit threats of denunciation to the police and deportation[25]. Debt bondage also falls within this means element as a form of 'economic coercion' and is a common 'means' and exploitative practice prevalent in labour trafficking in the UK and for forced criminality[26]. Debt bondage is when a person's labour is demanded as a means of repayment for a loan and the value of the labour is not reasonably applied toward the debt or the debt is otherwise continuously inflated[27]. It can occur where an excessive amount is charged for substandard accommodation, or where significant deductions are made from an individual's 'salary'. Even where a set payment schedule is agreed to and repaid by the victim, the imposition of such a debt is illegal[28]. Evidence shows that debt bondage in itself can be strong enough to ensure that people comply with instructions from traffickers without being physically attacked or confined[29].

1.14

Deception and fraud are examples of less direct means and will generally relate to the nature of the promised work or service and the conditions under which

---

22 Home Office, *Victims of modern slavery – Competent Authority guidance* (21 March 2016) p 33.
23 LA Malone, 'Economic Hardship as Coercion Under the Protocol on International Trafficking in Persons by Organised Crime Elements' (2001) 25 *Fordham International Law Journal* 54 at 55.
24 *CN v United Kingdom* (2013) 56 EHRR 24, para 80.
25 *CN v United Kingdom* (2013) 56 EHRR 24, para 80; *CN and V v France* App No 67724/09 (11 October 2012), para 92 and *Siliadin v France* App No 73316/01 (26 October 2005), para 118. Forms of coercion used in cases of trafficked domestic workers are identified by the Office of the Special Representative and Co-ordinator for Combating Trafficking in Human Beings in *Trafficking in Human Beings Amounting to Torture and other Forms of Ill-treatment* (2013) at p 22.
26 *Trafficking for Forced Labour in the UK* (Anti-Slavery International, 2006).
27 Working under a debt bond is a 'slavery-like practice': see Supplementary Convention on the Abolition of Slavery, the Slave Trade and Practices Similar to Slavery 1956, Art 1(a).
28 Office of the Special Representative and Co-ordinator for Combating Trafficking in Human Beings, *Trafficking in Human Beings Amounting to Torture and other Forms of Ill-treatment* (2013) p 54. Debt bondage is a strong indicator of forced labour, as well as being a 'means' to bring victims into an exploitative situation. The OSCE Resource *Police Training Guide: Trafficking in Human Beings*, Publication Series Vol 12, at 66, states in respect of forced labour: 'When there is a disparity of income and the labour conditions between the country of origin of the potential victim and the country of destination where they are working. Victims of human trafficking cannot consent to exploitation and they must be treated in the same manner as if they were nationals of the State in which they are working'.
29 Office of the Special Representative and Co-ordinator for Combating Trafficking in Human Beings, *Trafficking in Human Beings Amounting to Torture and other Forms of Ill-treatment* (2013) p 55.

an individual is to undertake or perform a service[30]. For example, an individual may be recruited to work in the sex industry but on the basis of false, inaccurate or misleading information about the conditions of her work[31].

1.15

Abuse of power or of a position of vulnerability. The abuse of a position of vulnerability

> 'may be of any kind, whether physical, psychological, emotional, family-related, social or economic. The situation might, for example, involve insecurity or illegality of the victim's immigration status, economic dependence or fragile health. In short, the situation can be any state of hardship in which a human being is impelled to accept being exploited. Persons abusing such a situation flagrantly infringe human rights and violate human dignity and integrity, which no one can validly renounce'[32].

1.16

The EU Trafficking Directive defines a position of vulnerability as 'a situation in which the person concerned has no real or acceptable alternative but to submit to the abuse involved.' The various indicators of abuse of power or a position of vulnerability identified by international bodies[33] and the European Court of Human Rights[34] focus on the person's precarious financial, psychological, and social situation, illegal or precarious immigration status and on linguistic, physical, and social isolation of the victim[35]. A victim's poverty in his or her country of origin may constitute personal circumstances of which a trafficker may take advantage to secure the victim's consent to being exploited in the UK[36]. In the Netherlands the Supreme Court gave guidance on the concept of 'abuse of a vulnerable position', concerning six irregular migrants who, desperate for work and afraid of being discovered by authorities, approached a Chinese

---

30 The UN Office on Drugs and Crime (UNODC), *Abuse of a position of vulnerability and other 'means' within the definition of trafficking in persons* (2013) at 2.1.2.

31 Home Office, *Victims of modern slavery – Competent Authority guidance* (21 March 2016) p 33.

32 *Explanatory Report to the Council of Europe Convention on Action against Trafficking in Human Beings*, para 83.

33 For example International Labour Office, *Operational Indicators of Trafficking in Human Beings* (September 2009).

34 *Siliadin v France* (2006) 43 EHRR 16, paras 118–129.

35 UNODC, *Model Law against Trafficking in Persons*, released in 2009, suggests that a focus on the state of mind of the perpetrator, rather than that of the victim, could be more protective of the victims (see discussion in Anne T Gallagher, *The International Law of Human Trafficking* at p 33). Further guidance on this term is found in the UNODC Issue Paper, *Abuse of a position of vulnerability and other 'means' within the definition of trafficking in persons* (2013), as drafted by Dr Anne Gallagher.

36 *R v Khan* [2010] EWCA Crim 2880, [2011] Crim LR 336, para 18; EU Trafficking Directive, Art 2(2). The EU Trafficking Directive generally reproduces the definition of trafficking set out in the Palermo Protocol. It adopts the language of the Trafficking in Persons Protocol Interpretative note in defining 'position of vulnerability' as 'a situation in which the person concerned has no real or acceptable alternative but to submit to the abuse involved' (Art 2(2)). However, it is important to note a significant difference. Whereas the Interpretative Note refers to 'real and acceptable alternative', and appears to require that both elements be satisfied, the EU Trafficking Directive requires only that the alternative be 'real' or 'acceptable'.

restaurant owner for work. They were provided with accommodation and work that paid well below the minimum wage. The Supreme Court disagreed with the lower courts that the perpetrator must 'intentionally abuse' the vulnerable position of the victims. The Court held that 'conditional intent' is sufficient: it was enough that the perpetrator was aware of the state of affairs that must be assumed to give rise to power or a vulnerable position[37].

1.17

The giving or receiving of payments or benefits to achieve the consent of a person having control over another person: This term is opaque and there is little guidance on its meaning. It may extend beyond the situation in which legal control is exercised by one individual over another (for example, a parent over a child) to include de facto control (such as that which may be exercised by an employer over an employee). Presumably it is intended to bring within the definition practices such as payments made to parents in the course of child trafficking, but as the means element is redundant in child cases, the scope of this element remains unclear.

Third element of the trafficking definition: for the purpose of exploitation

1.18

This ingredient of the definition does not require that the intended exploitation actually takes place; a situation of trafficking can arise in the case of an adult victim subjected to an act by one of the means for the specified purpose of exploitation[38] and for a child victim that he was subjected to an act for the purpose of exploitation. The intention to exploit can be that of any of the individuals involved in either the act or the means, so it may be that of a final exploiter (eg the brothel owner or factory manager) or it may be that of a recruiter or a broker[39]. The trafficking instruments do not define exploitation. Instead they provide an open-ended list, which includes as a minimum the following:

(i) *forced labour or services, slavery or servitude*: these practices are discussed in Chapter 4[40];

---

37 Supreme Court, 27 October 2009, LJN: B17099408. See also L van Krimpen, 'The interpretation and implementation of labour exploitation in Dutch Case Law' in C Rijken (ed), *Combating Trafficking in Human Beings for Labour Exploitation* (WLP, 2011) p 498.

38 *Explanatory Report to the Council of Europe Convention on Action against Trafficking in Human Beings*, para 87.

39 Anne T Gallagher, *The International Law of Human Trafficking* (Cambridge University Press, 2010) p 33.

40 The terms 'forced labour', 'slavery' and 'servitude' should be interpreted consistently with other international instruments. This assumption is supported by the saving clauses in the Palermo Protocol (Art 14) and the ECAT (Art 40) which affirm their consistency with existing rights, obligations and responsibilities under international law and, in the case of ECAT, its consistency with the Palermo Protocol (Art 39).

(ii) *exploitation of the prostitution of others*: this has been interpreted to cover any acts to obtain profit from prostitution, such as pimping[41] and 'the unlawful obtaining of financial or other material benefit from the prostitution of another person'[42];

(iii) *other forms of sexual exploitation*: this term has been defined as 'any actual or attempted abuse of a position of vulnerability, differential power or trust, for sexual purposes, including but not limited to, profiting monetarily, socially or politically from the sexual exploitation of another'[43]. Forced, child and servile marriages have been identified as forms of sexual exploitation[44]. The inclusion of servile marriage as a form of sexual exploitation shows that receiving or intending to receive sexual gratification from an individual constitutes such exploitation where the individual's consent is ineffective because one of the means contained in the trafficking definition has been used;

(iv) *practices similar to slavery*: this term is adopted from the 1956 Supplementary Convention on the Abolition of Slavery, the Slave Trade and Institutions and Practices similar to Slavery. This Convention defined the following as practices similar to slavery: debt bondage, serfdom, servile or forced marriage[45] and exploitation of children[46];

(v) *exploitation for criminal activities:* this should be understood as the exploitation of a person to commit, inter alia, pick-pocketing, shop-lifting, drug trafficking and other similar activities which are subject to penalties and imply financial gain[47]. The Court of Appeal has included within these offences both drug production[48] and controlling prostitution for gain[49].

---

41 Working Group on Trafficking in Persons, 'Analysis of Key Concepts of the Trafficking in Persons Protocol' (9 December 2009) CTOC/COP/WG.4/2010/2, paras 9–12.

42 UNODC, *Model Law against Trafficking in Persons*, p 13.

43 UN Secretary-General's Bulletin, 'Special Measures for Protection from Sexual Exploitation and Sexual Abuse,' UN Doc ST/SGB/2003/13, 9 October 2003. For further discussion see Anne T Gallagher, *The International Law of Human Trafficking* at p 39.

44 Forum on Marriage and the Rights of Women and Girls, *Early Marriage: Sexual Exploitation and the Human Rights of Girls* (2001); ECPAT UK, *Stolen Futures: Trafficking for Forced Child Marriage in the UK* (2009) p 20.

45 See *Joint UN Commentary on the EU Directive – A Human Rights-Based Approach* (2011) p 104. Forced marriage is defined in the UK in the Family Law Act 1996, as amended by the Forced Marriage Act 2007, as: 'A person ("A") is forced into a marriage if another person ("B") forces A to enter into a marriage (whether with B or another person) without A's free and full consent. It does not matter whether the conduct of B which forces A to enter into the marriage is directed against A, B or another person.' Force is defined to include coercion by threats or other psychological means. These marriages, as well as being forms of sexual exploitation, are also recognised as forms of domestic servitude: ECPAT UK, *Stolen Futures: Trafficking for Forced Child Marriage in the UK* (2009) p 20 and OSCE, *Unprotected Work, Invisible Exploitation: Trafficking for the Purpose of Domestic Servitude*, p 44.

46 This was included in the EU Trafficking Directive, preamble (11) and Art 2(3).

47 'Any institution or practice whereby a child or young person under the age of 18 years, is delivered by either or both of his natural parents, or by his guardian, to another person, whether for reward or not, with a view to the exploitation of the child or young person or of his labour': Supplementary Convention on the Abolition of Slavery, the Slave Trade and Institutions and Practices similar to Slavery 1956, Art 1(d).

48 *R v L* [2013] EWCA Crim 991, [2014] 1 All ER 113.

49 *R v LM* [2010] EWCA Crim 2327, [2011] 1 Cr App Rep 135.

Exploitation of children

1.19

The European Commission has stated that child exploitation includes:

- procuring or offering a child for illicit or criminal activities (including the trafficking or production of drugs and begging);

- using children in armed conflict;

- using children for work that by its nature or the circumstances in which it is carried out is likely to harm the health and safety of children;

- the employment or use of a child who has not yet reached the applicable working age;

- other forms of exploitation; and illegal adoption[50].

1.20

The UN Convention on the Rights of the Child and its optional protocol provide a comprehensive framework for the protection of the rights and dignity of children. It should be considered, in its entirety, as a tool for understanding and responding to the trafficking and related exploitation of children. Whilst the Convention on the Rights of the Child does not make express reference to child trafficking, the Committee on the Rights of the Child has regularly raised and pronounced on trafficking-related issues in its concluding observations, and has found trafficking and child prostitution to directly implicate Arts 34 and 35[51]. The optional protocol refers to trafficking in its preamble, and Art 2 of the optional protocol defines the sale of children sufficiently broadly to encompass most child trafficking situations.

Definition of victims of slavery, servitude and forced or compulsory labour

1.21

There is now provision in the Competent Authority Guidance[52] for victims of slavery, servitude and forced or compulsory labour, where the victims have not been trafficked.

---

50 European Commission – DG Justice, Freedom and Security (JLS), *Recommendations on Identification and Referral to Services of Victims of Trafficking in Human Beings* (Brussels, 2007) p 5. This echoes the definitions found in the ILO's International Programme on the Elimination of Child Labour (IPEC) in its operations, which incorporated the ILO Convention to Eliminate the Worst Forms of Child Labour (June 1999) (ILO Convention No. 182), defining (in Art 3) the worst forms of child labour to be prohibited as illustrations of exploitation of children in the context of child trafficking. Articles 32 and 33 of the UN Convention on the Rights of the Child 1989 also recognise this form of child exploitation.

51 For further discussion see AT Gallagher, *The International Law of Human Trafficking* (Cambridge University Press, 2010) p 66.

52 Home Office, *Victims of modern slavery – Competent Authority guidance* (21 March 2016) p 39.

Overview of definition

1.22

The definition of modern slavery as forced or compulsory labour has two constituent elements:

(i)   means: threat of a penalty, eg threat or use of force, coercion, abduction, fraud, deception, abuse of power or vulnerability;

(ii)   service: as a result of the means an individual provides a service for benefit, eg begging, sexual services, manual labour or domestic service.

Servitude is an aggravated form of forced or compulsory labour.

The concept of ownership is what makes slavery distinct. It is a form of servitude with the additional concept of ownership[53].

The 'means' element of the definition of modern slavery

1.23

Coercion. The Competent Authority guidance gives the same examples of psychological coercion as are given for trafficking, but in addition includes 'anger or displeasure from the person considered by the victim to be his or her partner'[54].

1.24

Threat of a penalty. The Competent Authority guidance acknowledges that 'penalty' may go as far as physical violence or restraint, but it can also cover subtler forms, of a psychological nature, such as threats to denounce victims to the police or immigration authorities when their employment status is illegal. Consent is a factor in forced and compulsory labour, but a victim may have given consent in a situation where he felt he had no viable alternative, in which case he could still be subject to forced or compulsory labour[55].

Smuggling legislation

1.25

It is important to understand the difference between: (i) those individuals who have been smuggled; and (ii) those who have been trafficked, where the potential victim is a non-UK national who has no leave to enter or remain

---

53 Ibid p 41.
54 Ibid pp 41–42.
55 Ibid p 41.

in the UK. The definitions frequently become conflated. Often victims will believe they are being smuggled but become trafficked through transit or at their destination country. Factors such as political instability, economic pressures and environmental issues are often the catalysts for migrants seeking to come to the UK. Illegal migrants often rely on organised criminal networks to facilitate their passage to the UK, leading to higher risk of exploitation and further blurring of the distinction between trafficking and smuggling.

1.26

Smuggling is characterised by illegal entry and international movement only, either secretly or by deception, whether for profit or otherwise. The UN Protocol against the Smuggling of Migrants by Land, Sea and Air, adopted in 2000, defines human smuggling as:

> '... the procurement, in order to obtain, directly or indirectly, a financial or other material benefit, of the illegal entry of a person into a state party of which the person is not a national'.

1.27

For an individual to fall within the definition of 'trafficking', he must have been moved for the purpose of exploitation. The definition enables many different facilitators within the process to be caught, so even where the potential victim was originally being 'smuggled' into the UK, en route this can become trafficking either by the initial smuggler or by others in the 'smuggling' chain.

2 Determination of trafficking status

Introduction

2.1

Where there is a credible suspicion that a person is a victim of trafficking and/or modern slavery an obligation to identify and investigate arises under both the Council of Europe Convention on Action against Trafficking in Human Beings (referred to throughout this work as 'ECAT') and European Convention on Human Rights ('ECHR'), Art 4[1].

2.2

Rights arising under ECHR, Art 4 are enshrined in the Human Rights Act 1998, Sch 1. The UK government has not, however, incorporated ECAT directly into UK law through either primary or secondary legislation. Nevertheless, it is clearly-stated government policy and practice to comply with its provisions. To give effect to the UK's obligations under ECAT, guidance to 'frontline staff'[2] and 'competent authorities' has been issued and published[3].

2.3

The identification mechanism in place in the UK for potential victims of trafficking is the National Referral Mechanism ('NRM'). The NRM for potential victims of trafficking provides for a 'first responder' to refer a potential victim of trafficking to the 'competent authority' to make an initial reasonable

---

1   See *R (on the application of H) v Secretary of State for the Home Department* [2016] EWCA Civ 565, [2016] Imm AR 1272; and *J v Austria* (58216/12) (17 January 2017, unreported), ECtHR (EHRLR 326 *J v Austria* App No 58216/12) at 107. These obligations must be construed consistently with international human rights and trafficking obligations under Directive 2011/36/EU of the European Parliament and of the Council of 5 April 2011 on preventing and combating trafficking in human beings and protecting its victims, and replacing Council Framework Decision 2002/629/JHA (the 'EU Trafficking Directive') and ECAT. Similarly, immigration and enforcement policies are to be construed consistently with ECHR, Art 4.

2   Home Office, *Victims of modern slavery – frontline staff guidance* (18 March 2016); Home Office, *Victims of modern slavery – Competent Authority guidance* (21 March 2016).

3   *R (on the application of Hoang) v Secretary of State for the Home Department* [2015] EWHC 1725 (Admin), [2015] All ER (D) 228 (Jun). The SSHD appealed to the Court of Appeal solely in respect of the ECHR, Art 4 findings. The remainder of the case, which related to public law breaches of policy, the legal test and approach for a reasonable grounds decision were not appealed and remain good law. References in this chapter to *R (on the application of Hoang)* are to the parts which were not overturned by the Court of Appeal in *R (on the application of H) v Secretary of State for the Home Department* [2016] EWCA Civ 565.

grounds decision. If the decision is positive then a 'recovery and reflection' period of at least 45 days is granted. If the decision is negative it can only be challenged by way of judicial review[4]. Following a reasonable grounds decision the competent authorities are required to 'investigate' the claim and make a 'conclusive grounds' decision. If the conclusive grounds decision is positive the victim may require further support and assistance to aid recovery, advice in relation to compensation or in respect of a residence permit. If the decision is negative, again the only challenge lies by way of judicial review.

2.4

The identification process is of critical importance as it not only affects the position of the victim of trafficking, but it also affects the ability of the state to mount effective prosecutions against traffickers. A victim of trafficking is entitled to a series of rights under ECAT and these include the right to assistance to aid recovery (Art 12); to a residence permit in the circumstances laid down in Art 14; to information about and access to compensation procedures (Art 15); for any return to her country to be carried out with 'due regard for the rights, safety and dignity of that person' (Art 16); and the right not to be prosecuted for offences directly connected with the experience of being trafficked (Art 28)[5].

National Referral Mechanism

2.5

The NRM is a framework for identifying and referring potential victims of modern slavery and ensuring they receive the appropriate support. It was implemented in 2009 for victims of trafficking to give effect to obligations arising under ECAT[6] and extended to include victims of modern slavery on 31 June 2015[7]. According to the Home Office:

> 'It is designed to make it easier for all the different agencies that could be involved in a trafficking case (for example, the police, Home Office – including Border Force, UK Visas and Immigration and Immigration Enforcement – the National Crime Agency, local authorities, and non-governmental organisations) to co-operate, share information about potential victims and facilitate their access to advice, accommodation and support'[8].

---

4   In respect of foreign nationals, note that the reasonable grounds decision is not an 'immigration decision' and therefore attracts no right of appeal. The Administrative Court is the appropriate court in which to commence proceedings (see para **2.123** below).

5   See *R (on the application of SF) v Secretary of State for the Home Department* [2015] EWHC 2705 (Admin), [2016] 1 WLR 1439.

6   ECAT was signed by the UK on 23 March 2007, and entered into force on 1 April 2009.

7   It was introduced in 2009 in respect of victims of trafficking and extended from 31 July 2015 to include all victims of modern slavery following implementation of the Modern Slavery Act 2015: see www.nationalcrimeagency.gov.uk/about-us/what-we-do/specialist-capabilities/uk-human-trafficking-centre/national-referral-mechanism, last accessed 14 December 2017.

8   *Victims of modern slavery – Competent Authority guidance* (21 March 2016).

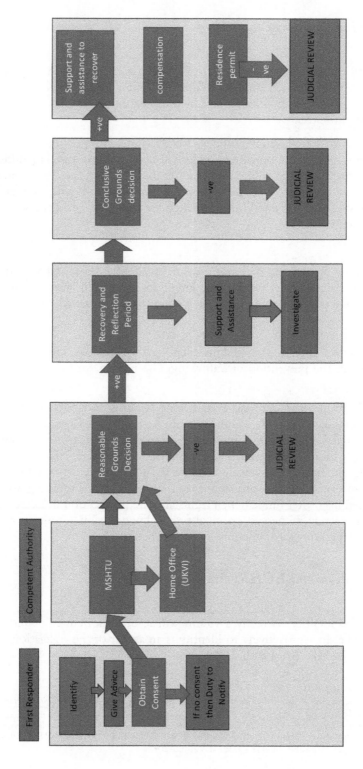

Identifying victims of trafficking

2.6

Article 10 of ECAT requires states to provide the competent authorities with 'persons who are trained and qualified in preventing and combating trafficking in human beings, in identifying and helping victims, including children'. The state is required to:

> 'ensure that the different authorities collaborate with each other as well as with relevant support organisations, so that victims can be identified in a procedure duly taking into account the special situation of women and child victims and, in appropriate cases, issued with residence permits under the conditions provided for in Article 14 of the present Convention'[9].

2.7

The purpose behind this definition was to ensure that those public authorities who may have contact with trafficking victims would have within them appropriately trained people to enable victims to be identified[10].

2.8

An integrated approach to victim identification enables victim protection and assists in the prevention of trafficking. The Explanatory Report to ECAT explains:

> '127. To protect and assist trafficking victims it is of paramount importance to identify them correctly. Article 10 seeks to allow such identification so that victims can be given the benefit of the measures provided for in Chapter III. Identification of victims is crucial, is often tricky and necessitates detailed enquiries. Failure to identify a trafficking victim correctly will probably mean that victim's continuing to be denied his or her fundamental rights and the prosecution to be denied the necessary witness in criminal proceedings to gain a conviction of the perpetrator for trafficking in human beings'.

Identification and ECHR, Art 4

2.9

A failure to identify correctly a victim will result in a denial of fundamental rights[11]. The duty proactively to identify is an aspect of the obligations arising under the ECHR, Art 4 and:

---

9   ECAT, Art 10.
10   CETS, *Explanatory Report to the Council of Europe Convention on Action against Trafficking in Human Beings* pp 129–130.
11   *Explanatory Report to the Council of Europe Convention on Action against Trafficking in Human Beings* p 127, see also *R (on the application of SF) v Secretary of State for the Home Department* [2015] EWHC 2705 (Admin), [2016] 1 WLR 1439 at 100 see also 2, 106–107.

'entails a procedural obligation to investigate situations of potential trafficking. The requirement to investigate does not depend on a complaint from a victim or next of kin: once the matter has come to the attention of the authorities they must act of their own motion'[12].

2.10

'The investigation must fulfil the requirements of independence and impartiality, promptness and reasonable expedition and urgency where there is a possibility of removing the individual concerned from a harmful situation. The investigation must also be capable of leading to the identification and punishment of individuals responsible ... authorities must take all reasonable steps available to them to secure evidence concerning the incident'[13].

2.11

In *R (on the application of H)*[14] the Court of Appeal determined that the only procedural obligation imposed by ECHR, Art 4 (as distinct from policy requirements) at the identification stage was on the police to investigate. The subsequent ECtHR decision in *J v Austria* makes clear that Art 4 includes a positive obligation to identify and support (potential) victims of trafficking as part of the requirement for 'protection'[15].

Indicators of trafficking

2.12

A proactive approach to identification is required. Failure to recognise a victim at the outset can result in the victim being treated as an irregular migrant and/or a criminal, resulting in the victim being detained and/or peremptorily removed from the UK[16]. The initiation of an inquiry should not depend on a report or accusation by the victim[17].

2.13

To ensure effective identification of victims of trafficking it is important that the indicators of trafficking are understood and recognised by those, including

---

12   *Rantsev v Cyprus & Russia* (2010) 51 EHRR 1 at 296, 288.

13   *J v Austria* (2017) App No 58216/12 at 107.

14   *R (on the application of H) v Secretary of State for the Home Department* [2016] EWCA Civ 565, [2016] Imm AR 1272.

15   See *J v Austria* (2017) App No 58216/12 at 109 and see the court's comments under the heading 'Whether the positive obligations to identify and support the applicants had been complied with' at 110–111.

16   GRETA, 'Report concerning the implementation of the Council of Europe Convention on Action against Trafficking in Human Beings by the United Kingdom' (7 October 2016) GRETA(2016)21 at para 226.

17   EU Trafficking Directive, Recital (15).

legal practitioners, who may come into contact with potential victims of trafficking. It is essential to focus on the strength of the indicators of modern slavery or trafficking rather than any immigration or criminality concerns[18]. It is also important to recognise that British and EEA nationals may also be victims of trafficking[19].

2.14

Different forms of modern day slavery and trafficking can give rise to different indicators. The UN Office on Drugs and Crime (UNODC) and United Nations Global Initiative to Fight Trafficking (UNGIFT)[20] have produced a set of indicators that, if present, should lead to an investigation:

General indicators	*People who have been trafficked may:* • Believe that they must work against their will • Be unable to leave their work environment • Show signs that their movements are being controlled • Feel that they cannot leave • Show fear or anxiety • Be subjected to violence or threats of violence against themselves or against their family members and loved ones • Suffer injuries that appear to be the result of an assault • Suffer injuries or impairments typical of certain jobs or control measures • Suffer injuries that appear to be the result of the application of control measures • Be distrustful of the authorities • Be threatened with being handed over to the authorities • Be afraid of revealing their immigration status • Not be in possession of their passports or other travel or identity documents, as those documents are being held by someone else

---

18   For criticism of the overemphasis on immigration and criminal factors rather than trafficking indicators see David Bolt Independent Chief Inspector of Borders and Immigration, *An Inspection of Border Force's Identification and Treatment of Potential Victims of Modern Slavery'* (February 2017), available at www.gov.uk/government/uploads/system/uploads/attachment_data/file/614203/Potential-Victims-of-Modern-Slavery-_Inspection-report.pdf.

19   The inspection report found that there was 'limited awareness or recognition of the risk that EEA nationals could be victims of modern slavery' at para 7.9.

20   See www.unodc.org/pdf/HT_indicators_E_LOWRES.pdf, last accessed 11 January 2018.

	• Have false identity or travel documents
	• Be found in or connected to a type of location likely to be used for exploiting people
	• Be unfamiliar with the local language
	• Not know their home or work address
	• Allow others to speak for them when addressed directly
	• Act as if they were instructed by someone else
	• Be forced to work under certain conditions
	• Be disciplined through punishment
	• Be unable to negotiate working conditions
	• Receive little or no payment
	• Have no access to their earnings
	• Work excessively long hours over long periods
	• Not have any days off
	• Live in poor or substandard accommodations
	• Have no access to medical care
	• Have limited or no social interaction
	• Have limited contact with their families or with people outside of their immediate environment
	• Be unable to communicate freely with others
	• Be under the perception that they are bonded by debt
	• Be in a situation of dependence
	• Come from a place known to be a source of human trafficking
	• Have had the fees for their transport to the country of destination paid for by facilitators, whom they must payback by working or providing services in the destination
	• Have acted on the basis of false promises
Children	*Children who have been trafficked may:*
	• Have no access to their parents or guardians
	• Look intimidated and behave in a way that does not correspond with behaviour typical of children their age

- Have no friends of their own age outside of work
- Have no access to education
- Have no time for playing
- Live apart from other children and in substandard accommodations
- Eat apart from other members of the 'family'
- Be given only leftovers to eat
- Be engaged in work that is not suitable for children
- Travel unaccompanied by adults
- Travel in groups with persons who are not relatives

The following might also indicate that children have been trafficked:

- The presence of child-sized clothing typically worn for doing manual or sex work
- The presence of toys, beds and children's clothing in inappropriate places such as brothels and factories
- The claim made by an adult that he or she has 'found' an unaccompanied child
- The finding of unaccompanied children carrying telephone numbers for calling taxis
- The discovery of cases involving illegal adoption
- Have no choice of accommodation
- Never leave the work premises without their employer
- Be unable to move freely
- Be subject to security measures designed to keep them on the work premises
- Be disciplined through fines
- Be subjected to insults, abuse, threats or violence
- Lack basic training and professional licences

The following might also indicate that people have been trafficked for labour exploitation:

- Notices have been posted in languages other than the local language.
- There are no health and safety notices.

	• The employer or manager is unable to show the documents required for employing workers from other countries.
	• The employer or manager is unable to show records of wages paid to workers.
	• The health and safety equipment is of poor quality or is missing.
	• Equipment is designed or has been modified so that it can be operated by children.
	• There is evidence that labour laws are being breached.
	• There is evidence that workers must pay for tools, food or accommodation or that those costs are being deducted from their wages.
Domestic servitude	*People who have been trafficked for the purpose of domestic servitude may:* • Live with a family • Not eat with the rest of the family • Have no private space • Sleep in a shared or inappropriate space • Be reported missing by their employer even though they are still living in their employer's house • Never or rarely leave the house for social reasons • Never leave the house without their employer • Be given only leftovers to eat • Be subjected to insults, abuse, threats or violence
Sexual exploitation	*People who have been trafficked for the purpose of sexual exploitation may:* • Be of any age, although the age may vary according to the location and the market • Move from one brothel to the next or work in various locations • Be escorted whenever they go to and return from work and other outside activities • Have tattoos or other marks indicating 'ownership' by their exploiters

- Work long hours or have few if any days off
- Sleep where they work
- Live or travel in a group, sometimes with other women who do not speak the same language
- Have very few items of clothing
- Have clothes that are mostly the kind typically worn for doing sex work
- Only know how to say sex-related words in the local language or in the language of the client group
- Have no cash of their own
- Be unable to show an identity document

The following might also indicate that children have been trafficked:

- There is evidence that suspected victims have had unprotected and/or violent sex.
- There is evidence that suspected victims cannot refuse unprotected and/or violent sex.
- There is evidence that a person has been bought and sold.
- There is evidence that groups of women are under the control of others.
- Advertisements are placed for brothels or similar places offering the services of women of a particular ethnicity or nationality.
- It is reported that sex workers provide services to a clientele of a particular ethnicity or nationality.
- It is reported by clients that sex workers do not smile.

Labour exploitation	People who have been trafficked for the purpose of labour exploitation are typically made to work in sectors such as agriculture, construction, entertainment, service industry and manufacturing (in sweatshops). *People who have been trafficked for labour exploitation may:* • Live in groups in the same place where they work and leave those premises infrequently, if at all. • Live in degraded, unsuitable places, such as in agricultural or industrial buildings.

	• Not be dressed adequately for the work they do: for example, they may lack protective equipment or warm clothing
	• Be given only leftovers to eat
	• Have no access to their earnings
	• Have no labour contract
	• Work excessively long hours
	• Depend on their employer for a number of services, including work, transportation and accommodation
Begging and petty crime	*People who have been trafficked for the purpose of begging or committing petty crimes may:* • Be children, elderly persons or disabled migrants who tend to beg in public places and on public transport • Be children carrying and/or selling illicit drugs • Have physical impairments that appear to be the result of mutilation • Be children of the same nationality or ethnicity who move in large groups with only a few adults • Be unaccompanied minors who have been 'found' by an adult of the same nationality or ethnicity • Move in groups while travelling on public transport: for example, they may walk up and down the length of trains • Participate in the activities of organized criminal gangs • Be part of large groups of children who have the same adult guardian • Be punished if they do not collect or steal enough • Live with members of their gang • Travel with members of their gang to the country of destination • Live, as gang members, with adults who are not their parents • Move daily in large groups and over considerable distances

> *The following might also indicate that people have been trafficked for begging or for committing petty crimes:*
>
> - New forms of gang-related crime appear.
>
> - There is evidence that the group of suspected victims has moved, over a period of time, through a number of countries.
>
> - There is evidence that suspected victims have been involved in begging or in committing petty crimes in another country.

Experiences of victims

2.15

As recognised by the ECAT Explanatory Report, the identification process is a process that might take time[21]. For many victims, the identification process is stressful[22], and can be a source of risk if the victim is still under the control of the trafficker. Although some victims escape and seek assistance, others may be 'discovered' either in the trafficking situation or shortly afterwards, for example during an immigration raid or police raid.

2.16

One key to identifying victims of trafficking is an understanding of the power relationships in place and the effects of trafficking. It is well recognised that, certainly when first encountered, victims of trafficking may not tell the truth and often both fear the authorities trying to assist them and may try to protect their abuser[23]. This means a very different approach is required than a simple 'credibility assessment' (see below).

2.17

How the potential victims are treated during the identification process can materially affect their experience of identification, their recovery and the quality of information and evidence they are able to give[24]. These outcomes in turn impact on the ability of the authorities to protect victims, and prevent and prosecute trafficking. It is essential to try to build a relationship of trust with the victim and understand the fears and beliefs he may hold. Time should be taken to ensure that the victim properly understands the process and the potential

---

21 *Explanatory Report to the Council of Europe Convention on Action against Trafficking in Human Beings* pp 128, 131.

22 R Surtees, *Listening to Victims: Experiences of Identification, Return and Assistance in South-Eastern Europe* (International Centre for Migration Policy Development, 2007) (hereafter *Listening to Victims*).

23 This is true even for those who self-identify.

24 *Listening to Victims* p 68.

consequences and outcomes. Consideration should be given to the location of interviews, the emotional and physical state of the victim, the presence of others (particularly family members), interpreters, and the gender of the interviewer and interpreter (do not simply assume that a woman will feel more comfortable with a woman or vice versa but take time to ask). All interviews should be conducted according to safety and ethical standards[25].

2.18

Non-verbal communication and body language can be very important in determining whether there are indicators of trafficking, particularly if the potential trafficker is present[26]. The potential victim may look nervous and his behaviour may suggest that he is controlled by another. These behaviours can be positive indicators that the person might be trafficked.

2.19

Potential victims of trafficking and modern slavery may experience fear and suspicion (particularly of being returned to their trafficking situation by the authorities or punished by a trafficker still controlling them)[27]. They can be in shock, confused and disoriented, suffering post-traumatic stress disorder or marked depression[28], can lack understanding of the process, or the language skills and experience of state or NGO assistance – all deficits which can hinder their identification as a victim of modern slavery[29]. On the other hand, some victims have a positive experience of discovery including feelings of relief, safety and comfort[30]. On discovery they may feel desperation and agitation which can affect their presentation[31], ashamed and blamed or responsible for what has happened to them[32], anger, anxiety and disappointment (particularly for those who had been in less exploitative conditions or able to earn and save some money despite the exploitation)[33].

2.20

Victims of trafficking have often been lied to. These lies can encompass the nature and legality of their work, their immigration status, details of the journey and even their current location. Some victims will be wary of the authorities because of experiences in their home country, or what they have been told by the traffickers.

---

25 See the World Health Organisation's 'WHO Ethical and safety recommendations for interviewing trafficked women', Zimmerman (2003), available at www.who.int/mip/2003/other_documents/en/Ethical_Safety-GWH.pdf. Also refer to the ABE and PEACE model techniques set out in Chapter 6 below.

26 Home Office, *Victims of modern slavery – frontline staff guidance* (18 March 2016).

27 *Listening to Victims* p 57.

28 *Listening to Victims* p 61.

29 *Listening to Victims* p 62.

30 *Listening to Victims* p 62.

31 *Listening to Victims* p 64.

32 *Listening to Victims*, p 65.

33 *Listening to Victims*, p 67.

The experiences of victims can lead to difficulties in their accurate narration of events and their circumstances.

Difficulty	Possible reasons
Reluctance to come forward with information/unwilling to disclose	<ul><li>debt bondage;</li><li>under threat of something happening to family overseas;</li><li>told that the authorities will harm them or put them in prison if they do not do as they are told;</li><li>fear of punishment or reprisals at hands of traffickers or authorities;</li><li>fear of deportation (eg if involved in illegal activities);</li><li>consequence of juju or witchcraft or other rituals leading to a belief that bad things will happen if the person discloses;</li><li>discrimination or stigma from community or family (eg sexual exploitation can often lead to a woman being ostracised);</li><li>fear of being accused as complicit in their situation;</li><li>fear of being seen as 'colluding' with their exploiter;</li><li>they may be in a situation of dependency, perhaps due to their age;</li><li>they may suffer from Stockholm syndrome, where due to unequal power, victims create a false emotional or psychological attachment to their controller.</li></ul>
Not recognise themselves as having been trafficked or enslaved	<ul><li>may see their situation as a stepping stone to a better life;</li><li>may not be aware of support structures and their entitlements and feel that they are dependent on traffickers;</li><li>may have been groomed;</li><li>may see their current situation as temporary and blame it on their lack of understanding of the culture and labour market in the UK;</li></ul>

	• children may not understand what modern slavery means;
	• children may not have the same cultural understanding of childhood as is held in the UK and feel they are young adults responsible for earning money for their family; they may see an exploitative situation as a sacrifice to be made for their family.
Tell their story with obvious errors	• It is not uncommon for traffickers or modern slavery facilitators to provide stories for victims to tell if approached by the authorities;
	• errors or lack of reality may be because their initial stories are composed by others and learnt;
	• mental and physical ill-health may impact on their recall ability

2.21

Common misconceptions about the behaviour of victims of trafficking, often arising from the same causes as above, include:

- the person did not take the opportunity to leave and therefore is not being coerced;
- UK nationals cannot be victims of modern slavery[34];
- crossing a border is required in order to be trafficked[35];
- it cannot be slavery where the trafficker and victim are married, related, living together or lovers[36];
- the person has a better life than previously and therefore is not a victim;
- a rejection of help means a person is not a victim.

The conduct of traffickers

2.22

The common modus operandi of traffickers is dealt with in depth in Chapter 15. 'Grooming' of victims is common. Traffickers frequently target victims with

---

34 UK nationals can and have been victims of modern slavery.

35 A border crossing is not required: trafficking can occur within a country.

36 Children are often trafficked by and to family members for the purpose of domestic servitude. The 'boyfriend' model is common in cases of sexual exploitation.

a noticeable vulnerability, for example, poverty, youth, emotional neediness, low self-confidence or irregular immigration status. The trafficker will then obtain information about the potential victim and often appear as a friend or sponsor who will promise a better life. Traffickers may pose as the victim's friend or boyfriend, promise schooling, buy gifts or provide drugs or alcohol. The victim is then likely to be isolated either within his home country or by being taken abroad and the trafficker will seek to groom or intimidate so as to obtain control of the victim. Once the victim has been 'groomed' the trafficker will often resort to more violent or psychologically coercive measures to retain control over the victim[37]. There is an increasing use by traffickers of methods to engender trust and confidence including the gifting of money to encourage the victim's trust[38].

2.23

To obtain and keep control over victims it is common for agents and traffickers to use threats against the victim's family, a control model especially effective against children in order to manipulate and control the victim. The fear of reprisal on themselves or their family can have a huge impact on whether a potential victim of trafficking is willing to cooperate[39]. Unaccompanied migrant children are also often targets of trafficking because they are without a guardian or parent, leaving them highly vulnerable.

2.24

Victims of trafficking are also often held in 'debt bondage' and this bond is commonly held over the family abroad. Debt bondage occurs where the person is forced to work, often for little or no money, to pay off a debt, often characterised as passage and living costs with compound interest added. Such victims face coercion, intimidation or violence against them or loved ones if they try to leave before the 'debt' has been repaid[40].

'Credibility' and mitigating factors

2.25

In assessing credibility, the guidance recognises that it is 'generally unnecessary and sometimes counter-productive, to focus on minor or peripheral facts that are not material to the claim'[41].

---

37   Home Office, *Victims of modern slavery – frontline staff guidance* (18 March 2016) p 20.
38   Bernie Gravett, former Superintendent with the Metropolitan Police.
39   Home Office, *Victims of modern slavery – frontline staff guidance* (18 March 2016) p 20.
40   For more information see eg Anti-Slavery International, at www.antislavery.org/slavery-today/debt-bondage/, last accessed 14 December 2017.
41   *Victims of modern slavery – Competent Authority guidance* (21 March 2016) p 97.

2.26

The competent authority is directed to assess the material facts based on:

- whether the person is coherent and consistent with any part-written or verbal statements;

- how well the evidence submitted fits together and whether it is contradictory;

- whether the facts are consistent with claims made by witnesses and any documentary evidence.

2.27

If there is 'insufficient evidence to support a claim', for example 'where the case is lacking key details, such as who exploited them or where the exploitation took place', the competent authority is entitled to question whether the relevant threshold is met. It must also consider whether more information is needed before that decision can be reached[42].

2.28

It is suggested that it would be appropriate to assume that a victim will be able to give a greater level of detail than a person who has not had the experience and will be able to recount the central elements in a broadly consistent manner. This is internally inconsistent with the remainder of the guidance which explains and outlines a myriad of reasons why this cannot be assumed. However, this rationale is being used increasingly to discount the experiences of victims.

2.29

Before making a finding of adverse credibility at any stage of the process, the competent authority should[43]:

- consider whether it is necessary to seek further information or evidence;

- consider whether any inconsistencies in the evidence or any failure to disclose matters promptly can be explained by any mitigating circumstances[44];

- refer back to the first responder or other expert witnesses to seek clarification of inconsistencies.

---

42 Ibid p 97.
43 Ibid p 98.
44 *R (on the application of Hoang) v Secretary of State for the Home Department* [2015] EWHC 1725 (Admin), [2015] All ER (D) 228 (Jun) at paras 81–83.

2.30

There are a number of recognised good reasons (including the nature of trafficking and the trauma it can cause[45]) why a victim of trafficking may not immediately be able to advance a coherent, consistent and detailed account of what has happened to him. Inconsistencies or delay in coming forward with detail are not necessarily reasons for finding lack of credibility, and later disclosure of more detail to a trusted person should not be seen as necessarily manipulative or untrue, because it can be the result of an effective recovery period and/or the establishment of trust[46].

2.31

Many of these factors are explicitly recognised in the guidance, which includes the following non-exhaustive list[47]:

- trauma (mental, psychological, or emotional);
- inability to express themselves clearly;
- mistrust of authorities;
- feelings of shame;
- painful memories;
- age;
- ongoing nature of abuse through childhood (in child cases);
- fear of traffickers or modern slavery facilitators, violence or witchcraft (juju).

2.32

Many of the symptoms of PTSD such as flashbacks, intrusive thoughts, hypervigilance, shame and low self-esteem, as well as the fear of (and resultant inability to deal appropriately with) authority figures, can have direct effect on the ability to give clear and consistent testimony. Dissociation (a psychological defence mechanism manifested as a perceived detachment of the mind from the emotional state and the body which often occurs in the aftermath of severe trauma) can lead to particularly severe difficulties in the context of giving testimony[48].

---

45   *R (on the application of Hoang) v Secretary of State for the Home Department* [2015] EWHC 1725 (Admin), [2015] All ER (D) 228 (Jun) at para 82b.

46   *R (on the application of Hoang) v Secretary of State for the Home Department* [2015] EWHC 1725 (Admin), [2015] All ER (D) 228 (Jun) at para 82c, *R (on the application of SF) v Secretary of State for the Home Department* [2015] EWHC 2705 (Admin), [2016] 1 WLR 1439 at 79, *Victims of modern slavery – Competent Authority guidance* (21 March 2016) p 99.

47   Home Office, *Victims of modern slavery – Competent Authority guidance* (21 March 2016) p 99.

48   C Katona and L Howard, 'The mental health difficulties experienced by victims of human trafficking (modern slavery) and the impact this has on their ability to provide testimony' (Helen Bamber Foundation, Briefing Paper, February 2017), available at www.helenbamber.org/wp-content/uploads/2017/02/Briefing-Paper-Difficulties-in-providing-testimony-victims-of-modern-slavery.pdf.

2.33

Expert evidence and evidence from support organisations (see below) are recognised as being of assistance to the competent authority in determining trafficking status. The guidance recognises the role and expertise of first responders and other experts and reflects the fact that these organisations know, from their own expertise and experience, how trafficking works, which enables them to test the cogency of the account of the individual concerned. It also enables them to explain why and how those who have been trafficked may, because of their experiences, give inconsistent accounts or fail to mention something of importance at an early stage[49].

2.34

Corroboration at either the reasonable grounds or conclusive grounds stage is not required, because there is no requirement for it at common law or under any relevant statute[50].

2.35

The current strong emphasis placed on 'credibility' can lead to individual decision makers focusing on the individual credibility of the potential victim of trafficking without evaluating the objective context in which the trafficking took place and without properly investigating the facts as required by ECAT, Art 10. Despite the clear Home Office guidance, expert opinion and decisions of the courts, competent authorities routinely fail to deal with factors that mitigate inconsistent evidence or delays in disclosure[51]. The consequences are that victims who are subject to coercion and control, suffering mental health difficulties, who experienced out of the ordinary situations and/or have been groomed and are unable to disclose, are likely to be rejected as victims of trafficking. This puts the UK in breach of its obligations under the Convention.

---

49 *R (on the application of SF) v Secretary of State for the Home Department* [2015] EWHC 2705 (Admin), [2016] 1 WLR 1439.

50 See *R (on the application of M) v Secretary of State for the Home Department* [2015] EWHC 2467 (Admin) at 61 and *R (on the application of SF) v Secretary of State for the Home Department* [2015] EWHC 2705 (Admin), [2016] 1 WLR 1439 at 191.

51 See eg *R (on the application of FK) v Secretary of State for the Home Department* [2016] EWHC 56 (Admin) at para 31; *R (on the application of Hoang) v Secretary of State for the Home Department* [2015] EWHC 1725 (Admin), [2015] All ER (D) 228 (Jun) (in a reasonable grounds context); *R (on the application of M) v Secretary of State for the Home Department* [2015] EWHC 2467 (Admin) (in a conclusive grounds context); Children's Commissioner, 'If only someone had listened' (Office of the Children's Commissioner's Inquiry into Child Sexual Exploitation in Gangs and Groups, Final report November 2013), available at www.childrenscommissioner.gov.uk/wp-content/uploads/2017/07/If_only_someone_had_listened.pdf.

Expert evidence

Evidence from support organisations

2.36

Support organisations hold a special position in the victim status determination process because of their own experience and knowledge, both of the trafficking process and the victim.

2.37

Victims of trafficking often do not trust or are afraid of the police or immigration officials. Support organisations are likely to have spent more time over a longer period with the individual and established a greater degree of trust[52].

2.38

In recognition of this special status the guidance requires this evidence to be given 'due weight' although the competent authority is not bound to accept it[53]. If a report from a support organisation is available, there is an imperative requirement that the competent authority obtain one[54].

Evidence from other experts

2.39

Expert evidence is often relied on to explain to the competent authority how the approach to evidence of a trafficked person has to be viewed differently from Refugee Convention witnesses or other classes of victims. As recognised by the civil courts in this context[55], if expert evidence is ignored there is a great risk that the person alleged to be trafficked will be disbelieved, because his or her account is inconsistent. The consequence of this is that he would not be treated fairly, as the crucial effect of the trauma of having been trafficked would have been ignored in appraising his evidence.

2.40

As recognised by Silber J in *R (on the application of SF)*:

---

52   *R (on the application of SF) v Secretary of State for the Home Department* [2015] EWHC 2705 (Admin), [2016] 1 WLR 1439 at para 145.

53   Home Office, *Victims of modern slavery – Competent Authority guidance* (21 March 2016) p 101; *R (on the application of SF) v Secretary of State for the Home Department* [2015] EWHC 2705 (Admin), [2016] 1 WLR 1439 at para 148.

54   *AB v Secretary of State for the Home Department* [2015] EWHC 1490 (Admin) at paras 40–41.

55   Note the different approach of the criminal courts; see *R v N; R v L* [2012] EWCA Crim 189, [2013] QB 379 at para 86(a); and *R v Joseph* [2017] EWCA Crim 36, [2017] 1 WLR 3153 at para 122.

'these expert reports are not to be regarded as "trump cards" for the claimant, but they must be evaluated but if they are not accepted, explanations have to be put forward for rejecting them. The fact finder may well be helped by expert evidence explaining the difficulties confronting those who have been trafficked in putting forward a prompt and consistent claim by setting out the known reasons why trafficking victims might give inconsistent accounts or delayed accounts'[56].

2.41

All expert evidence relied on should state the experience and qualifications of the person providing the evidence. If the evidence is from a medical practitioner, the practitioner should be qualified in the appropriate field. The report should refer to the relevant physical or mental health condition, when and how it has been diagnosed and why that condition and any treatment relating to it is relevant to human trafficking or modern slavery[57].

2.42

The letter of instruction will be disclosable.

2.43

If there are clear, robust reasons why the reasonable or conclusive grounds test is not met, there is no requirement to accept the assessment of an expert report simply because it states that the reasonable or conclusive grounds test is met[58].

2.44

The guidance notes that the individual writing the report may not have access to the full range of information available to the competent authority[59]. If the competent authority has additional information on which it intends to rely to reject the report of an expert, as a matter of fairness this should be disclosed and the expert asked to comment prior to the decision.

2.45

The guidance also notes that 'Any evidence supplied must be capable of being verified by the competent authority where appropriate'. It is therefore important that reports are properly and adequately sourced. Where the expert is giving his opinion as an expert, this should be made clear. There is a failure to understand that an expert is very often the 'source' of the information precisely because of his knowledge or expertise. Expert evidence is dealt with in Chapters 5 and 7.

56   R *(on the application of SF) v Secretary of State for the Home Department* [2015] EWHC 2705 (Admin), [2016] 1 WLR 1439 at para 156.
57   Home Office, *Victims of modern slavery – Competent Authority guidance* (21 March 2016) pp 101–102.
58   Home Office, *Victims of modern slavery – Competent Authority guidance* (21 March 2016) p 101.
59   Home Office, *Victims of modern slavery – Competent Authority guidance* (21 March 2016) p 101.

2.46

The competent authority is required to evaluate any expert evidence and decide how far it stands up to a proper evaluation[60]. In other words, the competent authority must 'grapple with' the evidence which requires the competent authority to recognise the conclusions of the report, engage with them and explain, if rejecting the report, however briefly why the competent authority disagreed with them'. A failure to do this will amount to a failure to have sufficient regard to policy, and irrationally failing adequately to take into account the expert opinion[61].

First responders

2.47

The following key steps for frontline staff in the NRM process are outlined in *Victims of modern slavery – frontline staff guidance*[62].

2.48

Under the UK system only a 'first responder' can make a referral to the 'competent authority'. First responders are currently:

- the Home Office;

- local authorities;

- Health and Social Care Trusts (HSC Trusts);

- police;

- National Crime Agency (NCA);

- Trafficking Awareness Raising Alliance (TARA);

- Migrant Help;

- Kalayaan;

- Gangmasters Licensing Agency;

- Medaille Trust;

---

60   *R (on the application of AA (Iraq)) v Secretary of State* [2012] EWCA Civ 23 at 74, (2012) Times, 5 March.
61   *AB v Secretary of State for the Home Department* [2015] EWHC 1490 (Admin) at para 41.
62   See   www.antislaverycommissioner.co.uk/media/1057/victims-of-modern-slavery-frontline-staff-guidance-v3.pdf, last accessed 14 December 2017.

- Salvation Army;

- Barnardos;

- National Society for the Prevention of Cruelty to Children (NSPCC);

- Unseen UK;

- New Pathways;

- BAWSO;

- Refugee Council.

2.49

Notably missing from this list are medical and legal professionals and prison officers, who cannot make direct referrals to the NRM[63]. Concern that someone might be a victim of trafficking should prompt contact with one of the bodies above and a request for a referral to be made.

2.50

The 'first responder' is required to complete an NRM referral form. Forms[64] should be sent to the National Crime Agency Modern Slavery and Human Trafficking Unit (MSHTU) by email to nrm@nrm@nca.x.gsi.gov.uk or by fax to 0870 496 5534.

2.51

First responders should ensure that the relevant forms are signed by the victim. In the case of an adult, informed consent is required for a referral. This requires the first responder clearly to explain to the potential victim what the NRM is, the referral process, what support is available through the NRM, and the potential outcomes. Good explanations can overcome some of the reasons why a victim may refuse to give consent, for example through a lack of understanding or fear of the authorities. Consent is not required in the case of a child[65].

2.52

Potential victims who were trafficked as children but are now adults should have their cases assessed as if they were a child against the child indicators but will be required to consent to referral[66].

---

63 This has been criticised by GRETA (see fn 16 above) at para 141.
64 Available at www.gov.uk/government/publications/human-trafficking-victims-referral-and-assessment-forms.
65 Home Office, *Victims of modern slavery – frontline staff guidance* (18 March 2016) p 40.
66 Home Office, *Victims of modern slavery – frontline staff guidance* (18 March 2016) p 42.

2.53

The form is not to be used as an interview record[67], but as a means for the first responder to provide as much information as possible, including documentary evidence where available, to enable a decision to be reached. First responders should avoid placing victims of trafficking under unnecessary additional stress or further trauma. If the first responder is unable to use an accredited interpreter to fill out the form this should be made clear on the form. In trafficking cases best practice suggests that members of the community should not be used to interpret an account of trafficking by victims. Similarly, caution should be used when working with interpreters who lack experience of trafficked victims when filling out the NRM referral form. The first responder must ensure that it does not place the victim at further risk of harm, including reprisals or shame and further trauma.

Duty to notify

2.54

From 1 November 2015 specified public authorities are required to notify the Home Office about any potential victims of modern slavery they encounter in England and Wales[68]. The information to be provided during this process is set out in the Modern Slavery Act 2015 (Duty to Notify) Regulations 2015[69]. The notification can be done either by completing an NRM form or, in the case of a victim who does not consent to the NRM, by completing an MS1 Form and sending it to dutytonotify@homeoffice.gsi.gov.uk within one month of identification (absent exceptional circumstances). Although the duty to notify applies to both children and adults, children do not need to consent to enter the NRM, so potential child victims should be referred into the NRM in all cases (rather than making an MS1 notification).

---

67 As it is not an interview, and is completed by someone other than the victim, it should also not be relied on to undermine the credibility of the victim.

68 Modern Slavery Act 2015, s 52. The 'duty to notify' provision is set out in s 52, and applies to the following public authorities in England and Wales at the time of publication (additional public authorities may be added by regulations): (a) a chief officer of police for a police area, (b) the chief constable of the British Transport Police Force, (c) the National Crime Agency, (d) a county council, (e) a county borough council, (f) a district council, (g) a London borough council, (h) the Greater London Authority, (i) the Common Council of the City of London, (j) the Council of the Isles of Scilly, (k) the Gangmasters and Labour Abuse Authority. Home Office staff within UK Visas and Immigration, Border Force and Immigration Enforcement are also required, as a matter of Home Office policy, to comply with the duty to notify guidance: see www.gov.uk/government/uploads/system/uploads/attachment_data/file/508817/Duty_to_Notify_Guidance__Version_2.0_.pdf.

69 SI 2015/1743.

Competent authorities

2.55

The UK has designated the following to be 'competent authorities' with the responsibility to take decisions relevant to victims of trafficking:

(1)   the National Crime Agency (NCA) Modern Slavery and Human Trafficking Unit (MSHTU);

(2)   the Home Office (UK Visas and Immigration).

2.56

MSHTU will decide the case itself or, if the case involves an EEA or non-EEA national subject to immigration control they will refer the case to the most appropriate competent authority within the Home Office, who will then make the reasonable and conclusive grounds decisions[70].

Reasonable grounds decision

2.57

The 'reasonable grounds' decision is designed as an initial filter to identify potential victims. The burden of identifying a victim of trafficking or modern slavery rests on the state and a failure to identify may cause the state to be in breach of ECHR, Art 4. At the reasonable grounds stage the issue is not whether the victim can prove that he has been trafficked to the decision-maker's satisfaction, but whether taken in the round, all available evidence demonstrates that there are reasonable grounds to believe that the person has been trafficked[71].

2.58

This initial filter should not be elevated to detailed summary determination of the ultimate credibility of the case advanced[72]. At this stage in the process the victim will often not have had an opportunity to 'recover' and access support and advice. Thus, all of the possible reasons why a victim of trafficking might give an incomplete or inconsistent account are far more likely to be present. The victim may not yet have built a relationship of trust and confidence with anyone. Fear of authorities, post-traumatic stress disorder, shame, a desire to protect others, or fears arising from immigration status may impact on the individual's ability to recall concrete facts. Similarly, the decision-maker may

---

70   Home Office, *Victims of modern slavery – Competent Authority guidance* (21 March 2016) p 22. MSHTU also handles the data on NRM referrals: see www.nationalcrimeagency.gov.uk/about-us/what-we-do/specialist-capabilities/uk-human-trafficking-centre/national-referral-mechanism.

71   *R (on the application of Hoang) v Secretary of State for the Home Department* [2015] EWHC 1725 (Admin), [2015] All ER (D) 228 (Jun) at paras 71–72.

72   Ibid para 74.

not have had time to undertake adequate inquiries from other relevant agencies such as social services, support agencies or the police[73].

2.59

It is for these reasons that the guidance cautions against being too quick to assume that an account which has some holes or inconsistencies in it is therefore not credible, at the initial 'reasonable grounds' stage. At this stage in the process it is not necessary to identify what means, method or form of exploitation have or might have been employed.

Standard and burden of proof

2.60

The test applied by the competent authority at the reasonable grounds stage is whether the statement 'I suspect but cannot prove' the person is a victim of human trafficking/modern slavery is true, and whether a reasonable person, having regard to the information known to the decision maker, would think that there are reasonable grounds to believe that the individual had been a victim of human trafficking or modern slavery.

2.61

Current guidance[74] states:

> 'Reasonable suspicion would not normally be met on the basis of an unsubstantiated claim alone, without reliable, credible, precise and up to date:
>
> - intelligence or information
> - evidence of some specific behaviour by the person concerned.
>
> Where reliable, credible, precise and up to date intelligence, information or evidence is present, it must be considered in reaching a reasonable grounds decision'.

2.62

The way this guidance is framed unfortunately tends to lead to individual decision-makers imposing a burden of proof on the victim and placing an overemphasis on credibility and corroboration, in breach of the remainder of the guidance (see paras **2.25–2.35** above on credibility).

---

73 Ibid para 75.
74 Home Office, *Victims of modern slavery – Competent Authority guidance* (21 March 2016) p 51.

2.63

Provided there are reasonable grounds for belief, then the question of whether there are also reasonable grounds for disbelief is irrelevant. It does not become relevant until the conclusive grounds stage of the process[75].

Assessment

2.64

The decision-maker should first identify evidence and matters that might lead to reasonable grounds for suspecting that the individual is a victim of trafficking. He should then critically examine the evidence to decide whether those grounds did in fact exist, bearing in mind the circumstances identified as mitigating for discrepancies, lack of credulity and delays in disclosure[76].

2.65

Regard should be had to the possible explanations for credibility gaps and/or evidentiary gaps. The guidance cautions against being too quick to assume that an account which has some holes or inconsistencies in it is not credible at this stage (see paras **2.25–2.35** above on credibility)[77].

2.66

Competent authorities should use published and recognised reports which address the propensity of trafficking in the home country[78]. Although these sources are not defined, we would suggest that they should include, as a minimum:

- US Trafficking in Persons Report (produced annually)[79];

- any relevant UK country of information reports [COI] produced by the Home Office;

- NRM statistics[80];

- police intelligence/reports and guidance, eg Child Exploitation and Online Protection reports[81];

---

75   *R (on the application of Hoang) v Secretary of State for the Home Department* [2015] EWHC 1725 (Admin), [2015] All ER (D) 228 (Jun).

76   See *R (on the application of Hoang) v Secretary of State for the Home Department* [2015] EWHC 1725 (Admin), [2015] All ER (D) 228 (Jun) at para 116; *R (on the application of SF) v Secretary of State for the Home Department* [2015] EWHC 2705 (Admin), [2016] 1 WLR 1439 at para 117.

77   *R (on the application of Hoang) v Secretary of State for the Home Department* [2015] EWHC 1725 (Admin), [2015] All ER (D) 228 (Jun) at para 75.

78   *R (on the application of Hoang) v Secretary of State for the Home Department* [2015] EWHC 1725 (Admin), [2015] All ER (D) 228 (Jun), summarising Competent Authority Guidance at 48f, 85–86, 90–94.

79   Available at www.state.gov/j/tip/rls/tiprpt/.

80   Available at www.nationalcrimeagency.gov.uk/publications/national-referral-mechanism-statistics.

81   Available at www.ceop.police.uk/safety-centre/.

- Association of Chief Police Officers guidance on cannabis[82].

2.67

Notwithstanding this, if possible, it is recommended that practitioners explicitly refer to any relevant information that the competent authority should take into account when making a decision.

2.68

As a matter of good practice we would also suggest that regard should be had to reports produced by specialist NGOs, such as ECPAT, Anti-Slavery International and the NSPCC.

2.69

The competent authority tends to cite from the US TIP report and reach an initial decision on whether trafficking of the type described from the country described occurs, but often fails to apply that information to the account given by the individual. This is an impermissible approach[83].

2.70

Provision is made for interviews at the reasonable grounds stage[84], although it is anticipated that it is 'more likely' that the reasonable grounds decision will be based on evidence from the first responder than an interview.

2.71

In foreign national cases it is becoming more prevalent for decision-makers to require interviews (see paras **2.25–2.35** above on credibility). We would suggest that where 'further enquiries' or an interview are necessary, the reasonable grounds test will almost invariably be met.

2.72

Although credibility is relevant to the existence or otherwise of 'reasonable grounds', a decision-maker does not have to (and may be unable to) form a concluded view on credibility at the 'reasonable grounds' stage of the decision-making process under the National Referral Mechanism[85].

---

82 Available at www.wsmp.org.uk/documents/wsmp/Trafficking%20Guidance/160810%20ACPO%20 lead's%20position%20on%20CYP%20recovered%20from%20cannabis%20farms.pdf.

83 For an example of this see *R (on the application of Hoang) v Secretary of State for the Home Department* [2015] EWHC 1725 (Admin), [2015] All ER (D) 228 (Jun) at paras 86–94, where the decision-maker dismissed the case on the grounds that what happened to the claimant was 'intrinsically incredible' or the result of a chance encounter with gangs without recognising that the circumstances described were consistent with established and recognised patterns of trafficking activity (para 93).

84 Home Office, *Victims of modern slavery – Competent Authority guidance* (21 March 2016) p 53.

85 *R (on the application of Hoang) v Secretary of State for the Home Department* [2015] EWHC 1725 (Admin), [2015] All ER (D) 228 (Jun).

Timing of decision

2.73

The decision should be taken within five days of receipt of the referral to the decision-maker (either MSHTU or the Home Office) or 'as soon as possible' where the person is in detention[86]. A failure to take a decision within this time may result in a victim being unlawfully detained[87] or being unable to access rights to which he is entitled[88].

2.74

A positive decision must be taken as soon as there is sufficient information to do so *even* if it is likely that further information will be provided. The same is not true of a negative decision. If it is likely the decision will be negative the competent authority is required to contact the first responder and/or support providers, police and local authority (as relevant), discuss the decision and give them the opportunity to provide any further information or evidence that is available. In line with ECAT, a multi-agency collaborative approach is required[89].

Relevance of criminal investigations to the NRM decision

2.75

A victim of trafficking will be a victim of crime[90]. It is not necessary for there to be an ongoing criminal investigation or proof that an offence has taken place to find that there are reasonable grounds to believe an individual is a victim of trafficking or slavery.

---

86   Home Office, *Victims of modern slavery – Competent Authority guidance* (21 March 2016) p 50. Practitioners are of the view that it is intended that where a person is detained the decision will be prioritised and made more swiftly than the five days rather than the detention itself being used to suggest that it is not 'possible' to make a decision sooner.

87   See eg *R (on the application of XYL) v Secretary of State for the Home Department* [2017] EWHC 773 (Admin).

88   *R (on the application of SF) v Secretary of State for the Home Department* [2015] EWHC 2705 (Admin), [2016] 1 WLR 1439 at para 107, there in the context of a conclusive grounds decision.

89   ECAT, Art 10(1).

90   Prior to the commencement of the Modern Slavery Act 2015, Part 1, trafficking offences in the UK were contained in the following legislation: the Sexual Offences Act 2003, s 59A (as amended by the Protection of Freedoms Act 2012); the Asylum and Immigration (Treatment of Claimants) Act 2004, s 4 (as amended by the Protection of Freedoms Act 2012); the Criminal Justice (Scotland) Act 2003, s 22 (as amended by the Criminal Justice and Licensing (Scotland) Act 2010, s 46); the Criminal Justice and Licensing (Scotland) Act 2010, s 47. Part 1 of the Modern Slavery Act 2015 introduces the consolidated slavery and trafficking offences, tougher penalties and sentencing rules, ensures the main offences are subject to the toughest asset recovery regime under the Proceeds of Crime Act 2002, introduces bespoke slavery and trafficking reparation orders, and provides for the detention and then forfeiture of vehicles, ships and aircraft used for the purposes of trafficking. See also Home Office, *Victims of modern slavery – Competent Authority guidance* (21 March 2016) p 52.

2.76

The competent authority guidance asserts that if there is no evidence of a crime or that the person requires time to decide whether to cooperate in a criminal investigation the competent authority is entitled to take this into account at the reasonable grounds stage. This approach is potentially premature and inconsistent with the recognition in Art 13 that a victim may require time to recover and escape the influence of the traffickers and/or to take an informed decision on cooperating with the competent authorities.

2.77

Furthermore, decisions to prosecute are taken where the prosecutor is 'satisfied that there is sufficient evidence to provide a realistic prospect of conviction'[91]. This entails making the jury or magistrate sure of the guilt of the defendant, or of proving his or her guilt beyond reasonable doubt. This test is significantly higher than 'I suspect but cannot prove' or the 'balance of probabilities (see below), and therefore reliance on a decision not to prosecute as indicative that a person had not been trafficked would more than likely be unlawful[92].

Consequences of positive reasonable grounds decision

2.78

Where a positive reasonable grounds decision is made the person will be notified but will not receive reasons for that decision. The competent authority is also required to inform other relevant agencies of the decision including:

- the first responder;

- the support provider and the Salvation Army, TARA or Migrant Help or Women's Aid (depending on the location of the victim);

- the local authority in the case of children.

If the Home Office was the competent authority, the MSHTU should also be notified.

Recovery and reflection period

2.79

A positive reasonable grounds decision should trigger support for a minimum of 45 days. This is known as the 'recovery and reflection' period[93]. ECAT, Art

---

91   The Code for Crown Prosecutors at para 4.5.
92   See eg *R (on the application of SF) v Secretary of State for the Home Department* [2015] EWHC 2705 (Admin), [2016] 1 WLR 1439 at paras 115–118.
93   This period can be extended if necessary.

12 requires that victims are assisted in their physical, psychological and social recovery, which should include at the least the following:

- standards of living capable of ensuring their subsistence, through such measures as: appropriate and secure accommodation, psychological and material assistance;

- access to emergency medical treatment;

- translation and interpretation services, when appropriate;

- counselling and information, in particular as regards their legal rights and the services available to them, in a language that they can understand;

- assistance to enable their rights and interests to be presented and considered at appropriate stages of criminal proceedings against offenders;

- access to education for children.

2.80

The purpose of the recovery and reflection period is to enable the person concerned to recover and escape the influence of the traffickers and/or to take an informed decision on cooperating with the competent authorities. The period of time granted (unless a positive conclusive grounds decision is made: see below) must be sufficient to enable these objectives to be achieved[94]. A foreign national potential victim of trafficking is protected during this time from expulsion from the UK, shall be authorised to stay in the UK and will normally be granted either temporary admission or temporary release if necessary.

2.81

All potential victims of trafficking are entitled to the measures prescribed by ECAT, Art 12. The right to such support is not dependent on the victim reporting trafficking/slavery to the police, nor does it require there to be an active investigation. Many trafficking/slavery victims are extremely reluctant to report matters to the police because they are so frightened of their traffickers.

2.82

Decisions taken in providing such support and assistance must take account of the victim's safety and protection needs. For example, the victim may need to be accommodated in a safe house away from the area in which she was found.

2.83

Victims lawfully resident within the territory are also entitled to medical

---

94   ECAT, Art 13(1).

and other assistance and access to the labour market, vocational training and education[95].

2.84

The EU Trafficking Directive also requires assistance and support be provided to victims before, during and for an appropriate period of time after the conclusion of criminal proceedings[96]. Such assistance should commence as soon as there is a reasonable grounds indication for believing an individual might have been subject to an offence[97] but must not be conditional on cooperation with any investigation, prosecution or trial[98]. Support must take into account the individual needs of the victims[99] and be provided on a consensual basis[100].

2.85

In both Scotland[101] and Northern Ireland[102] statutory provision for support and accommodation of victims of trafficking has been made. In both countries:

- support and accommodation are not conditional on cooperation, require consent, must take into account safety and protection needs and must meet the assessed personal needs of the individual[103];

- the types of support referred to in ECAT, Art 12 are explicitly referenced[104].

2.86

In Scotland the legislation provides for:

- mandatory provision of support and assistance from the date of a reasonable grounds decision until either the end of a period made in regulations[105] or a negative conclusive grounds decision[106];

- a discretion to provide support prior to the reasonable grounds decision and at other times including after the conclusive grounds decision[107].

---

95 ECAT, Art 12(3) and (4).
96 EU Trafficking Directive, Art 11(1)–(2).
97 EU Trafficking Directive, Art 11(2).
98 EU Trafficking Directive, Art 11(3).
99 EU Trafficking Directive, Art 11(7).
100 EU Trafficking Directive, Art 11(5).
101 Human Trafficking and Exploitation (Scotland) Act 2015.
102 Human Trafficking and Exploitation (Criminal Justice and Support for Victims) Act (Northern Ireland) 2015.
103 Human Trafficking and Exploitation (Criminal Justice and Support for Victims) Act (Northern Ireland) 2015, s 18(5); Human Trafficking and Exploitation (Scotland) Act 2015, s 9(1) and (5).
104 Human Trafficking and Exploitation (Criminal Justice and Support for Victims) Act (Northern Ireland) 2015, s 18(7); Human Trafficking and Exploitation (Scotland) Act 2015, s 9(4).
105 Human Trafficking and Exploitation (Scotland) Act 2015 power to make regulations in s 9(2)(b)(i) and 9(8) is in force but no such regulations have yet been made. The consultation document is available at www.gov.scot/Publications/2017/09/7631.
106 Human Trafficking and Exploitation (Scotland) Act 2015, s 9(1)–(2) (not yet in force).
107 Human Trafficking and Exploitation (Scotland) Act 2015, s 9(3) (not yet in force).

2.87

In Northern Ireland:

- legislation provides for support and accommodation for at least 45 days (even if a negative decision is made within that time)[108];

- provision of support may continue even if the person leaves Northern Ireland[109] or is determined on conclusive grounds not to be a victim of trafficking[110];

- specific provision is made for assistance and support for exiting prostitution[111].

2.88

In contrast, in England and Wales there is currently no statutory basis for the provision of support. Guidance relating to the identification and support of victims required by the Modern Slavery Act 2015[112] has not been produced, nor have any regulations been made by the Home Secretary relating to provision of support and assistance to victims[113].

2.89

At the time of writing there are two Bills pending before Parliament: the Human Trafficking (Child Protection) Bill 2017–19, which aims to make provision for the creation of secure safe houses for children who have been subjected to human trafficking and connected purposes; and the Modern Slavery (Victim Support) Bill [HL] 2017–19, which seeks to amend the Modern Slavery Act 2015 so as to create a statutory duty to provide support and assistance to potential victims of trafficking for 45 days and a further period of 12 months following confirmation of their status as a victim of trafficking.

2.90

The Modern Slavery (Victim Support) Bill aims to ensure:

- support until conclusion of the identification process (including during any process for reconsideration of the decision);

- a minimum period of 45 days' reflection and recovery during which support will be provided;

---

108 Human Trafficking and Exploitation (Criminal Justice and Support for Victims) Act (Northern Ireland) 2015, s 18(3) and (4).
109 Human Trafficking and Exploitation (Criminal Justice and Support for Victims) Act (Northern Ireland) 2015, s 18(8).
110 Human Trafficking and Exploitation (Criminal Justice and Support for Victims) Act (Northern Ireland) 2015, s 18(9).
111 Human Trafficking and Exploitation (Criminal Justice and Support for Victims) Act (Northern Ireland) 2015, s 19.
112 Modern Slavery Act 2015, s 49.
113 The power to make regulations derives from the Modern Slavery Act 2015, s 50.

- a discretionary power to continue support if necessary;

- temporary admission whilst under consideration by NRM[114].

2.91

The police should be notified as soon as possible of a positive reasonable grounds decision and generally the competent authority should ask the police to notify prosecutors as soon as the decision is made. In the case of a child, the immediate priority is to safeguard the child and promote his welfare[115].

Relevance of trafficking decisions in other proceedings

2.92

Chapter 7 considers the interplay of reasonable or conclusive grounds decisions with criminal proceedings, where the person referred is positively or negatively identified as a potential victim of trafficking, or conclusively is a victim of trafficking.

2.93

Chapter 10 sets out the relevance of a trafficking NRM decision in the asylum, human rights and immigration context. In summary, a negative decision on an asylum claim should not be made until after any conclusive grounds decision, as it may have a bearing on the decision. This does not preclude the Home Office making a positive decision (for example, if all nationals of a particular country qualify for protection there would be no reason to delay a grant of protection).

2.94

Chapter 11 considers in detail the consequence of this decision in the context of immigration detention and bail. In summary, where a positive reasonable grounds decision has been made the decision should be recorded on the Case Information Database. The Home Office will need to consider whether to grant temporary admission (to a person encountered and not detained) or temporary release (if a decision to detain has previously been taken) for the 45-day period, unless the person already has leave to remain of some form for the same period or more. The guidance is clear that a potential victim of trafficking will normally need to be released on temporary admission or temporary release unless the detention can be justified on the grounds of public order. This is a very different test to the usual test for immigration detention. See Chapter 11 for further detail.

---

114 Modern Slavery (Victim Support) Bill (HL Bill 4) introduced in the House of Lords on 26 June 2017, cl 48A(7).
115 Home Office, *Victims of modern slavery – Competent Authority guidance* (21 March 2016) p 109.

Negative reasonable grounds decision

2.95

Where a decision is negative a second appropriately trained caseworker or manager must review the decision. If the person has claimed asylum the second decision-maker must not be directly involved in the asylum decision[116].

2.96

The consequences of a negative decision are very serious for a victim. The account is dismissed as so incredible that the person is not entitled to the limited protections of the recovery and reflection period: a short time and safe space designed to enable a victim to obtain psychological, practical and legal advice which could in turn enable them to participate more fully in the determination process before a conclusive grounds decision is reached[117].

2.97

In practice, a person accommodated by a support agency will be required to leave his accommodation. It is therefore imperative that the potential victim of trafficking obtains legal advice as soon as possible as to whether there are grounds to challenge the decision.

Conclusive grounds decision

Standard of proof

2.98

The standard of proof for a conclusive grounds decision is the balance of probabilities. The test applied is whether 'on the balance of probabilities', 'there are sufficient grounds to decide that the individual being considered is a victim of human trafficking or modern slavery'. The guidance means that the competent authority has to consider that it is more likely than not that trafficking or modern slavery has 'happened'. It is important to remember that the purpose of the trafficking does not have to have been achieved for a person to qualify[118].

---

116 The competent authority may similarly review positive decisions, but is not required to do so.
117 *R (on the application of Hoang) v Secretary of State for the Home Department* [2015] EWHC 1725 (Admin), [2015] All ER (D) 228 (Jun).
118 Home Office, *Victims of modern slavery – Competent Authority guidance* (21 March 2016) p 65.

2.99

The guidance demands a high standard of reasoning from the competent authority, and rightly demands that if a decision is to turn on a lack of credibility, the competent authority must carefully analyse the relevant factors and explain its reasoning about credibility in its decision[119].

Assessment

2.100

At the conclusive grounds stage the competent authority is required to take into account every factor telling in favour of the potential victim of trafficking[120]. The guidance requires the competent authority to have before it all 'necessary information' before making a negative decision. The guidance notes[121]:

'The Competent Authority must make every effort to secure all available information that could prove useful in establishing if there are conclusive grounds.

If they cannot make a conclusive grounds decision based on the evidence available, they must gather evidence or make further enquiries during the 45 day recovery and reflection period.

The Competent Authority must gather this information, where appropriate, from:

- the first responder
- support provider
- police'.

2.101

To make its decision, it must weigh the strength of the indicators or evidence presented, including the credibility of the claim, and use common sense and logic based on the particular circumstances of each case.

2.102

An investigation into whether or not the individual is a victim of trafficking should then be undertaken. Under both ECAT and the ECHR, Art 4 there is

---

119 *R (on the application of M) v Secretary of State for the Home Department* [2015] EWHC 2467 (Admin) at para 55.
120 *R (on the application of SF) v Secretary of State for the Home Department* [2015] EWHC 2705 (Admin), [2016] 1 WLR 1439 at para 130.
121 Home Office, *Victims of modern slavery – Competent Authority guidance* (21 March 2016) p 65.

a clear obligation to investigate potential situations of trafficking. This is not simply a criminal investigation, as suggested by the Court of Appeal in *R (on the application of H)*[122], but an investigation designed to determine the status and protection needs of the victim[123]. Unfortunately, in the absence of a report to police or a proactive investigation, currently no real investigation is undertaken at all.

2.103

The individual should have the opportunity to deal with adverse inferences prior to a decision being made. This may require an interview. Adverse inferences should be put to the individual in writing where an interview could have a detrimental impact, and the benefits of an interview must be balanced against the potential to re-traumatise the victim[124].

2.104

Where the victim is a witness in an ongoing prosecution any interview should be conducted by an officer who is Achieving Best Evidence (ABE) trained. It is important that the competent authority is not seen to offer or appear to offer potential inducements to the victim, as these could undermine the credibility of any evidence obtained and adversely affect the prosecution's likelihood of a conviction[125].

2.105

Children should be interviewed only if absolutely necessary and in any event only by trained specialist child protection police or social work professionals[126]. The competent authority should avoid interviewing a child for the purpose of reaching a decision under the NRM if:

- there are specialists in other agencies capable of doing so;

- the modern slavery issues have already been clarified as part of the asylum process.

2.106

As with the reasonable grounds decision, before the competent authority reaches a negative conclusion, it must first refer back to the first responder or other expert witnesses to clarify any inconsistencies in the claim[127].

---

122 *R (on the application of H) v Secretary of State for the Home Department* [2016] EWCA Civ 565, [2016] Imm AR 1272 at para 39.
123 *J v Austria* (2017) App No 58216/12 at paras 109–111.
124 Home Office, *Victims of modern slavery – Competent Authority guidance* (21 March 2016) p 66.
125 Ibid p 67.
126 Ibid p 68.
127 Ibid p 97.

Timing of decision

2.107

The expectation is that a conclusive grounds decision will be made as soon as possible following the recovery and reflection period. However, the actual timescale will be based on all the circumstances of the case[128].

Consequences of positive conclusive grounds decision

2.108

If a positive decision is made, the individual will be recognised either as 'a victim of modern slavery (human trafficking)' or as 'a victim of modern slavery (slavery, servitude or forced and compulsory labour)'[129].

2.109

Where the decision relates to an adult, the decision will be served on the individual or his representative. A decision should not be served on a child under any circumstances, but on his representative. Additionally, the decision should be served on the first responder, any relevant support provider and any relevant local authority[130].

2.110

As with a reasonable grounds decision, the competent authority must notify the police and ask the police to notify the Crown Prosecution Service as soon as the decision is made[131].

2.111

Article 14 of ECAT requires states to make provision for the grant of a residence permit. This is incorporated into domestic law via policy.

2.112

Discretionary leave to remain (DLR) will be considered automatically where the individual has received a positive conclusive grounds decision. Discretionary leave to remain may be granted owing to:

- *Personal circumstances* where the person can demonstrate 'particularly compelling personal circumstances';

---

128 Ibid p 64.
129 Ibid p 70.
130 Ibid p 70.
131 Ibid p 71.

- *Pursuing compensation* where this results in a need to stay in the UK[132];

- *Helping police with enquiries* where the person has agreed to cooperate with the enquiry **and** the police make a formal request for leave to be granted.

2.113

'Personal circumstances' is perhaps the most disputed of these grounds with the Home Office demonstrating reluctance to recognise the vulnerability and ongoing needs of victims of trafficking and the lack of ability to return in dignity and safety.

2.114

There is a broad discretion about whether to grant DLR and if so for how long[133]. The period of leave will depend on the individual facts of the case and should be for the amount of time required, without further grants of discretionary leave being necessary in most cases. However, leave should normally be granted for a minimum of 12 months, and normally no more than 30 months. Shorter or longer periods may be granted if the facts of the case justify it, in accordance with the discretionary leave guidance[134]. Provision is made for the grant of indefinite leave to remain where a longer period of leave to remain is appropriate, for example, because it is in the best interests of a child or because there are other particularly exceptional compelling or compassionate reasons in the case[135].

2.115

Mishandling of a claim by the competent authority is a factor that should be taken into account when determining the period of leave to be granted[136]. Where expert medical evidence demonstrates that a particular period of leave to remain is required to undertake treatment, the decision-maker is required adequately to engage with that material and, in exercising his discretion take into account and afford appropriate weight to those conclusions[137].

---

132 See eg *R v Chief Immigration Officer, ex p Quaquah* [2000] HRLR 325; *R (on the application of Byndloss) v Secretary of State for the Home Department* [2017] UKSC 42, [2017] 1 WLR 2380 for examples of presence being required to pursue civil proceedings and the types of difficulties that result from litigating from abroad.

133 *IT (Sierra Leone) v Secretary of State for the Home Department* [2010] EWCA Civ 787 at 15; *R (on the application of Alladin) v Secretary of State for the Home Department* [2014] EWCA Civ 1334, [2015] Imm AR 237 at 53; *R (on the application of FT) v Secretary of State for the Home Department ('rolling review'; challenging leave granted)* [2017] UKUT 331 (IAC) at 65.

134 Home Office, *Victims of modern slavery – Competent Authority guidance* (21 March 2016) pp 77–78.

135 Home Office, *Asylum Policy Instruction: Discretionary Leave* (August 2015) sections 5.3–5.4.

136 *R (on the application of FT)* at 74.

137 *R (on the application of FT)* at 97, noting it was irrational to grant leave for the purpose of obtaining medical treatment for a shorter period than necessary to undertake that treatment.

2.116

However, if the trafficking experience took place some time ago, or if support could be accessed in another country, the competent authority is entitled to take those factors into account in determining whether the victim requires a grant of leave to remain in the UK due to compelling personal circumstances[138].

2.117

In England and Wales, the Modern Slavery (Victim Support) Bill[139] would require:

- continuation of support for a period of 12 months following the end of the reflection and recovery period[140] or the date of the conclusive grounds decision (whichever is the latest)[141];

- any grant of leave also to enable recourse to public funds where necessary[142];

- a discretionary power to extend support and leave to remain after the 12 months[143].

Negative conclusive grounds

2.118

Where a negative conclusive grounds decision is made, the competent authority must send a reasoned decision to the victim and notify the first responder, support provider and local authority (where relevant)[144]. As with a reasonable grounds decision, the competent authority must notify the police and ask the police to notify the Crown Prosecution Service as soon as the decision is made[145].

2.119

Any relevant immigration issues will need to be concluded and practitioners should note that it is open to the Immigration and Asylum Chamber of the Tribunal to reach its own decisions as to whether a person is a victim of trafficking, requires leave to remain to avoid a human rights breach[146], is a refugee or otherwise in need of protection.

---

138 Home Office, *Victims of modern slavery – Competent Authority guidance* (21 March 2016) p 103.
139 Modern Slavery (Victim Support) Bill.
140 Modern Slavery (Victim Support) Bill, cl 48B(2)(b).
141 Modern Slavery (Victim Support) Bill, cl 48B(4).
142 Modern Slavery (Victim Support) Bill, cl 48B(5) and (6).
143 Modern Slavery (Victim Support) Bill, cl 48B(6) and (8).
144 Home Office, *Victims of modern slavery – Competent Authority guidance* (21 March 2016) p 86.
145 Ibid pp 86–87.
146 Most commonly ECHR, Art 3, 4 or 8.

2.120

Assisted voluntary return may be requested at any point in the process by a person who does not wish to remain in the UK. Following a negative conclusive grounds decision the Home Office must inform the individual of this opportunity and the options available to make a voluntary return[147]. The individual should be notified of any programmes specifically aimed at victims of modern slavery[148].

Challenging negative decisions

2.121

First responders can ask the competent authority to review a negative decision[149]. There is no policy allowing legal advisers to make such requests but they should be proactive in asking first responders to make a reconsideration request and provide additional evidence if necessary. A refusal to review a decision requested by a representative is potentially incompatible with the requirement on the State to identify victims of trafficking as soon as a credible allegation is received. For example, if a reasonable grounds decision was made on the basis of a lack of indicators and the legal representative had evidence of additional indicators, the competent authority should not simply refuse to accept the evidence because it had not arrived through specified channels.

2.122

Challenges to negative reasonable and conclusive grounds decisions are brought in the Administrative Court by way of judicial review[150]. Challenges to refusals to issue residence permits are also by way of judicial review but should be brought in the Upper Tribunal[151]. An application for anonymity under the Civil Procedure Rules, r 39.2 should be made. A claim challenging the negative conclusive grounds decision must be made promptly and in any event within three months of the decision.

---

147 Note that not all schemes apply to all potential victims, for example in criminal cases.
148 Home Office, *Victims of modern slavery – Competent Authority guidance* (21 March 2016) p 118; see www. gov.uk/return-home-voluntarily for more information.
149 Home Office, *Victims of modern slavery – Competent Authority guidance* (21 March 2016) p 91.
150 This includes immigration cases (where otherwise judicial review proceedings would be commenced in the Upper Tribunal) because a negative reasonable grounds decision is not related to the Immigration Acts and is explicitly stated not to be an immigration decision: Home Office, *Victims of modern slavery – Competent Authority guidance* (21 March 2016) p 55.
151 Such decisions 'otherwise relating to leave to enter or remain in the United Kingdom outside the immigration rules' (see Consolidated Direction given in accordance with the Constitutional Reform Act 2005, Sch 2, Part 1 and the Tribunals, Courts and Enforcement Act 2007, s 18, available at www. judiciary.gov.uk/wp-content/uploads/2013/10/lcj-direction-jr-iac-21-08-2013-updated-2.pdf).

Victims who go missing

2.123

Victims who go missing present particular problems for practitioners, including in respect of Legal Aid and instructions. As a matter of good practice you should seek a retainer and your client's instructions about what she wishes you to do if those circumstances were to arise[152].

2.124

In cases involving persons who go missing where a decision on either reasonable or conclusive grounds has not yet been taken and:

- the evidence available is insufficient to meet the relevant standard of proof; and

- it is not possible to gather more information because the victim is missing,

the competent authority is required to take the following steps[153]:

(i) **Action 1**: report the potential victim of human trafficking or modern slavery as a vulnerable missing person to the police and arrange for a missing person marker to be added to the police national computer;

(ii) **Action 2**: notify the following that the case has been suspended:

- first responder;

- the support provider (all supported adult and family cases) (and the Salvation Army if support was being provided in England and Wales);

- the local authority (in the case of children);

(iii) **Action 3**: if the potential victim is the subject of criminal proceedings, several agencies need to be notified as soon as the reasonable or conclusive grounds decision is suspended. The competent authority must ensure that the police (in Scotland, the National Human Trafficking Unit) are notified of the suspended reasonable or conclusive grounds decision as soon as they make it. Generally the competent authority should ask the police to notify prosecutors (the Crown Prosecution Service) (or the Crown Office and Procurator Fiscals Service in Scotland or Prosecution Service

---

152 There is no requirement to obtain fresh instructions at each stage of proceedings (see eg *Donsland Ltd v Hoogstraten* [2002] EWCA Civ 253, [2002] PNLR 28 at para 19, per Tuckey LJ). However, there may be specific issues on which specific instructions are required. In general it is likely that a judicial review relating to an historic decision (eg a reasonable or conclusive grounds decision) could be concluded, but any associated damages claim would have to be stayed.

153 The steps are the same at both the reasonable and conclusive grounds stages. See Home Office, *Victims of modern slavery – Competent Authority guidance* (21 March 2016) pp 62 and 89.

in Northern Ireland) of the suspended reasonable or conclusive grounds decision as soon as they make it[154];

(iv) **Home Office action only**: Home Office staff must:

- register the case as a 'PVoT suspended absconder' on the Case Information Database;

- ensure that the case has been flagged on the Case Information Database as having had the issue of human trafficking or modern slavery raised, so that the person is recognised as potentially at risk if he is encountered again.

2.125

The guidance for both reasonable or conclusive grounds decisions also states that if 'sufficient information' is available a decision should be made. In light of the above it is clear that the policy intended that only positive decisions would be made as it is not possible to gather more information where a person has gone missing[155].

2.126

Furthermore, we would suggest that if the decision-maker does not know why the person has gone missing, it is entirely possible that he may have been re-trafficked. In many cases a victim will turn up months later in a cannabis farm or a brothel[156]. The Court of Appeal, in the context of a criminal appeal, has taken a precautionary approach when considering cases where victims have gone missing[157]. In such circumstances an order should be sought, at the very least, agreeing a set of minimum standards and actions should the individual be discovered, eg that he will be treated as a potential victim of trafficking, his legal representative/support provider will be notified, he will not be removed for a specified period of time etc.

2.127

The competent authority guidance also states that 'If someone who has claimed asylum goes missing it may be appropriate to treat their claim as withdrawn.' We would respectfully disagree and suggest that the asylum claim should be stayed pending the reappearance of the victim, for the same reasons.

---

154 Home Office, *Victims of modern slavery – Competent Authority guidance* (21 March 2016) pp 62 and 129.

155 In practice, UK Visas and Immigration is currently also making negative decisions in such circumstances. We would suggest that this is generally in breach of its own policy save in the most exceptional cases.

156 See eg 'Heading Back to Harm: A study on trafficked and unaccompanied children going missing from care in the UK' (ECPAT and Missing People, November 2016) reporting that over 25% of trafficked children in the UK went missing, available at www.ecpat.org.uk/heading-back-to-harm-a-study-on-trafficked-and-unaccompanied-children-going-missing-from-care-in-the-uk, last accessed 6 December 2017.

157 *R v Okedare* [2014] EWCA Crim 228, [2014] 1 WLR 4071 at paras 23–34. The Administrative Court has taken a similar approach in judicial review proceedings – however, those cases are unreported.

Asylum seekers

2.128

Where a person is referred to the NRM and has an asylum claim no decision should be taken on the asylum claim pending resolution of the NRM process[158]. This does not prevent the Home Office from conducting status interviews. A status interview technically is an interview to determine identity, nationality or citizenship and immigration status in the UK. The current interpretation by both the Home Office and the courts is that there is nothing to prevent an asylum interview taking place prior to completion of the identification[159].

2.129

The approach taken by the Home Office is that normal procedures should be carried out and that the asylum interview 'may provide information that is also relevant to the NRM decision where trafficking or modern slavery issues are clarified and investigated as part of the asylum process'[160]. As there are often cross overs between the reasons the individual is seeking asylum and the trafficking, all the reasons why it may not be appropriate to interview a potential victim of trafficking logically equally apply to the asylum interview. Therefore, we are of the view that, unless significant and appropriate modifications are made to the process, interviewing asylum applicants prior to a rest and recovery period is unsafe.

2.130

Specialist immigration advice should be sought if the potential victim of trafficking is subject to the Dublin Regulations. Current guidance suggests that where an individual is an asylum seeker subject to the 'third country' procedures under Dublin III Regulation (EU) No 604/2013, the UK is not required to provide support and protection in the UK while his trafficking or modern slavery case is considered under the NRM[161]. This is wrong. The duty to identify arises when a credible allegation arises. If a person is a victim or potential victim of trafficking positive obligations arise under both ECAT and ECHR, Art 4[162]. In principle, the two procedures can and do run parallel to each other. Practitioners should note that referral under the NRM process does not suspend time limits for the purposes of ECAT, Art 27[163].

---

158 Home Office, *Victims of modern slavery – Competent Authority guidance* (21 March 2016) pp 71 and 116.

159 *R (on the application of XYL) v Secretary of State for the Home Department* [2017] EWHC 773 (Admin) at para 22, see also Home Office, *Enforcement and Instructions Guidance* ch 9, at 8.1.

160 Home Office, *Victims of modern slavery – Competent Authority guidance* (21 March 2016) p 115.

161 Home Office, *Victims of modern slavery – Competent Authority guidance* (21 March 2016) p 103.

162 *J v Austria* (2017) App No 58216/12. In *R (on the application of BG) v Secretary of State for the Home Department* [2016] EWHC 786 (Admin), [2016] Imm AR 928 Cranston J rejected an argument that once a reasonable ground decision had been made this overrode the requirements of the Dublin II Regulation because it was a 'residence permit'.

163 At the time of writing permission on this point has been granted but not determined in *CO/1758/2016*.

2.131

Decision-makers are referred to the 'latest guidance on Dublin III'. Unfortunately this has not been published, despite the Regulation having been in force for well over two years at the time of writing.

Historical victims

2.132

In circumstances where an individual has experienced trafficking a long time ago or prior to coming to the UK or on his journey, he still requires identification and protection under the NRM[164].

2.133

Where trafficking has occurred overseas the competent authority must in any event pass any details of the alleged trafficking or exploitation to the NRM Intelligence Hub so they can consider raising it with the authorities in the country where the offence was committed. This is to ensure that the Home Office's obligations under ECAT, Art 27 are met[165].

Grounds of challenge

2.134

The failure to incorporate ECAT directly into UK law means that it is not directly effective. Any challenge to decisions made by the competent authority will be based on general public law principles, including a failure to apply the published policy. As it is clear that the policy was published to give effect to ECAT it:

> 'should be taken to have intended to protect the victim's rights, combat trafficking and promote international co-operation (the objectives identified in the Convention) and to promote a human rights based approach'[166].

2.135

The standard of review has been the subject of much debate[167]. As trafficking and slavery cases involve fundamental rights (both in themselves and in the

164 *R (on the application of Atamewan) v Secretary of State for the Home Department* [2013] EWHC 2727 (Admin), [2014] 1 WLR 1959 at 69–80.
165 Home Office, *Victims of modern slavery – Competent Authority guidance* (21 March 2016) p 103.
166 *R (on the application of Hoang) v Secretary of State for the Home Department* [2015] EWHC 1725 (Admin), [2015] All ER (D) 228 (Jun) at para 53.
167 *R (on the application of SF) v Secretary of State for the Home Department* [2015] EWHC 2705 (Admin), [2016] 1 WLR 1439 at paras 84–107.

consequences flowing from positive recognition) the rationality of a gateway decision that a person is not the victim of trafficking requires a more heightened or a more rigorous level of scrutiny, both because it relates to fundamental rights and also because it arises in an area in which a court has the requisite knowledge. Consequently, the competent authority needs to ensure decisions show by their reasoning that every factor which tells in favour of the applicant has been properly taken into account[168].

2.136

Further, given the nature of the guidance, and the level of detail that it provides in relation to the consideration of credibility in trafficking claims, a high standard of reasoning is required from the competent authority in order to demonstrate a careful and conscientious analysis of the relevant factors which have to be taken into account when assessing credibility[169].

2.137

Broadly speaking the court can consider legality, rationality and procedural impropriety. The most common grounds of review in trafficking cases include:

- errors of law or fact[170];

- failure to give reasons[171];

- substantive unfairness[172];

- failure to take into account material considerations/taking into account immaterial considerations;

---

168 *R (on the application of SF) v Secretary of State for the Home Department* [2015] EWHC 2705 (Admin), [2016] 1 WLR 1439 at para 104.

169 *R (on the application of Hoang) v Secretary of State for the Home Department* [2015] EWHC 1725 (Admin), [2015] All ER (D) 228 (Jun) at para 48; *R (on the application of FK) v Secretary of State for the Home Department* [2016] EWHC 56 (Admin) at para 27.

170 For mistake of fact see *E v Secretary of State* [2004] QB 1044, per Carnwath LJ at 66, p 1071:
  '66.   In our view, the time has now come to accept that a mistake of fact giving rise to unfairness is a separate head of challenge in an appeal on a point of law, at least in those statutory contexts where the parties share an interest in co-operating to achieve the correct result. …Without seeking to lay down a precise code, the ordinary requirements for a finding of unfairness are apparent from the above analysis of CICB. First, there must have been a mistake as to an existing fact, including a mistake as to the availability of evidence on a particular matter. Secondly, the fact or evidence must have been "established", in the sense that it was uncontentious and objectively verifiable. Thirdly, the appellant (or his advisers) must not have been responsible for the mistake. Fourthly, the mistake must have played a material (not necessarily decisive) part in the Tribunal's reasoning'.

171 Lord Carnwath (with whom Moore-Bick and Etherton LJJ agreed) in *R (on the application of YH) v Secretary of State* [2010] EWCA Civ 116, [2010] 4 All ER 448 at 24 explained 'the need for decisions to show by their reasoning that every factor which tells in favour of the applicant has been properly taken into account'. See also *R (on the application of SF) v Secretary of State for the Home Department* [2015] EWHC 2705 (Admin), [2016] 1 WLR 1439 at para 104.

172 See eg *E v Secretary of State for the Home Department* [2004] EWCA Civ 49, [2004] QB 1044, where unfairness resulted from a misunderstanding or ignorance of a relevant fact.

- irrationality[173];

- breach of policy[174];

- breaches of human rights (ECHR, Arts 4 and 8 most commonly arising in trafficking claims).

2.138

The question whether the correct legal test has been applied is one of 'substance not semantics'[175]. This means it is not sufficient for the competent authority to merely state that it has applied the correct test; it must also do so in practice.

2.139

A victim of trafficking is entitled to understand how the competent authority guidance has been applied[176].

2.140

There is a contentious issue as to whether the failure to identify and investigate results in a public authority acting in a way which is incompatible with a Convention right under Art 4, which is unlawfulness proscribed by the Human Rights Act 1998, s 6(1)[177]. The Court of Appeal has indicated that this merely requires a police investigation where relevant and is not the responsibility of the 'Secretary of State for the Home Department' acting as the 'Competent Authority'[178]. However this appears to be based on a misunderstanding of the interrelationship between the National Crime Agency and the Home Office as 'competent authorities' and the requirements of the protective limb of Art 4 as subsequently clarified in *J v Austria*. We are of the view that *R (on the application of H)* is an incorrect statement of the law.

---

173 See *R (on the application of SF) v Secretary of State for the Home Department* [2015] EWHC 2705 (Admin), [2016] 1 WLR 1439 at para 180 citing *R (on the application of M) v Secretary of State for the Home Department* [2015] EWHC 2467 (Admin), in which it was held to be irrational to accept the claimant's evidence showing one of the requirements was satisfied but then reject the same evidence in respect of another aspect of the definition.

174 A failure by a public authority to follow its own established policy without good reason can be an error of law: *Lumba v Secretary of State* [2011] UKSC 12, [2012] AC 245. See *R (on the application of M)* [2015] EWHC 1725 (Admin) at 53 for breach of policy in a trafficking case.

175 *R (on the application of Hoang) v Secretary of State for the Home Department* [2015] EWHC 1725 (Admin), [2015] All ER (D) 228 (Jun).

176 *R (on the application of FK) v Secretary of State for the Home Department* [2016] EWHC 56 (Admin) per Dove J at para 32.

177 See Lord Hoffmann in *Miss Behavin' v Belfast City Council* [2007] 1 WLR 1420 at 14 and 15, as applied in *R (on the application of SF) v Secretary of State for the Home Department*.

178 *R (on the application of H) v Secretary of State for the Home Department* [2016] EWCA Civ 565, [2016] Imm AR 1272.

2.141

If a challenge is successful the court will not (absent exceptional circumstances) substitute its own view of the merits of a decision, but will instead 'quash' the decision and remit it to the competent authority to retake[179].

---

179 See eg *R (on the application of FT) v Secretary of State for the Home Department* [2017] UKUT 331 (IAC).

3   Age disputes in immigration and criminal proceedings

Introduction

3.1

The United Nations Declaration on the Rights of the Child 1959 and the UN Convention on the Rights of the Child 1989 ('UNCRC') both require that a child enjoy special protection[1]. The guiding principle for safeguarding and promoting the welfare of children is contained in UNCRC, Art 3:

> 'In all actions concerning children, whether undertaken by public or private social welfare institutions, courts of law, administrative authorities or legislative bodies, the best interests of the child should be of primary consideration.'

The principle of 'best interests' appears repeatedly throughout the UNCRC, for example in Arts 9, 18, 20 and 21. Whilst the UNCRC is not directly incorporated into the domestic law article by article in their exact terms, the aims of the UNCRC and the best interests approach to affording children special protection are recognised across the different areas of law, including social welfare, education, immigration and crime[2]. The special protection afforded under the UNCRC and in domestic law is predicated on an individual being in fact a child.

3.2

So who is a child? Article 1 of the UNCRC defines a child as a human being who is under the age of 18. The UK's domestic law adopts the same definition in almost all circumstances, although criminal law makes a distinction between those who are children and those who are young persons (persons of 16 and 17 years of age) for the purposes of how they are dealt with in the youth justice system.

---

1   For discussion, see *R (on the application of HC) v Secretary of State for the Home Department* [2013] EWHC 982 (Admin), [2014] 1 WLR 1234.

2   See *ZH (Tanzania) v Secretary of State for the Home Department* [2011] UKSC 4, [2011] 2 AC 166; *R (on the application of HC) v Secretary of State for the Home Department* [2013] EWHC 982 (Admin), [2014] 1 WLR 1234; *R (on the application of Mathieson) v Secretary of State for Work and Pensions* [2015] UKSC 47, [2015] 1 WLR 3250; *R (on the application of SG) v Secretary of State for Work and Pensions* [2015] UKSC 16, [2015] 1 WLR 1449.

3.3

More often than not, the fact of age has a significant bearing on how the state approaches different aspects of a child's social, emotional and developmental existence. Age is itself an immutable characteristic. Determining a person's age, however, is not an easy forensic task, particularly in the context of children who arrive in the UK unaccompanied or trafficked.

3.4

Age disputes commonly arise in circumstances where putative children arrive unaccompanied in the UK to seek asylum or other forms of international protection, or where they are trafficked to the UK for the purposes of exploitation[3]. These children often have no identifying information on them. In other cases their documents may be false or they may have been told to lie about their age to evade the attention of the authorities[4]. Some may also have been given a false history by their traffickers or agents, which may include a false date of birth showing that they are adults in order to make it easier to provide them with false identity documents and to facilitate their travel[5]. There are then some who do have some documentary evidence corroborative of their claimed age, but the evidence may require translation or need to have its provenance verified, having regard to information about the manner in which the document was issued and by whom.

3.5

This chapter will look at the following issues:

- the importance and relevance of age in domestic law;

- how age is assessed;

- the approach to be taken by the courts.

Importance and relevance of age in the context of social welfare law

3.6

The Supreme Court has held in *R (on the application of A) v Croydon London Borough Council*[6] that a person's age is an objective fact which admits only a

---

3   See for example, the first three appellants in the linked appeals in *R v L* [2013] EWCA Crim 991, [2014] 1 All ER 113.

4   See CPS Legal Guidance, Human Trafficking and Smuggling: Prosecution of Defendants (children and adults) charged with offences who might be Trafficked Victims, available at www.cps.gov.uk/legal-guidance/human-trafficking-smuggling-and-slavery.

5   ECPAT, 'UK's Submission to the Joint Committee on Human Rights inquiry into the human rights of unaccompanied migrant children and young people in the UK' (2012) para 36.

6   [2009] UKSC 8, [2009] 1 WLR 2557.

right or a wrong answer[7]. It is not a matter of subjective evaluation by an individual decision-maker, and certainly not a summary one without proper inquiries. The precedent fact of age is a gateway decision that unlocks access to the child of child-centred accommodation, support, and special protection in the immigration and youth justice context.

3.7

The *A v Croydon* case itself concerned a local authority children's services department, which was obliged to provide an unaccompanied asylum-seeking child with accommodation and support under the Children Act 1989, s 20 because there was no-one with parental responsibility and no family or friend able to take care of the child. Section 105 of the Children Act 1989 defines a child objectively as someone under 18. If a person is a child, it unlocks a host of special protections that adult asylum-seekers cannot access.

3.8

Children who are taken into 'voluntary care', as s 20 accommodation is often described, are entitled to a suite of further special protection measures from the local authority. The authority is obliged to:

- arrange accommodation suitable to the child's needs and age;
- make educational provision for the child, whether the child is of statutory school age or beyond;
- support the child to access legal representation for immigration advice; and
- care for the child generally as a reasonable parent would do.

Once accommodated, the child is considered 'looked after' by the local authority under the Children Act 1989, s 22. The duty to promote and safeguard all aspects of the child's welfare is engaged and requires a best interests approach to care planning for the child.

3.9

Accommodation arrangements are often highly dependent on the child's age. Whilst there are no hard and fast rules and arrangements should be made in accordance with the child's needs, children aged 15 and under tend to be placed in foster care, whereas 16- and 17-year-olds tend to be placed in supported lodgings.

3.10

Educational placements are also determined by the precise age of the child. For example, children under 16 are of statutory school age, and the local authority,

---

7   Per Lady Hale at [27] and [33], Lord Hope at [52]–[54].

acting as corporate parent, is obliged in law to enrol the looked after child in education, whether in a school or otherwise in an alternative facility. There are continuing duties to promote the child's educational achievement beyond statutory school age, if the child is looked after by the local authority.

3.11

The duties owed to 'looked after' children who are in voluntary care continue beyond the child's 18th birthday. When they turn 18, if they have been looked after by the local authority, whether under a care order or under s 20 accommodation arrangements for 13 weeks or more, with at least one day being when the child is over the age of 16, they acquire status as former relevant children (defined under the Children Act 1989, s 23C(1)). Under s 23C(4), they continue to receive assistance from the local authority. The assistance given can include continued suitable accommodation arrangements in accordance with the former relevant child's needs, support to access education and vocational training and general advice and assistance, as a reasonable parent would provide for a child transitioning into adulthood. See paras 1.8 and 1.10 of the *Children Act 1989 Guidance and Regulations: Transition to Adulthood*[8]. These leaving care duties continue until at least the former relevant child's 21st birthday and, in circumstances where they remain in education or are returning to education, the duties can continue up to the former relevant child's 25th birthday.

Importance and relevance of age in the context of immigration law

3.12

The objective fact of age also plays a significant role in the context of the Home Office's exercise of immigration powers, both in the context of decisions relating to the grant or refusal of leave to remain in respect of children and in the context of decisions to detain.

3.13

In all decisions concerning children, the Home Office is obliged to have due regard to the need to safeguard and promote the welfare of the child pursuant to the Borders, Citizenship and Immigration Act 2009, s 55. Section 55(6) defines children as those under the age of 18. Section 55 came into being after the UK lifted its reservation on the UNCRC in respect of immigration matters concerning children. The language of s 55 mirrors the obligation owed by local authorities, health authorities, police, and the youth offending team under the Children Act 2004, s 11.

---

8 Department for Education (revised January 2015).

3.14

Specific immigration rules recognise and afford the special protection status required by children. For example, para 350 of the Immigration Rules[9] requires that in the case of unaccompanied children, particular priority and care is given to the handling of their cases. Paragraphs 352 and 352ZA set out the requirements for undertaking asylum interviews with children, including the requirement that the child be given an opportunity to have an appropriate adult present for the interview. Only decision-makers who have received specialist training can make decisions in asylum claims from children, and they must also observe a wealth of guidance on the different approach to be taken to assessing the credibility of child asylum seekers, having regard to the child's age and maturity and recognising that more weight may need to be given to objective evidence than to the child's subjective fears.

3.15

More importantly, in the context of immigration detention, by an amendment to the detention powers, the Immigration Act 1971, Sch 2, para 18B now prohibits the detention of an individual who is objectively and in fact a child. Deprivation of such a child's liberty would constitute a false imprisonment whether or not the Home Office reasonably believed or suspected him or her to be an adult at the time[10]. Where a dispute about age arises, the Home Office's policy is to presume that the person is a child (albeit age disputed) pending inquiries unless, and only unless the person's physical appearance *strongly* suggests that he or she is *significantly* over the age of 18. The Home Office's policy describes this as affording the putative child the benefit of the doubt. Unsurprisingly, there has been litigation around the meaning of the policy and what 'significantly over' 18 means. As observed by Munby J (as he then was) in *R (on the application of A) (disputed children) v Secretary of State for the Home Department*[11], in the context of group litigation relating to the immigration detention of age disputed asylum-seeking children:

> 'Plainly the matter [as to age] cannot rest on the mere assertion, however obviously ludicrous, of the asylum seeker. If, for example, I was to present myself – an obviously middle-aged, some might say elderly, man – at Heathrow and claim to be a child, my claim to be a child would rightly be rejected on the spot. But other cases may be far less clear cut and may take time to resolve. So the Secretary of State has to have a policy'.

9   Published 29 February 2016.
10 *R (on the application of Ali) (Sudan) v Secretary of State for the Home Department* [2017] EWCA Civ 138, [2017] 1 WLR 2894.
11 [2007] EWHC 2494 (Admin) at para [5].

Importance and relevance of age in the context of youth justice

3.16

The importance of establishing the right answer as to the objective fact of age is self-evident in the youth justice context. In General Comment No 10 (2007) on *Children's Rights in Juvenile Justice*[12], the Committee on the Rights of the Child stated that children differ from adults in their physical and psychological development, and their emotional and educational needs. Such differences constitute the basis for the lesser culpability of children in conflict with the law. These and other differences are the reasons for a separate juvenile justice system and 'require a different treatment for children'. The protection of the best interests of the child may mean that the traditional objectives of criminal justice, such as repression/retribution, must give way to rehabilitation and restorative justice objectives in dealing with child offenders[13].

3.17

Articles 37 and 40 of the UNCRC are of particular importance in this context, as the former deals with detention and the latter with juvenile justice[14]:

'17.1 Article 37(a) provides that "no child shall be deprived of his or her liberty unlawfully or arbitrarily. The arrest, detention or imprisonment of a child shall be in conformity with the law and shall be used only as a measure of last resort and for the shortest appropriate period of time". Article 37(c) provides that, "every child deprived of liberty shall be treated with humanity and respect for the inherent dignity of the human person, and in a manner which takes into account the needs of persons of his or her age".

17.2 This is echoed in Article 40 which in essence provides that any child of under 18 accused of, or guilty of, breaking the law must be treated with dignity and respect, and they have a range of minimum

---

12 CRC/C/GC/10 (25 April 2007), available at http://docstore.ohchr.org/SelfServices/FilesHandler.ash x?enc=6QkG1d%2fPPRiCAqhKb7yhsqIkirKQZLK2M58R F%2f5F0vEZN%2bo3pfhJYL%2b%2fo2i7 llJgP6EjqSGKnB2CPSr6g7ed2P0M8AO57Tg1kfwde7vhIIwc0tRQLDmAZWHVA9bVwzD%2b (last accessed 6 December 2017).

13 The Supreme Court has held that the General Comments of the CRC provide 'authoritative guidance' on the effect of the provisions of the CRC: *R (on the application of Mathieson) v Secretary of State for Work and Pensions* [2015] UKSC 47, [2015] 1 WLR 3250 at [39], endorsing *R (on the application of SG) v Secretary of State for Work and Pensions* [2015] UKSC 16, [2015] 1 WLR 1449 at [105]–[106].

14 The essential safeguards in the UNCRC concerning children in conflict with the law are supplemented by many other specific instruments. See eg The United Nations Standard Minimum Rules for the Administration of Juvenile Justice ('the Beijing Rules' 1985); the United Nations Guidelines for the Prevention of Juvenile Delinquency ('the Riyadh Guidelines'); the United Nations Rules for the Protection of Juveniles Deprived of their Liberty ('the Havana Rules'); the UN Guidelines for Action on Children in the Criminal Justice System ('the Vienna Guidelines', 1997); and the UN Model Strategies and Practical Measures on the Elimination of Violence against Children in the Field of Crime Prevention and Criminal Justice (2014).

procedural rights which must be provided in a manner which takes account of their age and situation. Article 40(2)(b) describes the seven bare minimum requirements ("at least the following guarantees"), including the right to have the matter determined by a competent, independent and impartial authority or judicial body in a fair hearing according to the law, bearing in mind the best interests of the child, taking into account his or her age or situation; and the right to have his or her privacy fully respected at all stages of the proceedings.

17.3 Article 40(3) requires that State parties shall seek to promote the establishment of laws, procedures, authorities and institutions specifically applicable to children, rather than treating them in the same manner and through the same mechanisms as adult suspects or adult offenders'.

3.18

Domestic law concerning youth justice has also long recognised the need to have regard to a child's welfare. The principal aim of the youth justice system is to prevent offending by young people, as enshrined in the Crime and Disorder Act 1998, s 27(1). Thus the approach to youth defendants is necessarily different. 'Child' and 'young person' have technical meaning within the criminal justice framework. A 'child' is defined as someone under the age of 14 years[15]. A 'young person' is someone who has attained 14 but not yet 18. The age of criminal responsibility is 10 years old[16]. Sentencing guidelines are often guided by age. The fact of age is significant for how the criminal justice system deals with a person, as is evident from the following.

Decision to prosecute

3.19

The Crown Prosecution Service has detailed guidance (*The CPS:Youth Offenders*) on prosecuting young defendants. The public interest test for prosecution demands different considerations than in the context of an adult, requiring the CPS to make a decision which considers the best interests and welfare of both the accused and the victim (if the latter is also a child): see Chapter 5.

First appearances

3.20

The child's first court appearance in respect of an offence will be in the youth court unless the case is an exceptional one where he is jointly charged with an

---

15 Children and Young Persons Act (CYPA) 1933, s 107(1) and CYPA 1963, s 70(1).
16 CYPA 1933, s 50.

adult; charged with aiding and abetting an adult to commit an offence (or vice versa); or charged with an offence which arises out of circumstances which are the same as (or connected with) those which resulted in the charge faced by an adult accused. The child has no right to elect a Crown Court trial and can only be sent to the Crown Court if the magistrates have decided that they should not accept jurisdiction. Even then, the Crown Court has power to put in place additional safeguards in the trial process. These include, generally, the exclusion of the public, reporting restrictions and the attendance of parent or guardian if a juvenile is under 16.

Bail

3.21

Although the criteria for granting bail under the Bail Act 1976 are virtually the same for adults and children, there are a number of important differences which put the primacy of protection of the welfare of the child at their heart. For example, the court has a discretion to refuse bail where this is necessary for a juvenile's welfare or protection[17]. A parent or guardian may be asked to act as surety as a condition of bail[18].

3.22

What bail package a person can access for a realistic bail application can also turn on the fact of age. A lone child, for whom no one has parental responsibility, will necessarily meet the criteria for local authority accommodation under the Children Act 1989, s 20. Through the Youth Offending Team, the child defendant could seek to access accommodation with accompanying wrap-around support to meet his full range of needs. Being in the local authority's care would – in and of itself – provide a great measure of assurance of compliance with bail conditions. All this would put the child in good stead for a realistic application for bail and likely grant of bail.

3.23

Even if bail is refused to a child, the court approaches remand significantly differently for children as opposed to adults. If bail is withheld from a child[19], he is remanded to local authority accommodation or to youth detention accommodation[20]. This includes 17-year-olds who, under the previous framework under the Children and Young Persons Act 1969, could be remanded to an adult prison. The Legal Aid, Sentencing and Punishment of Offenders Act ('LASPO') 2012, ss 98–102 also strengthened protections for youth

---

17 Bail Act 1976, Sch 1, para 1.
18 Bail Act 1976, s 3(7).
19 Child, for the purposes of LASPO 2012, means a person under the age of 18: s 91(6).
20 LASPO 2012, ss 91–107.

defendants, setting a more rigorous threshold for the court to satisfy before a child can be remanded to youth detention accommodation instead of local authority secure accommodation. These provisions marked a significant step in recognising the importance of differentiating the needs and welfare issues relating to youth offenders as compared to adult offenders, acknowledging the importance of safeguarding the welfare of *all children* under 18[21] and the material difference in restrictions between a youth detention and local authority secure accommodation environment. All these contribute to creating a *child-friendly* justice system which ensures effective participation of the child in the trial process irrespective of the nature and gravity of the offence. A lone putative child, wrongly deemed to be an adult, self-evidently will be deprived of these precautionary and protective measures.

Mode of trial

3.24

The great majority of juveniles are tried and sentenced in youth courts, which are, by virtue of the Children and Young Persons Act ('CYPA') 1933, s 45, a special subset of the magistrates' courts and a court of summary jurisdiction. Youth courts sit for the purpose of hearing any charge against a child or a young person or for the purpose of exercising any other jurisdiction conferred on youth courts by or under any Act. There is a statutory assumption that the youth court is the most appropriate forum to try youth defendants, having regard to the best interests and welfare of the child, the importance of a child's effective participation and a fair trial. This manifests in the material difference in trial environment and process in the youth court as compared to adult courts. Youth courts are essentially private places; members of the public are not allowed in and there are reporting restrictions[22]. Victims of crime are able to attend youth court hearings if they want to but must make a request of the court if they wish to do so. Magistrates hearing cases in the youth court receive training to approach the trial process in a child-centred manner notwithstanding the gravity of crimes which may come before them. Importantly, the youth court has jurisdiction to try offences which, in the case of an adult, are triable only on indictment (with the exception of homicide and certain firearms offences). Whereas an adult may never be tried summarily for an offence triable only on indictment and has a right to elect trial on indictment for an offence triable either way, a child may be (and normally is) tried summarily for an indictable offence, whatever his wishes as to mode of trial may be. The youth defendant, in other words, has no right to elect a Crown Court trial and if sent to the Crown Court for trial this is only because the magistrates have decided that they should not accept jurisdiction.

---

21 See *R (on the application of HC) v Secretary of State for the Home Department* [2013] EWHC 982 (Admin), [2014] 1 WLR 1234.
22 CYPA 1933, ss 47 and 49.

3.25

If the court gets the answer to age wrong (ie in its determination of age before a decision on mode of trial) this may result in a putative child, wrongly deemed to be an adult, being committed to the Crown Court to be tried by a jury in circumstances where, had the correct facts as to age been ascertained, the Crown Court would have no lawful jurisdiction over the putative youth defendant. The adverse consequence is compounded by the Crown Court having no statutory power to remit the youth defendant's case back to the youth court for trial.

3.26

Once the youth court has declined jurisdiction and the matter has presented itself to the Crown Court, it stays in the Crown Court, irrespective of whether the factual basis of committal no longer exists or was wrong, flawed and unreliable. Thus even in a case where committal to the Crown Court was solely on the basis of deemed adulthood (which was factually wrong and renders the committal invalid), the Crown Court is unable to remedy the invalid committal by remitting the youth defendant back to a specialist court designed specifically with youth defendants in mind. The Crown Court can, of course, make its own assessment of the youth defendant's age but can only use its powers to direct such special measures as may be required. The trial would still proceed in the Crown Court. This means that the onus for redressing the prejudice caused falls heavily (and almost exclusively) on the defendant if the court's inquiry of age was legally flawed or factually wrong. The only tangible way by which the youth defendant could re-access the youth court is by way of a successful judicial review against the youth court's decision to commit predicated on an unlawful and factually erroneous deeming of his adulthood.

Assessing age

3.27

There is no proven scientific process by which age can be precisely determined. Dental and wrist x-rays have long been criticised for the wide margin of error both by courts and by the Royal College of Paediatrics and Child Health, in particular, in 1999 and again in 2004. Most recently, in *R (on the application of ZM) v Croydon London Borough Council*[23], the Upper Tribunal acting as a judicial review court concluded that age cannot be accurately assessed from dental x-rays and maturity.

3.28

As long ago as 2003, local authority children's services developed a pro forma identifying the domains of inquiries relevant to a more holistic determination

---

23 [2016] UKUT 559 (IAC).

of a person's age, adopting a model from the needs assessment framework which focuses on child development. This model acknowledges that physical appearance and demeanour are highly risky and unreliable factors for determining age. This is acknowledged to be particularly so in borderline cases where the young person falls between 16 and 20 years' old because of ethnic, cultural and situational influences that may make certain people appear older than their actual age[24]. Indeed, the notes to the pro forma developed by local authorities to assess age highlight under guidance notes to the heading 'Physical Appearance, Demeanour' that these factors can only serve as initial indicators of age and do not determine and end the process of inquiry:

> 'An initial hypothesis of age range is formed based on height, facial features (facial hair, skin lines / folds etc) voice tone and general impression.

> It is important to consider racial differences here e.g. It is normal in some cultures for boys to have facial hair at an early age and for girls to develop at different ages.

> Life experiences and trauma may impact on the aging process, bear this in mind.

> Demeanour, it is essential to take account of how the person presents, style, attitude and authority and relate this to the culture of the country of origin and events preceeding [sic] the interview, journey experiences etc.

> It is useful to establish the length of time that the person has taken to arrive in the UK from the time they left their country of origin and include this into the age calculation'.

3.29

Local authority guidance on assessing age has been refined by case law over more than a decade. This led to the development of core common and accepted principles for the factual inquiry into age going beyond a determination of age based on physical appearance and demeanour. The principles, often referred to as the '*Merton* guidelines'[25], are summarised in *MVN v London Borough of Greenwich*[26]:

---

24 *R (on the application of CJ) v Cardiff County Council* [2011] EWHC 23 (Admin), [2011] LGR 301 at [129]. In *R (on the application of HBH) v Secretary of State for the Home Department* [2009] EWHC 928 (Admin), the Administrative Court held that the methodology used to assess HBH's age was flawed because the court relied on an assessment limited to his appearance and demeanour.

25 Named after the case of *R (on the application of B) v Merton London Borough Council* [2003] EWHC 1689 (Admin).

26 [2015] EWHC 1942 (Admin).

'30.1 The assessment must be a holistic one and must start with an open mind, with no imposition on the child to prove his age.

30.2 Assessments of age should normally be carried out by two assessors in the first place because two heads are better than one.

30.3 The assessment may need to be undertaken over a period of time because it is important for the assessors to first establish a rapport with the putative young person. This is all the more important in cases of potential trafficking where mistrust of authorities or fear of repercussion from traffickers may delay disclosure.

30.4 Physical appearance and demeanour are notoriously unreliable factors not determinative of age. Thus except in clear cases, age cannot be determined solely from appearance.

30.5 Cultural, ethnic and racial context of the young person being assessed must be considered as these may reflect in their presentation as well as their descriptions of their lives.

30.6 General credibility is not to be determinative of age. It is more likely that a young person who tells a consistent account of his life which supports his claimed age will be the age he claims to be. Conversely, young people may lie for reasons unrelated to age but related to their claims for protection or the reasons they had to leave their country of origin.

30.7 The child should be afforded the benefit of the doubt where evidence can tip one way or the other.

30.8 Local authority decision-makers, as well as courts, should take everything material into account. The source of information will frequently go well beyond that of the individual and include objective evidence of the country context and expert testimony.

30.9 Credibility assessments should not be carried out in isolation without considering other relevant evidence such as reports regarding a country that corroborates a person's explanation of their understanding of age.

30.10 All available evidence must be assessed in the round.

30.11 Safeguards should be in place to ensure the young person understands the purpose of the interview.

30.12 If the decision-maker forms a view that the young person may be lying, he should be given the opportunity to address the matters that may lead to that view. Adverse provisional conclusions as to a putative child's age should be put to him, so that he may have the opportunity to deal with them and rectify misunderstandings.

30.13 The local authority is obliged to give reasons for its decision, although these need not be long or elaborate'.

3.30

These well-trodden principles have now been adopted and enshrined in a comprehensive set of practice guidance published by the Association for Directors of Children's Services ('ADCS'), published in April 2015[27]. The guidance was developed over more than three years of consultation with stakeholders, including the Home Office, children's rights charities, the Children's Commissioner, social workers and lawyers representing age dispute claimants.

3.31

The ADCS has also agreed and published a joint protocol with the Home Office on the process by which age disputes are to be determined where they arise in the immigration context (most frequently in the context of immigration detention)[28]. The protocol was agreed and published in recognition of the importance and relevance of age to a breadth of areas of a putative child's life and decision-making by state authorities. The objective of the joint working protocol is to ensure a consistent approach. In that protocol, the Home Office acknowledges the expertise of social workers in carrying out assessments having regard to child development and well-being, and the default position will normally be for the local authority to do an assessment where that is deemed necessary. The *Merton* framework for assessing age and that set out in the ADCS guidance are accepted by the Home Office to be the standard for a proper age assessment.

3.32

The only comparable equivalent guidance in the criminal justice context are the Crown Prosecution Service's Youth Offenders Guidance[29] and the CPS Guidance on prosecuting victims of trafficking. The CPS Youth Offenders Guidance states as follows:

'*Determining Age*

Where anyone is brought before any court and it appears that they are a child or young person, the court shall make due enquiry as to their

---

27 ADCS, *Age Assessment Guidance* (October 2015), available at http://adcs.org.uk/assets/documentation/Age_Assessment_Guidance_2015_Final.pdf (last accessed 6 December 2017).

28 ADCS/Home Office, *Age Assessment: Joint Working Guidance* (June 2015), available at www.gov.uk/government/uploads/system/uploads/attachment_data/file/432724/Age_Assessment_Joint_Working_Guidance__April_2015__Final_agreed_v2_EXT.pdf (last accessed 6 December 2017).

29 Available at www.cps.gov.uk/legal/v_to_z/youth_offenders/#a41 (last accessed 6 December 2017).

age, and the age presumed or declared by the court is deemed to be their true age: section 99 Children and Young Persons Act 1933 and section 150 Magistrates' Courts Act 1980. The statutory provisions for sentencing also refer to the age of the defendant on conviction. Such age will be deemed to be that which it appears to the court to be after considering any available evidence: section 164(1) Powers of the Criminal Courts (Sentencing) Act 2000. The sentence or order will not be invalid if it is subsequently established that the defendant is in fact a different age that makes him or her ineligible for such a sentence: *R v Brown* [1989] CLR 750.

The Court should consider any evidence of age that is available at the hearing of the case. Where there is a dispute as to age which is material, it is better for the court to adjourn for more detailed inquiries if there is any doubt about the matter: *R v Steed* 1990.[30]

Prosecutors should assist the court by:

—   adducing relevant documents that indicate a date of birth such as a list of antecedents, PNC printout, custody record, copies of passports, identity cards;

—   inviting the court to hear oral evidence from the defendant and any accompanying adult(s) as to the age of the defendant and cross examining where such evidence is inconclusive or inconsistent with other evidence, including the defendant's appearance and demeanour.

—   Where the defendant appears to have entered the UK without satisfactory evidence of identity and age, additional evidence should be available from UKBA or the local authority. *R on the application of R v London Borough of Merton* [2003] EWHC 1689 (Admin) gives guidance to local authorities on the conduct of an assessment of age of a person claiming to be under 18, which includes guidance on assessing appearance and demeanour, credibility, social history and family composition, education, developmental considerations, ethnic and cultural background. See also the Immigration Law Practitioners Association Publications: When is a child not a child? Asylum, age disputes and the process of age assessment, and chapter 3 of Working with Refugee Children: Current Issues in Best Practice.'

3.33

The CPS guidance on prosecuting victims of trafficking expands on the above guidance by specifically highlighting the need for due inquiries to be made

---

30   (1990–91) 12 Cr App Rep (S) 230, [1990] Crim LR 816.

under the CYPA 1933, s 99, explicitly stating that any dispute of age ought to be addressed at the first court appearance. If that did not happen, the guidance directs the CPS to consider the matter at the Plea and Case Management Hearing (now Plea and Trial Preparation Hearing), clearly acknowledging and highlighting the importance of age, particularly in the context of defendants who may have been child victims of trafficking.

3.34

There is no comparable guidance issued for Youth Offending Teams, although they are statutorily the responsibility of local authority children's services, and thus the ADCS guidance which local authority children's services are obliged to follow ought also to be applied to Youth Offending Teams.

Approach to be taken by a court to determine age in a social welfare and immigration law context

3.35

In *R (on the application of A) v Croydon London Borough Council*, the Supreme Court held in relation to 'the question whether a person is a "child"' that:

'there is a right or a wrong answer. It may be difficult to determine what the answer is. The decision-makers may have to do their best on the basis of less than perfect or conclusive evidence. But that is true of many questions of fact which regularly come before the courts. That does not prevent them from being questions for the courts rather than for other kinds of decision-makers'[31].

3.36

There is no statutory process in the context of social welfare or immigration law for determining age. This is why the *A v Croydon* judgment was so significant. As a consequence of the Supreme Court's judgment, the Administrative Court is now seised of the jurisdiction through judicial review to determine the objective fact of a putative child's age where local authority obligations and immigration powers are engaged.

3.37

That the primary remedy is judicial review, however, does not dictate the issue for the court to decide or the way in which it should do so. The public authority, whether the children's services authority or the Home Office, has to make its own determination in the first instance and it is only if this is disputed that the

---

31 [2009] UKSC 8, [2009] 1 WLR 2557 per Lady Hale at [27].

court may have to intervene. As Lady Hale observed in *A v Croydon*, 'the better the quality of the initial decision-making, the less likely it is that the court will come to any different decision upon the evidence'[32]. However, and ultimately, if there is a disagreement over the factual answer arrived at by the local authority (or the Home Office), the putative child may apply for permission to bring a judicial review in the Administrative Court to resolve the dispute.

3.38

The task of the Administrative Court is not to determine whether the local authority's or the Home Office's assessment of age is right or wrong but, rather, the more fundamental question – how old is the child?[33] This requires a fact-finding exercise on the basis of all the evidence made available to the court. There is no burden on either the child or the public authority to prove the correctness of their assertion on age[34]. As the claim is brought by way of judicial review, the child applicant still needs to satisfy the Administrative Court that the case is arguable to obtain permission to proceed to trial. The test for permission is as formulated by the Court of Appeal in *R (on the application of FZ) v Croydon London Borough Council*[35]:

> 'whether the material before the court raises a factual case which, taken at its highest, could not properly succeed in a contested factual hearing. If so, permission should be refused. If not, permission should normally be granted, subject to other discretionary factors, such as delay.'

3.39

Because it is rarely the case that the fact of age can be determined by documentary evidence, the Court at trial will receive a range of evidence, much of which will be opinion evidence from professionals as well as lay persons who have had contact over time with the putative child. This includes, for example, key workers, foster carers, volunteers at charitable organisations, counsellors, social workers, and medical professionals. The putative child would normally give evidence unless he is unable to do so.

3.40

In practice, the judicial review court has not exerted exclusive jurisdiction over age disputes. The immigration appeals tribunals continue to examine the fact of age in the context of appeals against the Home Office's refusal of asylum where the question as to whether someone is a child or not bears on the assessment of risk of persecution and the need for international protection. The difference

---

32 Ibid per Lady Hale at [33].
33 *R (on the application of F) v Lewisham London Borough Council* [2009] EWHC 3542 (Admin), [2010] 1 FLR 1463.
34 *R (on the application of CJ) v Cardiff County Council* [2011] EWHC 23 (Admin), [2011] LGR 301, above.
35 [2011] EWCA Civ 59, [2011] PTSR 748.

between a judicial review court determination of age and a finding of age by the immigration appeals tribunal is that the latter has no power to make declarations that are binding *in rem* (ie concerning age) on all organs of the state. By contrast, at the conclusion of judicial review proceedings, the judicial review court will make a declaration as the fact of a child's age which binds the state, including public authorities who were not party to the proceedings.

Approach of criminal court to age disputes

3.41

Although a number of sections in existing statutes refer to procedures for the determination of age in criminal proceedings, the guidance provided is very general in nature. The main provision on determining age is CYPA 1933, s 99(1), which states:

> 'Where a person, whether charged with an offence or not, is brought before *any court* otherwise than for the purpose of giving evidence, and it appears to the court that he is a child or young person, the court *shall make due inquiry* as to the age of that person and *for that purpose shall take such evidence as may be forthcoming at the hearing of the case*, but an order or judgment of the court shall not be invalidated by any subsequent proof that the age of that person has not been correctly stated to the court, and the age presumed or declared by the court to be the age of the person so brought before it shall, for the purposes of this Act, be deemed to be the true age of that person, and where it appears to the court that the person so brought before it has attained the [age of eighteen] years, that person shall for the purposes of this Act be deemed not to be a child or young person.'

3.42

In the context of the youth justice system, this and other associated provisions place the responsibility for reaching a defendant's age on the magistrate or court before which the defendant is appearing. This approach conforms with the Supreme Court's decision in *A v Croydon* (above) as to there being a right or wrong answer to the question of age. Given that the age of a defendant is a very material factor at various stages of the criminal justice system, it is plain that such inquiry into the question of age must be one which is capable of arriving at the right answer so far as is possible.

3.43

The plain meaning of the phrase 'due inquiry' in CYPA 1933, s 99(1) obliges the magistrate or a court to undertake a fact-finding exercise as to the objective fact of the defendant's age if a reasonable magistrate or judge could conclude that the defendant may be a child or a young person.

3.44

The use of the word 'appears' in CYPA 1933, s 99(1) may suggest that a judge could simply consider whether on the basis of his or her appearance the defendant was a child. However, that would be inadequate to satisfy the obligation to carry out a 'due inquiry' for reasons stated in the long line of case law established by the judicial review court, which recognise that physical appearance and demeanour are highly risky factors to rely on in borderline cases, particularly where a young person falls in the grey area of 16 to 20 years' old.

3.45

When the principles for assessing age[36], established over more than a decade in the local authority context, are considered in the round, it is clear that the inquiry necessary to inform the criminal court of the right decision on age (insofar as this is possible) is one that requires a process of rigorous scrutiny. Such an approach requires decisions on age to 'show by their reasoning that every factor which might tell in favour of the claimed age has been properly taken into account'[37]. This is 'axiomatic' in decisions which if made incorrectly may fundamentally and adversely impact on a putative child's ability to participate effectively in the trial process.

3.46

The necessary corollary to an approach of rigorous scrutiny is the obligation to ensure that all relevant parties to the proceedings, and in particular the putative child subject to the inquiry, are afforded a fair opportunity to adduce such evidence as is relevant and available in order to achieve, insofar as is possible, the right answer as to the fact of age.

3.47

Although, it could arguably be fuller, the advice provided in the CPS *Legal Guidance on Youth Offenders*[38] as to the role of the CPS in this process does seek to conform to this approach:

> '[p]rosecutors should assist the court by:
>
> — adducing relevant documents that indicate a date of birth such as a list of antecedents, PNC printout, custody record, copies of passports, identity cards;
>
> — inviting the court to hear oral evidence from the defendant and any accompanying adult(s) as to the age of the defendant and cross

---

36 Outlined at §23 of Ms Twite's statement.
37 *R (on the application of YH) v Secretary of State for the Home Department* [2010] EWCA Civ 116 at [24].
38 Available at www.cps.gov.uk/legal/v_to_z/youth_offenders/#a41 (last accessed 6 December 2017).

examining where such evidence is inconclusive or inconsistent with other evidence, including the defendants' appearance and demeanour'.

3.48

Critically, the CPS guidance recognises the right of the putative child to be heard. This conforms with a core principle underpinning the youth justice system, ie the right of the child to be heard in any court proceedings to which he is a party, and to participate effectively[39]. See also para [34] of *ZH (Tanzania) v Secretary of State for the Home Department*[40], where Baroness Hale said:

'acknowledging that the best interests of the child must be a primary consideration ... immediately raises the question of how these are to be discovered. An important part of this is discovering the child's own view'.

3.49

Effective participation by the child is essential to a proper due inquiry of the fact of the putative child defendant's age. It is a cornerstone of a fair trial[41]. It is unrealistic to expect that all available evidence of age will be available at the first appearance of the putative child before the court. This may particularly be so where the child has only recently arrived in the UK or has been brought to the court following events such as an immigration enforcement, or an arrest following a police search of a cannabis farm. To ensure effective participation of the child in the first important decision in the trial process – the deeming of age for the purposes of determining bail and remand, venue, jurisdiction and mode of trial – it is of paramount importance that the parties, and in particular the putative child, are afforded a reasonable opportunity to adduce evidence, including of a documentary and expert nature, to assist the court in the inquiry process on age. This will almost always necessitate an adjournment, an approach supported by criminal cases[42]. A refusal to adjourn for these purposes should be the rare exception to the norm.

3.50

There are other sources of evidence, including from social work professionals with expertise and experience in assessing age. In the absence of verifiable documentary proof of age, the youth court should invite the Youth Offending Team to refer the putative child defendant to the local authority for an opinion on age to be provided by a qualified social work professional with the training and experience to do so. It is similarly open to the CPS or the defendant

---

39 UN CRC, Arts 12 and 40.
40 [2011] UKSC 4, [2011] 2 AC 166.
41 *R v G* [2003] UKHL 50, [2004] 1 AC 1034.
42 See *R v Steed* [1990] 12 Cr App Rep (S) 230 and *R v Farmer* [2002] EWCA Crim 2128.

himself to do the same, the courts having acknowledged that local authority social workers have developed some expertise and experience in undertaking a holistic assessment of age. That said, local authority age assessments ought not to become a mandatory part of the criminal court's inquiry into age. The local authority's ADCS guidance (referred to above) warns against conducting age assessments in any and all cases where a putative child is unable to prove age by verified documents. An age assessment should only be undertaken where there is 'significant doubt'. This is consistent with the advice of the Committee on the Rights of the Child at [39] of General Comment No 10, (see para **3.16** above). The ADCS guidance provides for a local authority to decide, when asked, not to undertake an age assessment on the basis that it does not have significant doubt that the child is the age claimed. If that decision is reasoned, it ought to provide weighty evidence in favour of deeming the putative child a child, age claimed (or at least under 18). The approach adopted in the ADCS guidance, which demonstrates the importance of a precautionary and protective approach to decisions as to whether age should be disputed, and if so assessed, is adopted in this context. Where age assessments are conducted by local authority children's services, they should not be the only evidence considered by a magistrate or a court. After all, local authority age assessments are themselves subject to judicial review, and the ultimate decision-maker is the court, exercising an inquisitorial function.

3.51

Pending the completion of the inquiry, the presumption in favour of childhood ought to be afforded to the putative child in accordance with the precautionary approach advocated for in General Comments No 6 and 10 and the ADCS guidance on age. Even if a local authority bail package is not immediately available, this would at least ensure that the putative youth defendant is remanded under LASPO 2012 to local authority accommodation unless the rigorous threshold for a youth detention centre is met. All this serves to preserve the status quo in a precautionary manner having due regard to the putative child's best interests as a primary consideration.

4 Criminal offences of trafficking

Introduction

4.1

When considering charges in relation to acts of human trafficking, modern slavery, servitude or forced or compulsory labour, from the point of view of a prosecutor or defence representative, a range of offences may be relevant. The Modern Slavery Act 2015 (MSA 2015) includes two key substantive offences: slavery, servitude or forced and compulsory labour in s 1, and human trafficking in s 2. These were a consolidation of existing offences from earlier statutes, as well as an attempt to address a lacuna identified in *CN v UK*[1], with the aim of simplifying enforcement[2]. Section 4 of the MSA 2015 also creates an offence of committing any offence with intent to commit either of these substantive offences.

4.2

It would be impossible to predict the full range of other offences which different factual circumstances might make relevant. Those which may be expected to arise most commonly (either as possible charges worthy of consideration when making a charging decision, or as alternative counts on the same indictment as MSA offences) are examined in turn below.

4.3

As a matter of principle, where the essence of an allegation is most properly characterised as human trafficking, or as slavery, servitude, or forced labour and compulsory labour, it will be most appropriate that it be charged as such. This applies even where other offences are also made out on the facts, and even if such other offences carry the same maximum penalty: the Code for Crown Prosecutors stipulates that prosecutors should select charges that, among other things, enable the case to be presented clearly and simply[3]. It may be that the use of some of the offences discussed below in the context of trafficking and modern slavery becomes less common as the scope and application of the MSA offences becomes better known.

---

1   App No 4239/08 (13 February 2013).
2   584 HC Official Report (6th series) col 197, 8 July 2014 (Tracey Crouch).
3   See para 6.1(c).

Offences under the Modern Slavery Act 2015

Slavery, servitude and forced or compulsory labour: MSA 2015, s 1

4.4

Section 1 of the MSA 2015 provides as follows:

'(1) A person commits an offence if –

(a) the person holds another person in slavery or servitude and the circumstances are such that the person knows or ought to know that the other person is held in slavery or servitude, or

(b) the person requires another person to perform forced or compulsory labour and the circumstances are such that the person knows or ought to know that the other person is being required to perform forced or compulsory labour.

(2) In subsection (1) the references to holding a person in slavery or servitude or requiring a person to perform forced or compulsory labour are to be construed in accordance with Article 4 of the Human Rights Convention.

(3) In determining whether a person is being held in slavery or servitude or required to perform forced or compulsory labour, regard may be had to all the circumstances.

(4) For example, regard may be had –

(a) to any of the person's personal circumstances (such as the person being a child, the person's family relationships, and any mental or physical illness) which may make the person more vulnerable than other persons;

(b) to any work or services provided by the person, including work or services provided in circumstances which constitute exploitation within section 3(3) to (6).

(5) The consent of a person (whether an adult or a child) to any of the acts alleged to constitute holding the person in slavery or servitude, or requiring the person to perform forced or compulsory labour, does not preclude a determination that the person is being held in slavery or servitude, or required to perform forced or compulsory labour.'

Section 1(1)

4.5

In order for an offence to have been committed under this provision actual slavery, servitude or compulsory labour has to have taken place. This is materially different from the offence of human trafficking in the MSA 2015, s 2, which can be committed 'with a view' to exploitation even where that exploitation has not in fact taken place.

Section 1(2)

4.6

Slavery, servitude, and forced or compulsory labour are to be construed in accordance with the ECHR, Art 4. In doing so, case law from the European Court of Human Rights (ECtHR) will be authoritative. There is a hierarchy of denial of personal autonomy, in which slavery is the most severe, followed by servitude, and with forced or compulsory labour being the least severe[4].

4.7

The definition of slavery adopted by the Strasbourg court is taken from the 1927 Slavery Convention (Convention to Suppress the Slave Trade and Slavery), which provides that 'slavery is the status or condition of a person over whom any or all of the powers attaching to the right of ownership are exercised'[5]. Courts have generally been slow to find that slavery is established in any particular case, perhaps in part because it is not necessary to do so when a finding of servitude or of forced or compulsory labour will have the same effect. Where applicable, sentences can be determined based on the actual facts of the offence, without having to determine whether or not such facts cross the boundary from (for example) servitude to slavery.

4.8

As to servitude, it was said in *Siliadin v France*[6] that this does not involve any claim to proprietary rights over the victim, but refers to an obligation to provide one's services, and includes an obligation to live on the other person's property and the impossibility of changing one's status[7]. It was also said that the concept of servitude is to be linked to that of slavery[8].

4.9

More recently, however, the ECtHR appears to have broadened the definition of servitude somewhat. In *CN and V v France*[9], it was held that servitude is an aggravated form of forced or compulsory labour: the fundamental additional

---

4 *R v SK* [2011] EWCA Crim 1691, [2013] QB 82 at [24]. This case concerned the offence under the Asylum and Immigration (Treatment of Claimants etc) Act 2004, s 4. This offence was a precursor to the MSA 2015, s 2, and an element of it was an intention to exploit – exploitation including behaviour that contravenes Art 4.
5 *Siliadin v France* App No 73316/01 (26 July 2005), (2006) 43 EHRR 106 at [122].
6 Ibid.
7 Ibid at [123].
8 Ibid.
9 App No 67724/09 (11 October 2012).

feature required for forced or compulsory labour to become servitude is 'the victim's feeling that their condition is permanent and that the situation is unlikely to change'. Whilst that feeling *may* be brought about by the objective features previously identified, it would also be sufficient to amount to servitude if that feeling is brought about or kept alive by the perpetrators (apparently regardless of the means used to bring it about)[10].

4.10

The definition of forced or compulsory labour, meaning work or service exacted under the menace of any penalty, and for which the worker has not offered himself voluntarily, has its origins in the International Labour Organisation's Convention 29 concerning Forced or Compulsory Labour[11]. 'Forced' suggests some kind of physical or mental constraint[12]. Whilst many forms of labour are 'compulsory' in some sense – such as that required under a contract, where sanctions will apply if the contract is not performed – it will not be 'compulsory labour' for the purposes of the ECHR (and therefore for the purposes of the MSA 2015, s 1) if the worker has offered himself voluntarily[13]. Apparent consent will not always be sufficient. Consent may most obviously be vitiated where the employer has abused his power or taken advantage of the vulnerability of the workers[14]. Consent may also prove insufficient on more mundane facts[15]. Other factors should also be taken into account, including the type and amount of work involved, and whether a 'disproportionate burden' is imposed[16].

4.11

The 'menace of penalty' may go as far as a threat of physical force, or it may be more subtle, such as a threat of denunciation to immigration authorities[17]. It may be direct or indirect, including by force of circumstances[18]. A comparatively minor threat, such as the risk of not being able to qualify into your chosen profession if you refuse to perform unpaid tasks during training, can amount to a menace of penalty[19]. Extremely low pay can be relevant evidence, but may not amount to coercion in itself[20].

---

10 *CN and V v France* App No 67724/09 (11 October 2012) at [91].
11 *Van de Mussele v Belgium* App No 8919/80 (23 November 1983), (1984) 6 EHRR 163 at [32]. Although in *Van de Mussele* the ECtHR seemed keen to allow room for the definition of forced or compulsory labour in the ECHR to vary somewhat from that in the ILO's Convention 29, in later cases this definition has been accepted without further discussion (eg *Siliadin v France* at [117]).
12 *Van de Mussele v Belgium* at [34].
13 Ibid.
14 *Chowdury v Greece* App No 21884/15 (30 March 2017) at [96].
15 As in *Van der Mussele v Belgium*, where the applicant had voluntarily entered his profession, knowing it would involve a certain amount of compulsory pro bono work: because he had no choice but to accept this work if he wished to pursue his chosen career, the choice was not sufficiently free that he could be held to have offered himself voluntarily for the pro bono work.
16 *CN and V v France* App No 67724/09 (11 October 2012) at [74].
17 Ibid at [77].
18 *R v SK* [2011] EWCA Crim 1691, [2013] QB 82 at [42].
19 *Van der Mussele v Belgium* at [35].
20 *R v SK* [2011] EWCA Crim 1691, [2013] QB 82 at [42]. However, consideration should be given to the later ECtHR judgment of *Chowdury v Greece* App No 21884/15 (30 March 2017).

Section 1(3) and (4)

4.12

In considering 'all of the circumstances', as required by the MSA 2015, s 1(3), one is first directed to questions of the victim's vulnerability. It is important to make clear that 'abuse of a position of vulnerability' is one of the possible 'means' by which a trafficking offence may be committed – it is not, in itself, an element of a slavery, servitude or forced or compulsory labour offence. However, it is clearly relevant, by virtue of s 1(4)(a), and is discussed in Chapter 1.

4.13

The ECtHR has repeatedly emphasised the wide array of circumstances which may be relevant, finding breaches of the Convention where states have taken too narrow a view. In *CN v United Kingdom*[21], the subtle means of coercion which might be employed were highlighted, including the taking of identity documents, retention of wages, and threat of denunciation (both implicit and explicit)[22]. Other factors which may be relevant would include working conditions, standard of accommodation if provided, and the passage of time: work which may have been voluntary initially may be seen to be forced or compulsory labour after wages have been retained for a lengthy period[23].

Section 1(5)

4.14

Section 1(5) makes clear that consent may not preclude a finding of slavery, servitude, or forced or compulsory labour: this is discussed at para 4.7 above in the context of compulsory labour, but the same considerations would apply (it is submitted *a fortiori*) in the context of slavery or servitude.

Human trafficking: MSA 2015, s 2

4.15

This offence is created by the MSA 2015, s 2:

> **'2 Human trafficking**
>
> (1) A person commits an offence if the person arranges or facilitates the travel of another person ('V') with a view to V being exploited.
>
> (2) It is irrelevant whether V consents to the travel (whether V is an adult or a child).

---

21 App No 4239/08 (13 February 2013).
22 *CN v United Kingdom* App No 4239/08 (13 November 2012) at [80].
23 *Chowdury v Greece* App No 21884/15 (30 March 2017) at [94] and [97].

(3) A person may in particular arrange or facilitate V's travel by recruiting V, transporting or transferring V, harbouring or receiving V, or transferring or exchanging control over V.

(4) A person arranges or facilitates V's travel with a view to V being exploited only if—

(a)   the person intends to exploit V (in any part of the world) during or after the travel, or

(b)   the person knows or ought to know that another person is likely to exploit V (in any part of the world) during or after the travel.

(5) "Travel" means—

(a)   arriving in, or entering, any country,

(b)   departing from any country,

(c)   travelling within any country.

(6) A person who is a UK national commits an offence under this section regardless of—

(a)   where the arranging or facilitating takes place, or

(b)   where the travel takes place.

(7) A person who is not a UK national commits an offence under this section if—

(a)   any part of the arranging or facilitating takes place in the United Kingdom, or

(b)   the travel consists of arrival in or entry into, departure from, or travel within, the United Kingdom'.

Elements of the offence

4.16

Section 2 provides for a single offence of human trafficking. It includes sexual and non-sexual exploitation.

Facilitating travel for exploitation

4.17

Section 2(1) makes it a criminal offence to arrange or facilitate the travel of another person with a view to his being exploited. Travel is defined in s 2(5) as arriving in, entering, departing, or travelling within any country.

Consent irrelevant

4.18

Section 2(2) makes it clear that with a human trafficking offence the victim's consent to his travel (whether an adult or a child) is irrelevant.

Arranging or facilitating

4.19

Section 2(3) gives examples of what may amount to arranging or facilitating another person's travel. This includes recruiting, transporting, transferring, harbouring, receiving or exchanging control of that person. The language reflects the definitions of trafficking set out in the Council of Europe Convention on Action against Trafficking in Human Beings ('ECAT') and the associated Palermo Protocol.

4.20

Section 2(3) is a poorly drafted provision. It is unclear whether there is a required nexus between arranging or facilitating 'travel' and the 'recruitment, transportation or transferring, harbouring, receiving or exchanging control over the victim'. Recruiters and those transferring the victim, harbouring or receiving the victim may have no involvement in the arranging or facilitation of the travel of the victim but do intend to exploit the victim, or know or ought to know that the victim will be exploited. These individuals may not be caught by the human trafficking offence.

4.21

What is not clear, given the inclusion of the word 'may' in the subsection, is whether, where a person who harbours the individual but who has no role in the travel to the place in which the victim is harboured for onward travel will be guilty of the offence. Likewise, receiving and transferring or exchanging control of a victim may not be caught by the natural wording of the MSA 2015. If those acts are not caught by the subsection, it will not be compliant with ECHR, Art 4.

Mens rea

4.22

Section 2(4) provides that the arranging or facilitating is done with a view to the exploitation of the victim if the perpetrator either:

— intends to exploit the victim; or

— knows or ought to know that any other person is likely to exploit the victim.

It is irrelevant where in the world that exploitation might take place.

4.23

The phrase 'with a view to' exploitation means either that the defendant intends to exploit the victim during or after travel, or knows or ought to know someone else is likely to do so. What does not seem to be captured by this is exploitation or a view to exploitation in situ prior to travel.

Extra territorial effect

4.24

Section 2(6) makes the offence extra-territorial in relation to UK nationals. It does not matter where in the world a UK national arranges or facilitates the travel. It does not matter what the country of arrival, entry, travel or departure is. In the Explanatory Notes to the MSA 2015, the example given is that if a UK national trafficks a person from Spain to France, he could be prosecuted in England and Wales for this offence.

4.25

Section 2(7) provides for a more limited territorial reach in relation to non-UK nationals. If any part of the arranging or facilitating takes place in the UK, non-UK nationals will commit an offence. Likewise, if the UK is the country of arrival, entry, travel or departure, a non-UK national will commit an offence.

4.26

Travel can be caught by this offence whether it is cross border or within any country[24]. It can immediately be seen that the scope of the offence is very broad. There is no minimum distance required for a journey to count as 'travel', although journeys involving truly minimal distances (such as walking between rooms) may well be excluded[25]. It therefore appears that, for example, an occupier who accepts a person into his house (ie harbours or receives them) after a journey of a few miles, with a view to exploiting them, would be guilty of this offence.

Exploitation: MSA 2015, s 3

4.27

Exploitation is defined exhaustively in the MSA 2015, s 3. It covers the following:

---

24 MSA 2015, s 2(5).
25 *R v Ali* [2015] EWCA Crim 1279, [2015] 2 Cr App Rep 457 at [80]. This was a case concerning the Sexual Offences Act (SOA) 2003, s 58 (trafficking within the UK for sexual exploitation), one of the precursors to the MSA 2015, s 2.

(i)   offences under the MSA 2015, s 1, sexual offences under the SOA 2003, Pt 1 or the Protection of Children Act 1978, s1(1)(a) (indecent photographs), and organ harvesting and related activities under the Human Tissue Act 2004, ss 32 and 33;

(ii)   activities that would amount to such offences if committed in England and Wales;

(iii)   the use of force, threats or deception designed to induce the victim to provide services or benefits (MSA 2015, s 3(5));

(iv)   the use or attempted use of a person to obtain services or benefits when that person has been chosen because he is a child or vulnerable adult, and would otherwise be likely to refuse (MSA 2015, s 3(6)).

4.28

The definition is, with minor variations, an amalgamation of the definitions of exploitation in the two predecessor offences (trafficking for sexual exploitation under the SOA 2003, s 59A, and trafficking for exploitation under the Asylum and Immigration (Treatment of Claimants, etc) Act 2004, s 4). It may be that the offences under s 3(5) and 3(6) add little, since most behaviour falling within either of those descriptions would also amount to an offence under the MSA 2015, s 1.

4.29

This offence has a broad territorial scope: a UK national will be guilty of it regardless of where the travel, or the arranging or facilitating of it, takes place; a non-UK national will be guilty of it if any part of the travel, or its arranging or facilitation, takes place in the UK[26].

Sentencing

Principles

4.30

The offences under MSA 2015, ss 1 and 2 both carry the same maximum sentence (life imprisonment) when tried on indictment, and are also triable summarily with a maximum sentence of six months[27]. Both are listed in the Criminal Justice Act 2003, Schs 15 and 15B and therefore extended sentences under s 226A of that Act are available, and life sentences under ss 224A (for a second listed offence) and 225 (for dangerous offenders) may apply. There

---

26 MSA 2015, s 2(6) and (7).
27 MSA 2015, s 5(1).

is no Sentencing Guideline in respect of these offences, nor has the Court of Appeal yet considered sentence in cases arising under them. There is, however, guidance to be gained from the predecessor offences.

4.31

Section 71 of the Coroners and Justice Act 2009 was in broadly the same terms as the MSA, s 1, although it should be noted that the statutory maximum penalty for that offence was 14 years: the increased maximum penalty now applicable shows that Parliament's intention is that longer sentences should be imposed[28].

4.32

In considering sentences under the Coroners and Justice Act 2009, s 71, Lord Judge CJ noted that although the three forms of this offence do fall into a hierarchy, it does not necessarily follow that the maximum sentence for servitude must always be lower than that for slavery (and so on)[29]. There must be a deterrent element to sentences, given how hard it is for victims to complain, let alone bring their treatment to the attention of the authorities, and sentences 'must also emphasise that there is no victim so vulnerable to exploitation, that he or she somehow becomes invisible or unknown to or somehow beyond the protection of the law'[30]. These remarks would appear equally applicable to trafficking offences.

4.33

Section 2 of the MSA 2015, on the other hand, is not a like-for-like replacement of any one earlier provision, but a combination of the SOA 2003, s 59A and the Asylum and Immigration (Treatment of Claimants, etc) Act 2004, s 4. Section 59A was itself a replacement for several more specific offences (trafficking for sexual exploitation into the UK, within the UK, out of the UK, and outside the UK) under the SOA 2003, ss 57–59. Additional care is therefore required when looking at sentences imposed under any of these previous provisions. Again, the MSA 2015, s 2 offence provides for a maximum penalty, indicative that longer sentences will be imposed.

4.34

Trafficking for sexual exploitation may, all other things being equal, attract a heavier sentence than trafficking for other exploitation[31]. There is a Sentencing Council definitive guideline (as part of the sexual offences guidelines) for

---

28 *R v Joyce* [2017] EWCA Crim 337 at [26].
29 *A-G's Reference (Nos 2-5 of 2013) (William Connors)* [2013] EWCA Crim 324, [2013] 2 Cr App Rep (S) 71 at [8].
30 Ibid at [10].
31 *A-G's Reference (Nos 37, 38 and 65 of 2010) (Khan)* [2010] EWCA Crim 2880, [2011] 2 Cr App Rep (S) 31 at [16].

offences under the SOA 2003, s 59A, which will remain applicable to offences committed before the MSA 2015 came into force, and can provide some assistance when sentencing for trafficking for sexual exploitation under the MSA 2015, s 2, if the increased maximum sentence is taken into account.

4.35

Offenders convicted under the SOA 2003, ss 57–59A or the Asylum and Immigration (Treatment of Claimants, etc) Act 2004, s 4 often fell to be sentenced not just for the arranging or facilitating of travel, but for the exploitation of the victim itself after transportation, because, in practice, defendants tended to be involved in that aspect of the exploitation as well. For this reason, many of the considerations relevant to sentencing decisions under these provisions were also relevant to sentencing for offences under the Coroners and Justice Act 2009, s 71. These sentencing considerations will be of relevance in the context of the new provisions.

4.36

The Court of Appeal identified a number of factors which were relevant to sentencing for trafficking offences under the Asylum and Immigration (Treatment of Claimants, etc) Act 2004, s 4: the nature and degree of coercion used to recruit workers; the nature and degree of exploitation exercised once they arrived (involving comparison both with what was promised, and with common standards in the UK); the level and methods of control exercised to prevent the worker from leaving; the worker's physical, psychological and, most commonly, economic vulnerability; the degree of physical, psychological and financial harm suffered by the worker; the level of organisation and planning and the offender's role within that organisation; the financial rewards for the offender; and the number of people exploited. Previous similar convictions were of course also relevant[32].

4.37

In a later forced labour case, an almost identical list of factors was said to be relevant, although the court did not expressly refer to the previous decision. Working conditions were listed as a separate factor. It was also noted that deliberate targeting of vulnerable victims is an aggravating feature[33]. In *R v Connors*[34], C was convicted after a trial of one count of conspiring to require a person to perform forced or compulsory labour. Workers were forced to work long hours, seven days a week, for around £10 a day. They were not provided with proper equipment. They were given very poor accommodation. They were subjected to threats of, and occasional use of, violence, over a one-year indictment period. Their offending behaviour was aggravated by the

---

32 Ibid at [17].
33 At [9].
34 [2013] EWCA Crim 324, [2013] 2 Cr App Rep (S) 451.

victims' pre-existing vulnerability. The Crown Court imposed a six and a half year sentence of imprisonment for the head of the household. For him, the offending was a way of life. He had raised others so that they committed the offence with him. He had £370,000 in his bank account when arrested. The Court of Appeal said that the sentence was lenient but not unduly lenient. Permission was refused to refer sentences of three years' imprisonment each for: (1) a defendant who was 17 at the start of the indictment, brought into the criminality by his father; and (2) another defendant who intervened to prevent violence and used some machinery and outside help on jobs to reduce the reliance on exploited labour[35]. It was subsequently noted that this case was not intended to be a guideline case: substantial weight was given to the view of the judge who had presided over a lengthy trial[36].

4.38

In *R v Connors (Josie)*[37], leave to appeal against sentence was refused for a defendant sentenced to a total of 11 years' imprisonment for two counts of holding a person in servitude (along with forced labour counts in respect of the same victims), and one of assault occasioning actual bodily harm. The workers were malnourished, lived in a caravan with no washing or toilet facilities, worked 16-hour days with no pay or breaks, were periodically seriously assaulted and were threatened with murder if they ran away. One worker had been kept by the family for seven years, and had been forced back to work three days after breaking his foot[38].

4.39

In *A-G's Reference (No 35 of 2016) (Rafiq)*[39], a trafficking case, the court did not change the sentence of 27 months' imprisonment. In that appeal, the company director had, for at least a year, employed workers whom he knew had been trafficked into the UK. The workers had been paid only £10 a week. They were housed in very overcrowded and squalid conditions. A large number of strong character witnesses spoke to his positive qualities. He was not a primary offender in the trafficking. There was no credit for a guilty plea.

4.40

In *R v Khan*[40] the Court of Appeal held that three years' imprisonment was unduly lenient. Two brothers effectively ran a restaurant employing nine vulnerable men. They were recruited overseas with false promises. The defendants obtained

---

35 Ibid.
36 At [48].
37 [2013] EWCA Crim 368.
38 Ibid. Sentences for other defendants are also considered in that case. For other cases considering sentencing under the Coroners and Justice Act 2009, s 71, see *A-G's Reference (Nos 146 and 147 of 2015) (Edet)* [2016] EWCA Crim 347, and *R v Joyce* [2017] EWCA Crim 337.
39 [2016] EWCA Crim 1368.
40 [2010] EWCA Crim 2880.

fraudulent visas for them. The victims' documents and savings were taken. They were threatened with violence (although none was used) and forced to work up to 13 hours a day, 6 or 7 days a week. The defendants had many testimonials of good character, but the conspiracy had lasted for over four years. The court held that a sentence of five years after trial would have been appropriate (although four years was imposed, taking account of double jeopardy).

4.41

Cases concerning trafficking for sexual exploitation are likely to be of less assistance than the definitive guideline.

Committing any offence with intent to commit an offence under s 2

4.42

Section 4 of the MSA 2015 creates an offence of committing any offence with the intention of committing an offence under the MSA 2015, s 2. At first blush it is hard to see what the purpose of this offence is, in the sense that such behaviour would also generally amount to either an attempted s 2 trafficking offence, or an offence of assisting or encouraging a s 2 offence. However, in an appropriate case s 4 may be an appropriate means of enabling trafficking to be taken into consideration as an aggravating feature of a second substantive offence. This section will thus have strategic application for prosecution and defence practitioners alike.

4.43

Technically, s 4 creates two offences, since there are different maximum sentences applicable: in general, the maximum is 10 years, but where the offence which is committed is kidnapping or false imprisonment, it is life imprisonment[41].

Unlawful restriction of liberty

4.44

Three offences that share the common feature of unlawful restriction of the victim's liberty are kidnapping, false imprisonment and child abduction. These offences may arise in a slavery, servitude, forced labour or compulsory labour or trafficking context. Where the criminal offence can properly be construed as either an MSA 2015, s 1 or s 2 offence then that would be the appropriate charge. However, where one or more of the elements cannot be made out in these offences it may be appropriate to consider alternative charges.

---

41 MSA 2015, s 5(3).

Kidnapping and false imprisonment

4.45

These two common law offences, although separate offences with distinct elements, are often considered in the same cases.

Kidnapping – elements of the offence

4.46

The elements of kidnapping are as follows:

(i)   deprivation of personal liberty;

(ii)   the taking or carrying away of one person by another;

(iii) by force (or threat of force) or fraud;

(iv)   without the consent of the person so taken or carried away;

(v)   without lawful excuse[42].

4.47

The 'taking or carrying away' need not involve the victim being taken or carried very far: about 100 yards was sufficient in *R v Wellard*[43]. The victim himself can be the driver of the vehicle which carries her away, or indeed can walk the relevant journey, as long as she does so as a result of force or fraud[44]. However, if the defendant merely induces the victim by fraud to take a journey on which the defendant does not accompany her, then this can neither amount to either 'a taking and carrying away', nor to a deprivation of liberty[45].

4.48

A lack of consent may be inferred where (for example) the victim is too young to understand what it is he is consenting to. The consent of a parent in such a situation is not relevant to kidnapping (although if there is parental consent, it may give rise to a defence of lawful excuse)[46]. If the victim initially consents to the taking or carrying away, but that consent is later withdrawn, the offence

---

42 These elements are largely derived from the speech of Lord Brandon of Oakbrook, with which the rest of their Lordships materially agreed, in *R v D* [1984] AC 778 at 800. Although deprivation of liberty was not one of the elements enumerated in *D*, it was mentioned, and the Court of Appeal in *R v Hendy-Freegard* [2007] EWCA Crim 1236, [2008] QB 57 at [42] confirmed that this remained a necessary element of the offence. In respect of what is item (iii) on this list, Lord Brandon referred only to force or fraud, but it was clarified in *R v Archer* [2011] EWCA Crim 2252, [2012] Crim LR 292 at [27]–[30], that this includes a threat of force.

43 (1978) 67 Cr App Rep 364 at 367.

44 *R v Archer* [2011] EWCA Crim 2252, [2012] Crim LR 292 (victim drove himself and the defendant); *R v Wellard* (1978) 67 Cr App Rep 364 (victim walked with the defendant).

45 *R v Hendy-Freegard* [2007] EWCA Crim 1236, [2008] QB 57 at [58].

46 *R v D* [1984] AC 778 at 806.

is committed by the use of force to maintain the kidnapping[47]. However, the requirement of force, threat of force, or fraud remains even where the victim is a child, and it is not hard to imagine cases in which force, threat or fraud may not be needed to induce a child (or an adult with impaired development) to go with the defendant[48]. In such cases the offence would not be made out, although a child abduction offence might be.

4.49

There is authority that a 'lawful excuse' must amount to necessity to be sufficient for a defence[49]. However, this decision has been rightly criticised as too restrictive (for example, criminalising the father who carries his child away after a visit to a grandmother's house)[50], and it seems unlikely it would be followed.

4.50

Both kidnapping and false imprisonment are described in the cases as offences of recklessness[51].

False imprisonment – elements of the offence

4.51

False imprisonment 'consists in the unlawful and intentional or reckless restraint of a victim's freedom of movement from a particular place. In other words it is unlawful detention which stops the victim moving away as he would wish to move'[52]. This restraint may be physical, but may also be by deliberate intimidation[53]. Indeed it may be that even intimidation is not required, as long as the victim is compelled to remain[54].

4.52

The mens rea of false imprisonment is intention or reckless restraint of the victim's freedom of movement from a particular place[55]. The defendant's belief

---

47 *R v Lewis* (1993) 14 Cr App Rep (S) 744. This decision seems dubious – the different elements of the offence would appear not to coincide if the taking or carrying away occurs when there is consent. *R v Nnamdi* [2005] EWCA Crim 74 supports the view that they do need to coincide. In such circumstances it may be that false imprisonment is a more realistic charge.
48 *Re HM (vulnerable adult) (abduction)* [2010] EWHC 870 (Fam), [2010] 2 FLR 1057 at [60].
49 *R v Henman* [1987] Crim LR 333.
50 See the commentary in [1987] Crim LR 333.
51 *R v Hutchins* [1988] Crim LR 379.
52 *R v Rahman* (1985) 81 Cr App Rep 349 at 353–354.
53 *R v James* [1997] 34 LS Gaz R 27.
54 This would appear to be the effect of *Hunter v Johnson* (1884) 13 QBD 225, where it was unlawful for a school to detain a boy outside school hours, with no suggestion of violence or intimidation. Although it is not expressly described to be a case of false imprisonment, that is the logical inference.
55 *R v Hutchins* [1988] Crim LR 379.

that he is acting in the victim's best interests does not amount to a defence, even if accepted[56].

Sentence

4.53

Both offences are triable only on indictment, and the maximum sentence is life imprisonment[57]. Extended sentences under the Criminal Justice Act 2003, s 226A are available, but automatic life sentences for second offences do not apply[58]. No guidelines have been issued by the Sentencing Council in respect of these offences.

4.54

Approximate guidance on kidnapping was given some years ago in *R v Spence and Thomas*[59], in which it was said that at the lower end of the scale events arising out of family disputes scarcely qualified as kidnapping; whereas, at the other end, there were carefully planned abductions where the victim was used as a hostage or ransom money demanded – for such offences sentences of eight years and up (significantly more where serious aggravating features were present) would be appropriate. The facts of that case, which would now be seen as almost archetypal trafficking (victim taken by force from Southampton to London with the intention of making her work as a prostitute, but rescued on arrival in London), were said to fall between those two extremes, and sentences of six years' and four years' imprisonment respectively for two defendants (the former more culpable and with a worse record) were appropriate, in place of sentences for eight years' and six years' imprisonment[60].

4.55

More recently, the guidance given in *Spence* for the upper end of the scale has been overtaken by more recent cases. In a Court of Appeal decision in December 2014, sentences starting around 10 years were appropriate where violence had been used and money demanded[61]. Relevant factors were identified in such cases. Not all factors would be apposite in a trafficking context, but those that would include: the length and circumstances of detention, including any method of restraint; the extent of any violence used; involvement of weapons; the effect on the victim and others; the extent of planning; the use of torture or humiliation; and whether the victim was particularly vulnerable[62]. There is a

---

56 Eg *R v Saker* [2011] EWCA Crim 1196, [2012] 1 Cr App Rep (S) 87.

57 Confirmed in respect of false imprisonment by *R v Szczerba* [2002] EWCA Crim 440, [2002] 2 Cr App Rep (S) 86 at [15]–[19].

58 False imprisonment and kidnapping both appearing in the CJA 2003, Sch 15, but not in Sch 15B.

59 (1983) 5 Cr App Rep (S) 413.

60 *R v Spence and Thomas* (1983) 5 Cr App Rep (S) 413.

61 *A-G's Reference (Nos 92 and 93 of 2014) (R v Gibney)* [2014] EWCA Crim 2713, [2015] 1 Cr App Rep (S) 44 at [17] and [22].

62 Ibid at [19].

tension between this case and *A-G's Reference (Nos 102 and 103 of 2014) (R v Perkins)*[63], decided only a fortnight later, where it was held that 'cases involving hostage-taking and demands for ransom will attract figures close to the 16-year starting point; others, where such behaviour has been absent, will still attract double figures, regardless of the degree of violence meted out'.

4.56

In, *R v Pearson-Gaballonie*, seven years' imprisonment in total was appropriate for offences of actual bodily harm ('ABH'), making threats to kill, and false imprisonment, where the defendant's 24 year-old sister-in-law was expected to look after the defendant's six children and clean, was kept in the house naked against her will, beaten regularly, and had her hair cut off, over 'a substantial period'. The sentence in respect of the false imprisonment itself was four years' imprisonment, consecutive with a further three years in respect of some of the counts of ABH[64].

4.57

In *A-G's Reference (No 6 of 2004)*[65], the defendant brought a number of young women and girls to the UK in breach of immigration laws, coerced them to work as prostitutes, incited the rape of one. Three of the victims were held to have been kidnapped (albeit by fraud, rather than by force). Consecutive sentences were appropriate for the sexual offences, kidnapping, and immigration offences, giving a total of 23 years' imprisonment. Of this, 10 years was attributable to the kidnapping.

Child abduction

4.58

As mentioned above, an offence under the Child Abduction Act 1984, s 2 might be used in place of a kidnapping charge, especially where the element of force, threat or fraud is absent. Section 2(1) is in the following terms:

> 'Subject to subsection (3) below, a person, other than one mentioned in subsection (2) below commits an offence if, without lawful authority or reasonable excuse, he takes or detains a child under the age of sixteen—
>
> (a)   so as to remove him from the lawful control of any person having lawful control of the child; or
>
> (b)   so as to keep him out of the lawful control of any person entitled to lawful control of the child.'

---

63 [2014] EWCA Crim 2922, [2015] 1 Cr App Rep (S) 55 at [29].

64 [2007] EWCA Crim 3504. See also *A-G's Reference (No 9 of 2014) (R v R (David))* [2014] EWCA Crim 952, in which a sentence for six-and-a-half years' imprisonment was upheld for false imprisonment and ABH.

65 [2004] EWCA Crim 1275, [2005] 1 Cr App Rep (S) 19.

4.59

Broadly speaking, the persons mentioned in s 2(2), who cannot be guilty of this offence, are parents and guardians. Section 2(3) provides defences which are discussed below.

4.60

There are two ways of committing the offence, as set out in s 2(1)(a) and (b), and an offence under sub-s (1)(a) is not committed by an unlawful taking or detention after the victim has already been removed from the lawful control of, for example, his parents[66].

4.61

By virtue of the Child Abduction Act 1984, s 3(a), 'taking' is defined broadly: 'a person shall be regarded as taking a child if he causes or induces the child to accompany him or any other person or causes the child to be taken'. Section 3(c) provides a similarly broad definition of 'detaining'. The consent of the child is irrelevant to the offence – even if one cause of the child being removed from or kept out of the lawful control of the relevant person is the child's own free choice, the offence will still be committed if the defendant's actions are an effective cause of the child accompanying him[67].

4.62

The taking or detention of the child must be intentional or reckless – but it is not part of the offence to prove that the defendant knew that by doing so he was removing or keeping the child from the lawful control of someone else. In some cases, a lack of such knowledge might be linked to a reasonable excuse, however[68]. The burden of proving that there was no lawful authority or reasonable excuse is on the Crown[69]. What can amount to a 'reasonable excuse' is not defined by statute. At present there is no restriction imposed on the defence by case law. Case law concerning 'reasonable excuse' in other contexts is indicative of the likely scope of the defence but at the moment there is scope for the boundaries to be tested by the courts. There are three defences under the Child Abduction Act 1984, s 2(3), two of which (the defendant being, or reasonably believing that he is, the father of a child whose parents were not married at the time of birth) are unlikely to be relevant in trafficking or slavery cases. However, the third is provided for through s 2(3)(b): it is a defence for a defendant to prove that he believed the child to be 16 or over. This belief need not be reasonable, as long as it is honestly held[70]. Thus, in the context of abduction, if a defendant believed the victim was 16 or over then conduct

---

66 *Foster v DPP* [2004] EWHC 2955 (Admin), [2005] 1 WLR 1400.
67 *R v A (child abduction)* [2000] 1 Cr App Rep 418 at 422–424.
68 *Foster v DPP* [2004] EWHC 2955 (Admin), [2005] 1 WLR 1400 at [27].
69 *R v Berry* [1996] 2 Cr App Rep 226 at 229.
70 *R v Heys* [2011] EWCA Crim 2112 at [6].

sufficient to amount to kidnapping is required before the defendant's behaviour is criminalised. No offence is therefore established if force or fraud sufficient for a kidnapping has not been proved, and a belief that the victim is 16 or over can be proved by the defendant.

Sentence

4.63

The offence is triable either way, with a maximum sentence of seven years' imprisonment if tried on indictment, and six months' imprisonment if tried summarily[71]. It has been noted that the disparity between this and the maximum life sentence for kidnapping seems illogical, and that in the worst cases of child abduction the maximum sentence may be too low[72]. Although the case of *R v RH* sets out a detailed approach to sentencing child abduction cases in general, akin to a full sentencing guideline[73], little guidance is available for sentencing in cases with slavery or trafficking elements. In such cases more assistance may be gained from the cases already referred to in relation to other offences, with suitable adjustment made for: (a) the increased seriousness of an offence committed against a child; but also (b) the absence of features such as force or fraud.

Immigration offences

4.64

Trafficking can go hand in glove with breaches of immigration law, albeit it will be recalled that the offence does not require a crossing of national borders. Immigration offences may be apposite where trafficking occurs from a state outside the UK and in certain other circumstances where defendants' actions engage with immigration law. Immigration crime is a minefield. Those prosecuting and defending in immigration crime would be well advised to read the judgment in *R v Boateng*[74]. This case is instructive in that it shows the various ways in which mistakes can be made by a prosecutor in indicting immigration offences and in which mistakes can be made by defence representatives.

4.65

The offence of primary importance here is under the Immigration Act 1971, s 25, which sets out that:

'(1) A person commits an offence if he—

---

71 Child Abduction Act 1984, s 4(1).
72 *R v Kayani* [2011] EWCA Crim 2871, [2012] 2 All ER 641 at [5] and [16].
73 *R v RH* [2016] EWCA Crim 1754, [2017] 4 WLR 81 especially [7]–[14].
74 [2016] EWCA Crim 57, [2016] 2 Cr App Rep 43.

(a) does an act which facilitates the commission of a breach or attempted breach of immigration law by an individual who is not a citizen of the European Union,

(b) knows or has reasonable cause for believing that the act facilitates the commission of a breach or attempted breach of immigration law by the individual, and

(c) knows or has reasonable cause for believing that the individual is not a citizen of the European Union.'

4.66

It is notable that this section as originally enacted, and as in force until as recently as 2003, was concerned with securing or facilitating entry into the UK of illegal entrants, and related matters. The 'immigration law' the breach of which is facilitated must be one which controls entitlement of non-nationals to enter, transit across or be in the state[75], so it does not include, for example, laws which create document offences[76]. The breach which the defendant facilitates need not actually be completed by the third party, nor does it need to amount to an offence[77].

4.67

There was for a time doubt over whether this offence required that the person who facilitated had been dishonest, as was suggested by some of the dicta in *R v Kaile*[78]. However, this has been clarified in later cases: on the facts of *Kaile* dishonesty by the third party was necessary, since the prosecution case was that the breach facilitated was an offence under the Immigration Act 1971, ss 24A or 26 (an element of which is deception). However, if the defendant is alleged to have facilitated some other breach, and such a breach (if considered in isolation) can occur without dishonesty on the part of the third party, then the offence under s 25 does not require such dishonesty either[79].

---

75 Immigration Act 1971, s 25(2).
76 *R v Kapoor* [2012] EWCA Crim 435, [2012] 2 All ER 1205 at [36].
77 *R v Javaherifard* [2005] EWCA Crim 3231 at [37] and [44].
78 [2009] EWCA Crim 2868 at [16].
79 *R v Boateng* [2016] EWCA Crim 57 at [27]. Note: *Boateng* concerned facilitating the entry of a third party without leave, when leave was required. In that case the particulars of the illegal entry in a s 25 offence should have been framed by reference to s 3 of the Immigration Act 1971 (the general prohibition on entry without leave). What of a deceptive entrant (someone gaining leave by deception) when the person whose entry is facilitated is not dishonest himself (eg a child)? It is arguable in such a case that there is no breach of s 3, because leave has been obtained (albeit by deception); so the particulars of the illegal entry in a s 25 offence should not be framed by reference to s 3. On the other hand, the entry into the UK was undoubtedly illegal. The definition of 'illegal entrant' (in the Immigration Act 1971, s 33(1) as amended by the Immigration and Asylum Act 1996, Sch 2, para 4(1)) follows: 'illegal entrant … means a person … entering or seeking to enter [or who has entered the UK] by means which include deception by another person'. Rather than particularising the breach of immigration law by reference to s 3, it is suggested that the breach should be framed by reference to s 33(1). Alternatively, when prosecuting such a case, best practice may well be to invite the Secretary of State to review the grant of leave on the basis that it was obtained by deception with a view to revoking or curtailing leave. In those circumstances, the breach could be framed by reference to s 3.

4.68

An indictment for a s 25 offence should generally, as a matter of good practice, specify which immigration law the defendant is said to have breached; this will usually be the Immigration Act 1971, s 3, the section providing the general provisions for regulation and control. However, a failure to do so will not necessarily be fatal, especially if it is expressly set out in the prosecution's opening[80]. Defence practitioners should be ready to request further particulars if it is not clear which immigration law is said to have been breached/targeted for breach: a lack of such a request was relevant when holding that an absence of particulars was not a fatal flaw[81].

4.69

It is possible to facilitate entry by actions occurring immediately after entry has occurred[82]. Actions which provide assistance to someone who is known by the defendant to be present in the UK illegally will only amount to an offence if the assistance is provided to the third party *qua* illegal entrant: providing food, money or accommodation to someone *qua* human being, simply to help avoid destitution, is no offence even if he is known to be an illegal entrant[83]. Whilst it would be hard for a defendant to make such an argument in cases where the exploitation of the third party is clear, it is perhaps less likely that a charge under s 25 would be the defendant's primary concern in such a case. Section 25 charges are more likely to be preferred (either alone or as a lesser alternative to a trafficking charge) where exploitation is less obvious, and thus such a defence more plausible.

Sentence

4.70

Offences under s 25 are triable either way, with the maximum penalty on indictment being 14 years' imprisonment. General guidance on aggravating factors was given in *R v Le, R v Stark*. Such factors included committing the offence for financial gain, duration of the offending when it was not a single incident, and the degree of planning and sophistication.[84] The particular features of trafficking cases were not considered. *Le and Stark* was also decided at a time when the maximum sentence for this offence was seven years' imprisonment,

---

80 *R v Dhall* [2013] EWCA Crim 1610 at [15].
81 Ibid.
82 *R v Javaherifard* [2005] EWCA Crim 3231 at [29]. Although this was a decision on s 25 after it had been amended to (so far as is relevant) its current form, it appears the decision owed a certain amount to the pre-2003 wording (which created offences such as 'facilitating ... the entry into the United Kingdom of ... an illegal immigrant'). Nonetheless, the principle that acts can be facilitated even after they have been completed, as long as it is sufficiently soon after, could still apply.
83 Ibid at [50].
84 [1999] 1 Cr App Rep (S) 422, especially 425.

so the specific sentences discussed would no longer be relevant. A more recent decision suggests that the appropriate range into which offences will routinely fall is 3–8 years' imprisonment, depending on which aggravating factors are present[85].

4.71

In *Plakici*[86] the sentence for the illegal entry element of the offending was five years' imprisonment (out of a total of 23). The maximum sentence was then 10 years' imprisonment, and the court broadly followed the approach of *Le and Stark*, so a sentence for such an offence today would probably be higher. In a case where the defendant had employed between 50 and 75 security guards who were not entitled to be in the country, and had taken advantage of their status to exploit them, paying wages around £3 per hour and on occasion requiring them to work for 24 hours or more, and where he had forged documents for the workers and made substantial profits over a five-year period, a sentence of four-and-a-half years' imprisonment was increased to eight years[87].

Offences related to the 'use' of victims of slavery and trafficking

4.72

There are a wide range of purposes for which victims are trafficked, or held in conditions of slavery, servitude, or forced or compulsory labour. Many such purposes are themselves illegal, so even where trafficking or restriction of liberty are not proved, other offences will often arise.

Sexual exploitation

4.73

Perhaps the most widely-recognised purpose for trafficking, etc is that of sexual exploitation, particularly forced prostitution. A number of offences may be relevant here: causing or inciting prostitution under the SOA 2003, s 52, and controlling prostitution under s 53 each carry a maximum penalty of seven years' imprisonment when tried on indictment. The sexual offences sentencing guideline applies.

---

85 *Khan* at [16].
86 [2004] EWCA Crim 1275, [2005] 1 Cr App Rep (S) 19.
87 *A-G's Reference No 28 of 2014 (R v Okoh)* [2014] EWCA Crim 1723. The conviction was not appealed in this case. It prima facie might have been the subject of an appeal against conviction however, the defendant had assisted the workers to avoid prohibitions on working in the UK, but not to breach an 'immigration law' as defined by the act (see para **4.55** above).

4.74

For the s 52 offence to be committed, the defendant must 'intentionally cause or incite another person to become a prostitute'. This means that it is an element of the offence that the complainant has not acted as a prostitute before, and also that the defendant knew this[88]. Where, therefore, a woman who worked as a prostitute in her home country is brought to the UK to do the same, there would be a complete defence.

4.75

'Controlling' prostitution under the SOA 2003, s 53 does not require force or coercion, only direction[89]. Both offences include a requirement that the defendant acts 'for or in the expectation of gain for himself or a third person'[90]. The fact that the gain may not be for defendants themselves highlights that care needs to be taken to ensure that these offences are not used to criminalise those who are forced into supervisory roles after having been the victims of trafficking themselves (as was the case in *R v LM*)[91].

4.76

Where the complainants are children, offences under the SOA 2003, ss 48, 49 and 50 may be charged – these cover causing or inciting sexual exploitation of a child; controlling it; and arranging or facilitating it, respectively. All are triable either way, with a 14-year maximum sentence on indictment. The sexual offences guideline applies.

4.77

'Sexual exploitation' in this context only covers prostitution and the creation of indecent images[92]. In each case, unless the complainant is under 13, it is a defence if the defendant reasonably believed the complainant was 18 – this may often be relevant in cases where the complainant is not previously known to the defendant, perhaps having been picked up off the street, whether in the UK or abroad.

4.78

Those whose sole involvement is as customers of exploited (adult) prostitutes are likely to be guilty of the strict liability offence under the SOA 2003, s 53A, punishable with a level 3 fine. Those who pay for sex from children will commit one of a number of offences under the SOA 2003, s 47, which (perhaps surprisingly) may attract a higher penalty, up to life imprisonment, than controlling such sexual exploitation.

---

88 *R v Ubolcharoen* [2009] EWCA Crim 3263 at [6].
89 *R v Massey* [2007] EWCA Crim 2664, [2008] 2 All ER 969.
90 SOA 2003, s 52(1)(b) and 53(1)(b).
91 [2010] EWCA Crim 2327, [2011] 1 Cr App Rep 135.
92 SOA 2003, s 51(2).

Drug offences

4.79

A number of cases have shown that forced or compulsory labour is often used in the production of cannabis and other drugs: whilst it may be difficult to show that those in control of such operations have committed an offence under the Misuse of Drugs Act 1971, s 4(2)(a) (producing a controlled drug), they are more likely to be concerned in the production (under the Misuse of Drugs Act 1971, s 4(2)(b)), or to have conspired with the worker or workers to commit a s 4(2)(a) offence, or an offence of cultivation of cannabis under s 6.

4.80

The maximum sentence varies depending on the class of drug, but for cannabis is 14 years' imprisonment. These offences are covered by the drug offences sentencing guideline. The defence of lack of knowledge (under the Misuse of Drugs Act 1971, s 28) is likely to be most commonly encountered.

Worker exploitation

4.81

A gangmaster is a person who supplies a worker to do agricultural work, gathering shellfish, or the processing and packaging of produce from such work[93]. A gangmaster must be licensed, pursuant to the Gangmasters (Licensing) Act 2004, s 6. Acting as a gangmaster without a licence, or having false documents to make others believe one is licensed, is punishable with up to 10 years' imprisonment[94]. This is clearly a very substantial penalty for an offence which is expressed as being concerned with regulatory failings: the true mischief at which it is aimed is, of course, the exploitation of workers which the licensing scheme seeks to prevent.

4.82

A list of factors relevant to sentencing, adapted from those set out in the context of trafficking offences, was provided by the Court of Appeal in *R v Morkunas*[95]. In that case the defendant had systematically exploited a significant number of workers over three years, reinforcing economic exploitation with threats and in some cases the use of violence (including one count of ABH of which he was convicted), and had profited to the tune of around £100,000[96]. A sentence of seven years' imprisonment was imposed for the Gangmasters (Licensing) Act

---

93 Gangmasters (Licensing) Act 2004, ss 3 and 4.
94 Gangmasters (Licensing) Act 2004, s 12.
95 [2014] EWCA Crim 2750 at [51]. See paras **3.36** and **4.37** for the list of factors for trafficking offences.
96 Ibid at [59]–[61].

2004 offence, after a 12.5% discount for plea with concurrent sentences for the other offences. This sentence was not interfered with (although the court commented that the judge could have taken a lower starting point for the Gangmasters (Licensing) Act 2004 offence and made the sentence for the ABH offence consecutive).

4.83

A gangmaster, whether licensed or not, can be in a position where he is expected to safeguard, or to not act against, the financial interests of his workers, particularly if he collects wages on their behalf. If he then makes unwarranted deductions from those wages, an offence of fraud by abuse of position (Fraud Act 2006, s 4) may be committed. This does not mean that all exploitative financial arrangements will amount to fraud: for example, the charging of excessive rents for accommodation that the worker is required to take was discussed and not considered to be sufficient[97].

4.84

An offence of failing to pay the national minimum wage is punishable only by way of a fine[98]. It may therefore be an attractive option for defendants to offer as an alternative plea, although no doubt prosecutors will be unlikely to accept it where the evidence of wider exploitation is sufficient.

Orders on conviction

Confiscation

4.85

Any offence from which the defendant benefits can be the subject of confiscation proceedings under the Proceeds of Crime Act 2002; this is likely to apply to a great many slavery and trafficking cases. A number of the offences discussed above are also 'lifestyle offences', listed in the Proceeds of Crime Act 2002, Sch 2, and therefore give rise to the various statutory assumptions in s 10. Offences under the MSA 2015, ss 1 and 2, the Immigration Act 1971, s 25, the SOA 2003, ss 48–50, 52 and 53, and the Misuse of Drugs Act 1971, s 4(2), are all 'lifestyle offences'. It should be noted that the assumptions also apply to any offence which forms part of a course of criminal activity, or is committed over a period of at least six months (providing that the defendant has benefited from it in the sum of at least £5,000)[99].

---

97 *R v Valujevs* [2014] EWCA Crim 2888, [2015] QB 745. It may be that other fraud offences could apply – for example, fraud by false representation where a trafficking victim is promised a good life at his destination – but of course the gain or loss involved in a fraud must be in money or property, which will often not apply.

98 National Minimum Wage Act 1998, s 31.

99 Proceeds of Crime Act 2002, s 75(2).

Forfeiture

4.86

Various forfeiture provisions may be relevant. Under the MSA 2015, s 11, a vehicle used for a trafficking offence under s 2 may be forfeited. The Immigration Act 1971, s 25C provides for a similar power in relation to offences contrary to s 25 of that Act. Section 27 of the Misuse of Drugs Act 1971 provides a wider power, allowing 'anything shown to the satisfaction of the court to relate to the offence' to be forfeited where an offence under that Act has been committed. In all cases, the general power under the Powers of Criminal Courts (Sentencing) Act 2000, s 143 allows property in the possession or control of the defendant at the time of his arrest, and used or intended to be used for committing or facilitating any offence, to be taken. Such forfeiture orders are part of the punishment of the offender, so should be taken into account when considering totality[100]. When defending it is worth bearing in mind that if an asset could form part of a defendant's recoverable amount in confiscation proceedings, by agreeing that it can be forfeited under s 143, the defendant will be at risk of the state recovering that money twice.

Civil orders

4.87

On or after conviction for an offence listed in the MSA 2015, Sch 1 (which broadly covers offences under the MSA 2015, the predecessors to those offences, and inchoate versions of those offences) the court can impose a 'slavery and traffic prevention order' ('STPO') (see ss 14–17). Such orders can impose prohibitions on the defendant doing anything described in the order, if necessary to protect others from harm as a result of further slavery or trafficking offences. Examples of possible prohibitions are given in the explanatory notes to the Act, including participating in particular kinds of business, acting as a gangmaster, visiting particular places, or working with children[101]. There is no restriction on the kind of prohibition that can be imposed, however.

4.88

The Act makes further provisions as to prohibition on foreign travel, and the requirement to provide one's name and address to police, but orders are not limited to these conditions. The court can also impose 'slavery and trafficking risk orders' ('STROs') by virtue of the MSA 2015, s 23 where the defendant has not been convicted, but has acted in a way that shows a risk of committing such offences; the main difference between prevention and risk orders is that the

---

100 *R v Buddo* (1982) 4 Cr App Rep (S) 268, [1982] Crim LR 837.
101 Explanatory notes, para 80.

latter can be made for shorter durations. The Home Office has issued guidance on STPOs and STROs, and forms to be used for applications[102].

4.89

Serious crime prevention orders ('SCPOs') can be imposed either by the Crown Court on conviction for a serious offence, or by the High Court if satisfied that the person has committed or facilitated the commission of such an offence (or acted in a way likely to do so)[103]. A serious offence is either one listed in the Serious Crime Act 2007, Sch 1, Part 1, which includes the majority of offences discussed in this chapter, or one which in the circumstances of the case is sufficiently serious to be treated as if it was listed[104]. SCPOs can contain a wider range of restrictions, requirements and other terms (as well as prohibitions) than STPOs and STROs, but cannot be in force for more than five years (although this does not prevent an application to the High Court for a new order in the same terms as the old one)[105]. They can only be made on application by the DPP or the director of the SFO[106].

4.90

The terms of an order must protect the public by preventing, restricting or disrupting the defendant's involvement in serious crime[107], and must be commensurate with the risk[108]. They must be precise, practicable and enforceable, and be preventative not punitive[109]. These general comments should, as a matter of principle, also apply to STPOs and STROs. Prosecution authorities have historically applied for SCPOs in circumstances where the facts of individual cases have rendered the applications inappropriate. It is important to look beyond the charge to the underlying facts and background circumstances when considering these orders.

4.91

Finally, sexual harm prevention orders (SHPOs) may be imposed on a defendant convicted of any of various sexual and indeed non-sexual offences, listed in the SOA 2003, Schs 3 and 5[110]. These schedules include all the sexual offences discussed above with the exception of the strict liability offence for customers of exploited prostitutes (SOA 2003, s 53A), and also include trafficking under the MSA 2015, s 2, kidnapping, false imprisonment, and child abduction.

---

102 Available at www.gov.uk/government/publications/slavery-and-trafficking-prevention-and-risk-orders.
103 Serious Crime Act 2007, ss 1, 2 and 19.
104 Serious Crime Act 2007, s 2(2).
105 Serious Crime Act 2007, s 16.
106 Serious Crime Act 2007, s 8.
107 Serious Crime Act 2007, s 1(1)(b).
108 *R v Hancox* [2010] EWCA Crim 102, [2010] 4 All ER 537 at [10].
109 Ibid at [11]–[12].
110 SOA 2003, s 103A.

Breach of any of these orders is an either way offence, with a maximum sentence of five years[111]. Guidance on sentencing for breach of an SCPO, likely to be applicable in other cases as well, was given in *R v Koli*[112].

Commentary on the MSA

4.92

As the Strasbourg Court made clear in *Chowdury v Greece*[113] to fulfil the positive obligation to criminalise and effectively punish any act referred to in ECHR, Article 4, States must establish a legislative and administrative framework that prohibits and punishes forced labour or compulsory labour, servitude and slavery. The court re-affirmed that trafficking falls within the scope of the ECHR, Art 4 and a legislative and administrative framework must be in place to punish any act of trafficking[114]. In *Rantsev v Cyprus and Russia*[115] the court held that human trafficking, within the meaning of the Palermo Protocol, Art 3(a) and ECAT, Art 4(a), fell within the scope of the ECHR, Art 4[116].

4.93

The EU Trafficking Directive, Art 2(1) requires Member States to take the necessary measures to ensure that the following intentional acts are punishable:

'The recruitment, transportation, transfer, harbouring or reception of persons, including the exchange or transfer of control over those persons, by means of the threat or use of force or other forms of coercion, of abduction, of fraud, of deception, of the abuse of position of power or of a position of vulnerability or of the giving or receiving of payments or benefits to achieve the consent of a person having control over another person, for the purpose of exploitation'.

4.94

This provision is dealt with at length in Chapter 1. The statutory language on the meaning of exploitation (MSA 2015, s 3) in s 3(4)–(6) does not mirror and/ or reflect all the 'means' envisaged under the EU Trafficking Directive, Art 2(1) and/or ECAT, Art 4. Whereas the language of the EU Trafficking Directive, Art 2(1) and ECAT, Art 4 envisages that the 'means' by which exploitation is committed can apply across *all forms* of exploitation, the MSA 2015, s 3(4)–(6) suggests that different means apply depending on what the form of exploitation

---

111 MSA 2015, s 30 (for STPOs and STROs), Serious Crime Act 2007, s 25 (for SCPOs), and SOA 2003, s 103I (for SHPOs).
112 [2012] EWCA Crim 1869, [2013] 1 Cr App Rep (S) 39.
113 App No 21884/15 (30 March 2017) at 105.
114 Ibid at para 86 and 87.
115 (2010) BHRC 313.
116 Para 282.

is. This is an approach that is completely at odds with the approach of the regional and international instruments defining trafficking and thus non-compliant with ECAT, Art 4 or the EU Trafficking Directive[117].

4.95

The wording of the MSA 2015, s 3(6) fails to deal with 'consent'. Section 3(6) does not adequately address the position in law (as per the EU Trafficking Directive, Art 2) that the question of consent is entirely irrelevant to determining whether a child has been exploited. Further, s 3(6) conflates the position of two distinct (although at times overlapping) groups of trafficked victims: children and those who are in a position of vulnerability. As made clear under Art 2(4) and preamble 11 of the EU Trafficking Directive, consent is not only irrelevant vis-à-vis children (in all circumstances), consent is also irrelevant in respect of adults where the 'means' of exploitation entails the use of force, threats, deception, coercion, abduction, abuse of power or a position of vulnerability, giving/receiving payments or benefits to achieve the consent of a person having control over another. Section 3(6) of the MSA 2015 does not reflect the true position on the (ir)relevance of consent in these circumstances.

4.96

Further, s 3(6)(b) establishes a subjective test, importing a measure of evaluative judgment. ECAT and the EU Trafficking Directive do not require an evaluative judgment. Where the victim is a child, and he is subjected to an action which amounts to exploitation, objectively, that child has been exploited. The test thus is an entirely *objective* test where children are concerned. It is irrelevant whether a reasonable adult may or may not have consented to the exploitation 'services' in the assessment of whether that child is an exploited child.

4.97

Another pressing problem with the MSA 2015 offences is one of enforcement: although there have been recent increases in detection and prosecution, a review of the MSA's effect carried out after one year concluded that the number of recorded modern slavery offences was less than 10% of the likely number of actual offences, and the number of prosecutions was less than 15% of the number of recorded offences[118].

4.98

There has also been criticism of the failure of the MSA 2015 to provide a standalone offence of exploitation: exploitation within s 3 is a necessary condition for a trafficking offence under s 2, and comprises relevant evidence when determining whether a s 1 offence has been committed, but does not

---

117 *CN v UK* and *CN and V v France* App No 67724/09 (11 October 2012).
118 C Haughey, *The Modern Slavery Act Review* (2016) p 12.

amount to an offence in itself[119]. The joint select committee on the Modern Slavery Bill proposed a standalone offence of exploitation[120].

4.99

It could be argued that such a standalone 'exploitation' offence is unnecessary. Given the definition of exploitation in s 3, behaviour caught by it would in many cases amount to one or more other criminal offences (including offences under the MSA 2015, s 1, various sexual offences, and secondary participation in Human Tissue Act 2004 offences). Such offences, however, may not always carry appropriate maximum penalties: sentences for Human Tissue Act offences vary up to a maximum of three years' imprisonment, which may not adequately reflect the gravity of controlling organ harvesting, for example.

4.100

In addition, whilst behaviour that amounts to exploitation under the MSA 2015, s 3 may *often* amount to another offence as well, it would not always. This is particularly true of the exploitation of children or vulnerable persons, as provided for by s 3(6). Any use or attempted use of such a person to obtain services or benefits amounts to exploitation, if he has been chosen because of his vulnerability and because he would otherwise be likely to refuse. This kind of exploitation would be unlikely to amount to another offence in most cases, unless the victim could be shown to have been forced to act as he did. Nor will it amount to trafficking unless there has been movement of the victim, or to forced or compulsory labour unless there is a menace of penalty[121].

4.101

During the passage of the Modern Slavery Bill, the government's position was that the offences in the Bill were sufficiently wide, and widening them further would undermine focus on the more serious offences that were the Bill's target[122]. This may merit review once the practical application of the Act is better understood.

---

119 See P Rook and R Ward, *Rook and Ward on Sexual Offences Law and Practice* (5th edn, Thompson Reuters, 2016).

120 Joint Committee on the Draft Modern Slavery Bill, *Draft Modern Slavery Bill Report* (2013–14, HL166, HC1019).

121 Joint Committee on the Draft Modern Slavery Bill, *Draft Modern Slavery Bill Report* (2013–14, HL166, HC1019) at [13]–[16].

122 Modern Slavery Bill Deb, 4 September 2014, cols 191–194 (Karen Bradley MP).

5 Criminal defences available to victims of trafficking

Introduction

5.1

The domestic safeguards in England and Wales concerning victims of human trafficking who are prosecuted for criminal offences stem from the Council of Europe Convention on Action against Trafficking in Human Beings 2005[1], ratified by the UK in December 2008 ('ECAT'), specifically Art 26, and EU Directive 2011/36/EU on Preventing and Combating Trafficking in Human Beings and Protecting its Victims ('the Trafficking EU Directive'), specifically Art 8.

5.2

Those international safeguards concern the 'non-punishment' and 'non-prosecution' of people who commit criminal offences who are also victims of trafficking.

5.3

Historically, those safeguards were implemented in England and Wales though the Crown Prosecution Service's 'guidance on suspects in a criminal case who might be victims of trafficking or slavery' ('the CPS guidance'), coupled with the remedy of abuse of process.

5.4

Since 31 July 2015, when the Modern Slavery Act ('MSA') 2015, s 45 came into force, the non-punishment protections have been further supplemented in England and Wales to include the statutory defence available to defendants facing certain non-excluded offences who are victims of slavery or trafficking exploitation.

---

1   CETS No 197.

111

International law protection

Palermo Protocol

5.5

The modern international law framework for the protection of victims of trafficking derives from the Palermo Protocol[2]. The Protocol supplements, and is interpreted together with, the UN Convention against Transnational Organized Crime[3]. Through the Preamble to the Protocol state parties declared:

> '... that effective action to prevent and combat trafficking in persons, especially women and children, requires a comprehensive international approach in the countries of origin, transit and destination that includes measures to prevent such trafficking, to punish the traffickers and to protect the victims of such trafficking, including by protecting their internationally recognized human rights ...'.

5.6

The Protocol defined and explained the concept of 'trafficking'[4]. There is no separate concept of slavery. Trafficking in international law includes the harbouring or receipt of persons by various means of compulsion[5] for exploitation. It therefore includes slavery as a form of trafficking.

5.7

Although the Protocol itself was silent on the non-punishment of trafficking victims, the Working Group on Trafficking in Persons in January 2010 prepared a background paper 'Non-punishment and non-prosecution of victims of trafficking in persons: administrative and judicial approaches to offences committed in the process of such trafficking'.

ECAT

5.8

ECAT came into force in the UK on 1 April 2009[6]. The UK complies with its provisions through various government policies and, in part, through the enactment of the MSA 2015.

---

2 The 2000 Protocol to Prevent, Suppress and Punish Trafficking in Persons, especially Women and Children.
3 Palermo Protocol, Art 1.1.
4 Palermo Protocol, Art 3.
5 See the commentary below in the context of ECAT.
6 It was ratified by the UK on 17 December 2008.

5.9

The purpose and scope of ECAT are set out in Arts 1.1 and 2 respectively:

'Article 1 Purposes of the Convention

1 The purposes of this Convention are:

a   to prevent and combat trafficking in human beings, while guaranteeing gender equality

b   to protect the human rights of the victims of trafficking, design a comprehensive framework for the protection and assistance of victims and witnesses, while guaranteeing gender equality, as well as to ensure effective investigation and prosecution;

c   to promote international cooperation on action against trafficking in human beings.

...

Article 2 Scope

This Convention shall apply to all forms of trafficking in human beings, whether national or transnational, whether or not connected with organised crime'.

5.10

Article 4 defines trafficking and the terms necessary to interpret the definition:

'Article 4 Definitions

For the purposes of this Convention:

a   "Trafficking in human beings" shall mean the recruitment, transportation, transfer, harbouring or receipt of persons, by means of the threat or use of force or other forms of coercion, of abduction, of fraud, of deception, of the abuse of power or of a position of vulnerability or of the giving or receiving of payments or benefits to achieve the consent of a person having control over another person, for the purpose of exploitation. Exploitation shall include, at a minimum, the exploitation of the prostitution of others or other forms of sexual exploitation, forced labour or services, slavery or practices similar to slavery, servitude or the removal of organs;

b   The consent of a victim of "trafficking in human beings" to the intended exploitation set forth in subparagraph (a) of this article shall be irrelevant where any of the means set forth in subparagraph (a) have been used;

c   The recruitment, transportation, transfer, harbouring or receipt of a child for the purpose of exploitation shall be considered "trafficking in human beings" even if this does not involve any of the means set forth in subparagraph (a) of this article;

d   "Child" shall mean any person under eighteen years of age;

e   "Victim" shall mean any natural person who is subject to trafficking in human beings as defined in this article'.

5.11

Article 26 comprises a 'non-punishment provision':

'Each Party shall, in accordance with the basic principles of its legal system, provide for the possibility of not imposing penalties on victims for their involvement in unlawful activities, to the extent that they have been compelled to do so'.

5.12

In England and Wales the UK provided for the 'possibility of not imposing penalties on victims for their involvement in unlawful activities, to the extent that they have been compelled to do so' through the implementation of CPS guidance. This guidance concerned when a victim of trafficking should not be prosecuted, first, on evidential grounds (where evidence of duress meant that there was no reasonable prospect of conviction) and, second, on public interest grounds, namely the status of the victim as a victim of trafficking and the nexus of compulsion between the trafficking and offending. For a discussion of the way in which Art 26 was implemented through the CPS guidance and the doctrine of abuse of process in the event that the CPS guidance was not followed, see *R v LM*; *R v MB*; *R v DG*; *R v Tabot*; and *R v Tijani*[7] ('*LM*') and *R v N*; *R v L*[8]. These cases are discussed below as they retain significance in the context of the current iteration of the CPS guidance and the law as it now stands.

The EU Trafficking Directive

5.13

The EU Trafficking Directive came into effect in the UK on 6 April 2013. It was introduced as '... part of global action against trafficking in human

---

7   [2010] EWCA Crim 2327, [2011] 1 Cr App Rep 12. See also *R v O* [2008] EWCA Crim 2835, (2008) Times, 2 October. At the time of *R v O* the UK had signed but not ratified ECAT, and was thus subject to the attenuated obligation under Art 18 of the Vienna Convention on the Law of Treaties to refrain from acts which would defeat its object and purpose.
8   [2012] EWCA Crim 189, [2012] 1 Cr App Rep 35.

beings …'[9]. In the preamble to the Directive the European Parliament and the Council set out: 'The Union is committed to the prevention of and fight against trafficking in human beings, and to the protection of the rights of trafficked persons'[10]. It sets out that children's interests must be a 'primary consideration' as 'Children are more vulnerable than adults and therefore at greater risk of becoming victims of trafficking in human beings'[11]. It also sets out that '… the validity of any possible consent to perform … labour or services [amounting to forced or compulsory labour] should be evaluated on a case-by-case basis. However, when a child is concerned, no possible consent should ever be considered valid'[12].

5.14

Recital (14) of the Preamble to the Directive says:

'Victims of trafficking in human beings should, in accordance with the basic principles of the legal systems of the relevant Member States, be protected from prosecution or punishment for criminal activities such as the use of false documents, or offences under legislation on prostitution or immigration, that they have been compelled to commit as a direct consequence of being subject to trafficking. The aim of such protection is to safeguard the human rights of victims, to avoid further victimisation and to encourage them to act as witnesses in criminal proceedings against the perpetrators. This safeguard should not exclude prosecution or punishment for offences that a person has voluntarily committed or participated in'.

5.15

Human trafficking is defined through Art 2 of the Directive, which outlines when Member States are required to punish those who commit acts of human trafficking:

'**2 Offences concerning trafficking in human beings**

1. Member States shall take the necessary measures to ensure that the following intentional acts are punishable:

The recruitment, transportation, transfer, harbouring or reception of persons, including the exchange or transfer of control over those persons, by means of the threat or use of force or other forms of coercion, of abduction, of fraud, of deception, of the abuse of power or

---

9   Preamble, Recital (2).
10 Preamble, Recital (4).
11 Preamble, Recital (8).
12 Preamble, Recital (11).

of a position of vulnerability or of the giving or receiving of payments or benefits to achieve the consent of a person having control over another person, for the purpose of exploitation.

2. A position of vulnerability means a situation in which the person concerned has no real or acceptable alternative but to submit to the abuse involved.

3. Exploitation shall include, as a minimum, the exploitation of the prostitution of others or other forms of sexual exploitation, forced labour or services, including begging, slavery or practices similar to slavery, servitude, or the exploitation of criminal activities, or the removal of organs.

4. The consent of a victim of trafficking in human beings to the exploitation, whether intended or actual, shall be irrelevant where any of the means set forth in paragraph 1 has been used.

5. When the conduct referred to in paragraph 1 involves a child, it shall be a punishable offence of trafficking in human beings even if none of the means set forth in paragraph 1 has been used.

6. For the purpose of this Directive, "child" shall mean any person below 18 years of age'.

5.16

Article 8 of the Directive is the provision which entitles a Member State not to prosecute or punish victims of trafficking who commit a criminal offence:

'8 Non-prosecution or non-application of penalties to the victim

Member States shall, in accordance with the basic principles of their legal systems, take the necessary measures to ensure that competent national authorities are entitled not to prosecute or impose penalties on victims of trafficking in human beings for their involvement in criminal activities which they have been compelled to commit as a direct consequence of being subjected to any of the acts referred to in Article 2'.

5.17

Article 8 protection is afforded through the CPS guidance (see below), to possible credible victims of trafficking who commit offences in England and Wales.

Domestic law protection

Prosecutorial staged inquiry

5.18

In *R v LM*[13] the court held that the word 'compelled' was not limited to the circumstances in which the English common law defences of duress and necessity apply. Further, ECAT, Art 26 must now be considered in the context of the EU Trafficking Directive, Art 8. The court also held[14] that prosecutors were required to conduct a three-stage inquiry when discharging their function:

> 'The first is: (1) is there a reason to believe that the person has been trafficked? If so, then (2) if there is clear evidence of a credible common law defence the case will be discontinued in the ordinary way on evidential grounds, but, importantly, (3) even where there is not, but the offence may have been committed as a result of compulsion arising from the trafficking, prosecutors should consider whether the public interest lies in proceeding to prosecute or not'.

It is clear that the inquiry does not merely stop at whether a common law defence of duress exists, but rather necessitates a further consideration of whether the public interest mandates prosecution, given the nefarious nature of trafficking.

5.19

With the enactment of the MSA 2015, s 45 prosecutors must now also ask whether there is clear evidence of a credible defence under s 45. Section 45 therefore needs to be interleaved into the existing three-stage test to create a new four-stage test. It is anticipated that further guidance will be introduced after the special court appeal hearing concerning the burden of proof *viz* s 45 (see below). In the event that the guidance were amended, the approach would likely be as follows:

- first, the evidence test of the CPS Code for Crown Prosecutors should be considered by reference to evidence of the common law defences of duress and necessity;

- second, it should then be considered by reference to evidence of a s 45 defence; and, if the evidence limb of the CPS Code test is satisfied;

- third, the specific rules for the guidance of prosecutors concerning the non-prosecution of credible victims of trafficking should be applied; and

- fourth, the court has the power to stay a prosecution for abuse of process.

---

13 [2010] EWCA Crim 237, [2011] 1 Cr App Rep 135.
14 At 10.

As a matter of good practice, CPS prosecutors should consider s 45 as part of the test now, in anticipation of the guidance being amended, given that Parliament has seen fit to strive to comply with its international law obligations through the enactment of s 45.

Is there reason to believe the person has been trafficked?

5.20

Chapter 1 explores the definition of trafficking, both in respect of adults and children (the definition differs significantly between the two). Chapter 2 sets out the identification process currently in place for victims of trafficking in the UK, the National Referral Mechanism. Not all victims are referred into this identification process.

5.21

In *R v L*[15] the court, when considering the weight to be applied to the trafficking identification decision taken under ECAT, Art 10, held:

> 'Whether the concluded decision of the competent authority is favourable or adverse to the individual it will have been made by an authority vested with the responsibility for investigating these issues, and although the court is not bound by the decision, unless there is evidence to contradict it, or significant evidence that was not considered, it is likely that the criminal courts will abide by it'.

The role of expert evidence in the identification of a victim is explored in Chapter 2 and below.

Compulsion and nexus

5.22

A common thread through the variety of non-punishment safeguards within the regional trafficking instruments and the MSA 2015, s 45 is the role of compulsion in the criminality, and whether there is a nexus between the trafficking of the victim and the criminal offending.

5.23

In *R v LM*[16] the court held that the word 'compelled' was not limited to the circumstances in which the English common law defences of duress and necessity apply.

---

15 [2013] EWCA Crim 991, [2013] 2 Cr App Rep 247 at para 28.
16 [2010] EWCA Crim 237, [2011] 1 Cr App Rep 135.

5.24

In *R v L* the court held[17]

> 'The reasoning is not always spelled out, and perhaps we should do so now. The criminality, or putting it another way, the culpability, of any victim of trafficking may be significantly diminished, and in some cases effectively extinguished, not merely because of age (always a relevant factor in the case of a child defendant) but because no realistic alternative was available to the exploited victim but to comply with the dominant force of another individual, or group of individuals'.

5.25

For the purposes of the MSA 2015, s 45, when considering whether a reasonable person would have acted as the defendant acted the jury will have to consider the nature of the compulsion in the context of the seriousness of the offence. The prosecution in argument in *R v Joseph*[18] suggested that a greater dominant force of compulsion would be needed to extinguish the higher criminality involved in serious offences. This, it is suggested, is a helpful way of analysing individual cases.

5.26

Compulsion for the purposes of non-punishment and duress thresholds should not become indistinguishable[19]. The term 'compulsion' in the regional trafficking instruments is directed to the particular state of 'trafficking' and to victims of human trafficking. The Explanatory Report to ECAT[20] provides, in respect of non-punishment:

> '273. In particular, the requirement that victims have been compelled to be involved in unlawful activities shall be understood as comprising, at a minimum, victims that have been subject to any of the illicit means referred to in Article 4, when such involvement results from compulsion'.

5.27

Those illicit means include, 'threat or use of force or other forms of coercion, of abduction, of fraud, of deception, of the abuse of power or of a position of vulnerability or of the giving or receiving of payments or benefits to achieve the consent'. The Explanatory Report also helpfully sets out what is meant by abuse of position of vulnerability, which is considered at length in Chapter 1.

---

17 [2013] EWCA Crim 991, [2013] 2 Cr App Rep 247 at para 13.
18 [2017] EWCA Crim 36, [2017] 1 Cr App Rep 33.
19 See *R v LM* [2010] EWCA Crim 237, [2011] 1 Cr App Rep 135 at para **5.18** above.
20 CETS, *Explanatory Report to the Council of Europe Convention on Action against Trafficking in Human Beings*.

Children

5.28

For the purposes of the MSA 2015, s 45, a child does not have to establish compulsion (or that there is an absence of compulsion, if the burden is reversed) in order to satisfy the provisions of the statutory defence: see below. However, the court does have to consider whether a reasonable person in the same situation as the person and having the person's relevant characteristics would do that act. Chapter 3 sets out in detail the special protections and provisions afforded to child victims of trafficking. The current CPS Guidance provides:

> 'When considering whether to prosecute a child victim of trafficking/ slavery, prosecutors will only need to consider whether or not the offence is committed as a direct consequence of, or in the course of trafficking/slavery'.

5.29

It is arguable that when applying the guidance, in order to satisfy the international law protections referred to above, a child does not have to be compelled to commit an offence before there will be a breach of international law if he is prosecuted for an offence. In the circumstances it would not be in the public interest to prosecute the child. However, it is also arguable that while compulsion is not a necessary element of trafficking with a child, some compulsion will be necessary before it will not be in the public interest to prosecute.

Duress

5.30

Duress provides a common law protection for victims of trafficking who commit offences. The scope of the defence was reconsidered by the House of Lords in *R v Hasan*[21]. Before analysing the elements of the defence, Lord Bingham observed in his speech, 'I find it unsurprising that the law in this and other jurisdictions should have been developed so as to confine the defence of duress within narrowly defined limits'[22].

5.31

The elements which must be established by a defendant are as follows:

- the defendant believed that there was a threat of death or serious injury[23];

---

21 [2005] UKHL 22 sub nom *R v Z* [2005] 2 AC 467.
22 At [21].
23 *R v Hasan* [2005] UKHL 22 at [21](2).

- this belief was reasonable, as well as genuinely held[24];

- the threat was to the defendant, a member of his immediate family, or to a person for whose safety he reasonably regarded himself as responsible[25];

- the defendant's criminal conduct was directly caused by the threat[26]; and

- a sober person of reasonable firmness, having the same characteristics as the defendant, would have responded in the same way[27]; the characteristics which may be taken into account are only those which realistically make a person less able to resist threats: age and possibly sex are relevant, as are pregnancy and physical or mental disabilities; other factors are not[28].

5.32

There are also a number of factors which preclude a defence of duress from succeeding. Duress is unavailable:

- as a defence to murder, attempted murder, and perhaps to treason involving the death of the sovereign[29];

- if there were some evasive action that the defendant could reasonably have been expected to take, in order to avoid the threat without committing the offence[30]: if the threat were not expected to be carried out almost immediately, 'there may be little if any room for doubt that he could have taken evasive action, whether by going to the police or in some other way'[31]; or

- where the defendant voluntarily associated with people engaged in criminality, in circumstances where he foresaw or ought reasonably to have foreseen the risk of being subject to violent compulsion: the 'gang exception'[32].

5.33

In *R v van Dao*[33], the Court of Appeal considered the case of a victim of trafficking who had been threatened with false imprisonment. The court was invited to expand the defence of duress:

---

24 Ibid at [23].
25 Ibid at [21](3). The inclusion of '… a person for whose safety the defendant would reasonably regard himself as responsible' was not decisively affirmed in *R v Hasan*, but it appeared to Lord Bingham to be consistent with the rationale of the defence. This issue does not arise in these cases.
26 Ibid at [21](5).
27 *R v Graham* (1982) 74 Cr App Rep 235, CA at 241; *Graham* was approved in *R v Howe* (1987) 85 Cr App Rep 32, HL, at 65–66.
28 *R v Bowen* [1996] 2 Cr App Rep 157, CA at 166.
29 *R v Hasan* [2005] UKHL 22 at [21(1)].
30 Ibid at [21](6).
31 Ibid at [28].
32 Ibid at [39].
33 [2012] EWCA Crim 1717, [2013] Crim LR 234.

'... better [to] ensure that domestic (English [and Welsh]) criminal law implemented the United Kingdom's obligations of protecting victims of trafficking contained in the [Convention] and, in particular, in Article 26'[34].

The judgment was delayed to allow the Court to consider the judgment in *R v N; R v L*[35]. Gross LJ (giving the judgment) held:

'The furthest we are prepared to go and essentially in deference to the arguments addressed to us, is to express a provisional view: namely, that we would have been strongly disinclined to accept that a threat of false imprisonment suffices for the defence of duress, without an accompanying threat of death or serious injury. We would be minded to regard any such widening of the defence as ill-advised. While accepting that the issue has not been resolved by authority, our provisional view is supported by pointers in the more recent authorities and, more especially, by considerations of policy there highlighted. Brief amplification follows'[36].

5.34

The court went on to note the observations of Hughes LJ in *LM* (above) and those of the court in *Re N; Re L* (above) (where the judgment of the court was handed down by Lord Judge CJ), citing in particular Lord Judge's dicta at [12] of *R v N; R v L*:

'... The logical conclusion of such elision would be to create a new form of immunity (albeit under a different name) *or to extend the defence of duress by removing the limitation inherent in it. Whatever form of trafficking is under consideration, that approach to these problems....would be fallacious*' (emphasis added)[37].

5.35

Gross LJ concluded that no modification should be made to the defences of duress and duress of circumstances in the context of victims of trafficking facing charges. In *R v Joseph*[38], Anti-Slavery International, a charity founded in 1839 to combat slavery, intervened with written submissions to argue that the Court of Appeal should reassess duress to bring it into line with the Modern Slavery Act 2015[39]. The court saw 'no reason to develop the law of duress in the way suggested'[40].

---

34 Ibid at [24](iv).
35 [2012] EWCA Crim 189, [2012] 1 Cr App Rep 35.
36 [2012] EWCA Crim 1717, [2013] Crim LR 234 at [33].
37 [2012] EWCA Crim 189, [2012] 1 Cr App Rep 35 at [54].
38 [2017] EWCA Crim 36, [2017] 1 Cr App Rep 33.
39 Ibid at 7.
40 Ibid at 24 ff, in particular at 28. The court there left open the possibility of revisiting the parameters of duress in a case post-dating the coming into force of the MSA 2015.

Modern Slavery Act 2015, s 45

5.36

Section 45 of the MSA 2015 came into force on 31 July 2015. It creates separate defences for adults and children who are victims of trafficking who commit certain criminal offences. The s 45 defence does not apply to offences which appear in the MSA 2015, Sch 4.

5.37

Where a victim of trafficking has committed one of the offences to which the defence in s 45 does not apply, reliance can still be placed on the non-punishment provisions within the regional trafficking instruments (ECAT and the EU Trafficking Directive) and whether the prosecution is in the public interest and/or is an abuse of process[41] still remain avenues available to the defence to halt the prosecution of the victim of trafficking.

5.38

It seems that Parliament intended that, after the s 45 defence came into force, abuse of process should still exist as a safeguard in relation to offences in Sch 4. In the Commons debate on second reading, the Home Secretary said[42]:

'The defence includes substantial safeguards against abuse and it will not apply to a number of serious offences – mainly violent and sexual offences – which are set out in the Bill. However, even in cases where the defence does not apply, prosecutors will still need to look carefully at all the circumstances to see whether it is in the public interest to prosecute victims'.

5.39

Section 45 is in the following terms:

'45 Defence for slavery or trafficking victims who commit an offence

(1) A person is not guilty of an offence if—

(a)　the person is aged 18 or over when the person does the act which constitutes the offence,

(b)　the person does that act because the person is compelled to do it,

(c)　the compulsion is attributable to slavery or to relevant exploitation, and

---

41　A failure to adhere to that guidance may be an abuse of process and lead to a stay of proceedings (whether or not the offence charged is exempted through Sch 4). This is a species of 'second limb' abuse of process (where it would be a misuse of the court's process to try a case, rather than where there cannot be a fair trial): *R v Horseferry Road Magistrates' Court, ex p Bennett* [1994] 1 AC 42, [1993] 3 All ER 138, HL.

42　607 HC Official Report (6th series) col 177, 8 July 2014, in the speech of the Home Secretary (Theresa May); see also Commons Committee Stage, 9th sitting, 607 HC Official Report (6th series) cols 365 and 391, 11 September 2014, junior Home Office minister Karen Bradley, and col 387, Sarah Teather.

(d)   a reasonable person in the same situation as the person and having the person's relevant characteristics would have no realistic alternative to doing that act.

(2) A person may be compelled to do something by another person or by the person's circumstances.

(3) Compulsion is attributable to slavery or to relevant exploitation only if—

(a)   it is, or is part of, conduct which constitutes an offence under section 1 or conduct which constitutes relevant exploitation, or

(b)   it is a direct consequence of a person being, or having been, a victim of slavery or a victim of relevant exploitation.

(4) A person is not guilty of an offence if—

(a)   the person is under the age of 18 when the person does the act which constitutes the offence,

(b)   the person does that act as a direct consequence of the person being, or having been, a victim of slavery or a victim of relevant exploitation, and

(c)   a reasonable person in the same situation as the person and having the person's relevant characteristics would do that act.

(5) For the purposes of this section—

"relevant characteristics" means age, sex and any physical or mental illness or disability;

"relevant exploitation" is exploitation (within the meaning of section 3) that is attributable to the exploited person being, or having been, a victim of human trafficking.

(6) In this section references to an act include an omission.

(7) Subsections (1) and (4) do not apply to an offence listed in Schedule 4.

(8) The Secretary of State may by regulations amend Schedule 4'.

5.40

By the MSA 2015, Sch 4, the s 45 defence is not available to the offences listed in this schedule[43].

---

43 A s 45 defence is not available for: (1) offences of attempting or conspiring to commit an offence listed in Sch 4; (2) offences of aiding, abetting, counselling or procuring an offence listed in Sch 4; or (3) offences under Part 2 of the Serious Crime Act 2007 (encouraging or assisting) where the offence (or one of the offences) which the person in question intends or believes would be committed is an offence listed in Sch 4.

Burden and standard of proof: s 45

5.41

The Court of Appeal is shortly to consider in a special court whether a reverse burden of proof applies to s 45, ie whether it is for the defendant to prove the elements of sub-s (1) in the case of an adult or sub-s (3) in the case of a child.

5.42

At the time of writing, the CPS guidance on s 45 identifies two burdens of proof applicable to the defence. First, an evidential burden rests with the defendant. On current guidance the defendant is required to show (some evidence) that they were compelled to commit the offence. It then falls to the prosecution to prove, so that a jury is sure, that they were not compelled to commit the offence. According to that guidance, in the event that the prosecution cannot disprove compulsion then it is for the defendant to prove on the balance of probabilities that the other limbs of the defence are made out. The guidance is in the following terms:

'In order to avail himself of a section 45 defence, the defendant will need:

— to adduce evidence to raise the issue of whether he was a victim of trafficking or slavery. It will then be for the Crown to prove beyond reasonable doubt that he was not a victim, if this is not accepted.

— for adults, to prove on a balance of probabilities that he was compelled to commit the offence (Whether the criminality is significantly diminished or effectively extinguished because no realistic alternative was available but to comply with the dominant force of another); and

— for adults, to prove on a balance of probabilities that the compulsion was as a direct consequence of his trafficking or slavery situation; and

— for adults, to prove on a balance of probabilities that a reasonable person with the same characteristics of the defendant and in the same position would have no realistic alternative but to commit the offence.

— for children, to prove on the balance of probabilities that a reasonable person in the same situation and with the same characteristics of the defendant, would do that act'.

5.43

There have been two Crown Court rulings which have led to juries being directed that such a reverse burden applies. In both cases the defendants were convicted. In *R v Danciu (aka Kreka)*[44], His Honour Judge Lucas QC held that, despite s 45 not being clear, despite competing submissions, and in reviewing the law in *R v Hunt*[45], the burden of proof was on the defendant. He derived some limited assistance from the (different) wording of the Immigration and Asylum Act 1999, s 31.

5.44

In *R v Maione*[46], Mr Recorder Rajah referred to *Kreka*. He acknowledged that he was not bound by that case, but concluded that the decision in *Kreka* was correct. The court also relied on what he considered to be Parliament's intention.

5.45

Kreka and *Maione* are to be the subject of a special court hearing before the Court of Appeal in 2018 to resolve where the burden of proof rests where a defence under the MSA 2015, s 45 has been raised.

5.46

In rebuttal to the present position set out in the CPS guidance, the court may consider the following:

- in *R v Hunt* it was held that it was for the prosecution to prove that the defendant possessed morphine in a proscribed form, and not for him to prove that he did not, where a preparation of morphine containing not more than 0.2 per cent of the drug as part of a compound containing other inert or active ingredients was not proscribed: s 45 is not analogous to the relevant provision of the Misuse of Drugs Act 1971 (where there was no reverse burden by necessary implication in any event);

- following *R v Lambert*[47], there is no 'necessary implication' in s 45;

- furthermore, *Hunt* was decided before the HRA 1998 came into force. Since the enactment of the 1998 Act a number of cases have considered when a reverse burden should apply. In *R v S*[48] the Court of Appeal reviewed authorities, including *Hunt* and those decided post-*Lambert*, and summarised the law as follows:

  'In our judgment, having regard to the authorities and, indeed, to general principle, as a matter of English law it is open to Parliament to provide that, in criminal proceedings in a given context, a legal (persuasive) burden be imposed upon an accused; but, if that is to be so, that is to

---

44 Crown Court at Wood Green.
45 [1987] AC 352.
46 Crown Court at Isleworth.
47 [2001] UKHL 37, [2001] 3 WLR 206, [2001] 2 Cr App Rep 511.
48 [2002] EWCA Crim 2558, [2003] 1 Cr App Rep 35.

be regarded as an exceptional course and sufficiently clear language is required. Ultimately, however, all depends on the interpretation of the particular statutory provision in question';

- *R v S* concerned the statutory defence to trade mark offences where '… it shall be for the defendant to show that he believed on reasonable grounds …' that there was no infringement. It is arguable that, with s 45, there is no 'sufficiently clear language'. Ultimately the interpretation of legislation is a matter of law for the courts. There is no question of the court showing deference or respect to the views of the government because of the subject matter of the legislation[49]. Lord Phillips, in *Thet v DPP*[50] stated:

  'I would, however, question the use of *Pepper v Hart* in the context of a criminal prosecution. Mr Chalk was not able to refer the court to any case in which *Pepper v Hart* has been used in that context. If a criminal statute is ambiguous, I would question whether it is appropriate by the use of *Pepper v Hart* to extend the ambit of the statute so as to impose criminal liability upon a defendant where, in the absence of the Parliamentary material, the court would not do so. It seems to me at least arguable that if a criminal statute is ambiguous, the defendant should have the benefit of the ambiguity';

- unlike the Immigration and Asylum Act 1999, s 31 defence, the word 'shows' does not appear in s 45. The interplay between s 31(1) and (7) of the 1999 Act explains why there is an evidential burden in relation to the first part of the defence under s 31 (namely whether someone is a refugee) and a legal burden in relation to the rest of the elements of the defence. There is no such interplay between the subsections of s 45.

5.47

In the event that the Court of Appeal finds that there is no reverse burden in s 45, the CPS will have to amend its guidance to reflect that decision.

Expert evidence: s 45 defence

5.48

In respect of adult defendants, in order to pray in aid of the s 45 defence, compulsion of the victim to commit the crime must exist (or if the burden is on the Crown – proven not to exist). Compulsion in the context of this statutory defence requires that a reasonable person in the same situation as the defendant with the person's relevant characteristics would have been so compelled. The defence involves both an objective element and a subjective element.

---

49 *R (on the application of Gillan) v Metropolitan Police Comr* [2004] EWCA Civ 1067, [2005] QB 388 at [30].
50 [2006] EWHC 2701 (Admin), [2007] 1 WLR 2022 at [15].

5.49

As with duress, psychiatric evidence might be admissible to show that a defendant was suffering from mental illness or impairment or a recognised psychiatric condition, provided that a reasonable person suffering from such illness might be more susceptible to compulsion. Such evidence might arguably assist the jury in deciding whether a reasonable person suffering from such condition in the same situation as the defendant might have committed the offence.

5.50

As with asylum and refugee cases, country evidence may be admissible to show what a person in the same situation as the defendant was enduring/had endured. Great care should be taken only to seek to admit evidence which is admissible and not self-serving or irrelevant[51]. There is a gulf presently between the prevalent use of expert evidence in immigration proceedings, and the situation in criminal proceedings, where such evidence is very rarely deployed. When representing defendants in criminal proceedings representatives should first consider the following:

(i)   is the expert being asked to provide an opinion on a matter which is outside the ordinary expertise of the jury?

(ii)   that the expert put forward should be suitably qualified to give expert testimony on the subject.

Is it in the public interest to prosecute the victim of trafficking?

5.51

The public interest test necessarily turns on the facts of individual cases. In each case it involves a careful analysis of the following:

- the seriousness of the offence: the more serious an offence is the greater the criminality or culpability that attaches to the offending; with a serious offence there will always be a greater need for prosecution in the public interest;

- the level of compulsion: with more serious offences and greater criminality or culpability, a higher dominant force of compulsion will be required to reduce the criminality or culpability of a suspect to a level at or below which he or she should not be prosecuted. The vulnerability of the defendant is highly relevant to this assessment of culpability;

---

51 See the commentary of Lord Judge in *R v N; R v L* [2012] EWCA Crim 189, [2013] QB 379 at 86c and the commentary of Lord Thomas in *R v Joseph* [2017] EWCA Crim 36, [2017] 1 Cr App Rep 33 at paras 87 and 88.

- the nexus of compulsion: for a prosecution not to be in the public interest there must be a link between the trafficking and the offending.

5.52

The CPS guidance (see below) is key to the public interest question. It helpfully assists in how the prosecution should address its mind to the public interest question in a case where the defendant is a victim of trafficking. It is essential that representatives for the Crown and the defendant consider this policy guidance in its entirety. A failure to follow the guidance will provide a strong basis for arguing that the prosecution is an abuse of the court process (see below).

5.53

When considering the public interest test the CPS has used the international and regional instruments definition of trafficking to ensure that the appropriate international and regional legal obligations are met. The CPS has avoided adopting Parliament's distinction between trafficking and slavery. This approach is very sensible, as there is concern that Parliament's artificial distinction between the two concepts may cause some potential victims of trafficking not to be identified as such[52].

5.54

The CPS guidance is as follows:

'The duty to make proper enquiries and to refer through the National Referral Mechanism (NRM)

In considering whether a suspect might be a victim of trafficking or slavery, as required in the first stage of the assessment, prosecutors should have regard to the duty of the prosecutor to make proper enquiries in criminal prosecutions involving individuals who may be victims of trafficking or slavery.

The enquiries should be made by:

- advising the law enforcement agency which investigated the original offence that it must investigate the suspect's trafficking / slavery situation; and

- advising that the suspect is referred through the NRM for victim identification (if this has not already occurred). All law enforcement

---

52 The reference to a trafficker having to facilitate the travel of a person to fulfil the elements of an offence of trafficking is, for example, unhelpful in the MSA 2015, s 2. The section sets out that the travel may be fulfilled by *inter alia* the receipt or harbouring of a person. However, the international definition of trafficking adopted in the regional instruments binding on the UK (whether under the Palermo Protocol, ECAT or the EU Trafficking Directive) does not require the 'travel' of a person: if he is recruited, received by someone or harboured by someone he will be a victim of trafficking if the other components of the definition are fulfilled. See Chapter 1, which deals with the definition at length.

officers are able to refer potential victims of trafficking/slavery to the NRM. ... Further information concerning the NRM can be found on the Council of Europe Convention on Action against Trafficking in Human Beings.

If an adult suspect does not consent to their referral, the charging decision should be made on whatever other information might be available, without the benefit of an NRM decision on their victim status (see below for further explanation).

These steps must be done regardless of what has been advised by the investigator or whether there is an indication of a guilty plea by the suspect's legal representative (see the section 'Early guilty plea' below). It should be noted that adults must consent to be referred to the NRM.

Referral to the NRM and NRM decisions

...

Prosecutors should take account of an NRM decision (reasonable grounds or conclusive grounds) regarding the status, or potential status, of the suspect as a victim of trafficking/slavery when considering the decision to prosecute; however a conclusive decision will carry more weight.

Where there is a reasonable grounds decision only, prosecutors should make enquiries about when a conclusive decision is likely to be made. If there is to be a delay, then prosecutors can take account of the reasonable grounds decision of the suspect but should additionally consider other evidence and the seriousness of the offence when considering the decision to prosecute.

...

Has the victim been compelled to commit an offence?

The following guidance on considering whether a victim has been compelled, as required in the third stage of the assessment, applies to adults only and does not apply to child victims of trafficking/slavery (see the section below 'Children and 'the means of trafficking'').

'Compulsion' includes all the means of trafficking defined by the United Nations Protocol on Trafficking (The United Nations Convention against Transnational Organised Crime 2000 supplemented by the Protocol to Prevent, Suppress and Punish Trafficking in Persons) : threats, use of force, fraud and deception, inducement, abuse of power or of a position of vulnerability, or use of debt bondage. It does not require physical force or constraint.

In considering whether a trafficking/slavery victim has been compelled to commit a crime, prosecutors should consider whether any of these means have been employed so that the victim has effectively lost the ability to consent to his / her actions or to act with free will.

The means of trafficking/slavery used in an individual case may not be sufficient to give rise to a defence of duress, but will be relevant when considering whether the public interest is met in deciding to prosecute or proceed with a prosecution.

In assessing whether the victim was compelled to commit the offence, prosecutors should consider whether:

- the offence committed was a direct consequence of, or in the course of trafficking/slavery and whether the criminality is significantly diminished or effectively extinguished because no realistic alternative was available but to comply with the dominant force of another.

Where a victim has been compelled to commit the offence, but not to a degree where duress is made out, it will generally not be in the public interest to prosecute unless the offence is serious or there are other aggravating factors.

If the defendant is a trafficking/slavery victim but the offence has been committed without reasonable compulsion occasioned by the trafficking/slavery, and there are no particular trafficking/slavery related public interest considerations, then the Full Code Test should be applied in the usual way.

Early guilty plea indicated

Where there is (1) an indication of an early guilty plea, (2) a full investigation has not been carried out and (3) the circumstances are such that there is suspicion of trafficking/slavery: at the first hearing prosecutors should request an adjournment for further investigation and ask that a plea is not formally entered.

Credible evidence of trafficking/slavery post-charge

In cases where a decision has already been taken to charge and prosecute a suspect, but further credible information or evidence comes to light, or the status of a suspect as a possible victim of trafficking/slavery is raised post-conviction, for example in mitigation or through a pre-sentence report, then prosecutors should seek an adjournment and ensure that the steps outlined in the section 'The duty to make proper enquiries and to refer through the National Referral Mechanism (NRM)' above are carried out.

Suspects who may be children – Additional requirements

Assessing age and trafficking/slavery status

In cases where the defendant may be a child victim of trafficking/slavery, two linked questions must be addressed:

1. what is the defendant's age?

2. what evidence is there to suggest that the defendant is a victim of trafficking/slavery?

If the defendant is a child victim of trafficking/slavery, the extent to which the crime alleged against the child was consequent on and integral to his / her being a victim of trafficking / slavery must be considered. In some cases the criminal offence is a manifestation of the exploitation. This might also arise in the case of an adult victim: see paragraph 20 of L, HVN, THN and T [2013] EWCA Crim 991.

Due Inquiry as to age

Section 99(1) of the Children and Young Persons Act 1933 directs the court to 'make due inquiry' about the defendant's age and 'take such evidence as may be forthcoming at the hearing of the case' for this purpose. Similar provisions require the court addressing the age question to consider 'any available evidence' (Section 150 of the Magistrates Court Act 1980; Section 1(6) of the Criminal Justice Act 1982; and Section 305(2) of the Criminal Justice Act 2003).

Where any issue as to the age of a defendant arises, it must be addressed at the first court appearance. The documentation accompanying the defendant to court should record his date of birth, whether as asserted by him, or as best known to the prosecution, or indeed both.

If age becomes or remains an issue at the Plea and Case Management Hearing in court, prosecutors should ensure that the appropriate age-assessment enquiries are carried out. This may require a request for an adjournment to the court.

Prosecutors should consider the separate CPS guidance concerning age assessment. See paragraphs 31 and 32 of L, HVN, THN and T [2013] EWCA Crim 991.

Presumption that a victim is a child

Article 10(3) of the Council of Europe Anti-Trafficking Convention provides: 'When the age of the victim is uncertain and there are reasons to believe that the victim is a child, he or she shall presume to be a child and shall be accorded special protection measures pending verification of his/her age'. If at the end of a 'due inquiry' into age the age of the defendant remains in doubt s/he must be treated as a child. See paragraph 25 of L, HVN, THN and T [2013] EWCA Crim 991. Section 51 Modern Slavery Act 2015 enshrines this in legislation.

Referring children through the NRM

In the case of suspects who are (or appear to be) children, the NRM referral should be made through the relevant social services department.

Children and "the means of trafficking"

In determining whether a child is a victim of trafficking/slavery, his or her consent to being trafficked or held in slavery is irrelevant and the means by which they are trafficked/held in slavery is also irrelevant. Therefore it is not necessary for any of the following to be present: threats, use of force, fraud and deception, inducement, abuse of power or of a position of vulnerability or use of debt bondage.

When considering whether to prosecute a child victim of trafficking/slavery, it is arguable that prosecutors will only need to consider whether or not the offence is committed as a direct consequence of, or in the course of trafficking/slavery. It is yet to be resolved whether compulsion is relevant to the decision whether or not to prosecute a victim in the public interest.

Guidance has been issued to police and Immigration authorities on identification of victims and the indicators that might suggest that someone is a trafficking/slavery victim. However, all decisions in the case remain the responsibility of the prosecutor.'

Abuse of process

5.55

The court's power to stay a prosecution is a power to ensure that the Crown has complied with its obligations and properly applied its mind to the possibility of not imposing penalties on victims. Where the Court of Appeal concludes that the trial court would have stayed the indictment had an application been made, the proper course is to quash the conviction[53].

5.56

In *R v L* the Lord Chief Justice held[54]:

'... In the context of an abuse of process argument on behalf of an alleged victim of trafficking, the court will reach its own decision on the basis of the material advanced in support of and against the continuation of the prosecution. Where a court considers issues relevant to age, trafficking and exploitation, the prosecution will be stayed if the court disagrees with the decision to prosecute. The fears that the exercise of the jurisdiction to stay will be inadequate are groundless'.

5.57

In *R v LM*, the court also stated[55] 'where trafficking is an obvious possibility, the police should enquire into it'. It arguably follows that, if it can be shown there was either no or inadequate inquiry into whether a defendant is a potential

---

53 *R v LM* [2010] EWCA Crim 237, [2011] 1 Cr App Rep 135 at §17.
54 [2013] EWCA Crim 991, [2013] 2 Cr App Rep 247 at para 17.
55 [2010] EWCA Crim 237, [2011] 1 Cr App Rep 135 at para 32.

victim of trafficking, the prosecution cannot discharge their responsibility and the decision to prosecute will be flawed.

Immigration and Asylum Act 1999, s 31

5.58

Many victims of international trafficking enter the UK as refugees (see Chapter 10 for a fuller exposition of trafficking victims meeting the definition of refugee). Where they do so by deception or where they commit an identity document offence, they may have a defence on the ground of their refugee status under the Immigration and Asylum Act 1999, s 31.

5.59

This is a defence which has frequently been overlooked by practitioners and judges. Lord Thomas CJ has made clear his views that where the defence is overlooked a referral of the relevant practitioner to his respective regulator is appropriate; see *R v Al Shabani*[56].

5.60

Section 31 derives from Art 31 of the Convention Relating to the Status of Refugees 1951[57], which provides as follows:

> '1. The Contracting States shall not impose penalties, on account of their illegal entry or presence, on refugees who, coming directly from a territory where their life or freedom was threatened in the sense of Article 1, enter or are present in their territory without authorization, provided they present themselves without delay to the authorities and show good cause for their illegal entry or presence'.

5.61

Section 31 is the domestic provision which incorporates Art 31 into the law of England and Wales. Section 31 has a limited application in that it only provides a defence to certain offences. The article itself should not be overlooked, because it is broader in scope than s 31. In rare cases in may be necessary for prosecutors to look beyond the section and consider the scope of Art 31 itself when considering charging a refugee. It may be necessary for defence practitioners (in an appropriately compelling case) to consider abuse of process as a remedy to a refugee being charged with an offence in circumstances where he should have been afforded refugee protection under Art 31 (but where s 31

---

56 [2015] EWCA Crim 1924.
57 189 UNTS 150.

does not apply)[58]. The Court of Appeal recently observed that s 31 may not provide the full protection encompassed in Art 31[59].

5.62

Section 31 is in the following terms:

'31 Defences based on Article 31(1) of the Refugee Convention

(1) It is a defence for a refugee charged with an offence to which this section applies to show that, having come to the United Kingdom directly from a country where his life or freedom was threatened (within the meaning of the Refugee Convention), he—

(a) presented himself to the authorities in the United Kingdom without delay;

(b) showed good cause for his illegal entry or presence; and

(c) made a claim for asylum as soon as was reasonably practicable after his arrival in the United Kingdom.

(2) If, in coming from the country where his life or freedom was threatened, the refugee stopped in another country outside the United Kingdom, subsection (1) applies only if he shows that he could not reasonably have expected to be given protection under the Refugee Convention in that other country.

(3) In England and Wales … the offences to which this section applies are any offence, and any attempt to commit an offence, under—

(a) Part I of the Forgery and Counterfeiting Act 1981 (forgery and connected offences);

(aa) section 4 or 6 of the Identity Documents Act 2010;

(b) section 24A of the 1971 Act (deception); or

---

58 See *R v Mirahessari* [2016] EWCA Crim 1733, in which refugees were charged with the 19th century offence of obstructing an engine when they breached Channel Tunnel security and tried to walk from Calais to Folkestone. In that case the appellants sought unsuccessfully to deploy abuse of process through their being charged with an offence to which the refugee defence does not attach.

59 In *R v Ordu* [2017] EWCA Crim 4, [2017] 1 Cr App Rep 21 at 4 (Edis J giving the judgment of the Court), it was noted: 'The [Immigration and Asylum Act] 1999 came into force in November 1999 following a decision of the Divisional Court in *R v Uxbridge Magistrates Court ex p. Adimi* [2001] QB 667, which had been decided on 29 July 1999. Section 31 was an attempt to comply with the treaty obligations of the United Kingdom under Article 31(1) of the Refugee Convention and was introduced by amendment to the Bill which became the Act because of the decision in *Adimi*. Until that date UK criminal law did not comply with the treaty obligations of the UK, and the introduction of s 31 was an attempt by Parliament to rectify the position. It was not, at least initially, successful because the plain words of s 31(2) appeared to remove the defence from those who had stopped over in a safe country while travelling, while Article 31 affords such people protection. That being so, s 31 as so construed failed to comply fully with the treaty obligation.'

(c)   section 26(1)(d) of the 1971 Act (falsification of documents).

…

(5) A refugee who has made a claim for asylum is not entitled to the defence provided by subsection (1) in relation to any offence committed by him after making that claim.

(6) 'Refugee' has the same meaning as it has for the purposes of the Refugee Convention.

(7) If the Secretary of State has refused to grant a claim for asylum made by a person who claims that he has a defence under subsection (1), that person is to be taken not to be a refugee unless he shows that he is.

…',

Application of s 31

5.63

In order for a defendant to avail himself of a s 31 defence:

- the defendant needs to satisfy an evidential burden that he was a refugee (a refugee being '… a person who has left his own country owing to a well-founded fear of being persecuted for reasons of race, religion, nationality, membership of a particular social group or political opinion'): see *R v Makuwa*[60]; the legal burden then vests in the Crown to prove that a defendant is not a refugee (if the Crown does not accept that the defendant is a refugee); or alternatively, where the Secretary of State has refused to grant a claim for asylum in respect of a defendant who claims that he has a defence under s 31(1), the legal burden vests in the defendant to show on the balance of probabilities that he is a refugee: see *R v Sadighpour*[61] and *R v Mateta*[62];

- the defendant then needs to prove (on the balance of probabilities) that he did not stop in any country in transit to the UK or, alternatively, that he could not reasonably have expected to be given protection under the Refugee Convention in the countries outside the UK in which he stopped; and, if so:

---

60 [2006] EWCA Crim 175, [2006] 1 WLR 2755 at 37.
61 [2012] EWCA Crim 2669, [2013] 1 Cr App Rep 269 (per Treacy LJ, who gave the judgment of the court, at 38–40).
62 [2013] EWCA Crim 1372, [2014] 1 WLR 1516 (Leveson and Fulford LJJ and Spencer J) at 10.

— to prove that he presented himself to the authorities in the UK without delay;

— to show good cause for his illegal entry or presence; and

— to prove that he made a claim for asylum as soon as was reasonably practicable after his arrival in the UK.

Section 31(2)

5.64

Section 31(2) is to be construed as providing immunity from prosecution to refugees who, fleeing from their country of persecution, make a short-term stopover in an intermediate country en route to the country of intended refuge[63]. In *R v Kamalanathan*[64] Thomas LJ (as he then was), giving the judgment of the court, said:

'[4] … A person could be, for example, making a short stopover or be still in the course of flight, if he had to be concealed in the intervening country whilst he was being pursued by foreign agents. It might be, in such circumstances, that the time could be very much more than the 3 hours that had occurred on the facts in *Asfaw*.

[5] The real question is, looking at all the circumstances: is the person in the course of a flight? Is he making a short-term stop over? Is he in transit? Whichever phrase is used, one has to see whether at the material time the person was here, not having come to this country either temporarily or permanently seeking to stop here, but was going on. That is a question of fact'.

Presenting without delay

5.65

In *R v Jaddi*[65] Hughes LJ (as he then was) giving the judgment of the court stated:

---

63 *R v Asfaw* [2008] UKHL 31, [2008] 1 AC 1061. The House of Lords decided that the IAA 1999, s 31 should be read so that it provided immunity, if the other conditions are fulfilled, from the imposition of criminal penalties for offences attributable to the attempt of a refugee to leave the country in the continuing course of a flight from persecution even after a short stopover in transit. This changed the law as it had previously been understood and explained in *R (on the application of Pepushi) v Crown Prosecution Service* [2004] EWHC 798 (Admin). The development of the law may be seen from *R v Kamalanathan* [2010] EWCA Crim 1335, *R v Abdalla* [2010] EWCA Crim 2400, [2011] 1 Cr App Rep 432, and *R v Mateta* [2013] EWCA Crim 1372, [2014] 1 WLR 1516.
64 [2010] EWCA Crim 1335.
65 [2012] EWCA Crim 2565.

'[26] … In very general terms, it seems to us that in the great majority of cases there will simply be no excuse for a genuine refugee not to make himself known immediately he arrives in the safe place – that is to say the arrivals immigration hall at a United Kingdom airport. Moreover, from the point of view of sensible immigration control, that makes sense. It is a great deal more difficult to discern whether a claim to be a refugee is genuine if it is not made until some time later and especially if it is only made when it is forced on the claimant by discovery that he is living illegally.

[30] … it is certainly open to a tribunal of fact to conclude and in many cases it may be the right conclusion, that there is simply no reason for such a traveller not to identify himself the moment he is in friendly official hands'.

5.66

R v Jaddi was considered by the court in *R v Mateta*[66]:

'These observations were not intended to detract from the principles in *R v Asfaw* and *R v Mohamed (Abdalla)* [viz there is no need for a voluntary exonerating act] or the other authorities to which we have referred: they do no more than make clear the very real importance of focussing on the particular facts and circumstances of each case'.

5.67

Most recently in *R v Z*[67] Hallett VP, giving the judgment of the court, accepted the submissions of the appellant and respondent that:

'27 … it was clearly arguable that the appellant did claim asylum at the first reasonably practicable moment. On any view, she claimed asylum within a matter of hours of landing in the United Kingdom and before she had left the airport …

28. It will be a question of fact in every case as to whether or not there is an excuse for a refugee not to make themselves known immediately they arrive in the immigration hall'.

Good cause

5.68

This condition '… has only a limited role in the article. It will be satisfied by a genuine refugee showing that he was reasonably travelling on false papers'[68].

---

66 *R v Mateta* [2013] EWCA Crim 1372, [2014] 1 WLR 1516.
67 [2016] EWCA Crim 1083.
68 See *R v Uxbridge Magistrates' Court and Another, ex p Adimi* [2001] QB 667 at 679; see also *Mateta* at 21(v).

Annex

5.69

Offences in relation to which the MSA 2015, s 45 defence is not available:

- false imprisonment;
- kidnapping;
- manslaughter;
- murder;
- perverting the course of justice;
- piracy;
- the following offences under the Offences against the Person Act 1861:
  - s 4 (soliciting murder);
  - s 16 (threats to kill);
  - s 18 (wounding with intent to cause grievous bodily harm);
  - s 20 (malicious wounding);
  - s 21 (attempting to choke, suffocate or strangle in order to commit or assist in committing an indictable offence);
  - s 22 (using drugs etc to commit or assist in the committing of an indictable offence);
  - s 23 (maliciously administering poison etc so as to endanger life or inflict grievous bodily harm);
  - s 27 (abandoning children);
  - s 28 (causing bodily injury by explosives);
  - s 29 (using explosives with intent to do grievous bodily harm);
  - s 30 (placing explosives with intent to do bodily injury);
  - s 31 (setting spring guns etc with intent to do grievous bodily harm);
  - s 32 (endangering safety of railway passengers);
  - s 35 (injuring persons by furious driving);
  - s 37 (assaulting officer preserving wreck);
  - s 38 (assault with intent to resist arrest);
- an offence under any of the following provisions of the Explosive Substances Act 1883:
  - s 2 (causing explosion likely to endanger life or property);

— s 3 (attempt to cause explosion, or making or keeping explosive with intent to endanger life or property);

— s 4 (making or possession of explosives under suspicious circumstances);

- child destruction;

- cruelty to children (Children and Young Persons Act 1933, s 1);

- control etc of quasi-military organisation (Public Order Act 1936, s 2);

- infanticide (Infanticide Act 1938, s 1);

- an offence under any of the following provisions of the Firearms Act 1968:

  — s 5 (possession of prohibited firearms);

  — s 16 (possession of firearm with intent to endanger life);

  — s 16A (possession of firearm with intent to cause fear of violence);

  — s 17(1); (use of firearm to resist arrest);

  — s 17(2); (possession of firearm at time of committing or being arrested for specified offence);

  — s 18 (carrying firearm with criminal intent);

- an offence under any of the following provisions of the Theft Act 1968:

  — s 8 (robbery or assault with intent to rob);

  — s 9 (burglary), where the offence is committed with intent to inflict grievous bodily harm on a person, or to do unlawful damage to a building or anything in it

  — s 10 (aggravated burglary);

  — s 12A (aggravated vehicle-taking), where the offence involves an accident which caused the death of any person

  — s 21 (blackmail);

- the following offences under the Criminal Damage Act 1971:

  — an offence of arson under s 1;

  — an offence under s 1(2) (destroying or damaging property) other than an offence of arson;

- assisting unlawful immigration to member state (Immigration Act 1971, s 25);

- penalty for fraudulent evasion of duty etc) in relation to goods prohibited to be imported under the Customs Consolidation Act 1876, s 42 (indecent or obscene articles) (Customs and Excise Management Act 1979, s 170);

- hostage-taking (Taking of Hostages Act 1982, s 1);

- an offence under the following provisions of the Aviation Security Act 1982:
  - — s 1 (hijacking);
  - — s 2 (destroying, damaging or endangering safety of aircraft);
  - — s 3 (other acts endangering or likely to endanger safety of aircraft);
  - — s 4 (offences in relation to certain dangerous articles);

- ill-treatment of patients (Mental Health Act 1983, s 127);

- abduction of child by parent etc or others (Child Abduction Act 1984, ss 1, 2);

- riot (Public Order Act 1986, s 1);

- violent disorder (Public Order Act 1986, s 2);

- torture (Criminal Justice Act 1988, s 134);

- causing death by dangerous driving (Road Traffic Act 1988, s 1);

- causing death by careless driving when under the influence of drink or drugs (Road Traffic Act 1988, s 3A);

- an offence under the following provisions of the Aviation and Maritime Security Act 1990:
  - — s 1 (endangering safety at aerodromes);
  - — s 9 (hijacking of ships);
  - — s 10 (seizing or exercising control of fixed platforms);
  - — s 11 (destroying fixed platforms or endangering their safety);
  - — s 12 (other acts endangering or likely to endanger safe navigation);
  - — s 13 (offences involving threats);

- offences relating to Channel Tunnel trains and the tunnel system (an offence under Part 2 of the Channel Tunnel (Security) Order 1994 (SI 1994/570));

- putting people in fear of violence (Protection from Harassment Act 1997, s 4);

- stalking involving fear of violence or serious alarm or distress (Protection from Harassment Act 1997, s 4A);

- racially or religiously aggravated assaults (Crime and Disorder Act 1998, s 29);

- racially or religiously aggravated offences under the Public Order Act 1986, ss 4 or 4A (Crime and Disorder Act 1998, s 31(1)(a) or (b));

- an offence under the following provisions of the Terrorism Act 2000:
  - — s 54 (weapons training);
  - — s 56 (directing terrorist organisation);
  - — s 57 (possession of article for terrorist purposes);
  - — s 59 (inciting terrorism overseas);
- genocide, crimes against humanity and war crimes and ancillary conduct (International Criminal Court Act 2001, ss 1, 2);
- an offence under the following provisions of the Anti-terrorism, Crime and Security Act 2001:
  - — s 47 (use of nuclear weapons);
  - — s 50 (assisting or inducing certain weapons-related acts overseas);
  - — s 113 (use of noxious substance or thing to cause harm or intimidate);
- female genital mutilation and related offences (Female Genital Mutilation Act 2003, ss 1, 2, 3);
- the following Sexual Offences Act 2003 offences:
  - — s 1 (rape);
  - — s 2 (assault by penetration);
  - — s 3 (sexual assault);
  - — s 4 (causing person to engage in sexual activity without consent);
  - — s 5 (rape of child under 13);
  - — s 6 (assault of child under 13 by penetration);
  - — s 7 (sexual assault of child under 13);
  - — s 8 (causing or inciting child under 13 to engage in sexual activity);
  - — s 9 (sexual activity with a child);
  - — s 10 (causing or inciting a child to engage in sexual activity);
  - — s 13 (child sex offences committed by children or young persons);
  - — s 14 (arranging or facilitating commission of child sex offence);
  - — s 15 (meeting a child following sexual grooming);
  - — s 16 (abuse of position of trust: sexual activity with a child);
  - — s 17 (abuse of position of trust: causing or inciting a child to engage in sexual activity);
  - — s 18 (abuse of position of trust: sexual activity in presence of child);

— s 19 (abuse of position of trust: causing a child to watch a sexual act);

— s 25 (sexual activity with a child family member);

— s 26 (inciting a child family member to engage in sexual activity);

— s 30 (sexual activity with a person with a mental disorder impeding choice);

— s 31 (causing or inciting a person with a mental disorder impeding choice to engage in sexual activity);

— s 32 (engaging in sexual activity in the presence of a person with a mental disorder impeding choice);

— s 33 (causing a person with a mental disorder impeding choice to watch a sexual act);

— s 34 (inducement, threat or deception to procure sexual activity with a person with a mental disorder);

— s 35 (causing a person with a mental disorder to engage in or agree to engage in sexual activity by inducement, threat or deception);

— s 36 (engaging in sexual activity in the presence, procured by inducement, threat or deception, of a person with a mental disorder);

— s 37 (causing a person with a mental disorder to watch a sexual act by inducement, threat or deception);

— s 38 (care workers: sexual activity with a person with a mental disorder);

— s 39 (care workers: causing or inciting sexual activity);

— s 40 (care workers: sexual activity in the presence of a person with a mental disorder);

— s 41 (care workers: causing a person with a mental disorder to watch a sexual act);

— s 47 (paying for sexual services of a child);

— s 48 (causing or inciting child prostitution or pornography);

— s 49 (controlling a child prostitute or a child involved in pornography);

— s 50 (arranging or facilitating child prostitution or pornography);

— s 61 (administering a substance with intent);

— s 62 (committing offence with intent to commit sexual offence);

— s 63 (trespass with intent to commit sexual offence);

— s 64 (sex with an adult relative: penetration);

— s 65 (sex with an adult relative: consenting to penetration);

— s 66 (exposure);

— s 67 (voyeurism);

— s 70 (sexual penetration of a corpse);

- causing or allowing a child or vulnerable adult to die or suffer serious physical harm (Domestic Violence, Crime and Victims Act 2004, s 5);

- an offence under the following provisions of the Terrorism Act 2006:

  — s 5 (preparation of terrorist acts);

  — s 6 (training for terrorism);

  — s 9 (making or possession of radioactive device or material);

  — s 10 (use of radioactive device or material for terrorist purposes);

  — s 11 (terrorist threats relating to radioactive devices etc);

- slavery, servitude and forced or compulsory labour (Modern Slavery Act 2015, s 1);

- human trafficking (Modern Slavery Act 2015, s 2).

6 Victims of human trafficking: at the police station

6.1

The first contact that victims of modern slavery may have with law enforcement is likely to be on arrest, particularly those involved in forced criminality. After arrest, they will be taken to a police station and there is an opportunity for early identification of the arrested person as a victim of trafficking which is often missed.

6.2

In any criminal case, the police station stage can be the most important part and influences greatly how the case develops. With potential victims of trafficking this stage of the case is even more important as the police have the opportunity to divert them from the criminal justice system or at least to refer them into the National Referral Mechanism ('NRM') at an early stage.

6.3

This stage of proceedings also provides the potential victim of trafficking with access to legal advice, perhaps for the first time. It is essential that legal representatives are aware of the basic trafficking indicators and can discuss the issues concerning a referral into the NRM at this early stage with their arrested client.

Arrival at the police station

Risk assessment

6.4

The first contact that an arrested potential victim of trafficking will have with police after his initial arrest will be with the custody officer who is responsible for the welfare of the detained person while in police custody. The custody officer is responsible for initiating a risk assessment to consider whether the detainee is likely to present specific risks to custody staff, any individual who may have contact with the detainee (eg legal advisers, medical staff) or themselves. This risk assessment must include the taking of reasonable steps to establish the detainee's identity and to obtain information about the detainee that is relevant to their safe custody, security and welfare and risk to others[1].

6.5

The current police risk assessment does not include any questions specifically designed to identify whether the arrested person may be a potential victim of trafficking and the process itself is unlikely to identify much more than whether the individual needs to see a health professional or has any mental health issues that require the services of an appropriate adult.

6.6

Whether the custody officer or arresting officers have any awareness of the issues that may identify the arrested individual as a potential victim of trafficking may depend on the extent of the briefing for the operation that led to the arrest, and the individual officer's experience and training.

6.7

If the operation leading to the arrest was a directed operation at a specific premises or group, it may be that the senior officers have made those engaged in the operation aware of the likelihood that potential victims of trafficking may be present and arrested at the scene. For instance, senior officers involved in the planning of a raid on a known cannabis factory which leads to the arrest of a number of young foreign nationals ought to have identified that possibility in advance. Consequently the police should be aware that any suspects arrested at the premises might be potential victims of trafficking and the officers subsequently dealing with them whilst in police detention should ensure that the issue is addressed and any necessary safeguards put in place.

6.8

If the arrest is opportunistic (eg a person arrested for pickpocketing on the street having been spotted by an officer), the identification of the individual as a potential victim of trafficking is likely to be more problematic and more reliant on the training of the custody officer or arresting officer to identify the warning signs.

Police training and development

6.9

Police recruitment and training varies across the country. Some forces require applicants to have completed an independently delivered training course called the Certificate of Knowledge in Policing ('CKP'), successful completion of

---

1   Police and Criminal Evidence Act ('PACE') 1984, Code C3.6.

which will enable the individual to transfer this externally recognised national qualification as evidence of the knowledge component for their Diploma in Policing. However, the syllabus for the CKP does not contain any specific input on modern slavery or human trafficking.

6.10

The College of Policing runs a course on protecting vulnerable people, which is an e-learning programme covering child abuse, child sexual exploitation, domestic abuse, female genital mutilation, forced marriage, honour-based violence, modern slavery, prostitution, serious sexual offences, stalking and harassment.

6.11

The College of Policing manages the content and delivery of detective training through the Professionalising Investigation Programme, which provides a structured development programme to embed and maintain investigative skills for police officers and police staff. It is to be hoped that, as awareness of the issues increases, the training of officers within these programmes will specifically deal with modern slavery and human trafficking.

6.12

Improved training for 'front line' officers and staff will lead to a greater number of potential victims of trafficking being identified. The training is required early in an officer's career and should be constantly updated with regard to changes in the forms of exploitation and methodology of the traffickers.

Provision of rights

6.13

On arrival at the police station, the arrested person will be informed by the custody officer of their legal rights under PACE 1984, which may be exercised at any stage during the period in custody. These rights include:

- the right to consult privately with a solicitor and to have free independent legal advice;
- the right to have someone informed of their arrest;
- the right to consult the Codes of Practice;
- the right to interpretation and translation and the right to communicate with their High Commission, Embassy or Consulate; and
- the right to be informed about the offence and any further offences for which they are arrested whilst in custody and why they have been arrested and detained[2].

---

2   PACE 1984, Code C3.1.

6.14

The detainee must also be given a written notice, which contains information to allow them to exercise these rights by setting out:

- the above rights;
- the arrangements for obtaining legal advice;
- the right to a copy of the custody record;
- the right to remain silent as set out in the caution;
- the right to have access to materials and documents which are essential to challenging the lawfulness of their arrest and detention for any offence;
- the maximum period for which they may be kept in police detention without being charged;
- when detention must be reviewed and when release is required;
- the right to medical assistance;
- the right, if they are prosecuted, to have access to the evidence in the case before their trial[3].

6.15

The notice should also briefly set out the detainee's other entitlements while in custody, by mentioning the provisions relating to the conduct of interviews, the circumstances in which an appropriate adult should be available to assist the detainee, and the statutory right to make representations whenever the need for his detention is reviewed. Finally the notice should list the entitlements concerning reasonable standards of physical comfort, adequate food and drink, access to toilets and washing facilities, clothing, medical attention, and exercise when practicable[4].

6.16

The custody officer or other custody staff as directed by the custody officer will ask the detainee whether he would like legal advice and want someone informed of his detention, with the detainee asked to sign the custody record to confirm his decisions.

6.17

The custody officer must also determine whether the detainee is, or might be, in need of medical treatment or attention, requires an appropriate adult or help to check documentation or requires an interpreter. The decision in respect of these matters must be recorded on the custody record[5].

---

3   PACE 1984, Code C3.2.
4   PACE 1984, Code C3.2.
5   PACE 1984, Code C3.5.

6.18

If the detainee appears to be someone who does not speak or understand English, the custody officer must ensure that without delay arrangements are made for the detainee to have the assistance of an interpreter and that the detainee is told clearly about his right to interpretation and translation.

6.19

The written notice given to the detainee must be in a language that the detainee understands and includes the right to interpretation and translation. If a translation of the notice is not available, the information in the notice must be given through an interpreter and a written translation provided without undue delay[6].

6.20

The right to free and independent legal advice will only be effective if it is exercised by the arrested person. Many people detained in the police station will not request the services of a solicitor and may therefore not obtain some of the protections that would be otherwise available to them at the police station. Whether a potential victim of trafficking is more or less inclined to request legal advice than any other detainee is unknown, although it is widely reported by victims of trafficking that they have little understanding of the procedures in the UK, particularly those who have come from isolated communities and they may not take up their entitlement to such advice.

6.21

Should the arrested person request legal advice, the police will ask whether they have a solicitor who they would like to contact. If they do not know a solicitor, the police will arrange for the duty solicitor to attend. In each situation the police will call the Defence Solicitor Call Centre ('DSCC'), who will contact the nominated firm or the duty solicitor.

Criminal Defence Direct

6.22

In some cases, despite asking to speak to a solicitor, the detained person may only be able to speak to an adviser at a call centre known as Criminal Defence Direct ('CDD'). Calls will be sent to CDD where the person is detained:

- in relation to any non-imprisonable offence;

- on a bench warrant for failing to appear and being held for production before the court, except where the existing solicitor acting has clear

---

6   PACE 1984, Code C3.12.

documentary evidence available that would result in the detainee being released from custody;

- on suspicion of driving with excess alcohol, who is taken to the police station to give a specimen (Road Traffic Act 1988, s 5); failure to provide a specimen (Road Traffic Act 1988, ss 6, 7, 7A); or driving whilst unfit/drunk in charge of a motor vehicle (Road Traffic Act 1988, s 4); or

- in relation to breach of police or court bail conditions[7].

6.23

Even in the above cases, a solicitor will be contacted if:

- the detainee is to be subject to an interview or an identification procedure;

- the detainee is eligible for assistance from an appropriate adult under the PACE Codes of Practice;

- the detainee is unable to communicate over the telephone;

- the detainee complains of serious maltreatment by the police;

- the investigation includes another alleged offence which allows a solicitor to advise;

- the solicitor is already at the same police station;

- the advice relates to an indictable offence; or

- the request is a Special Request[8].

In the case of potential victims of trafficking, it is likely that one of the exceptions above will apply such that the use of the CDD should be limited. One might expect that the potential victim of trafficking detained might require an appropriate adult or have difficulties in communication.

6.24

If the CDD is deployed, it is unlikely that the detained person would be identified by them as a potential victim of trafficking, given the limited and remote interaction on the telephone. The level of training provided for CDD staff in relation to identifying victims of trafficking is unknown. If the arrested potential victim of trafficking is directed to the CDD, because the offence is not imprisonable or they are in breach of bail, an opportunity to identify them as a potential victim of trafficking is missed.

---

7   See Chapter 15 regarding common offences linked to trafficking. Many victims who have been re-trafficked are often in breach of police or court bail.

8   A 'Special Request' is a request made to the solicitor by the DSCC to take the case even if it does not fall within the exceptions. Special Requests may include, for example, requests where CDD consider that, because of a conflict of interest, the request should be handled by a solicitor (instead of by a CDD telephone adviser) or considers that Advocacy Assistance is required.

Duty to attend the police station

6.25

Once called by the DSCC the solicitor will contact the police station by telephone and, if appropriate, also speak to the arrested person. The solicitor has a duty to attend at the police station to provide advice and attend all police interviews with the arrested person in connection with an offence. The solicitor must also attend at any identification parade, group identification or confrontation, and where the arrested person complains of serious maltreatment by the police[9]. Attendance at video identification parades is discretionary[10].

In general terms, once there is to be an interview the detained person will have face-to-face advice from a solicitor or accredited police station representative.

Arrival of the legal representative at the police station

6.26

On arrival at the police station the legal representative should obtain and read a copy of the custody record to ascertain the circumstances of the arrest and what has happened up to that point, while the detained person has been in police custody.

6.27

The legal representative should also obtain as much information from the interviewing officer as possible by way of disclosure about the alleged offence and the circumstances of the arrest. The police are not obliged to disclose anything to the representative but will provide at least some limited disclosure in all cases. The legal representative should consider the disclosure provided (usually but not always in written form) and ask further questions of the officer, which may or may not be answered. It is important to note what information is refused as well as what is provided.

6.28

This is an opportunity for the legal representative to gauge whether there may be any potential indicators of human trafficking. Legal representatives should be aware of the basic trafficking indicators and common types of offences where victims are exploited for criminality as well as certain types of victim profile, all of which should give cause for further enquiry. See Chapter 2 for further explanation on indicators of trafficking and Chapter 15 for common forms of forced criminality offences.

---

9   SCC 2017 Specification A9.38.
10 SCC 2017 Specification A9.40.

Interaction with the detained person

Interpreters

6.29

Although not the case with every potential victim of trafficking, it is likely that where the victim is a foreign national there will be language difficulties and instructions will need to be taken and advice given via an interpreter. If the custody officer assesses that the suspect does not understand English sufficiently well to be able to communicate effectively, he will seek the services of an interpreter.

6.30

Every interpreter working in the courts and police stations should be selected through the Ministry of Justice Framework Agreement or from the National Register of Public Service Interpreters in order to ensure a minimum and measurable standard of training and quality assurance. Such interpreters are subject to a Code of Conduct, standards of competence and professional skills, and disciplinary proceedings.

6.31

The arrangements must comply with the minimum requirements set out in Directive 2010/64/EU of the European Parliament and of the Council of 20 October 2010 on the right to interpretation and translation in criminal proceedings. The Directive states that the quality of interpretation and translation provided has to be sufficient to 'safeguard the fairness of the proceedings, in particular by ensuring that suspected or accused persons have knowledge of the cases against them and are able to exercise their right of defence'. Therefore the suspect must be able to understand their position and be able to communicate effectively with police officers, interviewers, solicitors and appropriate adults in the same way as a suspect who can speak and understand English and who would therefore not require an interpreter[11].

6.32

Equally, a written translation of all documents considered essential for the person to exercise their right of defence and to '*safeguard the fairness of the proceedings*' should be provided, which includes any decision to authorise a person to be detained and details of any offence(s) with which the person has been charged or for which they have been told they may be prosecuted.

6.33

All reasonable attempts should be made to make the suspect understand that interpretation and translation will be provided at public expense[12].

---

11 PACE 1984, Code C13.1A.
12 PACE 1984, Code C13.1B.

6.34

Consideration should be given to the gender and religious or cultural background of the interpreter. The views of the potential victim of trafficking should be taken into consideration, although this is not specifically set out in the PACE 1984 Codes of Practice (with the exception of seeking an alternative interpreter if the detainee complains about the adequacy of the translation from the interpreter in attendance).

6.35

The interpreter used to interpret witness statements should not also be used for the interview and private discussions between the legal adviser and the detainee. The adviser should consider whether there is a tension in using the same interpreter to interpret in the consultation as is used for the interview. It is possible to obtain public funding under the Police Station Advice and Assistance scheme for an interpreter to be obtained by the defence, although in practice there are problems in terms of locating suitable interpreters without an undue delay to the investigation and the time that the detainee remains in custody.

6.36

It is important that the interpreter understands that the discussions between the adviser and the detainee are confidential and subject to legal professional privilege. It would be a serious breach of the interpreter's professional ethics to inform police of what was discussed in such consultation. If such a situation arises, complaint must be made to their professional body, to the police and Ministry of Justice.

6.37

It is important that an interpreter used at a police station or in the course of investigations by other investigating agencies is not engaged to interpret in court. If, however, it is not possible to find another interpreter (for example, where the language is uncommon) the court and all parties must be notified of the intention to use the same interpreter for the court proceedings[13].

Initial meeting with the client

6.38

It is important to try to establish a rapport with the client, which is always more difficult via an interpreter. The client should be informed as to the status of the legal representative. If attending as duty solicitor, the representative should explain the nature of the duty scheme, as suspects are often under the impression that the duty solicitor is the 'police solicitor', obtained for them by the police.

---

13 *R (on the application of Bozturk) v Thames Magistrates' Court* (2001) Times, 26 June.

6.39

The role of the adviser should be explained, as should the fact that everything said in the consultation is confidential and subject to legal professional privilege and cannot be disclosed to others (except in very limited circumstances). It is also worth explaining that the solicitor is there to advise the suspect on the law and provide advice based on their instructions, if any, and is not there to suggest an account to put forward. Some suspects may not understand the purpose of having an adviser to assist them and some potential victims of trafficking may be wary or distrustful of their legal adviser. It is important to ensure that the client understands that the legal adviser is completely independent of the police, that he will not divulge information to the police and that the adviser is there to protect the interests of the client while in detention. It must be remembered that non-British victims of trafficking may come from countries which do not afford fair trial rights in practice, and therefore trust will need to be built with the client.

Identifying the client as a potential victim of trafficking: disclosure

6.40

The adviser should be alert to basic trafficking indicators[14]. The Law Society Practice Note, 'Criminal Prosecutions of Victims of Trafficking'[15], sets out a non-exhaustive list of offences that victims of trafficking are often arrested for, which includes cannabis cultivation, drug importation, immigration offences, document offences, prostitution, dishonesty offences including theft, pick-pocketing and begging.

6.41

The Practice Note also sets out a non-exhaustive list of common factors which may also assist in identifying possible victims, including:

- the suspected victim is from a place known to be a source of human trafficking;

- the possession of false identity or travel documents;

- showing signs of fear or anxiety;

- exhibiting distrust of the authorities;

- evidence of violence or threats of violence;

- fear of revealing immigration status;

---

14 See Chapter 2.
15 Available at www.lawsociety.org.uk/support-services/advice/practice-notes/criminal-prosecutions-of-victims-of-trafficking/, last accessed 14 December 2017.

- lack of knowledge of home or work address;

- signs that the individual's movements are being controlled or that they are taking instructions from a third party; and

- inconsistency about name and age.

6.42

If the adviser suspects that the detained person may be a victim of trafficking, the issue should be raised with the client and discussed. It is in the best interests of the suspect to declare that they are a victim of trafficking at this stage so that the legal protections afforded to them can be implemented.

6.43

However, it is common for victims of human trafficking and modern slavery not always to identify as such and not to make such disclosures to their solicitor or to police. They may often mistrust the authorities and their legal representatives (who they may consider to be in a position of authority, especially if called as duty solicitor). Many victims of trafficking will not wish to make such a disclosure to their legal adviser and may deny that they have been acting under the coercion of their trafficker. It is also common for a client to have been coached by the traffickers to give a particular account.

6.44

These discussions will rarely be straightforward. However, if disclosure can be made with the client's consent, it will trigger a duty on the police to investigate the matter and a referral into the NRM at this stage. The adviser should ensure that the notification is placed on the custody record.

6.45

The disclosure may prompt a further review of the safeguarding assessment regarding the medical needs of the suspect and consideration as to whether an appropriate adult is required, should an interview under caution take place.

6.46

While it is likely the police will seek to interview the suspect for the index offence, representations should be made to police that this is inappropriate and that the suspect should be referred into the NRM. Questioning in relation to the index offence will entail questioning as to their exploitation without the safeguards and special measures afforded to the client by an Achieving Best Evidence ('ABE') interview, where the potential victim of trafficking is treated as a potential victim of crime. Not every potential victim of trafficking will choose to co-operate with the ABE interview process.

Instructions not to disclose: the ethical dilemma

6.47

A potential victim of trafficking client may either not disclose that they are a trafficked individual, in circumstances where the objective evidence is that they have been trafficked, or give specific instructions to the legal adviser not to disclose that they have been trafficked and have been acting under the influence of their trafficker.

6.48

This situation raises issues of professional ethics and considerable caution is required. A referral of the client into the NRM is likely to be advantageous to the individual in many ways, not least in relation to a positive decision against charge on the index offence or in raising a modern slavery defence in due course should the matter proceed to trial. On the other hand for a client accused of a criminal offence, exposing their traffickers may involve a significant personal risk.

6.49

Adults cannot be referred into the NRM without their consent. Therefore, with an adult client who is refusing to agree to disclosure being made to police to trigger an NRM referral, the position is clear: no disclosure can be made.

6.50

Consent is not required for any client under the age of 18. The age of the client is not always obvious and at this stage the adviser has little option but to accept the client's instructions as to age.

6.51

A solicitor is professionally and legally obliged to keep the affairs of clients confidential. The obligations extend to all matters revealed to a solicitor, from whatever source, by a client, or someone acting on the client's behalf. In exceptional circumstances this general obligation of confidentiality may be overridden. However, certain communications are subject to legal professional privilege (LPP) and can never be disclosed unless statute permits it either expressly or by necessary implication[16].

6.52

LPP is a privilege against disclosure which ensures that clients know that certain documents and information provided to lawyers cannot be disclosed at all. It

---

16 See   www.lawsociety.org.uk/support-services/advice/practice-notes/aml/legal-professional-privilege/, last accessed 14 December 2017.

recognises the client's fundamental human right to be candid with his legal adviser, without fear of later disclosure to his prejudice. It is an absolute right and cannot be overridden by any other interest.

6.53

Generally confidentiality extends beyond LPP, which protects only those confidential communications falling under the definition of advice privilege or litigation privilege. Advice privilege includes communications between a lawyer, acting in his capacity as a lawyer, and a client, if they are both confidential and for the purpose of seeking legal advice from a solicitor or providing it to a client.

6.54

It is not always easy to identify what information is subject to privilege (and therefore cannot be overridden without a statutory exception) and what is merely confidential. Not all communications between a lawyer and client are privileged. The protection applies only to those communications which directly seek or provide advice or which are given in a legal context, that involve the lawyer using his legal skills and that are directly related to the performance of the lawyer's professional duties[17].

6.55

Information given to a legal adviser by the client in the consultation prior to a police interview is privileged. As such, if a client discloses that they are a victim of trafficking but specifically instructs the legal adviser not to disclose this information to police, regardless of the client's age, the legal adviser cannot make the disclosure.

6.56

The issue is perhaps more difficult where the adviser believes from his own assessment of the client that the client is a potential victim of trafficking under the age of 18, but the client does not confirm that to be the case. It is arguable that the legal adviser's belief of the client's status is not privileged, but confidential. This is a very fine line.

6.57

The Law Society Practice Note on this subject suggests that if a child client reveals information which indicates continuing sexual or other physical abuse but refuses to allow such disclosure of information to an appropriate authority, a conflict may arise between the duty of confidentiality and the adviser's ability to act with integrity (principle 2 of the SRA Handbook).

---

17 *Passmore on Privilege* (2nd edn, 2006).

6.58

Whether the adviser's duties conflict or not will depend on the materiality of the information in question. The adviser must consider whether the threat to the child's life or health, both mental and physical, is sufficiently serious to justify a breach of the duty of confidentiality[18].

6.59

In the vast majority of cases, it would not be appropriate for the adviser to make a disclosure to police which would lead to a referral to the NRM for a child client who has not specifically given consent for that disclosure. It would be an extremely rare case where the legal adviser makes such a disclosure based on discussions with the client without the client's consent.

6.60

A careful note should be made as to the information obtained and the reasons why no disclosure was made. The client should be encouraged to meet with an appropriate organisation after the police station attendance in the hope that he will subsequently allow a referral to take place.

Advice

6.61

If the legal adviser considers the client to be a potential victim of trafficking, the client should be encouraged to allow disclosure of that fact to the police for referral into the NRM. Such a disclosure imposes on police a duty to investigate the details of the disclosure (see below) and may stop, or at least suspend, the instant investigation. The client should be treated as a victim of crime. Even if the investigation into the index offence continues, the early disclosure will impact on the decision by the prosecuting authorities as to whether to prosecute the matter and may provide a more effective defence under the Modern Slavery Act ('MSA') 2015, s 45.

6.62

A defence under the MSA 2015, s 45 does not require an NRM referral, but the consequences of such a referral may provide evidence to support the s 45 defence, any application to stay proceedings as an abuse of process and/or a review of any decision to prosecute either initially or at a later stage. Gathering such evidence may be particularly difficult for defence lawyers, particularly where it may exist by way of intelligence-based sources on the operation of a particular trafficking gang, so the balance will be in favour of the client allowing a referral.

---

18 See www.lawsociety.org.uk/support-services/advice/practice-notes/criminal-prosecutions-of-victims-of-trafficking/, last accessed 14 December 2017.

6.63

Anyone advising on a matter where the client may be a potential victim of trafficking should consider the defence provided by the MSA 2015, s 45 and/ or duress. A full analysis of defences is set out in Chapter 5.

6.64

A person aged 18 or over at the time of the act which constitutes the offence is not guilty of an offence if he does that act because he is compelled to do it, the compulsion is attributable to slavery or to 'relevant exploitation', and a reasonable person in the same situation as the person and having the person's relevant characteristics would have no realistic alternative to doing that act[19].

6.65

A person may be compelled to do something by another person or by his circumstances[20]. Compulsion is attributable to slavery or to relevant exploitation only if it is, or is part of, conduct which constitutes an offence under the MSA 2015, s 1 or conduct which constitutes relevant exploitation, or it is a direct consequence of a person being, or having been, a victim of slavery or a victim of relevant exploitation[21].

6.66

A person under the age of 18 when he does the act which constitutes the offence is not guilty of an offence if he does that act as a direct consequence of being, or having been, a victim of slavery or a victim of relevant exploitation, and a reasonable person in the same situation as the person and having the person's relevant characteristics would do that act[22].

6.67

'Relevant characteristics' means age, sex and any physical or mental illness or disability. 'Relevant exploitation' is exploitation (within the meaning of the MSA 2015, s 3) that is attributable to the exploited person being, or having been, a victim of human trafficking[23].

6.68

The defences set out above do not apply if the offence under investigation falls within the MSA 2015, Sch 4[24]. If the offence under investigation falls within the

---

19 MSA 2015, s 45(1).
20 MSA 2015, s 45(2).
21 MSA 2015, s 45(3).
22 MSA 2015, s 45(4).
23 MSA 2015, s 45(5).
24 MSA 2015, s 45(7).

exceptions set out in Sch 4 (see the full list of exceptions, set out in the annex to Chapter 5), it will not preclude the engagement of the non–punishment legal framework or the Crown applying their guidance in deciding whether to prosecute (see Chapter 5).

6.69

If an interview is to proceed, the client should be advised as to the best options in dealing with the interview. This may include setting out sufficient information to mount the defence at a later stage or prepare the groundwork for representations to the prosecuting authority that it would be inappropriate to bring charges.

6.70

Much will depend on whether the client accepts that they are a victim of trafficking and have been acting under the influence of their trafficker. If they accept that, and disclosure has been made, but the interview proceeds, a prepared statement to that effect should be considered followed by a no comment interview. It would not necessarily be appropriate for the potential victim of trafficking to be probed about their disclosure in an investigative interview of this nature and answering questions may be problematic.

6.71

If the client refuses to disclose, or denies being a potential victim of trafficking, the client would most likely be best advised not to answer questions. Any answers that specifically deny or undermine the potential trafficking defence may be problematic (albeit not fatal) later at trial if by that stage disclosure has been made.

6.72

A refusal to answer questions in interview will invoke the *possibility* of adverse inferences being drawn in any subsequent trial if the jury (or tribunal in the magistrates' or youth court) believe that the fact not mentioned was relied on in the defence of those proceedings and it was a fact which in the circumstances existing at the time the accused could reasonably have been expected to mention when questioned[25].

6.73

Victims of trafficking may not want to disclose details regarding their exploitation for a number of complex cultural, religious and physiological reasons, which can include juju rituals, debt bondage and fear of reprisals. Full details on control methods are explored in Chapter 15.

---

25 Criminal Justice and Public Order Act 1994, s 34.

6.74

Whether a jury would subsequently draw an adverse inference from a silent interview cannot be known at the time of the interview. Indeed in the case of a vulnerable person who may be a victim of trafficking, there will be very good arguments to be deployed at trial that no inference should be drawn and that it was entirely reasonable for that person not to have answered questions and mentioned facts in interview that they later relied on at trial.

6.75

Whether the suspect could reasonably have been expected to mention a fact at the time of the interview or on charge is a question of fact and the court must have regard to 'the actual accused with such qualities, apprehensions, knowledge and advice as he is shown to have had at the time'[26].

6.76

The court will take into account such matters as the time of day that the interview took place, the age of the suspect, his experience, his mental capacity and state of health, his knowledge, personality; and the fact that they had received legal advice before allowing the possibility of an adverse inference being drawn by the jury.

6.77

A potential victim of trafficking is likely to be able to rely on a number of the above issues in order to justify the reasonableness of a decision not to mention facts in interview. It is possible that, during trial, expert evidence may be required to explain the special vulnerabilities of trafficked individuals, to ensure that the point is fully understood by the court.

6.78

The suspect cannot rely solely on the fact that he was advised to say nothing in interview by his legal adviser in order to avoid an adverse inference being drawn. What is important is not the quality of the advice but the effect of the advice on the suspect, and whether in the circumstances it was reasonable for him to take the advice and not answer questions.

6.79

The fact that the suspect has been advised by his legal representative to remain silent must be given 'appropriate weight' by the court. It is important that the decision to remain silent was genuinely made as a result of legal advice rather than because there was no innocent explanation or none that would stand up to scrutiny[27].

---

26 *R v Argent* (1997) 2 Cr App Rep 27.
27 *Condron v United Kingdom* (App No 35718/97) (2000) 31 EHRR 1, [2000] Crim LR 679; *R v Betts* [2001] EWCA Crim 224, [2001] 2 Cr App Rep 257.

6.80

Once it is shown that the advice (of whatever quality) has genuinely been relied on as the reason for the suspect remaining silent, adverse inference may still be allowed. It is not necessarily unreasonable to expect the suspect to mention the facts in question notwithstanding the advice received. What is reasonable depends on all the circumstances.

6.81

The fact that advice has been given to remain silent remains an important consideration but not one that automatically excludes an adverse inference. The defendant has a choice to accept or reject the advice and is warned in the caution that a failure to mention any facts that he relied on at trial might harm his defence.

6.82

Circumstances where a suspect could have good reason to rely on advice to remain silent, even if he has an innocent explanation for the allegations, would include where the suspect was vulnerable and might have real difficulty getting across what he wanted to say. Potential victims of trafficking are undoubtedly vulnerable and are likely to have understandable reasons as to why they may be reluctant to disclose certain information in interview even where that information may assist them in relation to setting out a defence under the MSA 2015, s 45 or in a wider context.

6.83

In circumstances where a potential victim of trafficking will not consent to a disclosure to police and for an NRM referral, and where they choose to remain silent in interview, it is important that legal representatives make detailed notes of instructions. The legal adviser should try to obtain as much information as possible from the potential victim of trafficking as to his fears and concerns. It may become relevant should the matter go to trial and a slavery defence is subsequently raised.

6.84

In order to rebut any potential adverse inference, the legal representative may be required to provide evidence regarding the instructions he obtained, his advice and the reason that the suspect did not want to answer questions. This *may* require a waiver of privilege, as the reasons for the advice will have to be explained. Any waiver will extend to the whole of the consultation and not merely the discrete piece of advice.

6.85

However, if the adverse inference to be drawn is that the suspect has recently made up an account in order to take advantage of the defence after charge, such inference can be rebutted by the legal adviser providing a statement as to the account given to him in the pre-interview discussion or producing a statement made by the defendant at that time. This will demonstrate that the account has not been made up subsequently, and may prevent privilege being waived for the whole of the consultation or at all[28].

6.86

Clearly such a decision needs careful consideration at trial as there remains a risk that privilege will have to be waived. Such a decision may be dependent on the content of the rest of the consultation and the importance of the jury understanding the reason for the defendant remaining silent in interview.

Positive obligations owed to a victim of trafficking by the state

6.87

When a defendant or suspect in criminal proceedings has been identified[29] as a potential victim of trafficking that individual could fall within the scope of the ECHR, Art 4. Article 4 is a prohibition on slavery and servitude (see Chapter 10 for a fuller account of this provision) and in *Rantsev v Cyprus and Russia*[30] the ECtHR held that trafficking in human beings fell within the scope of Art 4.

6.88

Article 4 carries with it positive obligations on the state to the victim of trafficking (or potential victim of trafficking). Article 4 requires Member States to penalise and prosecute effectively any act aimed at maintaining a person in a situation of slavery, servitude or forced or compulsory labour[31].

6.89

Article 4 may, in certain circumstances, require a state to take operational and protective measures to protect victims, or potential victims, of trafficking[32]. In order to establish that this positive obligation arises it must be demonstrated that the state authorities were aware, or ought to have been aware, of circumstances giving rise to a reasonable suspicion that an identified individual had been, or was at real and immediate risk of being, trafficked or exploited within the meaning of the Council of Europe Convention on Action against Trafficking

28 *R v Wilmot* (1988) 89 Cr App Rep 341.
29 Self-identification is not a pre-requisite to an individual meeting the definition of trafficking and coming within the scope of the different international, regional and domestic safeguards viz trafficking victims. This identification could be through the NRM (see Chapter 2) or by a statutory agency or other organisation supporting or assisting the potential victim.
30 App No 25965/04 (10 May 2010), paras 277 and 282.
31 *CN v United Kingdom* (2013) 56 EHRR 24, para 66; *Siliadin v France* App No 73316/01 (26 October 2005), para 112 and *CN and V v France* App No 67724/09 (11 October 2012), para 105.
32 *Rantsev* at para 286; *Osman v UK* (App No 87/1997/871/1083) at [115].

in Human Beings ('ECAT'), Art 4(a)[33]. Protection measures include facilitating the identification of victims by trained persons and assisting victims in their physical, psychological and social recovery[34].

6.90

There is a significant body of material in the public domain about the typology of trafficking within the UK. If a suspect fits this (eg a Vietnamese child recovered in a cannabis farm), it will be arguable that the Art 4 protection obligations are triggered at an early stage, such as upon arrest, and thus before the decision to charge[35]. See Chapter 15 for common trafficking victim profiles in the UK.

6.91

Article 4 entails a procedural obligation to investigate where there is a reasonable suspicion that an individual's rights under the article have been violated[36]. The duty to investigate does not depend on a complaint from the victim or next of kin; it is triggered as soon as the matter has come to the attention of the authorities, and the authorities must act of their own motion[37]. This obligation entails the relevant investigatory agencies asking the appropriate questions, making enquiries or further enquiries into the facts and background, and/or parts of the trafficking chain[38].

6.92

For the purposes of a criminal investigation, the relevant agencies required to meet this positive obligation will be the police and the Crown. The criminal investigation must be effective and capable of leading to the individuals responsible for the trafficking. Reasonable speed and diligence is required, although an investigation must be urgent if it is possible to remove the individual concerned from a damaging situation[39]. Promptness is required to avoid a negative impact on the victim's personal situation[40]. Authorities must take all reasonable steps to secure evidence concerning the incident[41].

6.93

Article 4 positive obligations and whether these have been fulfilled by state agencies is likely to be relevant to any challenge to the removal of a victim

---

33 *Rantsev* at para 286; *CN v United Kingdom*, para 67.

34 *Chowdhury v Greece* App No 21884/15 at para 110.

35 See, for example, Association of Chief Police Officers, *Position from ACPO Leads on Child Protection and Cannabis Cultivation on Children and Young People Recovered in Cannabis Farms*, available at http://new. ecpat.org.uk/sites/default/files/acpo_leads_position_on_cyp_recovered_from_cannabis_farms_final.pdf, last accessed 14 December 2017.

36 *Rantsev*, para 286; *CN v United Kingdom* (2013) 56 EHRR 24, para 69.

37 *Rantsev*, para 288; *J v Austria* App No 58216/12 (17 January 2017) at para 107.

38 *Rantsev*, paras 297, 303.

39 *Chowdhury v Greece*, para 89.

40 *LE v Greece* App No 71545/12 (21 April 2016), para 68.

41 In the context of Art 3, the positive obligation to secure evidence arose in *J v Austria* at para 107.

of trafficking from the UK or deportation decision (see Chapter 10), any challenge to a negative identification decision by the NRM (see Chapter 2) and/or prosecution of a potential victim of trafficking and any onward appeals of these decisions (see Chapters 7 and 9).

The NRM and the duty to notify

6.94

The NRM is a framework for identifying and referring potential victims of modern slavery and ensuring they receive the appropriate support. It was implemented in 2009 for victims of trafficking to give effect to obligations arising under ECAT, and extended to include victims of modern slavery on 31 June 2015 (see Chapter 2).

6.95

The police are first responders under the NRM. They have a further statutory duty under the MSA 2015. The duty applies to specified public authorities to respond to incidents of suspected trafficking and slavery. This is referred to as the duty to notify, and can be found in the MSA 2015, s 52.

6.96

Section 52 of the MSA 2015 is intended to further improve identification of victims by creating a statutory duty for specified public authorities to notify the Secretary of State where they have reasonable grounds to believe that a person may be a victim of slavery or human trafficking. The section requires that where a specified public authority to which the section applies has reasonable grounds to believe that a person may be a victim of slavery or human trafficking, it must notify the Home Office, regardless of whether the individual has consented to enter into the NRM.

6.97

The public authorities currently required[42] to report under the duty to notify are as follows:

- a chief officer of police for a police area;
- the chief constable of the British Transport Police Force ;
- the National Crime Agency;
- a county council;
- a county borough council;
- a district council;

---

42 Set out in MSA 2015, s 52.

- a London borough council;

- the Greater London Authority;

- the Common Council of the City of London;

- the Council of the Isles of Scilly;

- the Gangmasters and Labour Abuse Authority.

The police interview

6.98

In a situation where disclosure has been made to police that the client is a potential victim of trafficking but the officer in the case for the index offence continues with the interview under caution, the adviser should place on record at the start of the interview that the suspect has disclosed themselves to police as a potential victim of trafficking and that there is a duty upon the police to refer the client into the NRM. In the light of that process, an interview on the index offence is inappropriate.

6.99

Guidance has been issued, following the implementation of the MSA 2015, by the National College of Policing. It states:

> 'If a person is arrested and so enters the criminal justice system as a perpetrator, and officers discover during the PACE interview that the person committed a modern slavery offence through coercion and may also be a victim, the interview should continue and evidence be obtained. On conclusion of the interview, the person should be referred into the NRM if they consent. If appropriate, the person should be bailed for the offence under investigation. If, however, the person has been arrested for an offence outlined in Schedule 4, is illegally residing in the UK and is likely to abscond, bail should be withheld. Following the referral, a victim debrief and a subsequent interview in line with Achieving Best Evidence in Criminal Proceedings: Guidance on interviewing victims and witnesses, and guidance on using special measures should take place to identify additional perpetrators and to help officers gather further evidence'[43].

6.100

If disclosure is made during the course of the interview when it had not been made previously to the adviser, or in circumstances where the client had refused

---

43 See   www.app.college.police.uk/app-content/major-investigation-and-public-protection/modern-slavery/national-referral-mechanism/#responding-to-perpetrators-who-may-also-be-victims,   last accessed 11 January 2018.

to disclose it prior to interview, the adviser should consider interrupting the interview and request a further consultation with the client so that the matter can be clarified. At that point, disclosure can be made and representations made that the interview should not continue, regardless of the advice of the National College of Policing.

Age of potential victim of trafficking

6.101

The age of the potential victim of trafficking may be an issue and may not be known. It is common for victims of trafficking to be groomed to give a certain age if questioned by authority. The age given will depend on the modus operandi of the traffickers: some may be told to say that they are older than they actually are, and others to say that they are younger.

6.102

Generally if the potential victim of trafficking claims to be an adult, the legal adviser has to act on those instructions. However, if the adviser believes the potential victim of trafficking to be under 18, advice should be given to declare a proper age. Those under the age of 18 are treated more favourably in detention and would be entitled to the support of an appropriate adult.

6.103

The police are under an obligation to treat anyone who appears to be under the age of 18 as a juvenile unless there is clear evidence that they are older[44]. Full details on age assessment are explained in Chapter 3.

Appropriate adult

6.104

It is arguable that anyone identified as a potential victim of trafficking is potentially vulnerable and should be afforded the right to an appropriate adult. This is obviously true if the person is, or appears to be, under the age of 18, but should also apply to adults who have made such disclosure or where there is suspicion that they may be a potential victim of trafficking.

6.105

If an officer has any suspicion, or is told in good faith, that a person of any age may be mentally disordered or otherwise mentally vulnerable, in the absence

---

44 PACE 1984, Code C1.5.

of clear evidence to dispel that suspicion, the person shall be treated as such[45]. It is arguable that a potential victim of trafficking should be considered to be mentally vulnerable, which is defined in the PACE Code C as someone 'who, because of their mental state or capacity, may not understand the significance of what is said, of questions or of their replies'. This definition may fit potential victims of trafficking, but it is suggested that a change to the Code is desirable to specifically bring potential victims of trafficking within the definition of 'mentally vulnerable' people.

6.106

An appropriate adult in the case of a juvenile is:

- the parent, guardian or, if the juvenile is in the care of a local authority or voluntary organisation, a person representing that authority or organisation;

- a social worker of a local authority;

- failing these, some other responsible adult aged 18 or over who is not:

  — a police officer;

  — employed by the police;

  — under the direction or control of the chief officer of a police force; or

  — a person who provides services under contractual arrangements (but without being employed by the chief officer of a police force) to assist that force in relation to the discharge of its chief officer's functions, whether or not they are on duty at the time[46].

6.107

An appropriate adult in the case of a person who is mentally disordered or mentally vulnerable is:

- a relative, guardian or other person responsible for their care or custody;

- someone experienced in dealing with mentally disordered or mentally vulnerable people but who is not:

  — a police officer;

  — employed by the police;

  — under the direction or control of the chief officer of a police force; or

  — a person who provides services under contractual arrangements (but without being employed by the chief officer of a police force)

---

45 PACE 1984, Code C1.4.
46 PACE 1984, Code C1.7(a).

to assist that force in relation to the discharge of its chief officer's functions, whether or not they are on duty at the time;

- failing these, some other responsible adult aged 18 or over.

6.108

In the case of people who are mentally disordered or otherwise mentally vulnerable, it may be more satisfactory if the appropriate adult is someone experienced or trained in the care of such individuals, rather than a relative lacking such qualifications. However, if the detainee prefers a relative to a better qualified stranger, or objects to a particular person, his wishes should, if practicable, be respected[47].

6.109

A detainee should always be given an opportunity, when an appropriate adult is called to the police station, to consult privately with a solicitor in the appropriate adult's absence if he wants. An appropriate adult is not subject to legal privilege[48].

6.110

A solicitor or independent custody visitor who is present at the police station and acting in that capacity may not be the appropriate adult[49].

6.111

It is imperative that the adviser is content that the appropriate adult is appropriate. It may be, for example, that a juvenile potential victim of trafficking may request an appropriate adult who is linked to their trafficker. In such circumstances, it will be very difficult for the adviser or police to ascertain victim status as the client will not have disclosed being a potential victim of trafficking and most certainly would not in the presence of such an adult. The gender of the appropriate adult may be important to the potential victim of trafficking and their views should be taken into account if expressed.

After the interview

6.112

If disclosure of the suspect's status as a potential victim of trafficking has been made to police and the police have followed up with an NRM referral, no decision should be made to charge the suspect with any offences at that point.

---

47 PACE 1984, Code C Note 1D.
48 PACE 1984, Code C Note 1E.
49 PACE 1984, Code C Note 1F.

Representations must be made to this effect, relying on the EU Directives as to non-prosecution of victims of trafficking. It ought to be for the CPS to make such a decision, given the complicating feature of an NRM referral and assessment.

6.113

Where an NRM referral has been made by the police, the potential victim of trafficking should be collected and transported by a relevant first responder from the police station to safe and secure accommodation.

6.114

Where the police have no made NRM referral, legal representatives should take steps to ensure that they contact a first responder and have an NRM referral made immediately (see Chapter 2).

6.115

If the client has not made a trafficking disclosure and is to be charged, the legal adviser may provide further legal advice immediately following charge. However, attendance upon the client thereafter whilst fingerprints, photographs and swabs are taken will not meet the 'sufficient benefit test' for public funding, except where the client requires further assistance owing to his particular circumstances, in which case the relevant factors must be noted on file. It is arguable that such clients would be eligible to have the services of the legal adviser under public funds for this process of further disclosure.

6.116

The adviser may remain at the police station if required to make representations about bail, including conditions that may be attached to any police bail or bail to court following a decision to charge the suspect with criminal offences. For example, it will be important to ensure that bail conditions imposed do not place the client in potential danger from his suspected trafficker.

Police bail

6.117

Where no charging decision has been made but the investigation is continuing, the suspect must be released without bail unless the officer is satisfied that releasing the person on bail is necessary and proportionate in all the circumstances (having regard, in particular, to any conditions of bail which would be imposed), and a police officer of the rank of inspector or above authorises the release on bail (having considered any representations made by the person)[50].

---

50 PACE 1984, s 30A(1) and (1A).

6.118

Police bail conditions cannot include the taking of a security or surety to ensure the person's surrender to custody or any requirement to reside in a bail hostel[51]. Police bail conditions may be imposed only if they appear necessary to secure that the person surrenders to custody, to secure that the person does not commit an offence while on bail, to secure that the person does not interfere with witnesses or otherwise obstruct the course of justice, whether in relation to himself or any other person, or for the person's own protection or, if the person is under the age of 18, for the person's own welfare or in the person's own interests[52].

6.119

Once released on police bail the date or police station to which the person has to surrender can be changed, although the person must be given notice in writing of any changes[53].

6.120

The initial period of police bail cannot exceed 28 days beginning with the day after the day on which the person was arrested for the offence in relation to which bail is granted[54].

6.121

Police bail conditions can be varied by police[55] and if the person on bail wishes to apply to vary conditions, an application should initially be made to the police. If that is refused, an application can be made to the magistrates' court[56]. Public funding is available (if financially eligible) under the Advocacy Assistance scheme for such applications.

6.122

Police bail can be extended before the 28 days expires to three months by an officer of at least superintendent rank[57]. The police have to inform the person or his legal representative and give him an opportunity to make representations against such a decision[58].

---

51 PACE 1984, s 30A(3A).
52 PACE 1984, s 30A(3B).
53 PACE 1984, s 30B(6), (6A) and (7).
54 PACE 1984, s 30B(8), except in SFO investigations when the initial limit is three months (PACE 1984, s 47ZB(1)(a)).
55 PACE 1984, s 30CA.
56 PACE 1984, s 30CB.
57 PACE 1984, s 47ZD(2).
58 PACE 1984, s 47ZD(3), (4).

6.123

Bail can only be so extended if there are reasonable grounds for:

- suspecting the person in question to be guilty of the relevant offence;

- believing that further time is needed for making a decision as to whether to charge the person with the relevant offence, or otherwise, that further investigation is needed of any matter in connection with the relevant offence;

- believing that the decision as to whether to charge the person with the relevant offence is being made diligently and expeditiously, or otherwise, that the investigation is being conducted diligently and expeditiously; and

- believing that the release on bail of the person in question is necessary and proportionate in all the circumstances (having regard, in particular, to any conditions of bail which are, or are to be, imposed)[59].

6.124

Police bail can be extended up to six months on application to the magistrates' court prior to the end of the currently applicable bail period but only if the court has reasonable grounds for:

- believing that further time is needed for making a decision as to whether to charge the person with the relevant offence, or otherwise, that further investigation is needed of any matter in connection with the relevant offence;

- believing that the decision as to whether to charge the person with the relevant offence is being made diligently and expeditiously, or otherwise, that the investigation is being conducted diligently and expeditiously; and

- believing that the release on bail of the person in question is necessary and proportionate in all the circumstances (having regard, in particular, to any conditions of bail which are, or are to be, imposed)[60].

6.125

The court will only increase the bail period if the nature of the decision or further investigations means that that decision is unlikely to be made or those investigations completed if the current applicable bail period in relation to the person is not extended as requested[61].

6.126

In all other circumstances, where no charging decision has been made but the investigation continues, the person will be 'released under investigation' to which no conditions can be attached.

---

59 PACE 1984, s 47ZC(2)–(5).
60 PACE 1984, s 47ZG.
61 PACE 1984, s 47ZG(8).

6.127

Given these restrictions on police bail, it is likely that any potential victim of trafficking who has made a disclosure and been referred into the NRM will be released under investigation with no specific date to return.

6.128

It is important to keep in contact with the client throughout this period and ensure that they seek assistance from one of the appropriate organisations, whether or not they have disclosed themselves to be a potential victim of trafficking. A referral into the NRM can be made at any time by a relevant organisation and such a referral may well assist the client's case at whatever stage it is made.

6.129

The police may decide to release a potential victim of trafficking on police bail with protective conditions such as release to a suitable safe bail address not near the area of exploitation, although this cannot be a bail hostel. Often potential victims of trafficking go missing straight from their release from police custody as they will not wait to be met by someone from an organisation that might have been requested to help them. Victims may be met at the police station by people connected to their trafficker.

6.130

If bail conditions are imposed, it is important to ensure that they do not put the potential victim of trafficking in potential danger. It would be inappropriate to demand that the potential victim of trafficking sign on at a police station in an area of danger for them that is close to their trafficker or place of arrest. Further protective conditions and safeguarding are discussed in Chapters 8 and 11.

Limits on period of detention without charge

6.131

In the first instance a person shall not be kept in police detention for more than 24 hours without being charged. The time from which the period of detention of a person is to be calculated is the time at which that person arrives at the relevant police station, or the time 24 hours after the time of that person's arrest, whichever is the earlier[62].

6.132

A person who has not been charged within the 24-hour period shall be released either without bail unless the pre-conditions for bail are satisfied, in which case they may be released on police bail[63].

---

62 PACE 1984, s 41.
63 PACE 1984, s 41(7).

6.133

However, where a police officer of the rank of superintendent or above has reasonable grounds for believing that the detention of that person without charge is necessary to secure or preserve evidence relating to an offence for which he is under arrest or to obtain such evidence by questioning him; an offence for which he is under arrest is an indictable offence; and the investigation is being conducted diligently and expeditiously, he may authorise the keeping of that person in police detention for a period of up to 36 hours after the relevant time[64].

6.134

Any application for a warrant of further detention to detain a suspect beyond 36 hours has to be made to the magistrates' court. Representation at such a hearing is funded by Advocacy Assistance and is not means tested[65]. The maximum time that a person can be kept in detention is 96 hours[66].

The charging decision

6.135

According to the Crown Prosecutors' Guidance the police may charge:

- any summary only offence (including criminal damage where the value of the loss or damage is less than £5,000) irrespective of plea;

- any offence of retail theft (shoplifting) or attempted retail theft irrespective of plea provided it is suitable for sentence in the magistrates' court; and

- any either way offence anticipated as a guilty plea and suitable for sentence in a magistrates' court;

6.136

Good practice dictates that any case which involves indicators of modern slavery should be referred to the CPS for a charging decision as the issues are more complex, even if it might otherwise fall within the police charging remit. Legal advisers should press for this course at the police station by making representations to the investigating officer and the custody officer.

6.137

Publicly funded advice can be provided in the period after release from the police station and while a charging decision is being contemplated. Advice can

---

64 PACE 1984, s 42(10).
65 PACE 1984, ss 43 and 44.
66 PACE 1984, s 44.

be provided under the Legal Advice and Assistance scheme but this is strictly means tested and will only add to the fees the solicitors' firm receives for the representation if it takes the firm over the fee threshold into the exceptional fee bracket (see Chapter 13). Consequently, although in practice the work is likely not actually to be remunerated above the Police Station Advice Fixed Fee, funding is technically available for representations to be made to the police or the CPS to disposal of the case without charge.

6.138

Written representations can be submitted when the matter has been sent to the CPS for a decision on charge. Written representations[67] should include detailed reference to the Crown's obligations under the EU Directives on the non-punishment of trafficking victims[68] and to their own guidance on victims of human trafficking[69].

6.139

Defence representatives should endeavour to persuade the CPS that the client is a victim of trafficking and should not be prosecuted in the circumstances. Reference should be made to the availability of the slavery defence in the MSA 2015 and the Crown's EU Directive obligations not to proceed with the prosecution as not in the public interest (for full details of CPS charging decisions and guidance see Chapter 7).

6.140

Victims of trafficking ought to be largely protected from prosecution and punishment. This is accepted by the CPS published legal guidance, an important document that should be considered by the prosecutor pre-charge where there are indicators of trafficking present in respect of a suspect. This guidance is relevant irrespective of whether the suspect has self-identified as a victim of trafficking; indicators of trafficking are sufficient to prompt consideration of the guidance.

6.141

The guidance provides that prosecutors should be alert to particular circumstances or situations where a suspect or defendant might be a victim of trafficking or slavery. The guidance provides examples of common scenarios in which a suspect or defendant may also be a victim of trafficking. These examples include unaccompanied foreign national children committing offences of

---

67 Under The Code of Crown Prosecutors, para 3.3.
68 Directive 2011/36/EU of the European Parliament and of the Council of 5 April 2011 on preventing and combating trafficking in human beings and protecting its victims, replacing Council Framework Decision 2002/629/JHA.
69 Available at www.cps.gov.uk/legal/h_to_k/human_trafficking_and_smuggling/#a25, last accessed 14 December 2017.

pickpocketing or cultivation of cannabis, adults involved in offences relating to immigration documents, or controlling prostitution.

6.142

The CPS guidance says that the CPS should make proper enquiries in criminal prosecutions involving individuals who may be victims of trafficking or slavery. Specifically, it states that enquiries should be made by:

'advising the law enforcement agency which investigated the original offence that it must investigate the suspect's trafficking/slavery situation; and advising that the suspect is referred through the NRM for victim identification (if this has not already occurred). All law enforcement officers are able to refer potential victims of trafficking/slavery to the NRM.'

6.143

In addition to the CPS guidance specifically for 'Human Trafficking, Smuggling and Slavery', the general Code for Crown Prosecutors remains of application in every case. Crown Prosecutors are under a duty at all stages of a case to consider whether or not prosecution is in the public interest. The Code states that Prosecutors should not 'continue a prosecution which would be regarded by the courts as oppressive or unfair and an abuse of the court's process.' For further guidance on charging decision and the Crown's obligations see Chapters 5 and 7.

6.144

The Full Code test has two stages: the evidential stage, which if met, is followed by the public interest stage. At the evidential stage, Prosecutors must be satisfied that there is 'sufficient evidence to provide a realistic prospect of conviction against each suspect on each charge' including taking account of possible defences. Once the evidential stage test has been satisfied, a prosecutor must consider whether a prosecution is required in the 'public interest'.

Interviews where disclosure has been made

6.145

In circumstances where disclosure has been made to police that the suspect is a potential victim of trafficking and the suspect has been referred into the NRM, a request may be made for the individual to provide an interview about their trafficked status. These interviews should be attended by solicitors and funding is available under the Advice and Assistance Scheme subject to the client being financially eligible (which will likely be the case for the vast majority of potential victims of trafficking).

6.146

There is no obligation to co-operate in such interviews but co-operation may assist in providing information that could be used by authorities confirming the trafficked status of the individual and hence in any further representations that prosecution is inappropriate. However, in circumstances where the potential victim of trafficking has been charged or is still a suspect and is invited to provide an ABE interview whilst still a defendant or suspect in a case, it is routine that the investigating trafficking officer will provide information to the competent authority regarding their separate modern slavery investigation. This can in some cases be adverse and affect the competent authority's determination. The advice on whether a potential victim of trafficking suspect or defendant should co-operate in a parallel investigation is case specific.

The interviews will be conducted by specially trained officers and will be recorded on video as part of the Achieving Best Evidence process.

Police interviewing techniques with vulnerable witnesses

6.147

A training course called 'Investigative Interviewing' is available for those police officers who are likely to be required to conduct interviews with vulnerable complainants or to manage interviews in serious crime cases. This is based upon the best practice PEACE model[70] (see para **6.150** below).

6.148

The investigative interview process should create a managed conversation with the interviewee. It is not a linear process but should be constantly reviewed, remaining flexible and adaptable to changing circumstances. The process should not be undertaken with urgency, which is a challenge to many police officers who are under considerable pressure in terms of the time available to obtain witness and complainant evidence.

6.149

Investigative interviewing should be approached with an investigative mind-set. Accounts obtained from the person who is being interviewed should always be tested against what the interviewer already knows or what can be reasonably established. The main purpose of obtaining information in an interview is to further the enquiry by establishing facts. Interviewers should think about what they want to achieve by interviewing the complainant, witness or suspect, and set objectives which will help to corroborate or disprove information already

---

70 See College of Policing, at www.app.college.police.uk/app-content/investigations/investigative-interviewing/, last accessed 14 December 2017.

known. Investigators should try to fill the gaps in the investigation by testing and corroborating the information by other means where possible.

6.150

The PEACE mnemonic stands for:

- planning and preparation;
- engage and explain;
- account, clarification and challenge;
- closure; and
- evaluation.

6.151

Planning and preparation is one of the most important phases in effective interviewing. Prior to the interview, the interviewer prepares an interview plan containing all the necessary elements, including defining the aims and objects of the interview and assessing what information is available and from where it can be obtained.

6.152

Planning and preparation should be carried out no matter what type of interview is being considered, whether it is with a witness, complainant or suspect, as it ensures that the investigators are ready to conduct an effective and ethical interview.

6.153

In order to engage, the interview should open with an introduction appropriate to the circumstances in order that a suitable relationship may be formed, with the interviewer showing awareness of and responding to the welfare needs of the witness and any fears and expectations the witness may have. The reasons for the interview should be explained as should the routines to be followed and how it relates to the evidential process.

6.154

The process of 'account, clarification and challenge' involves obtaining from the witness the account, achieving quality information and fine detail. The interviewer summarises and recounts what the witness has said at each stage so that both parties have an agreed understanding of what has taken place.

6.155

The process should allow for 'free recall', letting the subject talk freely without interruption. In the 'Clarification' phase the interviewer seeks to clarify the pertinent parts of the account starting in a chronological fashion, but probing questions should be used as the interview proceeds.

6.156

Challenges are often required as there could be and often are inconsistencies in the account. However, the challenges should be in a structured manner. The interviewer should seek to establish 'the evidence chain' and identify weaknesses and inconsistencies. The challenge process should be conducted with complainants and witnesses in a sympathetic way.

6.157

The interviewer should ensure that there is a planned closure of the process. The complainant or witness should be given an opportunity to ask questions, and explanations – where legally available and practical – should be provided. This ensures that the complainant or witness knows what will happen next.

6.158

After each interview is completed the event and the material gathered should be fully evaluated. This includes consideration of whether the objectives were achieved, whether any further information is required and the need for any further enquiries or corroboration.

6.159

Where multiple interviews are taking place, the teams should confer to ensure every member is aware of all the facts and decisions taken as to whether re-interviews are necessary.

Achieving Best Evidence interviews

6.160

These interviews are generally conducted using the ABE process and are video recorded[71]. There is guidance to assist those responsible for conducting video-recorded interviews with vulnerable, intimidated and significant witnesses, as well as those tasked with preparing and supporting witnesses during the criminal justice process. The guidance incorporates best practice from local areas and the expertise of practitioners, charities and voluntary groups who support complainants and witnesses at a local level.

---

71 'Achieving Best Evidence in Criminal Proceedings Guidance on interviewing victims and witnesses, and guidance on using special measures' was produced by the Ministry of Justice in 2002, revised in 2007 and again in 2011. The full document is available at www.cps.gov.uk/publications/docs/best_evidence_in_criminal_proceedings.pdf, last accessed 14 December 2017.

6.161

Any video-recorded interview serves two primary purposes: evidence gathering for use in the investigation and in criminal proceedings; and to be used as the evidence-in-chief of the witness should the case go to court.

6.162

The Ministry of Justice guidance document outlines those who are defined as vulnerable. It states, that all children (those under 18) should always be deemed vulnerable. However, in respect of adults the guidance focuses on those adults with physical or mental health disabilities or issues. This follows the statutory definition of a vulnerable adult witness as someone who 'suffers from mental disorder within the meaning of the Mental Health Act 1983, or otherwise has a significant impairment of intelligence and social functioning' or who 'has a physical disability or is suffering from a physical disorder'[72] .

6.163

The guidance also outlines the procedures to be used in the case of intimidated witnesses. The assistance of these special measures is available if the court is satisfied that the quality of evidence given by the witness is likely to be diminished by reason of fear or distress on the part of the witness in connection with testifying in the proceedings[73].

6.164

In their determination the court must take into account:

- the nature and alleged circumstances of the offence to which the proceedings relate;

- the age of the witness;

- the social and cultural background and ethnic origins of the witness;

- the domestic and employment circumstances of the witness;

- any religious beliefs or political opinions of the witness;

- any behaviour towards the witness on the part of the accused, members of the family or associates of the accused, or any other person who is likely to be an accused or a witness in the proceedings[74].

6.165

Those who are victims of trafficking would fall within the definition of a witness requiring assistance due to fear or distress. However, the best practice

---

72 Youth Justice and Criminal Evidence Act 1999, s 16.
73 Youth Justice and Criminal Evidence Act 1999, s 17(1).
74 Youth Justice and Criminal Evidence Act 1999, s 17(2).

techniques are not always utilised in police investigations and do not seem to have been adopted by the Immigration agencies.

6.166

There are many benefits to an investigator regarding the video recording of interviews where disclosure of trafficking has been made. One of the main benefits is the reassurance to the interviewee that by recording his evidence on video, he will not be required to face his exploiter or trafficker in court at a later date. Additional benefits of the process include ensuring an accurate record of the interview, and a reduced likelihood of allegations that the witness was led by the interviewers in delivering his account.

7 Criminal court process

Introduction

7.1

All criminal practitioners need to be alive to the fact that a suspect or defendant might be a victim of trafficking or slavery. Assumptions should not be made by a prosecutor or defence representative that simply because of the subject's country of origin, or the type of alleged offence he faces, that considerations of trafficking/modern slavery are not applicable. Examples of forced criminality and other types of exploitation may not be immediately obvious. Organised crime networks and individuals who use human beings as commodities continually evolve and adapt their modus operandi to evade the attention of the authorities and to increase profitability[1].

7.2

General indicators of trafficking have been published by the United Nations Office on Drugs and Crime (see Chapter 2). The UN gives further, specific, guidance in relation to children, domestic servitude, sexual exploitation, labour exploitation, begging and petty crime[2]. Criminal practitioners should be familiar with these concepts and indicators, so they know what topics to explore through the police or with clients from the first opportunity onwards.

7.3

To assess the presence of trafficking and modern slavery indicators properly, full background details of a defendant need to be taken, as well as instructions concerning the offence itself. These are difficult tasks to conduct under the pressure and time limitations associated with practice in the magistrates' court. Cases are often, if not invariably, listed with many other first appearances. Consideration should be given to the sort of questions that need to be asked when liaising with the police (if prosecuting) or when taking instructions (if defending). Victims of modern slavery and human trafficking often do not identify themselves or present as victims, or avoid making disclosures due to fear of reprisal. Often victims are coached by their exploiters, as to the accounts they should give.

---

1   See Chapter 15 for full details on forced criminality, modus operandi and common forced criminality offences.
2   Available at www.unodc.org/pdf/HT_indicators_E_LOWRES.pdf, last accessed 14 December 2017.

7.4

When taking instructions detailed questions should be asked regarding background, methods of control used, such as debt bondage, the impact of cultural aspects of background (such as juju rituals), threats, sexual and physical abuse[3].

Police station and charge

7.5

Victims of trafficking are protected from prosecution and punishment by the Crown Prosecution Service ('CPS') published legal guidance. The guidance, safeguards and procedures stemming from the guidance are set out in detail in Chapter 5 and procedure at the police station is set out in Chapter 6. The guidance is a key document that should be considered by the prosecutor pre-charge where there are indicators of trafficking present in respect of a suspect(s). This guidance is relevant irrespective of whether the suspect has self-identified as a victim of trafficking – indicators of trafficking are sufficient to prompt consideration of the guidance.

7.6

The guidance provides that prosecutors should be alert to particular circumstances or situations where a suspect or defendant might be a victim of trafficking or slavery. The guidance provides examples of common scenarios in which a suspect or defendant may also be a victim of trafficking. These examples include unaccompanied foreign national children committing offences of pickpocketing or cultivation of cannabis[4], adults involved in offences relating to immigration documents[5], or controlling prostitution.

7.7

The guidance states that the CPS should make proper enquiries in criminal prosecutions involving individuals who may be victims of trafficking or slavery. The guidance specifies that the enquiries should be made by:

> 'advising the law enforcement agency which investigated the original offence that it must investigate the suspect's trafficking/slavery situation; and

---

3   See Chapter 15 for full details on control methods and modus operandi. Chapter 1 provides a breakdown of the definition. Chapters 2 and 8 highlight the particular vulnerabilities of victims of trafficking.

4   This form of exploitation is also commonly found in cases concerning adults and should not be overlooked.

5   False documents are also common with child victims of trafficking.

advising that the suspect is referred through the NRM for victim identification (if this has not already occurred). All law enforcement officers are able to refer potential victims of trafficking/slavery to the NRM'[6].

7.8

In addition to the CPS legal guidance specifically for 'Human Trafficking, Smuggling and Slavery', the general Code for Crown Prosecutors remains of application in every case[7]. Crown Prosecutors are under a duty *at all stages* of a case to consider whether or not prosecution is in the public interest. The Code sets out that prosecutors should not 'continue a prosecution which would be regarded by the courts as oppressive or unfair and an abuse of the court's process'.

7.9

The Full Code test has two stages: (i) the evidential stage, which if met, is followed by (ii) the public interest stage. At the evidential stage, prosecutors must be satisfied that there is 'sufficient evidence to provide a realistic prospect of conviction against each suspect on each charge'. Once the evidential stage test has been satisfied, a prosecutor must consider whether a prosecution is required in the 'public interest'.

7.10

Those representing clients at the police interview stage of proceedings should be ready to explore indicators of trafficking with a view to triggering an investigation into the suspect's status as a possible credible victim of trafficking from as early a stage as possible.

General position following charge

7.11

The CPS published legal guidance continues to apply post charge and throughout a case. Both prosecutors and defence practitioners should be alert to any evidence which suggests that a suspect or defendant might be a victim of trafficking. This will enable discontinuance to be considered, in the event that a defendant is a victim of trafficking whose culpability or criminality has been extinguished or significantly diminished by virtue of his trafficking status and that the nexus of the trafficking to the offending is present. The Crown may be

---

6   In any written representations made to the Crown concerning a case involving a suspected victim of trafficking or modern slavery it would be worthwhile considering including reference to the Full Code Test as well.

7   A detailed exposition of how the guidance should be applied is set out in Chapter 5.

privy to information during the preparation of the case which alerts them to the defendant potentially being a victim of trafficking. Irrespective of whether trafficking has been raised by the defendant, the Crown should re-evaluate the case in line with the guidance and re-assess the public interest question.

Magistrates' court

First appearance

7.12

The first appearance stage in a magistrates' court or youth court is a critical hearing for cases concerning victims of trafficking and modern slavery. This hearing usually takes place the day after the individual has been charged by the police, if the suspect is remanded in custody. In the majority of cases, because victims of trafficking will be a bail risk, a defendant will be produced at court in custody.

Assessing the evidence

7.13

The initial details of the prosecution case or 'IDPC' provided by the CPS to a defence representative will often only consist of a charge sheet, a list of antecedents and a short police case summary[8].

7.14

It is critical that defence representatives:

- consider whether there are indicators of trafficking or modern slavery;

- ascertain whether any referral has yet taken place to the National Referral Mechanism ('NRM')[9] by the police or any other first responder; and, if not, to invite a first responder to refer the case via the NRM if indicators are present. It may not assist the defendant to have the police to act as a first responder and refer the case into the NRM, as there may be a conflict of interest if the police do not consider indicators of trafficking are present and/or their impetus is to secure a prosecution;

- liaise with the prosecutor at court and ask him to review the case at this stage in the light of the CPS legal guidance on Human Trafficking,

---

8   MG5 document.
9   See Chapter 2, where the NRM process is set out in detail.

Smuggling and Slavery. The CPS may be assisted in having detailed representations from the defence in order to conduct this review, or may need to be invited to prompt the police to investigate the trafficking dimension of the case further in order to assist with this prosecutorial review.

7.15

At each stage of the court process, it is important for defence representatives to ensure that the prosecuting authority has engaged with the CPS legal guidance. In the event that the prosecutor is not the CPS, if the authority has trafficking/slavery guidance, that guidance should be compared against the CPS guidance to see whether it is fit for purpose. If the prosecuting body does not have any guidance, the authority should be invited to apply the CPS guidance.

7.16

If there are concerns that the guidance has not been applied by the prosecutor, this should be set out as one of the issues on the case management form. Often victims of trafficking are 'threshold charged'. This is the charging test which may only be applied where the suspect presents a substantial bail risk and not all the evidence is available at the time when he must be released from custody unless charged. Because of the nature of the threshold charge, by virtue of its definition and process it is unlikely that indicators of trafficking will have been explored adequately or at all. It is thus crucial that possible victims' circumstances are looked at carefully as soon as possible within the criminal process. Practitioners should never assume that trafficking indicators have been properly assessed at the pre-charge stage.

Entering of pleas

7.17

At the first appearance at a magistrates' court, defendants are asked to enter or give an indication of plea. There are significant incentives, in terms of credit for pleading guilty to an offence at an early stage. The Sentencing Guideline Council on 'Reduction in Sentence for a Guilty Plea'[10] highlights that 'Defendants who are going to plead guilty are encouraged to do so as early in the court process as possible'. For example, if a guilty plea is entered at the first stage of proceedings an individual would normally receive maximum credit, namely one-third reduction from a sentence. A sliding scale then applies. A plea at the first opportunity in the Crown Court will usually not attract credit of more than 20–25%, and a plea on the day of trial will usually attract no more than a 10% discount.

---

10 Guidance in force at 1 June 2017.

7.18

The first stage of proceedings is considered to be the first appearance at the magistrates' court. The Sentencing Guideline on credit for a guilty plea specifically provides exceptions to there being less than maximum credit available[11] where 'further information, assistance or advice [is] necessary before indicating plea'. Practitioners need to be robust and courts need to understand that the above incentives should not and are not meant to put undue pressure on a defendant whose circumstances need to be explored to see whether he is a credible victim of trafficking or modern slavery. There is nothing to prevent a defence representative from asserting that a guilty plea will be forthcoming in the event that MSA 2015, s 45 cannot be deployed and/or representations cannot be made to the prosecution in accordance with the guidance and/or an abuse of process submission is not successful.

7.19

It is vital that proper enquiries are made in cases involving individuals who may be credible victims of trafficking or slavery. The CPS guidance itself states that such steps of advising the law enforcement agency to investigate or refer the suspect/defendant to the NRM must be done 'regardless of what has been advised by the investigator or whether there is an indication of a guilty plea by the suspect's legal representative'. However, for the purposes of a referral into the NRM, an adult must consent to the referral.

Should a plea be entered if a trafficking identification decision from the NRM is still awaited?

7.20

If a representative considers that there are trafficking indicators, or a possible defence under the Modern Slavery Act ('MSA') 2015, then adjournment of arraignment should be sought[12]. It should be outlined that full credit for any guilty plea should be retained (see above). It is best practice that arraignment should only take place once a (conclusive) trafficking determination has been received. Both the CPS guidance[13] and the Judicial College guidance reaffirm that pleas should only be taken after a trafficking determination has been made.

7.21

Representatives should be mindful of custodial time limits and should be pro-active in obtaining an update from the competent authority on their identification

---

11 See F1 of the Definitive Guidelines on Reduction in Sentence for a Guilty Plea.
12 Note that if an individual at the magistrates' court provides no indication of plea, then this is often recorded a not guilty plea having been entered.
13 Available at www.cps.gov.uk/legal/h_to_k/human_trafficking_and_smuggling/, last accessed 14 December 2017.

decision. This obligation rests with both the defence and prosecution. Whilst the competent authority guidance gives an estimate timeframe for making a conclusive determination of 45 days[14], many decisions take considerably longer. Representatives should actively consider judicial review when the competent authority fails to make a timely identification decision where it has sufficient information to do so.

Completion of Better Case Management forms

7.22

Care needs to be taken when completing the Better Case Management ('BCM') form, which is submitted at the first appearance[15]. The form asks what the 'real issues in the case are'. Such a form is admissible at trial. In *R (on the application of Firth) v Epping Magistrates' Court*[16], the court considered that:

'7. The use of a case progression form is part of this process. It forms part of the court record. It records matters such as the date fixed for the trial, the estimated length of trial, the likely number of defence witnesses, and the names of prosecution witnesses.

It also had, at the relevant time, a box headed "trial issues"'.

'22. It does not infringe against the principle that a defendant is not required to incriminate himself for the court to require that the nature of the defence is made plain well before the trial. Of course, any requirement for disclosure of the nature of the defence must be a fair requirement, in the sense that it must not be extracted from a defendant in circumstances where the prosecution have no case and are trying to adopt Star Chamber processes to try to build a case, but the rules are designed to make sure that this does not occur.'

'33. Part of the purpose of early identification of the real issues is to avoid the time, expense and possible inconvenience of having to obtain evidence to prove aspects of the case which are not disputed.'

The impact of the above means that when completing the form, all matters that remain in issue, or that are not agreed, should be raised. In particular, if the commission of the act is not accepted, representatives need to be careful before simply saying that an MSA 2015 defence applies.

---

14 Home Office, *Victims of modern slavery – Competent Authority guidance* (21 March 2016), available at www. gov.uk/government/uploads/system/uploads/attachment_data/file/521763/Victims_of_modern_ slavery_-_Competent_Authority_guidance_v3_0.pdf, last accessed 14 December 2017.

15 And will be uploaded to the digital case if transferred to the Crown Court.

16 [2011] EWHC 388 (Admin), [2011] 1 WLR 1818.

What issues need to be outlined in BCM form?

7.23

It is best practice to set out in the BCM form whether there needs to be investigation or referral for a possible victim of trafficking or slavery. This is so that the court can identify any failures by the prosecutor to conduct all appropriate enquiries into whether the defendant is a victim of trafficking.

7.24

The failure to engage at early stages of proceedings, with the need for further investigation and referral into the NRM will cause delays, which arguably prejudices a defendant in the following ways:

- consideration of bail;

- impact on trial listing dates;

- impact on custody time limits;

- abuse of process submissions.

Be mindful before setting out 'defence under s 45'

7.25

It is vital to appreciate that the statutory defence within the MSA 2015, s 45 applies when an individual 'does the act which constitutes the offence'[17]. Therefore, if a representative were to complete the box by merely referring to a 'defence under section 45 MSA' being relied upon, it would imply an admission that the defendant committed the *actus reus*. If essential elements of the offence itself are to be challenged, this should be set out in the form. Equally, if the defendant accepts having committed the *actus reus*, then that should be accepted within the BCM form.

7.26

Furthermore, if at the first appearance it is clear that there are trafficking and modern slavery indicators, then that should be stated as the trial issue: ie at that stage in proceedings it may not be incumbent on practitioners to say whether the MSA 2015, s 45 will be relied upon as a defence, because consideration of the guidance would precede the application of the section. Practitioners could go as far as to say that an MSA defence may in due course apply, but it is an issue still being considered.

---

17 Even though there are admissions in the sense of accepting the 'actus reus,' trafficking and modern slavery cases raise a need to advise caution before entering any type of plea, if further information is required as to background and especially prior to any trafficking decision by the NRM.

Age assessment

7.27

If the age of the defendant is disputed issue then that should be raised within the BCM form[18]. If no *Merton* compliant age assessment has taken place, this is a matter of the utmost importance to raise with the court, as it will impact upon venue of trial, bail, application of the s 45 defence and sentencing. Chapter 3 explores age assessments and disputes to age in detail.

Challenging the decision to prosecute a victim of trafficking: raising an abuse of process

7.28

Chapter 5 sets out how the provisions concerning the non-punishment of trafficking victims (as provided in the Council of Europe Convention on Action against Trafficking in Human Beings ('ECAT'), Art 26 and Directive 2011/36/EU of the European Parliament and of the Council of 5 April 2011 on preventing and combating trafficking in human beings and protecting its victims, replacing Council Framework Decision 2002/629/JHA ('the EU Trafficking Directive'), Art 8) are applied in England and Wales. In this section we consider how these operate in practice in criminal proceedings where the defendant is a possible or identified credible victim of trafficking. In *R v N; R v L*[19], the court observed:

> 'Every vulnerable victim of exploitation will be protected by the criminal law…there is no victim, so vulnerable to exploitation, that he or she somehow becomes invisible or unknown to or somehow beyond the protection of the law. Exploitation of fellow human beings … represents deliberate degrading of a fellow human being or human beings'.

7.29

The court in *R v L*[20] provided guidance to the criminal courts on how those who may be or who are credible victims of human trafficking, who have become involved in criminal activities as a consequence, should be approached after criminal proceedings against them have begun. The court set out guidance concerning cases where the following issues arise: (1) the age of a victim or alleged victim of trafficking; (2) the status of a defendant as a possible victim of trafficking; and (3) whether the alleged offences were an aspect of the victim's exploitation. The court held that the Crown Court or magistrates' court must

---

18 Full guidance on age disputes can be found in Chapter 3.
19 [2012] EWCA Crim 189, [2013] QB 379 at paras [2]–[6].
20 [2013] EWCA Crim 991, [2014] 1 All ER 113.

resolve the issues in the context of the doctrine of abuse of process and the jurisdiction to stay a prosecution.

7.30

Where the asserted minor age of a putative child defendant is not accepted by the court, prosecution, police or local authority, it is likely that it will be necessary to consider judicial review to challenge the assessed age of the defendant during the course of criminal proceedings. This is addressed in Chapter 3.

7.31

The prosecution is responsible for deciding whether to prosecute an alleged victim of trafficking and whether or not to maintain the prosecution. The court considers the decision to prosecute through the exercise of the jurisdiction to stay proceedings. Thus the court protects the rights of a victim of trafficking by overseeing the decision of the prosecutor. The Lord Chief Justice in *R v L* described the role of the court as replicating its role in relation to *agents provocateurs*. The court 'stands between the prosecution and the victim of trafficking where the crimes are committed as an aspect of the victim's exploitation'[21].

7.32

In the context of an abuse of process argument on behalf of an alleged victim of trafficking, the court will reach its own decision on the basis of the material advanced in support of and against the continuation of the prosecution. Where a court considers issues relevant to age, trafficking and exploitation, the prosecution will be stayed if the court disagrees with the decision to prosecute[22]. Where the competent authority has identified a defendant as a victim of trafficking following his referral through the NRM (see Chapter 2), the court observed in *R v L* that the criminal court is not bound by this decision. However, the court held that unless there is evidence to contradict it, or significant evidence that was not considered by the competent authority, it is likely that the criminal court will abide by this decision[23].

7.33

In *R v L* it was argued on behalf of one of the appellants that abuse of process should be adapted by reference to dicta in the well-known proceeds of crime authority of *R v Waya*[24]. The court rejected this, stating, 'In short *Waya* did not provide an additional remedy to the well understood abuse of process remedies or widen the judicial review procedures to encompass situations

---

21   [2013] EWCA Crim 189 at para 16.
22   See *R v L* at para [17].
23   See para 28 of the judgment, reiterated by the criminal Court of Appeal in *R v Joseph* [2017] EWCA Crim 36, [2017] 1 WLR 3153.
24   *R v Waya* [2012] UKSC 51, [2013] 1 AC 294.

where a clear remedy is available at or before the criminal trial'[25]. The Court of Appeal put down a marker that the abuse of process jurisdiction within criminal proceedings provided potential victims of human trafficking with a remedy to challenge the decision to prosecute. In the light of this, although the discretion of the CPS to continue or discontinue criminal proceedings is reviewable by the Administrative Court on judicial review, this is only where it can be demonstrated that the decision was made regardless of or clearly contrary to a settled policy[26]. Following on from *R v L*, it would have to be established that the abuse of process jurisdiction within the criminal proceedings was not an appropriate alternative remedy.

7.34

The abuse of process submissions that can be run in the criminal courts should encompass an assessment of the decision to prosecute, which can be wider than that which could and would be undertaken by the Administrative Court. As stated by the Lord Chief Justice in *R v L*, modifying the position adopted by the Vice President in the earlier appeal of *R v LM*[27], the criminal court judge is not restricted to whether the decision of the prosecutor to prosecute was *Wednesbury* unreasonable[28]:

> '14. What, however, is required in the context of the prosecutorial decision to proceed is a level of protection from prosecution or punishment for trafficked victims who have been compelled to commit criminal offences. These arrangements should follow the "basic principles" of our legal system. In this jurisdiction that protection is provided by the exercise by the "abuse of process" jurisdiction'.

> '17. In the context of an abuse of process argument on behalf of an alleged victim of trafficking, the court will reach its own decision on the basis of the material advanced in support of and against the continuation of the prosecution. Where a court considers issues relevant to age, trafficking and exploitation, the prosecution will be stayed if the court disagrees with the decision to prosecute. The fears that the exercise of the jurisdiction to stay will be inadequate are groundless'.

7.35

The criminal court in the first instance therefore will not be limited to the evidence that was before the CPS when the decision was made to prosecute

---

25 See para 18 of the judgment.
26 *R v Chief Constable of the Kent County Constabulary, ex p L* [1993] 1 All ER 756 at 770d.
27 [2010] EWCA Crim 2327, [2011] 1 Cr App Rep 135.
28 In a human rights context the scope of the review by the Administrative Court may be wider than a *Wednesbury* analysis: see *R (on the application of Quila) v Secretary of State for the Home Department* [2011] UKSC 45, [2012] 1 AC 621 and *Bank Mellat v Her Majesty's Treasury* [2013] UKSC 39, [2014] AC 700.

an alleged victim, or to evidence considered by the prosecution when reviewing its prosecutorial decision. Instead a criminal court judge can and should consider all the evidence in support of and against the decision to prosecute the individual[29]. Furthermore, the line of authorities stemming from *R v O*[30] emphasise that the focus should be on whether the prosecution involves a breach of international law, rather than whether the decision is simply *Wednesbury* unreasonable[31].

7.36

The abuse of process submissions within the criminal court process can traverse public law arguments, as identified in *R v LM*. In preparing abuse of process submissions, over and above securing evidence concerning the factual question of whether the defendant is or is not a victim of trafficking and that there was a nexus between the trafficking and the offending, consideration should be given to whether the prosecuting authority applied its mind conscientiously to the question of public policy and reached an informed decision, including consideration of its own published guidance. If the exercise of judgement has not properly been carried out and would or might well have resulted in a decision not to prosecute, then there will be a breach of ECAT and hence grounds for a stay. Likewise, if a decision has been reached at which no reasonable prosecutor could arrive, there will be grounds for a stay.

7.37

Further, where in the course of the criminal proceedings, the police and/or the CPS had failed in their positive obligations to investigate pursuant to the ECHR, Art 4 (see Chapter 6) this will support an argument that the decision to prosecute is vitiated by Art 4 failings, particularly if there has been a failure to identify the victim or a failure to investigate the trafficking of the defendant (see Chapter 9).

7.38

If there have been failures by the Crown or the police to investigate whether an individual is a victim of trafficking or modern slavery, or to ensure a *Merton* compliant age assessment has taken place, it is appropriate even at such an early stage of proceedings to raise the possibility of an abuse of process application, as a result of the failure by the prosecuting authority to comply with its obligations. Identification of failures of the prosecution to consider issues such as age assessment or referral through the NRM needs to be raised at the earliest point possible in proceedings.

---

29 See Chapters 5 and 6 viz expert evidence.
30 [2011] EWCA Crim 2226.
31 See also *R v LZ* [2012] EWCA Crim 1867 and *R v Y* [2015] EWCA Crim 123.

Plea before venue: decision upon jurisdiction

7.39

If a charge is summary only, the proceedings are in the magistrates' court. The ethos of magistrates' court proceedings is that they are speedy. Summary only offences are relatively minor and normally lead to no more than a short custodial penalty, at most. Because of these factors, trafficking and modern slavery indicators are often ignored or overlooked in magistrates' court proceedings. The CPS's trafficking and modern slavery legal guidance applies equally to summary offences, as it does to indictable offences.

Some common summary only offences that might raise MSA 2015 defences and trafficking/modern slavery indicators are set out in Chapter 15.

7.40

When preparing a case involving trafficking/modern slavery that concerns a summary only offence, consideration should be given to applying for a certificate for counsel from the magistrates' court, given the complexity of preparation that will be required. Asking for the matter to be reserved to a District Judge rather than a lay bench should also be considered.

Either way offences

7.41

In relation to an either way offence, for example a charge of cultivation of cannabis, the magistrates will need to consider the most appropriate venue for trial through the 'plea before venue' procedure. The defendant is asked to give an indication of plea. If there are still outstanding trafficking or modern slavery determinations to be made, then 'no indication' is advisable.

7.42

The Sentencing Council has issued a definitive sentencing guideline on venue/ allocation, in accordance with the Coroners and Justice Act 2009, s 122(2) 'Allocation Guideline'[32], which sets out:

'In general, either way offences should be tried summarily unless:

(a)   the outcome would clearly be a sentence in excess of the court's powers for the offence(s) concerned after taking into account personal mitigation and any potential reduction for a guilty plea;

---

32   Published by the Sentencing Council and to apply for all cases involving adults at the magistrates' court and children/young persons charged with adults dealt with post-1 March 2016.

(b)   for reasons of unusual legal, procedural or factual complexity, the case should be tried in the Crown Court. This exception may apply in cases where a very substantial fine is the likely sentence. Other circumstances where this exception will apply are likely to be rare and case specific; the court will rely on the submissions of the parties to identify relevant cases'.

Given the complexity of issues that often arise where there are indicators of trafficking, exploitation and modern slavery, the Crown Court is likely to be the more appropriate venue for trying these cases. Practitioners should be aware of the Allocation Guideline when making submissions concerning venue.

Crown Court

7.43

The first appearance at the Crown Court after a case has been sent is the Pre-Trial Preparation Hearing or 'PTPH', which should be listed within 28 days of the first appearance. An indictment should be received at least seven days before the PTPH hearing, and the principal parts of the prosecution case should be served on the defence no fewer than seven days before the PTPH. If these items have not been received, the Crown Court and prosecution should be notified in advance of the PTPH.

Completion of PTPH form

7.44

Within a PTPH form, issues such as abuse of process, dismissal, fitness to plead, severance, arraignment, trial issues, witness requirements, reporting restrictions and special measures all need to be considered.

7.45

If the client is outlining a defence that they have been a victim of trafficking or modern slavery, or if aspects of sexual exploitation arise, then early consideration needs to be given to seeking reporting restrictions and an anonymity direction for all pre-trial hearings and trial. See Chapter 8 for special measures.

Fitness to plead: Crown Court

7.46

Early recognition of any concerns as to fitness to plead and to stand trial is vital in trafficking cases. The usual process in criminal proceedings includes a stage where a defendant is invited to enter a plea, whether guilty or not guilty. Fitness to plead is governed by procedure under the Criminal Procedure (Insanity) Act 1964, supplemented by the Domestic Violence Crime and Victims Act 2004 and the Criminal Procedure Rules 2015, rr 25.9 and 25.10. The law on fitness to plead is intended to deal with defendants in criminal proceedings who lack sufficient ability to participate meaningfully in a trial because of their mental or physical condition. The intention is to balance the rights of a defendant with vulnerabilities as against the need to protect the public. The court is able to make findings of fact as part of the process. The Law Commission published a Consultation Paper on unfitness to plead ('CP197') in October 2010 and reported in 2016. They concluded that 'the current law in this area is outdated, inconsistently applied and can lead to unfairness'. They also expressed the 'significant concerns' raised by the 'current lack of an effective legal framework for addressing participation difficulties experienced by young defendants in the youth court'. Their recommendations for reform have not, so far, been adopted[33].

The current test for unfitness to plead

7.47

The current test for whether a person is unfit to plead was laid down in 1836[34] in three parts:

(i)   whether the defendant is mute of malice or not;

(ii)   whether he can plead to the indictment or not;

(iii)   whether he is of sufficient intellect to comprehend the course of proceedings on the trial, so as to make a proper defence. This would include an ability to challenge a juror, to comprehend the evidence and to put forward a defence to the allegations.

7.48

The burden is usually on the defence to establish, on the balance of probabilities, that the defendant is unfit to plead[35]. However, where the issue is raised by the prosecution, the burden must be discharged beyond a reasonable doubt[36]. Over the course of more than a century, this test has been the subject of further clarification as follows:

(i)   the test is not limited to the ability to enter a plea but depends on the ability or otherwise to follow a trial[37];

(ii)   an accused person can be unfit to plead, even if not clinically insane[38];

---

33   Law Commission *Unfitness to Plead Report 2016*, available at www.lawcom.gov.uk/wp-content/uploads/2016/01/lc364_unfitness_vol-1.pdf, last accessed 14 December 2017.
34   *R v Pritchard* (1836) 7 C & P 303.
35   *R v Robertson* [1968] 1 WLR 1767, [1968] 3 All ER 557.
36   *R v Podola* [1960] 1 QB 325, [1959] 3 All ER 418.
37   *R v Marcantonio* [2016] EWCA Crim 14, [2016] 2 Cr App Rep 81.
38   *Governor of Stafford Prison, ex p Emery* [1909] 2 KB 81, 73 JP 284.

(iii) that the defendant suffers from a diagnosed mental illness does not mean he is inevitably unfit to plead. An assessment of the *Pritchard* criteria is not dependent on diagnosis, although a significant impairment may be good evidence to support a finding of unfitness[39];

(iv) the defendant does not have to suffer from a diagnosed illness or disorder within the international classification of diseases in order to be unfit to follow proceedings. There may be a combination of factors[40];

(v) loss of memory does not amount to unfitness to plead, providing the defendant can follow the proceedings[41];

(vi) making bad decisions as a result of a mental illness does not mean the defendant is unable to follow a trial[42].

Fitness to plead procedure

7.49

Since this is a special plea, the Crown Court procedure dictates that the judge must decide fitness as soon as it arises, based on a 'rigorous examination' of available evidence as against the *Pritchard* criteria[43]. The judge makes this decision alone on the written or oral evidence of two or more registered medical practitioners, at least one of whom must have been approved by the Secretary of State as having special experience in the diagnosis and treatment of mental disorder[44].

7.50

Generally the issue of fitness to plead is decided before trial, although there are cases where it arises during the trial and before disposal, including in cases where a second procedure should have been conducted[45]. If it arises at any time after sentence the procedure does not apply, as the process is concluded[46]. If the defendant is found fit to plead, the trial proceeds in the usual way. Where a decision is made that a defendant is unfit to plead, the appointment of an advocate to put the case for the defendant is mandatory and will include an assessment of expertise, which, if the allegation is of trafficking or the defendant

---

39 *R v Berry* (1977) 66 Cr App Rep 156.
40 *R v Berry* ibid.
41 *R v Podola* [1960] 1 QB 325, [1959] 3 All ER 418; *R v Norman* [2008] EWCA Crim 1810, [2009] 1 Cr App Rep 192.
42 *R v Walls* [2011] EWCA Crim 443, [2011] 2 Cr App Rep 61.
43 *Marcantonio* [2016] EWCA Crim 14, [2016] 2 Cr App Rep 81; *R v Ghulam* [2009] EWCA Crim 2285, [2010] 1 WLR 891.
44 Domestic Violence, Crime and Victims Act 2004, s 22.
45 *R (on the application of Hasani) v Blackfriars Crown Court* [2005] EHWC 3016 (Admin), [2006] 1 All ER 817.
46 *R v Webb* [1969] 2 QB 278, [1969] 2 All ER 626; *R v Burles* [1970] 2 QB 191; *R v Grant* [2008] EWCA Crim 1890; *R v B* [2008] EWCA Crim 1997, [2009] 1 Cr App Rep 261; *R v Orr* [2016] EWCA Crim 889, [2016] 4 WLR 132.

is a victim of trafficking, might well include an assessment of the advocate's experience in trafficking cases[47]. There will then be a trial of the fact of the allegation. Where one defendant is unfit and a co-defendant is not, the court must decide whether or not they can be tried together[48].

Trial of the acts or omissions

7.51

Following a decision by a judge that a defendant is unfit to plead, it is then for a jury to decide whether the defendant did the act or omission alleged[49]. Usual rules of evidence apply, including in relation to hearsay and bad character[50]. The prosecution will be required to disprove issues such as self-defence, accident or mistake as these can be raised on objective evidence[51]. However, it is rarely necessary to prove the mental element unless the act includes some purposive element such as concealing criminal property or voyeurism[52]. It follows that the jury cannot consider diminished responsibility or loss of control as part of their decision on the acts or omissions of the accused[53]. The defendant does not put forward a positive defence or give evidence as he is unfit to do so, although in some circumstances a defendant's police interview may be relevant, subject to whether the defendant understood the caution or not and suitable warnings from the trial judge[54]. If a finding that an accused person is unfit to plead is later quashed by the Court of Appeal, it is not possible to substitute an alternative verdict or order a retrial[55].

7.52

The jury is not asked whether the defendant is guilty or not guilty. It is directed that it must be sure that the defendant 'did the act or made the omission charged against him as the offence'. If it is so satisfied it must find accordingly[56]. If not it must acquit the defendant[57]. The procedure is approached as a method for public protection not a trial, so Art 6 rights have been held not to apply[58].

---

47   Criminal Procedure Rules 2015, SI 2015/1490, rr 25.9 and 25.10.
48   *R v B* [2008] EWCA Crim 1997, [2009] 1 WLR 1545.
49   Criminal Procedure (Insanity) Act 1964, s 4A(2).
50   *R v Chal* [2007] EWCA Crim 2647, [2008] 1 Cr App Rep 247; *R v Creed* [2011] EWCA Crim 144, [2011] Crim LR 644.
51   *R v Wells* [2015] EWCA Crim 2, [2015] 1 WLR 2797.
52   *R v Antoine* [2001] AC 340, [2000] 2 WLR 703; *R v Grant* [2001] EWCA Crim 2611, [2002] QB 1030; *R (on the application of Young) v Central Criminal Court* [2002] EWHC 548 (Admin), [2002] 2 Cr App Rep 178; *R v B* [2012] EWCA Crim 770, [2012] 3 All ER 1093.
53   *R v Antoine* [2001] AC 340, [2000] 2 WLR 703.
54   *R v Swinbourne* [2013] EWCA Crim 2329, (2014) 178 JP 34.
55   *R v McKenzie* [2011] EWCA Crim 1550, [2011] 1 WLR 2807.
56   Criminal Procedure (Insanity) Act 1964, s 4A(2) and (3).
57   *R v McKenzie* [2011] EWCA Crim 1550, [2011] 1 WLR 2807; *R v Chal* [2007] EWCA Crim 2647, [2008] 1 Cr App Rep 247.
58   *R v M* [2002] EWCA Crim 2024, [2002] 1 WLR 824; *R v H* [2003] UKHL 1, [2003] 1 All ER 497.

Disposal rather than sentence

7.53

If a defendant who has been found unfit to plead is then found to have done the act or made the omission charged then the court's powers are limited by the Criminal Procedure (Insanity) Act 1964, s 5 to three orders, as follows:

(i) a hospital order pursuant to the Mental Health Act ('MHA') 1983, s 37 on the written or oral evidence of two medical practitioners, at least one of whom must have been approved by the Secretary of State as having special experience in the diagnosis and treatment of mental disorder. An interim order can be made pending the paperwork. In order to make a hospital order, the court must be satisfied on the evidence of the approved clinician who would be in charge of the offender that suitable arrangements have been made for admission and treatment. A hospital order can be made with a restriction on release pursuant to the MHA 1983, s 41 if the court is satisfied that a restriction is necessary for the protection of the public. A restriction is usually made without limit of time and continues if the patient is subject to conditional release as part of treatment[59];

(ii) a supervision order;

(iii) an absolute discharge.

Fitness to plead: magistrates' and youth courts

7.54

There is no test for unfitness to plead in the magistrates' court or the youth court, so fitness to plead is never specifically considered. As a consequence this will mean that case preparation will not routinely include obtaining the types of assessments that would be required under the fitness to plead procedure in the Crown Court. If a defendant is unable effectively to participate in the trial process, this will affect the fairness of proceedings and could affect the welfare of any child defendant[60].

Abuse of process and fitness to plead

7.55

Where the defendant lacks capacity and is a victim of trafficking, representatives can and should deploy the abuse of process procedure to seek to stay any charges

---

59 *R v Blackwood* (1974) 59 Cr App Rep 170; *R v Lincolnshire (Kesteven) Justices, ex p O'Connor* [1983] 1 All ER 901; *R v Barker* [2002] EWCA Crim 1508, [2003] 1 Cr App Rep (S) 212; *R v Khelifi* [2006] EWCA Crim 770, [2006] 2 Cr App Rep (S) 650; *R v Vowles* [2015] 2 Cr App Rep (S) 39; *R v Turner* [2015] EWCA Crim 1249; *R v Marshall* [2015] EWCA Crim 474.

60 Children and Young Persons Act 1933, s 44.

on the basis that the accused cannot receive a fair trial. This process has been used successfully at appellate level[61]. Whilst the use of abuse of process in the lower courts is an exceptional remedy, rarely utilised, the appellate courts have set a benchmark in the context of slavery and trafficking and the lower courts should follow this line of authority. The approach of the appellate courts has been to quash convictions after it has been held that it was not in the public interest to prosecute a victim of trafficking. If evidence is available that the defendant is a victim of trafficking, even where there is no specific defence, it may well be appropriate to argue that the charges should be discontinued, and, if not, stayed as an abuse of the process of the court, to enable the defendant to be diverted to protection through the appropriate referral mechanisms. It is axiomatic that unfit defendants who are also victims of trafficking should not face a trial process unless it is in the public interest for them to be tried. The processes that have developed in the Crown Court and in the appellate courts ought to steer the lower courts to ensure the process is fair[62].

7.56

Aside from using the abuse of process procedure, the Law Commission's Unfitness to Plead Project is a useful resource. It exposed significant concerns over the inadequacies of the procedures to address unfitness to plead in the magistrates' and youth courts and the continuing need for better protection for defendants who lack capacity to engage in the trial process. Despite these observations, there has been no legislative change in this regard, it may well be helpful for advocates to refer to the Law Commission recommendations in making submissions in the youth court either on abuse of process or on alternative arrangements to accommodate a victim of trafficking who is also a defendant, where that defendant lacks capacity.

7.57

The following, taken from the Law Commission summary, may be of assistance in simplifying and streamlining proceedings as a matter of case management to ensure a defendant who is a victim of trafficking lacking capacity is not tried at all. If the defendant is tried, it should ensure that the trial process is fair and accommodates any vulnerabilities, or that the defendant is diverted away from the criminal justice system through referral mechanisms[63]:

'1.14 At the heart of our recommendations lies our belief that the normal criminal trial is the optimum process where a defendant faces

---

61 *R v Joseph* [2017] EWCA Crim 36, [2017] 1 WLR 3153; *R v LM* [2010] EWCA Crim 2327, [2011] 1 Cr App Rep 135; *R v N; R v L* [2012] EWCA Crim 189, [2013] QB 379 and *R v L* [2013] EWCA Crim 991, [2014] 1 All ER 113.

62 *CPS v P* [2008] 4 All ER 628 and see M Bevan, *Unfit To Plead in the Magistrates' and Youth Courts?*, available at www.criminallawandjustice.co.uk/features/Unfit-Plead-Magistrates-and-Youth-Courts.

63 Law Commission 2016, *Unfitness to Plead Summary*, available at www.lawcom.gov.uk/wp-content/uploads/2016/01/lc364_unfitness_summary_English.pdf, last accessed 14 December 2017.

an allegation in our criminal justice system. We consider that full trial is best not just for the defendant, but also for those affected by an offence and society more generally. This is because the full criminal process engages fair trial guarantees for all those involved, under article 6 of the European Convention on Human Rights ("ECHR"), and allows robust and transparent analysis of all the elements of the offence and any defence advanced. It also offers the broadest range of outcomes in terms of sentence and other ancillary orders.

1.15 Removing any defendant from that full trial process should, we consider, only be undertaken as a last resort. The decision to adopt alternative procedures should be made with great caution and only where it is in the best interests of the defendant, because he or she lacks the capacity to participate effectively in his or her trial. We consider that every effort should be made to afford a defendant whose capacity may be in doubt such adjustments to the proceedings as he or she reasonably requires to be able to participate in the full criminal process, and to maintain that capacity for the whole of the process. However, we do acknowledge that a very small number of defendants will never have the capacity to participate effectively in a trial.

1.16 We consider that the most important element of a framework to address issues of unfitness to plead is a legal test which accurately and efficiently identifies those defendants who, even considering available adjustments to trial, have such impairments in their ability to participate in proceedings that they could not fairly be tried ... We also consider it essential that those who, although unable to engage with the full trial process, have sufficient understanding and decision-making capacity to enter a plea of guilty, should be enabled to do so.

1.17 Assessment of such defendants is currently a time-consuming process and in some cases three or more expert reports are prepared, generally by psychiatrists or psychologists, before a defendant is found unfit to plead. The current arrangements often lead to substantial delays, causing uncertainty and anxiety to complainants, witnesses and the defendant. We consider that arrangements can be made to streamline this process, saving time and precious resources, without compromising the robustness or fairness of the outcome.

1.18 Following a finding by the court that a defendant lacks the capacity to participate effectively in the full criminal process, we take the view that the court should have the option not to embark on the alternative procedures for scrutinising the allegation. We have in mind, in particular, cases where a disposal imposed by the court is not necessary to protect the public, or to support the individual to avoid future concerning behaviour, and where it is concluded that it is not in the public interest for any further criminal hearing on the matter. We take this position because any procedure which protects the interests of the vulnerable individual, but appropriately scrutinises the allegation in order to justify imposing disposals on that individual, will inevitably be complex, and demanding of jurors, witnesses and defendants alike. In addition, such alternative procedures cannot result in conviction, because the defendant who cannot participate effectively is unable properly to defend him- or herself. As a result, the disposals available to the court are inevitably limited, and cannot involve punishment of the defendant.

1.19 For many individuals who are unfit to plead, the low level of seriousness of the original allegation and the arrangements which can be made in the community, without the court's intervention, mean that further action by a criminal court is unnecessary. We therefore recommend that diversion of such individuals out of the criminal justice system, once they have been found to lack capacity for trial, should be available where the court is satisfied that such an approach is in the interests of justice'.

Disposal of defendants suffering from a mental disorder

7.58

Although there is no system to decide unfitness to plead in the lower courts, there is a system for disposal for those defendants suffering from a mental disorder. This does not apply to those with developmental or intellectual issues or significant immaturity. In limited circumstances, under the MHA 1983, s 37(3), if the defendant is charged with an imprisonable offence and s/he is found to have done the act or made the omission as alleged, and s/he is suffering from a treatable mental disorder as defined by the Mental Health Act 1983, the summary court can impose a hospital order or a guardianship order (if the person is over 16).

7.59

The same requirements apply for reporting by medical practitioners, including at least one approved by the Secretary of State as having special experience in the diagnosis and treatment of mental disorder. The court can adjourn for the necessary medical reports to be prepared[64]. Given the limited sentencing options for summary-only offences, the irresistible inference is that vulnerable children and young people will choose to be sentenced rather than seek a disposal for treatment which may last a significantly longer period of time.

---

64   Powers of the Criminal Courts (Sentencing) Act 2000, s 11.

The role of expert evidence

7.60

In addition to evidence of abuse or injury, and other generally recognised areas of science and technology commonly adduced in the criminal courts, there are two areas which may well require expert evidence in cases involving victims of trafficking. This includes evidence of age[65] and evidence of how a trafficking gang and/or trafficker(s) might operate by reference to particular country or criminal practices[66]. In relation to age, it is generally accepted that children who are non-British victims of trafficking will not necessarily have any correct identifying documents, some may not know their exact age, others will have been told to lie. When age is not clear, the presumption is that the person is under 18[67], although courts are expected to make due enquiry using any available documentation, fingerprint record and oral evidence, including any expert assessment. A declaration as to age by a court is then regarded as the true age. However, see Chapter 3 in respect of the due process to be adopted in establishing age[68].

7.61

The mode of operation of a trafficking gang and the effect on the conduct of a victim may be an issue for expert evidence as, although prevalent, it is complex and highly likely to be outside the experience of a reasonable jury[69]. Care must be taken for the expert to provide expert evidence on the mode of operation of gangs in the factual context of the case, but the expert should not trespass into providing an opinion on the credibility of a defendant. Expert evidence is to be preferred over and above a 'myths direction' although it may also be helpful, particularly in cases involving sexual exploitation, for a judicial direction to deal with common misconceptions[70].

7.62

If the defence is raised that the defendant acted as a victim of trafficking, the consideration of whether 'a reasonable person in the same situation as the defendant and having the defendant's relevant characteristics would have no realistic alternative to doing that act' could, again require expert evidence.

---

65 See *R (on the application of A) v London Borough of Croydon, R (on the application of M) v London Borough of Lambeth* [2009] UKSC 8 in the context of housing. See also the CPS policy for prosecuting cases of human trafficking, available at www.cps.gov.uk/publications/docs/policy_for_prosecuting_cases_of_human_trafficking.pdf, last accessed 14 December 2017.

66 *R v Allad* [2014] EWCA Crim 421 evidence on the mode of operation of a carousel fraud. For forms of trafficking and expert evidence see, for example, Office for Victims of Crime Training and Technical Assistance Center, *Human Trafficking Task Force e-guide*, available at www.ovcttac.gov/taskforceguide/eguide/, last accessed 14 December 2017.

67 ECAT, Art 10.

68 Children and Young Persons Act 1933, s 99 and Magistrates' Courts Act 1980, s 150.

69 *R (on the application of AB) v Secretary of State for the Home Department* [2015] EWHC 1490 (Admin).

70 CPS, *Guidance on Rape and Sexual Offences and Societal Myths*, available at www.cps.gov.uk/legal/p_to_r/rape_and_sexual_offences/societal_myths/, last accessed 14 December 2017.

Again, care should be taken to ensure that the scope of the expert's instructions is appropriate. The 'relevant characteristics' are defined as 'age, sex and any physical or mental illness or disability', which must mean that the 'reasonable person' becomes the 'reasonable trafficking victim' in the given circumstances. Once the defence is raised, it will be a matter for the Crown to disprove it, although the burden of producing evidence of what was reasonable will be primarily for the defendant and it may require very particular expert evidence which might include regional trafficking reports[71].

Adducing expert evidence

7.63

Adducing expert evidence is dealt with in Part 19 of the Criminal Practice Direction (CPD). It is the duty of an expert to help the court to achieve the overriding objective that justice should be achieved[72]. This duty overrides the duty owed to the party providing the instructions or payment[73]. An 'expert' is described as 'a person who is required to give or prepare expert evidence for the purpose of criminal proceedings, including evidence required to determine fitness to plead or for the purpose of sentencing'[74]. Expert evidence is opinion evidence which must be objective and unbiased, and within the expert's area or areas of expertise[75].

7.64

Human trafficking indicators are many and varied and likely to be outside the experience of a jury and the judiciary. Expert evidence will need to be relevant to the particular case in hand, but much assistance can be provided by the material produced by the UN Office on Drugs and Crime as follows (the full table can be found in Chapter 2[76]).

Admissibility of expert evidence

7.65

In order to be admissible, expert opinion evidence must be relevant to the issue which the court is called upon to decide[77]. This essentially means it must

---

71 S Bird and P Southwell, 'Does the new "Slavery" Defence Offer Victims of Trafficking any Greater Protection?' (2015) 9 *Archbold Review* 7, available at www.archbolde-update.co.uk/PDF/2015/Archbold%209-15%20v%208%20press.pdf, last accessed 14 December 2017.
72 Criminal Procedure Rules 2015, r 19.2.
73 *The Ikarian Reefer* [1993] 2 Lloyds Rep 68; *R v Harris* [2005] EWCA Crim 1980.
74 Criminal Procedure Rules 2015, r 19.1.
75 Criminal Procedure Rules 2015, r 19.2.
76 UNODC, *HT Indicators Infographic*, available at www.unodc.org/pdf/HT_indicators_E_LOWRES.pdf, last accessed 14 December 2017.
77 *O'Brien v Chief Constable of South Wales Police* [2005] UKHL 26 at para 3.

be logically probative or dis-probative of some matter which requires proof[78]. A competent expert can only provide opinion evidence which is outside the knowledge and experience of the court[79] where there is a reliable scientific basis for the opinion[80]. Reports must comply with the Criminal Procedure Rules 2015, r 19.4 giving detail of the expert's 'qualifications, relevant experience and accreditation' and setting out the basis of the opinion[81]. Experts may give opinion evidence on the ultimate issue in a criminal trial but juries are directed that they are not bound to accept it. The exercise is not for the judgement of the expert but for the expert to provide material to enable the jury to reach their own conclusions to the requisite standard[82]. It may be possible, in some circumstances for an expert to give opinion evidence on the consistency of an account of a defendant relating to the circumstances of his trafficking situation; but the expert should remember his duty to the court and not simply proffer an opinion on an applicant's credibility without exploring areas of possible inconsistency[83].

7.66

Expert evidence which may not be admissible during a criminal trial may, however, still assist the competent authority in reaching trafficking identification decisions. It is important that evidence in support of a defendant's trafficking claim is submitted to the competent authority, such as medical reports, independent trafficking reports and reports from the specialist support provider or first responder.

7.67

It should be borne in mind that because of the way in which prosecutorial discretion is exercised (the prosecutor may consider evidence which would not be admissible in a criminal court) expert evidence might also be admissible in the context of an application to stay proceedings on the ground of abuse of process when it would not be admissible in a criminal trial.

7.68

Expert evidence may also assist the court when considering pre-trial applications such as severance, special measures and applications to move proceedings. Funding for prior authority for such reports should be applied for as soon possible after the first appearance.

---

78   Per Lord Simon of Glaisdale in *DPP v Kilbourne* [1973] AC 729.
79   Crim PD, 19 A.1.
80   *R v Dlugosz* [2013] EWCA Crim 2.
81   *R v H* [2014] EWCA Crim 1555, para [44].
82   *R v Pora* [2015] UKPC 9, [2016] 1 Cr App Rep 48.
83   See *R v Joseph* [2017] EWCA Crim 36 above, at para [67].

Indictment and severance

7.69

It may well be that a client has been advised to use an alias name. Ensure that the client's name has been correctly spelt and that the correct name is used on the indictment, if an alias name has been used.

7.70

If a defendant is charged with others, and there are indicators of trafficking/ modern slavery, careful consideration needs to be given to whether the defendant has or might have been charged with individuals responsible for trafficking/ exploiting them, exerting a form of control over them or is linked to the network responsible for his exploitation. In these circumstances an application for severance would in normal circumstances be raised at the PTPH and made as soon as possible. The Criminal Procedure Rules 2015, r 3.21 outlines that the application must be served as soon as practicable after becoming aware of the grounds for doing so, and that such an application has to be served on the court and each of the other parties.

7.71

The Indictments Act 1915, s 5 gives a discretion to the court to order severance. In circumstances where a defence of slavery is being raised and an allegation of slavery is being made against a co-defendant it is advisable to request a separate listing for mention to address pre-trial issues and applications without the co-defendant or his legal representative present.

7.72

Judges have detailed guidance from the Judicial College about how to deal with any suggestion that a defendant has been trafficked. If the NRM has not already been triggered, then the judge should adjourn for this to happen. Those representing the defendant should be aware of the risks to the defendant once the premise for severance has been disclosed – the safety of the defendant in custody needs to be ascertained and if necessary safeguarding measures adopted in prison if the defendant is detained in the same prison estate as either his co-defendants or others connected to the organised criminal network. Safeguarding issues should be raised with the court and prison service if the remand prison is the same, to avoid the victim defendant and co-defendant being transported to and from court together. Other protective measures could be sought for those on bail, such as non-contact with the co-defendant. If an application to sever is unsuccessful, other practical considerations should be made, such as how a defendant who is a victim of trafficking/slavery is produced at court, requesting that a dock officer sit between the defendants. In general, the Court of Appeal will interfere with the exercise of discretion for a refusal of severance as a ground of appeal, only if it can be shown that the trial judge took into account irrelevant considerations, ignored relevant issues and/or arrived at a manifestly unreasonable decision[84].

Arraignment

7.73

If at arraignment no reasonable grounds decision that the defendant is a victim of trafficking has been received from the competent authority, then arraignment should be postponed pending this decision. It should be submitted that full credit for a guilty plea should be retained until after that decision has been made. The reason for this is that:

> 'the decision of the competent authority as to whether a person had been trafficked for the purposes of exploitation is not binding on the court but, unless there was evidence to contradict it or significant evidence that had not been considered, it is likely that the criminal courts will abide by the decision'[85].

Defence statements

7.74

A defendant should[86] serve a defence statement 28 days after the disclosure of the material from the prosecution at Stage 1 of the Crown Court proceedings. Under the Criminal Procedure and Investigations Act 1996, s 6A, the defence statement should set out:

- the nature of the defence;

- what matters of fact they take issue with the Crown upon;

- why they take issue with it;

- any matters of fact they rely upon;

- any point of law, including any point as to the admissibility of evidence or an abuse of process, which he wishes to take;

- if an alibi is to be relied upon, details of it.

7.75

If abuse of process is a matter which may be raised, it should be set out as a potential issue within the defence statement. If, at the stage of serving a defence

---

84   *R v Moghal* (1977) 65 Cr App Rep 56.
85   *R v Joseph* [2017] EWCA Crim 36, above, para [28].
86   Criminal Procedure and Investigation Act 1996 (Defence Disclosure Time Limits) Regulation 2011, SI 2011/209 (in force from 28 February 2011).

of the authorities investigating the matter or any delay in referral to the NRM, that submissions opposing an extension of the custody time limits are made on this basis.

Bad character applications

7.81

The Crown may seek to introduce bad character against a defendant under the provisions of the Criminal Justice Act 2003, s 101.

7.82

One of the aspects of re-trafficking is that a person can be continually moved from different locations and in addition, even post-sentence, may be at risk of being re-trafficked. It is not uncommon in the sphere of trafficking and modern slavery for an individual to have unchallenged previous convictions that are in fact unsafe convictions or TICs.

7.83

One aspect to consider if the Crown are seeking to introduce 'bad character' is whether, in fact, the bad character allegations assist in illustrating previous exploitation. The provisions of the Criminal Justice Act 2003, s 101(1) govern the test for admissibility of bad character relating to a defendant. This sets out the provisions for admissibility as being:

'(a) all parties to the proceedings agree to the evidence being admissible,

(b) the evidence is adduced by the defendant himself or is given in answer to a question asked by him in cross-examination and intended to elicit it,

(c) it is important explanatory evidence,

(d) it is relevant to an important matter in issue between the defendant and the prosecution,

(e) it has substantial probative value in relation to an important matter in issue between the defendant and a co-defendant,

(f) it is evidence to correct a false impression given by the defendant, or

(g) the defendant has made an attack on another person's character.'

7.84

Aspects that should be considered when seeking to exclude any bad character are:

- Criminal Justice Act 2003, s 101(3): this provides that the court must not admit evidence under s 101(1)(d) or (g) if, on an application by the

211

defendant to exclude it, it appears to the court that the admission of the evidence would have such an adverse effect on the fairness of the proceedings that the court ought not to admit it;

- consideration should be given to how long ago the bad character subject matter was: see Criminal Justice Act 2003, s 101(4);

- in addition, it will be critical to examine in cases of a disputed age assessment whether or not the age assessments were lawfully made at the time of the convictions (ie not vitiated by a public law error: see Chapter 3).

Trial issues

7.85

When, post any conclusive grounds decision and abuse argument, might there still be a need for a trial? If a conclusive decision is negative, it does not mean that a defendant is unable to advance an MSA 2015, s 45 defence. The evidence will be independently assessed by the jury in the Crown Court or by the magistrates' court. However, the conclusive grounds decision is likely to be a good indicator of the merits of such a defence succeeding. It is therefore imperative that upon service of a negative identification decision (either reasonable grounds or conclusive grounds) advice is sought by counsel specialising in judicial review of these identification decisions, to advise whether there are grounds to challenge the identification decision in the Administrative Court (see Chapter 2).

7.86

Following a negative conclusive grounds decision, or a positive conclusive grounds decision where the prosecution has decided to proceed with a prosecution on evidential and public interest grounds, trafficking/slavery can and should still remain in issue at trial if, for example, a defence of duress or a defence under the MSA 2015, s 45 is advanced.

7.87

Initial witness requirements should be provided by the defence at the date of PTPH. A final list of witness requirements should normally be provided at stage 2 of the criminal proceedings in the Crown Court: on the same date as service of the defence statement.

7.88

One of the critical witnesses to require may well be the Officer in the Case, if there remain issues about the failure to investigate the trafficking/modern day slavery status or background position of the defendant. The College of Policing Guidance highlights that it is:

'the duty of a local police force (the primary legislative agency) to begin an investigation as soon as they believe a modern slavery crime may have been committed, regardless of whether a victim makes an allegation, whether a report is made, or whether consent to be entered into the national referral mechanism is provided or refused. A modern day slavery crime MUST NOT be approached as an employment or immigration issue at this stage'.

Questioning of the officer in the case

7.89

There may well be questions as to the following aspects of the case:

- whether there had been any consideration of trafficking or modern slavery pre-arrest in the pre-planning stages undertaken by the police, including the potential recovery of victims during the police operation (for instance, there are often pre-planning briefings when cannabis farms are raided on a large scale);

- surveillance of the property that may establish that the defendant never left the property or there was limited movement from the property under escort;

- whether there had been any consideration by the police of trafficking or modern slavery indicators at the point of the arrest of the defendant;

- evidence of an organised crime network, in which the defendant was clearly very low in the hierarchy and whether the police had actively analysed this evidence;

- whether there were any investigations into the telephones held by the defendant where it is alleged that the trafficker regularly contacted the defendant by telephone as a method of control;

- whether the defendant was interviewed, when a suspect, as a possible victim of trafficking or modern slavery;

- the stage at which an NRM referral was made;

- whether an NRM referral resulted in a crime record being set up (NB: this would contravene Home Office counting rules);

- if no crime record was created, confirmation as to why one had not been made[90];

- investigation of others linked to the address, or set out as having controlled the defendant.

---

90   See the strategic plan of Anti Slavery Commissioner 2015.

7.90

There are policing trafficking experts[91] who may be able to provide valuable expert evidence on what indicators of trafficking the police should have been alive to during the police operation and/or arrest and interview. The expert may also be able to evaluate the efficacy of the investigation into the trafficking of the defendant as undertaken by the police. This expert evidence can assist when cross examining the police, mounting an abuse of process submission and an MSA 2015, s 45 defence.

Exclusion of interview

7.91

If the police interview took place without an appropriate adult in place, and the defendant is considered to be a child or young person under 18, then it may be that exclusion of the police interview is appropriate, for example, under the Police and Criminal Evidence Act 1984, ss 78 and / or 76 and the PACE Code provisions, in particular, Code C.

Adverse inferences from failure to mention facts in police interview

7.92

Under the Criminal Justice and Public Order Act 1994, s 34, there is a power that exists to allow a jury to draw an adverse inference if an individual fails to mention facts that they later come to rely on in their defence. Such an adverse inference applies both to questions asked by an officer under caution pre-charge, or post-charge instances (such as within a police interview). Section 34(1) entails that such facts which 'in the circumstances existing at the time' the defendant 'could reasonably have been expected to mention.'

7.93

The prosecution and defence should consider before the start of the trial whether an adverse inference should be sought by the prosecution where there are background issues of trafficking and modern slavery. Where an individual has faced difficult circumstances of exploitation, coercion or is in fear of authority figures such as police or UK Border Agency staff, there may be reasons why an individual did not set out details of his full background circumstances or raise the MSA 2015 defence within the police interview or post-caution (see Chapter 2 re late disclosure).

---

91 Normally these are ex-detectives who were involved in high-profile trafficking and organised crime investigations.

7.94

In *R v Argent*[92] Lord Bingham highlighted that 'in the circumstances' should not be construed restrictively when assessing the application of s 34. Lord Bingham said:

> 'The time referred to is the time of questioning, and account must be taken of all the relevant circumstances existing at that time. The courts should not construe the expression "in the circumstances" restrictively: matters such as time of day, the defendant's age, experience, mental capacity, state of health, sobriety, tiredness, knowledge, personality and legal advice are all part of the relevant circumstances; and those are only examples of things which may be relevant. When reference is made to "the accused" attention is directed not to some hypothetical, reasonable accused of ordinary phlegm and fortitude but to the actual accused with such qualities, apprehensions, knowledge and advice as he is shown to have had at the time.
>
> Like so many other questions in criminal trials this is a question to be resolved by the jury in the exercise of their collective common-sense, experience and understanding of human nature. Sometimes they may conclude that it was reasonable for the defendant to have held his peace for reasons, such as, that he was tired, ill, frightened, drunk, drugged, unable to understand what was going on, suspicious of the police, afraid that his answer would not be fairly recorded, worried at committing himself without legal advice, acting on legal advice, or some other reason accepted by the jury.
>
> … This is an issue on which the judge may, and usually should, give appropriate directions. But he should ordinarily leave the issue to the jury to decide.'

7.95

Where the prosecution seeks an adverse inference direction under s 34 in the context of a defendant who contends that he is a victim of exploitation, the circumstances of the defendant's arrest and the demeanour of the defendant at the time of interview may be relevant matters to consider when questioning witnesses at trial, including officers present at the defendant's arrest and the defendant himself. In addition, this evidence may be the legitimate province of expert psychological, psychiatric or, trafficking evidence.

7.96

Further, consideration should be given to the state of health and/or fitness for interview of any defendant recovered in cannabis farms. The policing

---

92   [1997] 2 Cr App Rep 27.

guidance[93] clearly sets out the high levels of toxicity in premises modified for cannabis cultivation, which will have an impact on any individual exposed to this toxicity. As good practice any individual recovered in such premises should be evaluated by a Forensic Medical Examiner to ensure fitness to be interviewed.

Defendant giving evidence

7.97

There may be a real concern in a case where a defendant has a background of being subjected to trafficking or modern slavery exploitation about his ability to give evidence at trial. Special measures are addressed in Chapter 8.

7.98

A psychologist or psychiatrist might appropriately be instructed to provide an opinion on the ability of the defendant to give evidence, and, in particular, whether any adjustments to the trial process should be made (for example the defendant not sitting in the dock, the use of an intermediary or a greater number of breaks, etc): see Chapter 8.

7.99

Account needs to be taken of language needs, which may be overcome by use of an interpreter. Also, any learning difficulties or literacy issues a defendant may have should be addressed. An intermediary will usually be able to assist with this.

7.100

It is important at an early stage of proceedings to gauge the educational background of a defendant in his home country. It may well impact on the style of questions asked of a defendant and also the ability to understand questions and assimilate documents or schedules.

Pre-sentencing application to vacate a guilty plea

7.101

If, after a guilty plea but before sentence, it becomes apparent that an individual was a victim of trafficking/modern slavery, or had a defence

---

93   National Policing Improvement Agency, *Practical Advice on Tackling Commercial Cannabis Cultivation and Head Shops*, available at www.the-ata.org.uk/downloads/Cannabis_Cultivation_R.pdf, last accessed 14 December 2017.

available under the MSA 2015, s 45, but this was unknown to him for a good reason, then it might be appropriate for a court to entertain an application to vacate the guilty plea.

7.102

A defendant may apply at any time before sentence to vacate his plea of guilty, and it is for the court to decide whether justice requires that that should be permitted[94].

The Criminal Procedure Rules 2015, r 25.5 states that a party must apply in writing to both the Crown and the court 'as soon as practicable after becoming aware of the grounds for doing so'.

7.103

The principles, as set out within *DPP v Revitt*[95], were that

'it is likely to be appropriate to permit the withdrawal of an unequivocal plea of guilty if it becomes apparent that the defendant did not appreciate the elements of the offence to which he was pleading, or if it becomes apparent that the facts relied upon by the prosecution do not add up to the offence charged.'

7.104

The application must set out the following matters (see Criminal Procedure Rules 2015, r 25.5.3):

(i)   why it would be unjust for the guilty plea to remain unchanged;

(ii)   what, if any, evidence the applicant wishes to call;

(iii)   identify any proposed witness;

(iv)   indicate whether legal professional privilege is waived, specifying any material name and date.

Sentencing

7.105

When a victim of trafficking is convicted of an offence the background of trafficking, modern slavery or exploitation will be key to mitigation. A defendant may not have acted under duress, may not be able to rely on the MSA 2015, s 45 to provide him with a defence, and may not be able to cause the prosecution to

---

94   *S (an infant) v Manchester City Recorder* [1971] AC 481.
95   [2006] EWHC 2266 (Admin), [2006] 1 WLR 3172.

discontinue the case in the public interest. These are all issues which should be considered in the criminal proceedings (see above). Nevertheless, a defendant may still be a victim of exploitation or trafficking and the facts of that will self-evidently comprise mitigation.

7.106

The significance of such mitigation is exemplified in *R v N; R v L*[96]. There, sentences of an 18-month detention and training order and 20 months' detention in a Young Offender Institution were imposed in the separate cases in the Crown Court. They were reduced to a four-month DTO and 12 months' custody respectively: see [93] and [113].

7.107

In *R v L*[97] (where the judgment was again given by Lord Judge CJ) the court emphasised that where trafficking victims commit offences that are unconnected with their trafficking status, the facts of the trafficking can still amount to mitigation:

'These defendants are not safeguarded from prosecution or punishment for offences which were unconnected with the fact that they were being or have been trafficked, although we do not overlook that the fact that they have been trafficked may sometimes provide substantial mitigation.'

This spectrum of culpability was again highlighted when the court said that 'due allowance [was] to be made in the sentencing decision for their diminished culpability' (at [33]). This can be contrasted by those cases where the 'fact that the defendant was a victim of trafficking will provide no more than a colourable excuse for criminality which is unconnected to and does not arise from their victimisation.'

7.108

For many offences, Sentencing Guidelines apply. Section 125(1) of the Coroners and Justice Act 2009 provides[98]:

'Every court—

(a) must, in sentencing an offender, follow any sentencing guideline which is relevant to the offender's case, and

(b) must, in exercising any other function relating to the sentencing of offenders, follow any sentencing guidelines which are relevant to the exercise of the function,

---

96   [2012] EWCA Crim 189, [2012] 1 Cr App Rep 35, Judge LCJ giving the judgment of the Court.
97   [2013] EWCA Crim 991, [2014] 1 All ER 113 at para [14].
98   Offences committed after 6 April 2010.

Unless the court is satisfied that it would be contrary to the interests of justice to do so.'

7.109

A judge will need to determine the appropriate classification of an offence, in terms of the 'category of harm' and in addition the 'culpability demonstrated by the offender's role'. As highlighted by *R v L*[99], the backdrop of trafficking and modern slavery is pertinent to the issue of culpability.

7.110

Typical factors highlighting a lesser role (such as those in the drugs sentencing guideline) overlap with some of the issues that face those who have been subject to a backdrop of trafficking/exploitation:

- performs a limited function under direction;

- engaged by pressure, coercion, intimidation;

- involvement through naivety/exploitation;

- no influence on those above in a chain.

7.111

In the Sentencing Council Definitive Guideline on Drug Offences there is specific provision for the imposition of more lenient sentences on individuals who are properly characterised as drug mules, ie those who have been exploited by gangs and criminals heavily involved in the drugs trade[100].

7.112

The first question for the sentencing court to resolve will be whether there is evidence to support the submission that the defendant was a victim of trafficking on the relevant occasion and acting under the control of traffickers when he committed the offence[101].

7.113

In principle, the courts should consider non-punishment or reduced punishment having regard to the obligations under ECAT, Art 26 so there can be greater consideration of absolute or conditional discharges, community penalties or suspended sentences.

7.114

Sentencing outcomes will depend on the nature of the offence charged, which sentencing guidelines apply, including the guideline on a reduction for a guilty

---

99 [2013] EWCA Crim 991, [2014] 1 All ER 113.
100 So that the starting point was reduced from 10 years to 6 years.
101 *R v Khalifa* [2016] EWCA Crim 1967.

plea and guidelines on sentencing children. There is no Sentencing Council guideline which deals with victims of trafficking who commit a crime while they are victims (save in the context of drugs mules)[102]. It is also worth noting that powers under the Serious Organised Crime and Police Act 2005 provide immunity from prosecution or sentence discounts for those who co-operate with the authorities. Sentencing judges should take into account the age of the defendant when he became involved in the enterprise, the level of participation and the level of exploitation, taking a structured approach to the victims' relative involvement and culpability.[103]

7.115

More broadly, courts should consider the following: victims of trafficking are necessarily the subjects of duress, coercion or compulsion even where such a dominant force does not amount to a defence. Where such a defence is not available, for sentencing purposes, the influence of others in the commission of a crime may give rise to relevant mitigation. In particular, where that influence causes a defendant to be the subject of conduct amounting or akin to slavery or servitude, and/or where the individual may have been subject to oppression[104], material mitigation will be present. When considering mitigation in the context of exploitation it is helpful to consider the criteria used to sentence a *perpetrator* of offences of trafficking, slavery or servitude. In the same way that aggravating features of such an offence will increase the culpability of a defendant who is to be sentenced for trafficking offences, those aggravating features will serve to mitigate the criminal conduct of a victim of exploitation/trafficking[105]. In the same way, aggravating features of sexual offending are focused in part on victim vulnerability[106]. Whereas, when an offender has a particular vulnerability, this will amount to a mitigating factor.

7.116

A practical approach to mitigation on behalf of a victim of trafficking who has committed an offence is to consider the elements of the criminal offence of coercive control; see the Serious Crime Act 2015, s 76. The essential elements of the offence set out features of a trafficker or exploiter's criminal behaviour. Those elements may be looked at from the other end of the telescope as mitigating features of a trafficking victim's behaviour:

- is the coercion the product of repeated or 'continuous' (sic): continual/ continuing behaviour towards the defendant?

---

102 Sentencing Council Guideline for Drug Offenders, available at www.sentencingcouncil.org. uk/wp-content/uploads/Drug_Offences_Definitive_Guideline_final_web1.pdf and see www. sentencingcouncil.org.uk/news/item/courts-issued-with-new-guideline-for-sentencing-drug-offenders/, both last accessed 11 January 2018.

103 *R v N; R v L* [2012] EWCA Crim 189, [2013] QB 379.

104 *R v SK* [2011] EWCA Crim 1691, [2012] 1 All ER 1090.

105 *R v N; R v L* [2012] EWCA Crim 189, [2013] QB 379 .

106 *A-G's Reference (No 126 of 2014) (Jumale)* [2015] 1 Cr App Rep (S) 65.

- is the coercing person/exploiter personally connected to the defendant (ie do they live together as members of the same family or have they previously been in an intimate personal relationship with each other)?

- has the behaviour had a serious effect on the defendant?

- did the exploiter know or ought he to have known that the behaviour would have a serious effect on the defendant?

7.117

Further it is a useful to look at the following components of coercive behaviour when sentencing victims of trafficking who commit crime[107]. Coercive behaviour is a continuing act or a pattern of acts of assault, threats, humiliation and intimidation or other abuse that is used to harm, punish or frighten the victim and can capture a wide range of behaviour including isolation, monitoring, controlling movement, financial abuse, threats and force, including where it causes child neglect. The behaviour does not have to have occurred within a domestic setting, eg the home. The victim can be monitored by phone or social media from a distance.

7.118

Under sentencing guidelines for young offenders, immaturity may be as important as chronological age[108]. However, when a young person has committed a serious offence, immaturity when balanced against age may not result in a reduced sentence[109].

7.119

Following conviction and sentence, victims of trafficking may face a number of potential ancillary orders, including:

- deportation;

- confiscation;

- compensation;

- slavery and trafficking reparation orders: orders requiring the persons against whom they are made to pay compensation to the victim of a relevant offence for any harm resulting from that offence: MSA 2015, s 8;

- forfeiture and detention of vehicles, ships or aircraft: this applies to vehicles used or intended to be used in connection with an offence: see MSA 2015, ss 11 and 12;

---

107 F Gerry and L Harris, *Women in Prison: Is the Justice System Fit For Purpose* (Lexis Nexis, 2016), available at http://blogs.lexisnexis.co.uk/halsburyslawexchange/wp-content/uploads/sites/25/2016/11/SA-1016-077-Women-in-Prison-Paper-ONLINE-FINAL.pdf, last accessed 14 December 2017.
108 *R v N* [2010] 2 Cr App Rep 97.
109 *Asi-Akram* [2006] 1 Cr App Rep (S) 260; *R v B* [2006] EWCA Crim 330.

- slavery and trafficking prevention orders: post-conviction orders necessary for protecting persons from the physical or psychological harm which would be likely to occur if the defendant committed a slavery or human trafficking offence: see MSA 2015, ss 14–17;

- slavery and trafficking risk orders: orders where a person has acted in a way which means that there is a risk that he will commit a slavery or human trafficking offence to protect persons from the physical or psychological harm which would be likely to occur if the defendant committed a slavery or human trafficking offence: see MSA 2015, ss 23 and 24;

- sexual harm prevention orders and sexual risk orders, etc: see Anti-social Behaviour, Crime and Policing Act 2014, s 113(1), Sch 5, paras 1, 5;

- serious crime prevention orders: the Serious Crime Act 2007, ss 19(5) and 1(3) empower the Crown Court and High Court respectively to impose conditions considered appropriate for the stated purpose of protecting the public from serious crime: this is supplemented by the examples of the types of prohibitions, restrictions or requirements provided in the Serious Crime Act 2007, s 5;

- cash seizure and forfeiture orders;

- restraint orders which have the effect of freezing property anywhere in the world that may be liable to be sold to satisfy a confiscation order;

- deprivation of property orders: these enable the court to deprive an offender of property, used, or intended to be used to commit an offence, for example a vehicle;

- restraining orders on acquittal: these can be made if the court considers it necessary to do so to protect a person from harassment from the defendant: see Protection from Harassment Act 1997, s 5A;

- registration on the sex offenders' register: see the Sexual Offences Act 2003 (Notification Requirements) (England and Wales) Regulations 2012. The Home Office has introduced measures which will extend and strengthen the system of notification requirements placed on registered sex offenders (commonly referred to as the sex offenders' register). These measures came into force on 13 August 2012 and require all offenders subject to the notification requirements under the Sexual Offences Act 2003 to notify to the police.

Bail applications

7.120

Bail is a vital matter to consider, particularly given that the time it takes for a NRM conclusive grounds decision to be made is at least 45 days. Under the

Bail Act 1976, s 4, bail must be granted by a court to a person accused of an offence if none of the exceptions specified in Sch 1 applies.

7.121

The exceptions to the right to bail are where the court is satisfied that there are substantial grounds for believing that the defendant if released on bail would:

- fail to surrender to custody; or

- commit an offence while on bail; or

- interfere with witnesses or otherwise obstruct the course of justice, whether in relation to himself or any other person.

Children and young persons should be bailed to local authority care – this is why it is essential that at the stage of a first appearance any disputes as to the age of the defendant need to be raised.

7.122

In considering any bail application, consideration should be given to the use of electronic tagging. A curfew that has a minimum duration of nine hours amounts to a qualifying curfew under the provisions of the Criminal Justice Act 2003, s 240A. This would mean that if a defendant were convicted and sentenced at a later date, then the court must direct that the credit period, which is half the sum of the number of days a person has been on curfew, should count towards sentence.

7.123

In terms of any conditions such as registering at a local police station, there may be concerns as to the cost of travel for the defendant to continually travel to and from the location. Consideration should be had as to whether the signing in station and bail address are in an area where the victim's exploitation has taken place and where his traffickers operate. Protective conditions should be considered, such as no unsupervised use of phones or electronic equipment. It is common for victims who are being controlled or in debt bondage to make contact with their traffickers. For other safeguarding measures and considerations see Chapters 8 and 11.

7.124

In considering the ground that a defendant would, if released, fail to surrender to custody, account should be taken of whether the defendant has already been engaging with the authorities such as the UK Border Force, in terms of signing on provisions. Furthermore, it may be that the individual has been co-operating with police who may be investigating the individuals who have trafficked or placed the defendant into a position of modern slavery.

Absconders

7.125

In all criminal cases defendants are advised that a trial can proceed, and indeed that they can be convicted, in their absence. In *R v Jones*[110], the House of Lords considered that a judge has a discretion to start or continue a trial in a defendant's absence, but that this power was to be exercised with great caution, and with close regard to the overall fairness of the proceedings. The circumstances that a judge should have regard to are:

(i)   the nature and circumstances of the defendant's behaviour in absenting themselves from trial and whether the behaviour was voluntary;

(ii)   whether an adjournment would resolve the matter;

(iii)   the likely length of such an adjournment;

(iv)   whether the defendant, though absent, wished to be represented or had waived his right to representation;

(v)   whether the defendant's representatives were able to receive instructions from them, and the extent to which they would be able to present their defence;

(vi)   the extent of the disadvantage to the defendant in not being able to present their account of events;

(vii)   the risk of the jury reaching an improper conclusion about the absence of the defendant;

(viii)   the general public interest that a trial should take place within a reasonable time;

(ix)   the undesirability of having separate trials if there were co-defendants.

7.126

The Criminal Procedure Rules 2015, r 25.2 states:

'(b)   the Court must not proceed if the defendant is absent, unless the court is satisfied that—

(i)   the defendant has waived the right to attend, and

(ii)   the trial will be fair despite the defendant's absence'.

7.127

It is crucial to consider the position of individuals who may have been re-trafficked and who therefore may not have voluntarily chosen to absent themselves from trial. This is particularly important with children and young persons, given their high risk of re-trafficking. These are all factors which a

---

110 [2002] UKHL 5, [2003] 1 AC 1.

court needs to take into consideration in the determination of whether a trial can proceed in their absence.

7.128

If, for example, at date of trial, a representative has written instructions that have been signed, such as a proof of evidence, it will be a question for them if they consider the extent to which they are able to present the defence for the defendant. Without a signed proof of evidence, and a signed defence statement, it may be extremely difficult for a representative to continue at trial and as a result they would have to withdraw.

7.129

In some instances, a representative may become aware that his client has absconded in advance of trial. When an individual has been re-trafficked in advance of a defence statement being due to be submitted to the court it is best practice to notify the court if there are in effect 'non-compliance' issues. It would not be appropriate to wait until day of trial to set out non-compliance issues, if for example a client has failed to engage in attending any appointments/conferences with a solicitor from PTPH until trial and he cannot be contacted, this should trigger a notification.

7.130

Although *R v Okedare*[111] related to the position of absconders in the context of post-trial appeals against convictions and sentence, the case is relevant and should be considered in the context of individuals absconding at trial date. The court in *Okedare* dealt with one applicant, K, who had been arrested in relation to cannabis cultivation. The court considered that he 'may well have re-trafficked or simply absconded'. Because there had been written consent to the defence representatives as to a wish to appeal against conviction, there was nothing to suggest that the applicant wished to withdraw his appeal.

7.131

The court, in assessing the case, evaluated that 'in any event there remains the possibility that his disappearance was not his fault.' On account of this, the Court of Appeal considered that it had no option but to stay the application for permission to appeal, until the applicant was able to satisfy the evidential requirements as to whether or not he had in fact been trafficked and if he had been compelled to commit the offence for which he was tried.

7.132

The above is highly pertinent when a Crown Court or magistrates' court is considering whether trial in absence should take place, where an individual

---

111 [2014] EWCA Crim 228.

'may well have re-trafficked or simply absconded'. The issues at trial in relation to a defence under the MSA 2015 arguably cannot properly be dealt with if evidence of compulsion can only be met through the defendant giving evidence at trial. As a result, *Okedare* provides a basis for highlighting the need for an application to stay the proceedings in those circumstances.

8 Special measures for victims of trafficking

General principles

8.1

A potential victim of trafficking should be treated as a victim of a serious crime from the outset of preparation for any legal hearing, irrespective of which court or tribunal it is held in. It is essential that legal practitioners and judges recognise that special measures should always be put in place for victims of trafficking in order to enable them to give their best evidence.

Understanding the psychological impact of human trafficking

8.2

The following section of this chapter is drawn from 'Clinical Links Between Human Trafficking and Torture'[1] by the Helen Bamber Foundation, which is found at pp 45-117 of the OSCE publication, *Trafficking in Human Beings Amounting to Torture and other Forms of Ill-Treatment*[2].

8.3

Victims of trafficking suffer forms of psychological abuse and physical violence which have been found to share the same fundamental components as torture. The psychological consequences of these experiences are serious, and endure long after victims have left the control of their traffickers.

8.4

Mental health problems experienced by victims of trafficking include post-traumatic stress disorder (PTSD), depression, and anxiety[3]. While all of these problems can impair functioning, PTSD symptoms can result in particular difficulties for victims who are engaging in legal proceedings. Victims of trafficking are at particularly high risk of developing PTSD. This disorder develops after people have experienced traumatic events which are threatening

---

1   R Witkin, Helen Bamber Foundation, 'Clinical Links between Human Trafficking and Torture', Part II, in (2013) *Organization for Security and Cooperation in Europe* 45–117.

2   OSCE, Office of Special Representative and Co-ordinator for Combatting Trafficking in Human Beings in Partnership with the Ludwig Boltzmann Institute of Human Rights and the Helen Bamber Foundation, *Trafficking in Human Beings Amounting to Torture and other Forms of Ill-Treatment*, Occasional Paper Series no 5 (June 2013).

3   S Oram, M Abas, D Bick et al, 'Human trafficking and health: A survey of male and female survivors in England' (2016) 106(6) *American Journal of Public Health* 1073–78.

to their life or physical integrity, or if they have witnessed others being harmed in these ways. Victims report having been subjected to high levels of violence[4]. PTSD is more prevalent in people who have been intentionally harmed by other people, for example through sexual violence, serious physical assaults, and torture. The symptoms of PTSD include nightmares and flashbacks[5], panic attacks, dissociation[6], hyper-vigilance[7], intrusive thoughts and memories[8] and avoidance of any reminders of traumatic events. Additionally, victims may experience difficulties with regulating their emotions, trusting other people and forming safe relationships. Some victims experience problems with their identity, finding that their sense of self has changed as a result of their traumatic experiences. Depression is also common, leaving the person with symptoms including low mood, lack of enjoyment and interest, and negative thoughts and feelings. Victims often report distressing emotions and thoughts about themselves, such as self-blame, shame, and low self-esteem. Victims often believe that they are to blame in some way for what has happened to them[9], and some will struggle to find any meaning in life after their trafficking experiences. These problems can lead to significant long-term impairment for the victim, and in some cases can result in suicidal thoughts and behaviour. The interpretations a victim makes of their experiences can impact on their ability to provide full evidence; if a person blames themselves for some or all of their experiences, they may not disclose the full extent of their history, or identify these events as crimes against them.

---

4   L Ottisova, S Hemings, LM Howard et al, 'Prevalence and the risk of violence and the mental health, physical and sexual problems associated with human trafficking: an updated systematic review' (2016) 25(4) *Epidemiological and Psychiatric Services* 317–41.

5   Nightmares and flashbacks are the re-experiencing of a traumatic event. They feel to a person experiencing them as though they are occurring in the present moment and are associated with subjectively real sensory experiences.

6   Dissociation is a disruption in consciousness, where a person's thoughts, memories and sense of place are either partly or fully disconnected. While dissociated, a person's mind is elsewhere and he appears to lose their awareness of where he is. He may not hear questions he is being asked, lose eye contact with others or appear to be attending to sights or sounds which are not apparent to anyone else. His emotional state may also change suddenly and lack a clear link to what is happening in that moment. This can manifest itself in extreme emotion (such as sobbing or retching), or appearing to be blank and unresponsive, but can also appear as a form of emotional detachment, whereby descriptions that a person provides of his own traumatic experiences are recounted in an unemotional, almost 'deadpan' way.

7   Hyper-vigilance is a condition of being constantly 'on guard.' This can continue long after a victim has escaped the physical confines of their trafficking situation. Victims may also have an exaggerated startle response, and 'jump' more readily at certain trigger noises or situations. This can include specific noises that trigger flashbacks (eg shouting, doors being locked or unlocked), but can also be a reaction to any sudden loud noise.

8   Intrusive thoughts and memories can take the form of a continuous, anxious pre-occupation, or be experienced as a series of mental images and emotions that suddenly arise and feel beyond victims' control. Memory triggers that remind victims of traumatic experiences may give rise to intrusive thoughts which can increase at times of stress. They may go to great lengths to try and avoid these intrusive thoughts, for example victims may avoid recounting key details of distressing parts of their account so as to avoid the painful emotions associated with this memory.

9   It is common for victims to blame themselves for having been trafficked and suffering traumatic experiences. This can stem from traffickers' abusive statements and threats as well as internalised shame, self-blame and low self-esteem. This applies in the cases of victims who have suffered deception in being targeted by traffickers (for example being offered a job or love relationship that never materialised) but also in cases where victims have had no opportunity or power at any stage to avoid being trafficked.

8.5

It is important to consider the implications of PTSD in the context of a victim's ability to engage in providing a full account of his history and experiences. When a person with PTSD recalls a traumatic event, he experiences this recollection as if it is happening to him again in the present moment. For example, if asked about an incident of rape, the victim may see images of this as if it is occurring again, hear sounds that were heard at the time, and feel the physical sensations felt during the rape. The victim may also feel the same emotions, think the same thoughts and have the same bodily responses. Recalling a traumatic event can be re-traumatising for the victim, and lead to a deterioration in his mental health (see the best practice guidance below, which can support victims to feel safer).

8.6

It is useful for legal practitioners to know that PTSD is a memory disorder. This should be borne in mind when considering the consistency of accounts which have been provided by the victim at different stages. Traumatic memories are understood to be stored in a fragmented way in the brain, meaning that a victim who has PTSD may not be able to provide a coherent and chronological account of his history[10]. Providing a consistent account of traumatic events can be even more problematic if these memories trigger distressing negative feelings, such as shame, or if the person has dissociative symptoms[11]. All of the psychological problems outlined above may be exacerbated when victims are required to go through court proceedings, particularly in cases where they are asked to recount past traumatic events as part of this process[12].

8.7

In the context of preparing for a court or tribunal hearing, legal practitioners should bear in mind that victims may have undisclosed or non-visible physical injuries and health problems which can impede their ability to manage basic tasks and can cause them to feel ashamed or stigmatised. Some may have suffered head injuries which affect their cognitive function. Victims often feel unable to ask for help, or they lack awareness that there may be treatment available for their specific health needs. It should not be assumed that healthcare professionals who have worked with victims will have identified, or even considered, the full range of problems that may affect them. Healthcare records are rarely comprehensive, and significant health problems may have never been identified[13].

---

10 J Herlihy, L Jobson and S Turner, 'Just Tell Us What Happened to You: Autobiographical Memory and Seeking Asylum' (2012) 26 *Applied Cognitive Psychology* 661–76.

11 D Bognor, J Herlihy and CR Brewin, 'Impact of sexual violence on disclosure during Home Office interviews' (2007) 191 *British Journal of Psychiatry* 75–81.

12 C Katona and LM Howard, Briefing Paper: The mental health difficulties experienced by victims of human trafficking (modern slavery) and the impact this has on their ability to provide testimony (Helen Bamber Foundation and Kings College London 2017), see www.helenbamber.org/wp-content/uploads/2017/02/Briefing-Paper-Difficulties-in-providing-testimony-victims-of-modern-slavery.pdf.

13 C Ross, S Dimitrova, LM Howard et al, 'Human trafficking and health: a cross-sectional survey of NHS professionals contact with victims of human trafficking' (2015) *BMJ* 5, 8.

Understanding the psychological impact of human trafficking on children and young people

8.8

Children who have been trafficked commonly develop mental health problems such as PTSD, depression and anxiety disorders[14]. They will often have been exposed to traumatic events and multiple forms of maltreatment which can include physical, emotional and sexual abuse. Additionally, it should be recognised that at crucial stages of their development they will have lacked appropriate caregivers or a stable home in which their needs are met. In cases where adults with a duty of care to a child (for example parents, family members, foster carers or pastoral figures) have become perpetrators who abuse and exploit them, children's ability to form trusting and healthy relationships will have been fundamentally damaged. This can make it extremely difficult for them to trust any adults.

8.9

Disruption during children's crucial developmental years may mean that they lack the essential 'building blocks' of identity formation which are necessary tools for effective psychological recovery. Children also have a narrower range of previous life and learning experiences than adults, and therefore less capacity to make sense of, and recover from, their traumatic experiences. Those who have been exploited from an early age, or for a prolonged period of time, are highly likely to suffer complex, long-term mental health problems.

8.10

Acknowledging the psychological vulnerability of children and young people who have been trafficked is crucial to their well-being and ongoing protection. Tribunals have specific guidance to follow on special measures for parties and/or witnesses in proceedings who are under the age of 18. In any case where a young person's age is disputed by the UK authorities, he should be given the benefit of the doubt and be treated first and foremost as a vulnerable witness. From a developmental point of view, it is useful to bear in mind that the maturity 'cut off' point between the 'minor' age of 17 and the 'majority' age of 18 is arbitrary, and it is not always possible to determine the exact age of some young people in any case. Young adult victims of trafficking can be vulnerable because of their youth as well as their trafficking history and other factors[15]. Therefore special measures can be requested due to a victim's young age as well as any other reasons as to why he is vulnerable.

---

14 L Kiss, NS Pocock, V Naisanguansri et al, 'Health of men, women, and children in post-trafficking services in Cambodia, Thailand, and Vietnam: an observational cross-sectional study' (2015) *The Lancet* 3, 3, e154–e161.

15 N Stanley, S Oram, S Jakobowitz et al, 'The health needs and healthcare experiences of young people trafficked into the UK' (2016) 59 *Child Abuse and Neglect* 100–10.

Best practice methods of working with victims of trafficking for legal practitioners

General principles

8.11

Trafficking-related trauma can be considered to be *cumulative* because victims have often suffered human rights violations or circumstances of extreme vulnerability *prior to* having been trafficked, as well as during and after the trafficking process. It is the duty of legal practitioners to identify the individual vulnerabilities of their clients and therefore to be able to understand the specific challenges that can arise for them. In order to work with victims appropriately and effectively, their entire life history should be acknowledged and understood.

Expert medical evidence

8.12

It assists the court or tribunal to be provided with independent expert medical evidence which is produced in accordance with the Istanbul Protocol.[16] Medical documentation of physical and psychological injuries can help to minimise the risk of re-traumatisation from investigative questioning, and can also be critical in explaining the difficulties that the victim may face in giving a coherent and consistent account of past events. A medico-legal report can document any limitations on the victim's ability to give oral testimony and recommend specific conditions that should be put in place in order to support him with this[17]. However it should not be assumed that all medical experts have detailed knowledge of the court environment, or the scope of special measures which are available. Legal practitioners should provide specific instructions, and fully advise medical experts so that they are in a position to comment on the likely impact of the court or tribunal proceedings upon the victim, and make clinical recommendations on the special measures which are likely to assist. It should be noted that there are many cases in which victims of trafficking are unable to obtain expert medical evidence that meets the standard required for court purposes, and this can create an unfair disadvantage. Special measures should be requested in every case which involves victims of trafficking, whether or not medico-legal documentation is available.

Working appropriately and effectively with victims of trafficking

8.13

When working with victims in preparation for a court or tribunal hearing, it is important that legal practitioners refer to the guidance in the Trafficking

---

16 UN (1999) Istanbul Protocol (Manual on the effective investigation and documentation of torture and other cruel and inhuman degrading treatment or punishment).

17 *JL (medical reports – credibility) China* [2013] UKUT 00145 (IAC), at [26] and [27].

Survivor Care Standards, which are written by consensus of specialist human trafficking organisations throughout the UK and published by the Human Trafficking Foundation. These standards are endorsed by the UK Independent Anti-Slavery Commissioner, and the UK government has announced that they will be incorporated into the National Referral Mechanism victim care contract.

- Legal practitioners should work collaboratively, wherever possible, with independent advocates from trafficking-specialist NGOs and organisations in order to ensure that victims are supported before, during and after the court or tribunal process. Independent advocates can lend morale support to victims when they are having to disclose traumatic experiences. They may also be able to provide letters or reports which document the victim's profile, specific care requirements or trafficking history.

- Victims are likely to feel highly anxious about having to appear in a court or tribunal setting, particularly when people in a position of authority are speaking about them, and asking them direct questions relating to their history and credibility. There may also be cultural issues for them to overcome in appearing in court, and those who are speaking English as a second language, or require an interpreter, may feel that they are at a particular disadvantage. Factors that made victims originally vulnerable to trafficking can present challenges in the context of a court or tribunal hearing. For example, they may have undiagnosed learning difficulties, may come from a particularly sheltered cultural upbringing, or have a background of low socio-economic status with significant gaps in education. Many victims do not have the crucial support of close family members to rely upon. Therefore a sensitive approach is needed.

- Every person who is in the room with the victim and the legal practitioner should be vetted to ensure the victim's safety. Guidance on the appropriate use of interpreters is contained in the Trafficking Survivor Care Standards. It is important to ensure that any persons accompanying the victim (such as family members or friends) are asked to remain in the waiting room rather than accompanying the victim into the appointment room. If a victim requests that a particular person be with them in the room, this needs to be discussed with the victim without that person being present. Legal practitioners can then make an informed decision on whether the person's presence is necessary for the victim. It is important to bear in mind that friends and family members may be potential witnesses in the trafficking case, therefore they should not attend the appointment for that reason. In some cases family members, friends or associates of victims may be implicated in their trafficking without the victim realising it. Victims can also be particularly vulnerable to feeling dependent in controlling or abusive relationships. Of course, people who are accompanying the victim may be fully supportive of them and acting in their best interests, but it is good practice to avoid having them present in the room unless the victim feels unable to function without them there (for example because they need support with a disability or with overwhelming feelings of fear or they require assistance with a baby whom they cannot be apart from). In such cases practitioners should try to lend support to the victim to the extent that they will feel able to attend the appointment alone, either further on, or the next time.

- Psychological symptoms are rarely immediately obvious or visible. Victims may have developed psychological defence mechanisms which directly relate to a history of subjugation and enslavement. For example, they may be used to minimising injury or concealing it from others due to enforced secrecy imposed by traffickers. They may have become conditioned to minimising or even denying physical injuries, illnesses and conditions due to long-term experiences of exploitation and lack of access to healthcare. Many victims experience psychological distress, such as feelings of shame and humiliation, which prevent them from asserting their needs. Some victims are inhibited from speaking about their history because they fear that their PTSD symptoms (such as flashbacks or intrusive memories accompanied by psychological distress and physiological arousal) may be triggered and become overwhelming for them.

- Disclosure of rape and sexual violence is particularly distressing, and it is often the case that victims will not feel able to disclose the full extent of the sexual violence they have suffered. Practitioners should bear in mind that sexual violence can devastate victims' self-esteem and cause feelings of shame and self-blame. Even when they are giving evidence on non-related matters, victims may be suffering a profound fear of the subject being raised, whether it has been previously disclosed by them or not.

- Threats from traffickers against victims and their family members can operate to silence victims for years after they have left their direct control. Often traffickers have an intricate understanding of the victim and their family profile and this knowledge alone keeps victims in fear. Whether or not threats are recent, or likely to be carried out, they are of great significance to victims. Therefore it is important that they are fully supported by having their identity concealed (see para **8.24** below on anonymity applications).

- Some victims remain extremely afraid of departing from instructions given to them by traffickers or from promises/oaths they have been forced to make. This is particularly true of children and young people, but it can apply to any vulnerable person. Even after a victim has disclosed their history, they may still revert back to their initial fear of disobeying the trafficker, and feel unable to repeat it. Therefore a change of, or withdrawal from, an original account should not, by itself lead to the conclusion that the previous account was false.

- Victims may be emotionally controlled through the manipulation of their personal relationships with other people who are associated with the trafficker. There are many variations of this situation. One example is when young people who have grown up in domestic servitude are inhibited from giving evidence in court because traffickers have told them that their actions will harm the lives of the children of the family.

- Some victims of trafficking have been psychologically abused in a manner that leads them to form a traumatic bonding with traffickers (sometimes referred to as Stockholm Syndrome), which can prevent them from being able to make full sense of their experiences. This can arise from an isolated victim's dependency upon their trafficker for their physical and emotional survival, which can lead to the formation of an emotional attachment. Victims may adopt the world view of their abuser and internalise the abuser's opinion of them. Therefore they may act protectively towards their trafficker by denying the abuse for some time afterwards or experiencing confusion about whether they were abused at all.

- Some victims from West Africa may have been subjected to ritualised violence in 'juju' ceremonies performed by traffickers. These ceremonies utilise cultural beliefs in the ancient and omnipotent power of juju to terrorise victims, instilling deep fears to subjugate them in preparation for exploitation and to prevent them from ever telling anyone about their experiences. In these cases, victims who are talking about their experiences in any forum, including in conference with lawyers, providing information to the police and giving evidence in court, may be fearing phenomenal retribution in the form of illness or death of themselves and their loved ones. This can occur even in cases where the victim consciously believes the fear of juju to be irrational. It is useful to know that while this fear can diminish at times, it can return with its original force when the victim feels under pressure.

8.14

Victims will benefit from having all relevant information carefully explained to them as early as possible in the process. It will help them to be assured that special measures will be in place when they give their evidence. It is good practice to take time with the victim to check that information is fully understood and ensure that victims feel confident enough to be able to ask questions whenever they wish. Supporting victims to feel confident is key to successful legal work practice. It is important to recognise and acknowledge the individual strengths of each client, and to understand that they will know their own limits in the context of any question/answer session. They should know that they can take the time that they need to process their thoughts and answer questions, take a break if needed or come back to a particular point or issue later on if it is causing them distress. Mental health problems are far less likely to inhibit or distress a person when they know that the practitioner with whom they are working understands and acknowledges such problems. Experienced legal practitioners will be able to reassure clients that they have worked with victims of trafficking before, that mental health issues should never be a source of shame or embarrassment within any legal context, and that they are not expected to attempt to 'hide' or suppress their distress or anxiety in a court or tribunal setting.

8.15

The *Trafficking Survivor Care Standards* contain advice for practitioners from all disciplines who are working with victims, to enable them to minimise re-traumatisation and distress, establish a working relationship of trust and assist victims with disclosure[18].

8.16

The standards explain how practitioners from any discipline can:

- apply basic therapeutic principles to contact work with victims;

- provide a safe, calm, consistent environment and approach;

- build trust by demonstrating an interest in the victim's immediate safety, health and practical needs;

- ensure that the victim knows the professional role of each person who is working with him;

- support the victim by letting him know that he will be given an appropriate amount of time to be fully heard; and

- enable the victim to remain 'present' in the room, focusing on the 'here and now' so that he is not preoccupied with past or future fears and concerns.

8.17

From years of collective experience working with victims of trafficking, the Helen Bamber Foundation advises that:

> 'Establishing a relationship of mutual trust over time is of primary importance for the safety and well-being of people who have been trafficked. Take time to consider an account rather than dismissing anything that is said in the early stages of contact because it seems flawed. Those who work closely with victims over multiple sessions often find that the whole account becomes more coherent as a relationship of trust is established and the client feels able to speak more fully about their experiences. Over time, apparently inaccurate or inconsistent aspects of an account may be resolved and clarified'.

---

18   R Witkin and K Robjant, in *Trafficking Survivor Care Standards* (2015), Section B.3, 'Advice for Non-Clinicians working with Survivors who have Psychological Needs'.

Special measures in Immigration and Asylum Tribunal proceedings

8.18

The tribunal has wide-reaching powers under its own Procedural Rules[19], Practice Directions[20] and Guidance[21] to provide special measures in an appeal before it where the appellant or witness is a (potential) victim of trafficking and should therefore be treated as a vulnerable witness These powers include the power to appoint a litigation friend[22] in cases where the victim lacks capacity[23].

8.19

From the outset of any claim[24] or hearing, it is essential to identify the special measures that should be sought in an appeal before the court or tribunal to ensure that the victim has effective access to justice and that their voice is fully heard.

8.20

The Court of Appeal in AM (Afghanistan) v Secretary of State for the Home Department[25] gave guidance on the general approach to be adopted in law and practice by the Immigration and Asylum Tribunal[26] to the fair determination of claims for asylum from children, young people and other incapacitated or vulnerable persons whose ability to effectively participate in proceedings may be limited. The court observed that sufficient steps must be taken to ensure the appellant has obtained effective access to justice, and in particular that their voice can be heard in the proceedings that concern them[27]. In AM, the court held that the tribunal failed to adopt sufficient special measures. The court observed that the overriding objective in r 2 of the Tribunal Procedure Rules was ignored

---

19 Tribunal Procedure (First-Tier Tribunal) (Immigration and Asylum Chamber) Rules 2014, SI 2014/2604, and Tribunal Procedure (Upper Tribunal) Rules 2008, SI 2008/2698.

20 Practice Direction 'First-tier and Upper Tribunal Child, Vulnerable Adult and Sensitive Witnesses', issued by the Senior President, Sir Robert Carnwath, with the agreement of the Lord Chancellor on 30 October 2008.

21 In 2010 the Joint Presidential Guidance Note No 2 of 2010, 'Child, vulnerable adult and sensitive appellant guidance' was published and is a useful aide when making an application for special measures.

22 A litigation friend can be a parent or guardian, a family member or friend, a solicitor, a professional advocate, eg an Independent Mental Capacity Advocate, a Court of Protection deputy or someone who has a lasting or enduring power of attorney. It is also helpful for victims of trafficking to have the support of a trafficking-specialised and independent advocate from a reputable trafficking NGO.

23 As defined in the Mental Capacity Act, s 2.

24 Claim is used in two ways here. First, where a claim is being made for international protection and/ or asylum on behalf of a victim of trafficking, practitioners should consider prospectively what special measures may be needed at each stage of the process up until and including any appeal hearing (including at any interviews pre-decision). Second, prior to the issuing of a judicial review claim practitioners should consider what special measures need to be sought within the body of the claim or as interim relief (ie anonymity of the claim).

25 [2017] EWCA Civ 1123.

26 Both the First Tier and Upper Tribunal.

27 [2017] EWCA Civ 1123, para 16.

and there was a fundamental procedural unfairness, the court concluded that the proceedings were neither just nor fair.

Tribunal Guidance and Practice Directions

8.21

The key features[28] of the Practice Direction and Guidance note are:

(i) the early identification of issues of vulnerability is encouraged, if at all possible, before any substantive hearing through the use of a case management review hearing ('CMRH') or pre-hearing review. The purpose of early identification is to minimise exposure to harm of vulnerable individuals (Guidance [4] and [5]);

(ii) a person who is incapacitated or vulnerable will only need to attend as a witness to give oral evidence where the tribunal determines that 'the evidence is necessary to enable the fair hearing of the case and their welfare would not be prejudiced by doing so' (PD [2] and Guidance [8] and [9]);

(iii) where an incapacitated or vulnerable person does give oral evidence, detailed provision is to be made to ensure their welfare is protected before and during the hearing (PD [6] and [7] and Guidance [10]);

(iv) it is necessary to give special consideration to all of the personal circumstances of an incapacitated or vulnerable person in assessing their evidence (Guidance [10.2]–[15]); and

(v) relevant additional sources of guidance are identified in the Guidance, including from international bodies (Guidance Annex A [22]–[27]).

It will be expected that in any submissions seeking special measures, the Tribunal will be referred to the Guidance and Practice Direction. A failure of the Tribunal to follow the relevant practice direction and guidance for vulnerable witnesses will most likely be a material error of law[29]. This is particularly relevant in terms of the assessment of the credibility of the vulnerable witness/appellant (see Guidance at [13]–[15]).

The Tribunal Procedure Rules

8.22

The Procedure Rules provide an overriding objective at r 2, which requires the tribunal and the parties, as far as practicable, to ensure that an appellant is

---

28   AM (Afghanistan) v Secretary of State for the Home Department [2017] EWCA Civ 1123 at para 31.
29   AM (Afghanistan) v Secretary of State for the Home Department [2017] EWCA Civ 1123 at para 30.

able to participate fully in the proceedings and that there is flexibility which the tribunal can utilise to deal with a case fairly and justly. Within the rules themselves this flexibility and lack of formality is clear. The terms of rr 4 (case management), 10 (representation) and 14 (evidence and submissions) illustrate this: see AM (Afghanistan) v Secretary of State for the Home Department[30].

Examples of special measures

8.23

In AM (Afghanistan) v Secretary of State for the Home Department, the psychiatrist who had assessed AM proposed a series of arrangements to be put forward to the Tribunal if AM (contrary to his advice) were to give evidence. These arrangements were:

(i)   informal court dress for advocates and judge;

(ii)   informal venue for the hearing[31];

(iii)   informal seating arrangements, ie round tables or other seating that appears less confrontational and less adversarial[32];

(iv)   exclusion of members of the public when AM was giving evidence[33];

(v)   restriction of people present in the court room when AM was giving evidence to legal representatives, the judge, court clerk, and where he requests one, a nominated person to support him[34];

---

30   [2017] EWCA Civ 1123 at para 27.
31   Many victims are frightened of the power of the courts, especially those who have previous histories of prosecution or detention or prison, and those who fear the courts and authorities in their country of origin. Informal dress for court professionals and an informal venue for the hearing is very reassuring. It is helpful to use photographs and pictures which familiarise them with the layout early on in preparation for attendance at a hearing. Victims can feel well-prepared if they know in advance where the bathrooms are, and where the windows will be so that they can focus on a source of light and possibly a natural view.
32   The way that professionals are positioned in relation to victims in the court room or tribunal can have a profound effect in supporting and assisting them to be able to manage the proceedings. The best arrangements are those which avoid 'mirroring' any previous situations in which they may have been interrogated, interviewed, or had other negative experiences. In criminal cases in which the victim is a witness for the prosecution of a trafficker, it is helpful if they are able to meet with the judge and defending counsel prior to the hearing. Cross-examination can be harrowing for victims and a short meeting beforehand helps them to come to understand the need for an adversarial court process.
33   It is good practice to seek to secure exclusion of members of the public for the course of the entire appeal and any preliminary [CMRH] hearings where particulars of the trafficking are discussed. It is important to ensure that an application is made to keep the victim's name anonymous, and that the name is not recorded *anywhere* in court materials, including on the notices for court rooms and hearings.
34   It is helpful for victims to be accompanied before, during and after the hearing by appropriate, independent advocates from trafficking-specialist NGOs. This can be especially crucial to victims' well-being in relation to giving evidence. The use of independent advocates needs to be further established and recognised as best practice for victims of trafficking.

(vi)   questions asked by both parties to be open ended where possible and broken down so that each question is simple and self-contained[35];

(vii) points to be raised during cross-examination to be identified by the judge[36].

8.24

The above proposed arrangements are a useful guide on potential special measures appropriate in appeal hearings where a victim of trafficking is a part of the proceedings. In trafficking cases, where it is the appellant who is the victim, an application for anonymity should be made, ensuring that the name of the victim is neither on any court documents nor displayed in any public court room or on any hearing lists.

Special measures in criminal proceedings

Introduction

8.25

The court process is inevitably daunting, and complaining against traffickers may also put the witness or defendant at personal risk.

8.26

Council Framework Decision 2001/220/JHA of 15 March 2001 on the standing of victims in criminal proceedings establishes a set of victims' rights in criminal proceedings, which includes access without delay to legal counselling and to legal representation, including for the purpose of claiming compensation. The Decision confirms that:

- on the basis of an individual risk assessment carried out in accordance with national procedures, victims should be protected from retaliation, from intimidation, and from the risk of being re-trafficked;

---

35 Low self-esteem can inhibit victims from being able to speak with clarity, specificity or sufficient confidence, especially in response to direct questions. It is helpful to run through the process of questioning with victims prior to the hearing and explain that they can answer questions at their own pace and do not have to meet the same pace as the questioner. They should know how to tell the questioner if they do not understand a question or they need it to be put to them in a way that they can better understand. Victims may come from countries in which the status of the questioner would be so much higher than theirs, that any request for more repetition or clarity would be unthinkable to them.

36 The more predictable all aspects of the court or tribunal process, the better for the victim. Due to a history of being controlled and abused in unpredictable ways, victims are much more likely than the average person to be disturbed by anything unexpected, and they may easily become anxious that they will be blamed or criticised. If they are given the opportunity to make sense of court procedures and ask questions, this reduces the risk of them misinterpreting events within the court and becoming fearful, intimidated, and potentially re-traumatised by the process.

- victims of trafficking who have already suffered the abuse and degrading treatment which trafficking commonly entails, such as sexual exploitation, sexual abuse, rape, slavery-like practices or the removal of organs, should be protected from secondary victimisation and further trauma during the criminal proceedings. Unnecessary repetition of interviews during investigation, prosecution and trial should be avoided, for instance, where appropriate, through the production, as soon as possible in the proceedings, of video recordings of those interviews. To this end victims of trafficking should during criminal investigations and proceedings receive treatment that is appropriate to their individual needs. The assessment of their individual needs should take into consideration circumstances such as their age, whether they are pregnant, their health, any disability and other personal circumstances, as well as the physical and psychological consequences of the criminal activity to which the victim was subjected. Whether and how the treatment is applied is to be decided in accordance with grounds defined by national law, rules of judicial discretion, practice and guidance, on a case-by-case basis;

- assistance and support measures should be provided to victims on a consensual and informed basis. Victims should therefore be informed of the important aspects of those measures and they should not be imposed on the victims. A victim's refusal of assistance or support measures should not entail obligations for the competent authorities of the Member State concerned to provide the victim with alternative measures.

8.27

Procedural developments in England and Wales have included the use of interpreters, special measures to assist witnesses with communication other than translation, measures to adapt the court room and processes, and other support. Victim support measures might include protection for the individual and their family members, relocation, change of identity, protection from potential retaliation or intimidation for victims and their families[37]. Prosecutors are encouraged to meet witnesses in advance of trial. Regard should be had to the *Code of Practice for Victims of Crime*[38] (2015) which was developed following the Victim's Directive[39] and the Human Trafficking Directive[40], and which also incorporates the Child Sexual Exploitation Directive[41].

---

37 EU Trafficking Directive.
38 CPS (2015), available at https://cps.gov.uk/sites/default/files/documents/legal_guidance/OD_000049.pdf, last accessed 15 December 2017.
39 Directive 2012/29/EU of the European Parliament and of the Council of 25 October 2012 establishing minimum standards on the rights, support and protection of victims of crime, and replacing Council Framework Decision 2001/220/JHA.
40 Directive 2011/36/EU of the European Parliament and of the Council of 5 April 2011 on preventing and combating trafficking in human beings and protecting its victims, and replacing Council Framework Decision 2002/629/JHA.
41 Directive 2011/92/EU of the European Parliament and of the Council of 13 December 2011 on combating the sexual abuse and sexual exploitation of children and child pornography, and replacing Council Framework Decision 2004/68/JHA.

8.28

Guidance from the Crown Prosecution Service ('CPS') sets out the requirement for prosecutors to be 'alert to particular circumstances or situations where someone suspected of committing a criminal offence might also be a victim of trafficking or slavery'. There is a duty of the prosecutor to make 'proper enquiries' in criminal prosecutions involving individuals who may be victims of trafficking or slavery.

8.29

Aside from the unfitness to plead procedure for defendants and confirming the capacity of young children, all witnesses are presumed competent[42]. However, the traditional approach of requiring witness testimony in open court can be the subject of what are known as 'special measures'. These are procedural adaptations designed to achieve the best evidence from a particular person who may have particular issues that affect their effective participation[43]. Such adaptations as are necessary are used in order to ensure a fair trial[44]. It is a relatively bespoke exercise, which requires an understanding of the particular issues that arise in relation to the particular person in the particular trial[45].

8.30

In addition to the statutory criteria set out in the Youth Justice and Criminal Evidence Act ('YJCEA') 1999, ss 16–33 , detailed guidance is available in the *Equal Treatment Bench Book* (2013)[46], the Home Office Publication *Achieving Best Evidence* (2016)[47] and through the toolkits produced by *The Advocate's Gateway*[48].

Trauma – informed approach

8.31

There has been some progress in the context of trafficking to ensure that a criminal court is 'trauma informed', whether the victim encounters the court system as a complainant, witness or defendant. Trauma-informed procedures can

---

42 YJCEA 1999, s 53(3).
43 *R v Barker* [2010] EWCA Crim 4, [2011] Crim LR 233; *R v Lubemba* [2014] EWCA Crim 2064, [2015] 1 WLR 1579.
44 *R v Cox* [2012] EWCA Crim 549, [2012] 2 Cr App Rep 63.
45 *IA* [2013] EWCA Crim 1308.
46 A guide for judges, magistrates and all other judicial office holders, see www.judiciary.gov.uk/publications/equal-treatment-bench-book/, last accessed 15 December 2017.
47 The Home Office Guidance 'Achieving Best Evidence in Criminal Proceedings: Guidance for Vulnerable or Intimidated Witnesses, including Children' provides a detailed and recommended procedure. It considers planning interviews, decisions about whether the interview should be video recorded or a statement taken, preparing the witness for court and subsequent court appearances, pre-trial therapy and special measures.
48 The Advocate's Gateway, Toolkits 1 to 18, available at www.theadvocatesgateway.org/, last accessed 15 December 2017.

enhance victim engagement and decrease the potentially negative experiences which may stem from court procedure. Trauma may underlie the behaviour of trafficking victims, as it may in domestic violence or other abuse cases, and may be undiagnosed and untreated (see paras **8.3–8.6** above)[49].

8.32

Victims of trafficking as witnesses are often extremely traumatised individuals; many will have no experience or understanding of our criminal justice system. The CPS has issued practice guidance on the provision of therapy for vulnerable or intimidated witnesses prior to a criminal trial. It is possible for witnesses to engage in therapy prior to trial; many victims who are witnesses may already be engaging with therapy if they have had an NRM referral. The nature of the therapy should be explained and the CPS should be consulted so that consideration can be given to whether or not the provision of the therapy will have an impact on the criminal case. Records of therapy, including videos and tapes as well as notes and other contacts with the witness, must be maintained so that they can be produced if required by the court process, for example as part of the disclosure process. They should include details of the therapy(ies)/ treatment employed, details of those persons present and the content and length of the therapy sessions.

8.33

Pre-trial therapy for children has been the subject of guidance which may be relevant to victims of trafficking[50]. The purpose is to provide emotional support and counselling to decrease distress or psychological symptoms and behaviour, or improve personal functioning. The provision of this is not a decision for the police or prosecutors or defence advocates but a decision to be taken by those with care of the child alongside the relevant professionals providing therapeutic assessment and support.

8.34

In addition to traditionally recognised special measures or arrangements (set out below) and, in the absence of bespoke training for the judiciary, advocates can promote the concept of a trauma-informed court in cases where it is likely that witnesses or suspects are affected by trauma. Such an approach might include engaging other court stakeholders to make specific requests for any possible and reasonable adjustment to the proceedings. This might include court staff, other advocates and support workers. There may be occasions, particularly in relation

---

49 Office For Victims of Crime Training and Technical Assistance Center, *Human Trafficking Task Force e-guide*, available at www.ovcttac.gov/taskforceguide/eguide/, last accessed 15 December 2017.

50 Multi-agency guidance, *Provision of Therapy to Child Witnesses Prior to a Criminal Trial*, available at www.cps.gov.uk/publications/prosecution/therapychild.html, last accessed 15 December 2017 and *Safeguarding Children and Young People from Sexual Exploitation* (June 2009), available at www.gov.uk/ government/publications/child-sexual-exploitation-definition-and-guide-for-practitioners,   last accessed 15 December 2017.

to youths, where the judge can be invited to sit at the same level as the parties and not to wear robes, thus reducing the potential for intimidation by the process and/or the persons who habitually work in the criminal courts and may be insulated against trauma by their work experiences (see above the potential positive impact these measures can have for the victim). The purpose of such changes may reduce the risk of triggering trauma and encourage meaningful interaction[51]. Acknowledging and understanding the impact of trauma on court participants may lead to more successful interactions and outcomes[52].

Eligibility for special measures for witnesses in criminal proceedings

8.35

Child witnesses[53], whether for the defence or the prosecution, are automatically eligible for special measures[54]. Adult witnesses with physical or mental impairment, who are complainants of sexual offences, or witnesses to a 'relevant offence' or offences under the MSA 2015, ss 1 and 2 are also automatically eligible[55]. Other vulnerable witnesses may be eligible for special measures if the court is satisfied that the quality of their evidence would be diminished without some adaptation of the usual process[56].

8.36

Witnesses in fear or distress about testifying may be eligible for special measures providing the court is satisfied that the quality of their evidence is likely to be diminished by reason of that fear or distress[57]. This enables the court to take into account the social, cultural, domestic and employment circumstances, ethnic origin, religious beliefs or political opinions and any behaviour towards the witness on the part of an accused, his family or associates[58].

8.37

In relation to witnesses found to be in fear or distress about giving evidence and those giving evidence in relation to offences under the MSA 2015, ss 1 and 2, orders can be made for them to give evidence in private[59] with associated

---

51 The *Human Trafficking Task Force e-guide* contains some further practical suggestions.
52 SAMHSA, *Essential Components of Trauma Informed Judicial Practice*, available at www.nasmhpd.org/sites/default/files/JudgesEssential_5%201%202013finaldraft.pdf, last accessed 15 December 2017.
53 Those under the age of 18.
54 YJCEA 1999, s 19.
55 Ibid.
56 YJCEA 1999, ss 16 and 17.
57 YJCEA 1999, ss 16 and 17.
58 YJCEA 1999, s 17.
59 YJCEA 1999, s 25 as amended by the MSA 2015, s 46.

restrictions on reporting[60]. Other statutory special measures available under the YJCEA 1999 for eligible witnesses are pre-recorded video evidence in chief[61], pre-recorded cross examination (following a pilot)[62], restrictions on cross examination by the accused appearing in person[63], screens[64], live link[65], removal of wigs and gowns[66], assistance of an intermediary[67] and the use of aids to communication for young or incapacitated witnesses[68].

Child witnesses

8.38

Child witnesses are deemed eligible for numerous types of special measures as set out in the Youth Justice and Criminal Evidence Act 1999, ss 23–28, including pre-recorded evidence, an intermediary to assist with communication and/or aids to communication[69]. Guidance has been issued by the CPS that prosecutors must ensure that when dealing with cases involving children, the child is given appropriate support and there is consideration as to what is best for the child if a criminal prosecution proceeds. Examples given include the following:

- expediting cases and dealing with them with fairness and sensitivity;

- where children have been sexually exploited, treating them as victims of abuse;

- consideration of the use of children as witnesses, witness care and of special measures to enable them to give evidence in the best way possible in terms of quality of their evidence and reducing trauma to them;

- engaging with other authorities and agencies to safeguard children.

Applications for special measures for witnesses

8.39

Applications for a special measures direction must be made as soon as reasonably practicable and, in any event, within 28 days after a not guilty plea has been entered, citing the correct section that applies to eligibility. The relevant party must provide supporting material setting out the nature of the measures sought,

---

60 YJCEA 1999, s 46.
61 YJCEA 1999, s 27.
62 YJCEA 1999, s 28.
63 YJCEA 1999, ss 34–38.
64 YJCEA 1999, s 23.
65 YJCEA 1999, s 24.
66 YJCEA 1999, s 26.
67 YJCEA 1999, s 29.
68 YJCEA 1999, s 30.
69 YJCEA 1999, s 19(1).

the basis upon which the witness is eligible for assistance, the witness's views on the proposed measures and why such measures would be likely to improve the quality of the evidence[70].

In a summary or youth court trial, judges who have ruled on a special measures application do not need to recuse themselves from hearing the substantive matter[71].

Ground rules hearings

8.40

A ground rules hearing is commonly used by judges to make directions for the fair treatment and effective participation of vulnerable defendants and vulnerable witnesses. Courts must take reasonable steps to ensure the effective participation of vulnerable defendants and witnesses[72]. This might include removing wigs and gowns, screening and advance notice of questions the advocates plan to ask. The requirements for a ground rules hearing apply to vulnerable defendants in the same way that they do to vulnerable witnesses. Where the defendant is also a victim of trafficking, there are likely to be vulnerabilities which ought to be brought to the attention of the court at such a hearing so that any necessary adaptations can be considered (see the discussion of the psychological impact of human trafficking at paras 8.3–8.6 above). Measures can be adopted when evidence is given by witnesses so that a vulnerable defendant can follow the proceedings[73].

Special measures for accused persons/defendants who are victims of trafficking

8.41

In cases involving accused persons who are also victims of trafficking, case preparation requires attention to how the accused person's vulnerability is relevant. This raises issues in relation to the prosecution allegation, any defence raised and the procedure to deal with the accused's presentation in court[74]. The statutory framework for witnesses expressly excludes defendants from the assistance of special measures, save for that of a child with intellectual impairment, impairment of social functioning or a mental disorder who may

---

70 Criminal Procedure Rules 2015, r 18.
71 *KL and LK v DPP* (2002) 166 JP 369.
72 See Toolkits 1 and 1a.
73 *R v Cox* [2012] EWCA Crim 549, [2012] 2 Cr App Rep 63.
74 *R v S* [2008] EWCA Crim 6; *R v Braham* [2013] EWCA Crim 3, [2013] 1 Cr App Rep 481; *R v Thompson* [2014] EWCA Crim 836.

apply for an order to give evidence by live link[75]. A live link is not available for adult defendants[76].

8.42

Over the last two decades there has been a growing recognition that young defendants should have access to effective communication arrangements to enable them to fully participate in order to receive a fair trial[77]. In England and Wales, the Criminal Procedure Rules 2015, rr 3D–3G provide the current approach to children and vulnerable adults accused appearing in the Crown Court. This requires the particular vulnerability to be recognised and is intended to enable the accused person effectively to participate in the proceedings. This exercise ought to take into account the age, maturity, identified conditions and development of the accused person concerned and all other circumstances of the case[78].

8.43

The approach to be taken by criminal courts and the advocates is to ensure that the welfare of the child or otherwise vulnerable defendant is considered[79]. The process should be adapted to ensure the defendant can comprehend the proceedings and engage fully in his defence[80].

8.44

In relation to a defendant's evidence, the procedural expectation is that an application should be made pursuant to the Criminal Procedure Rules 2015, r 18 for a 'defendant's evidence direction' and that directions will be given to ensure the appropriate court adaptations are made and that the treatment and questioning of the defendant is approached in a suitable way to facilitate effective participation. The presumption is that adult defendants will be in court and, if they choose to give evidence, will do so in person but measures such as clearing the public gallery or regular breaks, the presence of a supporting person or the use of communication aids can be considered. Courts have inherent powers to ensure that a defendant receives a fair trial. These have been successfully deployed in the context of facilitating the participation of a vulnerable defendant by measures including directing that defendants have the assistance of an intermediary[81].

75 YJCEA 1999, s 33A.
76 *R v Ukpabio* [2007] EWCA Crim 2108, [2008] 1 Cr App Rep 101; *R (on the application of Hamberger) v Crown Prosecution Service* [2014] EWHC 2814 (Admin).
77 *R (on the application of D) v Camberwell Youth Court* [2005] UKHL 4, [2005] 1 All ER 999.
78 *R v H* [2006] EWCA Crim 853.
79 Children and Young Persons Act 1933, s 44.
80 *R (on the application of P) v West London Youth Court* [2005] EWHC 2583 (Admin), [2006] 1 All ER 477; *SC v UK* (2005) 40 EHRR 10.
81 *R (on the application of C) v Sevenoaks Youth Court* [2009] EWHC 3088 (Admin), [2010] 1 All ER 735; *R (on the application of P) v West London Youth Court* [2005] EWHC 2583 (Admin), [2006] 1 All ER 477.

8.45

The Criminal Practice Direction limits the use of intermediaries to those 'most in need'. However, the provision is not regularised, as the statutory provisions allowing for defendant intermediaries are not yet in force[82]. There is an obvious inequality in the approach to the prosecution witnesses as compared with defendants[83]. However, if a defendant is a victim of trafficking and has other vulnerabilities, the work of an intermediary can be invaluable in case preparation. A ground rules hearing will be an opportunity to apply for the directions to include the use of an intermediary, where the supporting evidence is sufficient to demonstrate the need. The burden falls on the defence team to ensure that the defendant's needs have been properly identified and assessed.

Child defendants

8.46

Directive (EU) 2016/800 of the European Parliament and of the Council of 11 May 2011 provides procedural safeguards for children who are suspects or accused persons in criminal proceedings or subject to a European arrest warrant: The purpose of the Directive is to ensure that children, meaning persons under the age of 18, who are suspects or accused persons in criminal proceedings, are able to understand and follow those proceedings, and to exercise their right to a fair trial, and to prevent children from reoffending and foster their social integration. The Directive establishes minimum rules on the protection of procedural rights of such children, which include the following[84]:

- a right to information;
- the right to have the holder of parental responsibility informed;
- assistance by a lawyer;
- the right to an individual assessment concerning protection, education, training and social integration;
- the right to a medical examination;
- audiovisual recording of questioning;
- a limitation on the deprivation of liberty;
- alternative measures to detention;
- separate detention from adults;

---

82 YJCEA 1999, ss 33BA and 33BB.
83 *R (on the application of OP) v Secretary of State for Justice* [2014] 1 Cr App Rep 70.
84 Directive (EU) 2016/800 of the European Parliament and of the Council of 11 May 2011 provides procedural safeguards for children who are suspects or accused persons in criminal proceedings, available at http://eur-lex.europa.eu/legal-content/EN/TXT/?uri=CELEX%3A32016L0800, last accessed 15 December 2017.

- timely and diligent treatment of cases;

- the right to protection of privacy;

- the right to be accompanied by the holder of parental responsibility during the proceedings;

- the right to appear in person and participate in their trial;

- the right to legal aid;

- effective remedies for breach of rights;

- specific training of law enforcement authorities and of detention facilities which handle cases involving children to a level appropriate to their contact with children with regard to children's rights, appropriate questioning techniques, child psychology, and communication in a language adapted to the child. This includes the judiciary, the legal profession and child support organisations.

Vulnerable adult defendants

8.47

The Children's Directive does not apply to vulnerable adults, but on 30 November 2009, the Council of the European Union adopted a Resolution on a roadmap for strengthening the procedural rights of all suspected or accused persons in criminal proceedings. Taking a step-by-step approach, the roadmap calls for the adoption of measures regarding the right to translation and interpretation, the right to information on rights and information about the charges, the right to legal advice and legal aid, the right to communicate with relatives, employers and consular authorities and special safeguards for suspected or accused persons who are vulnerable[85]. Some procedural rights have been adopted through Directives 2010/64/EU[86] on interpretation and translation, 2012/13/EU[87] on the right to information, 2013/48/EU[88] on access to a lawyer and having persons informed of arrest and 2016/343/EU[89] on strengthening the presumption of innocence and the right to be present at trial.

---

85 Resolution of the Council of 30 November 2009 on a Roadmap for strengthening procedural rights of suspected or accused persons in criminal proceedings (Text with EEA relevance).

86 Directive 2010/64/EU of the European Parliament and of the Council of 20 October 2010 on the right to interpretation and translation in criminal proceedings.

87 Directive 2012/13/EU of the European Parliament and of the Council of 22 May 2012 on the right to information in criminal proceedings.

88 Directive 2013/48/EU of the European Parliament and of the Council of 22 October 2013 on the right of access to a lawyer in criminal proceedings and in European arrest warrant proceedings, and on the right to have a third party informed upon deprivation of liberty and to communicate with third persons and with consular authorities while deprived of liberty.

89 Directive (EU) 2016/343 of the European Parliament and of the Council of 9 March 2016 on the strengthening of certain aspects of the presumption of innocence and of the right to be present at the trial in criminal proceedings.

Intermediaries

8.48

The Ministry of Justice provides a scheme of registered intermediaries for vulnerable witnesses. Independent intermediaries are available for instruction for vulnerable defendants, subject to funding. They are not expert witnesses. The approach is set out in Criminal Procedure Rules, r 3.9 and the Advocate's Gateway Toolkit 16 provides a step-by-step guide to the use of intermediaries in criminal proceedings as follows[90]:

- courts must take every reasonable step to encourage and to facilitate the attendance of witnesses and to facilitate the participation of any person, including the defendant;

- the function of the intermediary is to facilitate complete, accurate and coherent communication with the vulnerable witness or vulnerable defendant;

- intermediaries should be considered in every case involving a child witness or child defendant;

- a ground rules hearing must take place if the defendant is vulnerable or if a vulnerable witness is due to give evidence;

- where it is suggested that the witness or complainant should have the assistance of an intermediary, it is expected that the intermediary will meet the witness in advance, produce a report on the necessary adaptations and attend the ground rules hearing to discuss the approach with the court and the parties[91].

Witness anonymity

Sexual offences

8.49

By the Sexual Offences (Amendment) Act 1992, s 1, orders are automatic to protect the identity of complainants in alleged sexual offences listed in s 2. The prohibition can be lifted in limited circumstances:

- publicity is required by the accused to encourage witnesses to come forward, and the defence case would be seriously prejudiced otherwise; or

---

90   The Advocate's Gateway, Toolkit 16 'Intermediaries Step by Step' (10 April 2017), available at www.theadvocatesgateway.org/images/toolkits/16-intermediaries-step-by-step-2017.pdf, last accessed 15 December 2017.
91   The Advocate's Gateway, Toolkits 2 and 16.

- the prohibition imposes a substantial restriction on reporting and it is in the interests of justice to order otherwise.

8.50

It is worth noting that the common expression used that a witness has 'waived' anonymity is a misnomer. A witness cannot unilaterally waive a court order, although if a complainant does reveal his identity, this would be a powerful factor in lifting any order protecting identification.

Serious gang related crime

8.51

Investigation anonymity orders can be made in relation to specified witnesses pursuant to the Coroners and Justice Act 2009, ss 74–85, where the allegation is murder or manslaughter and the death was caused by shooting with a firearm or use of a knife. The police can apply for such an order to a Justice of the Peace, who must be satisfied that there are reasonable grounds for believing that a qualifying offence has been committed, the relevant person is aged between 11 and 30 and is likely to have been a member of a criminal group who is willing to assist but is fearing intimidation or harm and it is more likely than not that he will provide information that would assist the criminal investigation.

Necessity

8.52

Otherwise, witness anonymity is governed by the Coroners and Justice Act 2009, ss 86–90 and the Criminal Procedure Rules 2015, rr 18.18–18.22. It is a special measure of 'last practicable resort'[92]. The measure must be applied for in writing in advance and must satisfy three conditions:

(i) the anonymity order must be in the interests of justice where the witness would not otherwise give evidence and there would be no real harm to the public interest[93]; and

(ii) it must be necessary to protect the safety of the witness, another person, or to prevent serious damage to property[94]; and

(iii) it must be consistent with receiving a fair trial[95].

---

92 *R v Donovan* [2012] EWCA Crim 2749.
93 *R v Mayers* [2008] EWCA Crim 2989, [2009] 2 All ER 145.
94 *R v Powar* [2009] EWCA Crim 594, [2009] 2 Cr App Rep 120; *R v Khan* [2010] EWCA Crim 1692.
95 *R v Ford* [2010] EWCA Crim 2250, [2011] Crim LR 475; *R v Fox* [2010] EWCA Crim 1280; *Pesukic v Switzerland* [2012] ECHR 2031; *Horncastle v UK* [2014] ECHR 1394.

8.53

Withholding the name and address of a witness may be accompanied with necessary redacting from documents, use of a pseudonym, screens and voice alteration. Section 89(2) of the Coroners and Justice Act 2009 sets out a non-exhaustive list of factors for the court to consider, which is summarised below[96]. It is up to the court what weight to give to each factor, depending on the case in hand and dependent on what judicial directions are possible to maintain the safety of the trial[97]:

- the defendant's right to know the identity of the witness;

- the extent to which the credit of the witness is subject to challenge;

- any evidence of dishonesty;

- whether the witness's evidence is the sole or decisive evidence in the case[98];

- whether the evidence can be properly challenged without the witness being identified[99];

- other reasonably practicable means to protect the witness.

8.54

If a witness gives evidence anonymously, a judicial direction must be given to ensure there is no prejudice to the accused. This has in some cases gone beyond warning against speculation, specifically to direct that it has nothing to do with the accused[100].

Reporting identity of child witnesses and child defendants

8.55

For persons under the age of 18, in the youth court, reporting restrictions are automatic[101]. However, in trials on indictment, the power is discretionary. The Crown Court may make an order protecting the identification of children pursuant to the YJCEA 1999, s 45. The onus is on the court, but advocates should ensure an order is sought where the above anonymity restrictions do not apply. A s 45 order can only apply until the child is 18 unless the court makes a lifetime order pursuant to the YJCEA 1999, s 45A. The expectation is that a

96 *R v Taylor* [2010] EWCA Crim 830.
97 *R v Nazir* [2009] EWCA Crim 213; *R v Willett* [2011] EWCA Crim 2710, [2012] 2 Cr App Rep (S) 76; *R v Okuwa* [2010] EWCA Crim 832.
98 *R v Davis* [2008] UKHL 36, [2008] 1 AC 1128; *Al Khawaja v UK* (2012) 54 EHRR 807.
99 *R v Donovan* [2012] EWCA Crim 2749.
100 *R v Nazir* [2009] EWCA Crim 213; *R v Willett* [2011] EWCA Crim 2710, [2012] 2 Cr App Rep (S) 76 and see Crown Court Compendium, chs 3–8.
101 CYPA 1933, s 49.

defendant will be named, but the rights of the child have been said to 'trump' the rights of the public to know[102]. In relation to trafficked children there is a powerful argument against publicity, particularly where that identification could lead to re-trafficking.

Adult defendant anonymity

8.56

Save for the provisions of the Education Act 2011, which makes it a criminal offence to publish material identifying a teacher accused of a criminal offence against a child at their school until the teacher is charged, and save for the principles discussed in *R v GL and R v N* on 23 November 2017[103] (see para **9.35** ff), there is no specific power to anonymise an adult defendant. However, prosecution obligations to investigate whether a suspect is a victim of human trafficking suggest that the investigatory approach to such cases should take the approach of treating the suspect as a witness until charge[104].

8.57

The qualified right to privacy has some influence on restricting positive publication of ongoing investigations: current police guidance on releasing details and images of suspects depends on balancing the risk to the public and the legitimate purpose, necessity and proportionality[105].

8.58

Regulation of publicity to ensure a fair trial is governed by the Contempt of Court Act 1981, which can include postponing reporting of proceedings until the conclusion of the trial or related proceedings and restricting publicity of the defendant's identity where naming would lead to the complainant being identified (note that this is almost invariably achieved by not naming the complainant himself).

---

102 *R v Lee* [1993] 2 All ER 170, [1993] 1 WLR 103; *R v Cormick* [2015] EWCA Crim 110, [2015] 1 Cr App Rep (S) 483.

103 [2017] EWCA Crim 2129.

104 CPS guidance on suspects in a criminal case who might be victims of trafficking or slavery, available at www.cps.gov.uk/legal/h_to_k/human_trafficking_and_smuggling/#a25.

105 ACPO, *Guidance on releasing images of suspects or defendants*, available at http://library.college.police. uk/docs/acpo/ACPO-Guidance-Release-Images-Suspects-Media.pdf; ACPO, *Guidance from the Communication and Advisory Group* (2010), available at http://news.npcc.police.uk/Clients/NPCC/ ACPO%20CAG%20guidance.pdf; and ACPO, *Guidance on relationships with the media* (May 2013), available at www.npcc.police.uk/documents/reports/2013/201305-cop-media-rels.pdf, all accessed on 15 December 2017 See also CPS guidance on media relations, available at www.cps.gov.uk/publications/ agencies/mediaprotocol.html.

8.59

The Judicial College's guide, *Reporting Restrictions in the Criminal Courts*[106], is aimed at assisting the lower courts in reaching decisions as to whether they can or must depart from the open justice principle and, if so, to what extent. The Guide sets out the statutory exceptions to the open justice principles, both automatic and discretionary. It does not provide any specific guidance for cases in the Court of Appeal Criminal Division[107].

Applications to move proceedings

8.60

It is common that victims of forced criminality who raise modern slavery as a defence will be required to attend a court local to where they have offended or been apprehended. In those circumstances, it should be borne in mind that the victim, if on bail, will be required to travel to a 'danger or high risk area', where their traffickers may still operate. Not only does this raise safeguarding issues, but it also causes additional anxiety for the trafficking victim defendant.

8.61

Further consideration should be had to the means of the trafficking victim defendant, if the proceedings are being held in a court that is a considerable distance from his address. Victims of modern slavery should be accommodated in locations that are secure and safe. Many are housed a considerable distance away, and will have insufficient funds to travel to court. In such circumstances consideration must be given to an application to move the proceedings if this will not place the individual in further danger. Section 75 of the Senior Courts Act 1981 regulates the place of trial. Variation of venue is governed by s 76. The defendant or the prosecutor, if dissatisfied with the place of trial as fixed by the magistrates' court, or by the Crown Court, may apply to the Crown Court for a direction, or further direction, varying the place of trial; and the court shall take the matter into consideration and may endorse or refuse the application, or give a direction not in compliance with the terms of the direction sought, as the court thinks fit. Either party may apply for a change of venue. Reasons may include possible prejudice to a defendant, or where the nature of the case has provoked particular public hostility, but the reasons cannot include securing a multiracial jury[108]. Whilst witness or victim intimidation is not a specific criteria, it should be a factor the court can take into account in order to comply with the protective procedural requirements.

---

106 April 2015 (revised May 2016).
107 See Chapter 9 for anonymity for applicants in the Court of Appeal Criminal Division.
108 *R v Ford* [1989] QB 868, [1989] 3 All ER 445; *R v Bansall* [1985] Crim LR 151.

Applications to hold a Crown Court hearing in camera

8.62

In addition to an application for a court to be cleared as a special measure for vulnerable witnesses under the YJCEA 1999, there is a discretion to hold proceedings or parts of proceedings in the absence of the public and the press, known as 'in camera' where such a course is necessary for the administration of justice and national security. The Criminal Procedure Rules 2015, r 16.10 requires a prosecutor to make an application for proceedings to be held in camera for reasons of national security or for the protection of the identity of a witness or any other person. Given that trafficking can occur in the context of terrorism, this is a procedure that could arise in those types of cases.

9   Criminal appeal process

Introduction

9.1

It is a common occurrence that victims of human trafficking and modern slavery are overlooked by the criminal justice system, both post and pre-enactment of the Modern Slavery Act ('MSA') 2015[1]. This is often because victims do not make disclosures regarding their exploitation until after conviction, or because trafficking indicators have been overlooked by their legal representatives, the prosecution and the courts at the time of conviction. Trafficking in human beings remains a very serious concern, both in the UK and worldwide. The number of cases coming before the appellate courts demonstrates the underlying complexities and systemic failures in such cases.

9.2

It is important that prima facie unsafe convictions are challenged as soon as they come to light, for a number of reasons. Many foreign national victims will be subject to immigration proceedings, such as automatic deportation triggered by the conviction[2]. Many victims who decide to cooperate with the authorities into their trafficking situation and background circumstances may have numerous unchallenged convictions as a result of their exploitation and may have bad character for any subsequent criminal case against their traffickers, where they are a complainant. These convictions should be scrutinised with a view to challenging them, even if they are significantly out of time, or spent[3].

9.3

Setting aside convictions plays an important part in the rehabilitation and self-identification process for victims. Many may go on to enter into education or employment, certain types of convictions will directly affect eligibility onto a course or particular type of employment and hinder a victim's re-integration back into society. It is also necessary for convictions to be set aside before a defendant may qualify for compensation under the various schemes (see Chapter 12).

---

1   See the defence of slavery: MSA 2015, s 45.
2   See UK Borders Act 2007, s 32.
3   See Chapter 13 on funding and the sufficient benefit test.

Appeals to the Crown Court

9.4

There is an automatic right of appeal to the Crown Court against sentence and/or conviction in the magistrates' court. Notices of appeal[4] must be served within 21 days of the final disposal of the case[5].

9.5

A defendant may appeal from a magistrates' court to the Crown Court under the Magistrates' Courts Act 1980, s 108, only in the following circumstances:

(i)   if he pleaded guilty, against his sentence;

(ii) if he did not plead guilty, against the conviction and sentence.

9.6

This has historically caused problems for those defendants who have entered guilty pleas in the magistrates' court, barring them from appealing against their conviction to the Crown Court. It is a frequent event that victims of modern slavery involved in forced criminality are advised to plead guilty by trial representatives, or have entered pleas unrepresented. In these circumstances an application to the Criminal Cases Review Commission (CCRC) can be made. However, in certain circumstances consideration should be made into first seeking an application to reopen the proceedings under the Magistrates' Courts Act ('MCA') 1980, s 142, which, in comparison to a CCRC application and referral, can be dealt with in a matter of weeks, rather than months. Failing an unsuccessful application to re-open, an application to the CCRC can then be made.

Applications to re-open cases

9.7

Section 142 of the MCA 1980 confers upon the magistrates' court a power to rectify mistakes. Thus, s 142(2) enables a convicted defendant (whether he pleaded guilty or not guilty) to ask the magistrates to set the conviction aside.

9.8

The power of the magistrates' court to re-open a conviction is provided by the MCA 1980, s 142(2). This allows that:

---

4   See   www.justice.gov.uk/courts/procedure-rules/criminal/docs/october-2015/acc001-eng.pdf,   last accessed 14 December 2017.

5   Criminal Procedure Rules 2015, r 34.2(2).

'Where a person is convicted by a magistrates' court and it subsequently appears to the court that it would be in the interests of justice that the case should be heard again by different justices, the court may so direct'.

The applicable test is in the interests of justice, which has a broad application.

9.9

Section 142(2) was considered in *R v Croydon Youth Court, ex p DPP*[6], in which the defendant sought to reverse his guilty plea, relying upon s 142(2). The matter was re-opened and a re-hearing directed by different justices[7]. It was further considered in *R (on the application of Williamson) v City of Westminster Magistrates' Court*[8] where it was again held that the purpose of s 142(2) was to enable the court to correct mistakes, but in limited circumstances; it was not a power equivalent to a full appeal to the Crown Court or High Court, nor was it a power of general review. The court concluded that it did have the power to remit the matter in the circumstances of the case of *Williamson* itself, but declined to do so. The argument advanced was that the claimant received incompetent advice from his solicitor, in relation to the strength of CCTV evidence and misrepresentation of the existence of a witness relating to an allegation of being drunk and disorderly and assault. This case is arguably distinguishable from cases where a victim of trafficking is not advised by his representatives that he has a defence in law, or is not advised of his rights under the various legal frameworks for non-punishment and non-prosecution in the context of human trafficking (see Chapters 1 and 5).

9.10

There is no statutory time limit to making an application to re-open, although 28 days should be used as a guide. Applications made with significant delays may be refused on interests of justice grounds[9]. However, it is likely that applications to re-open convictions involving victims of human trafficking will be well outside 28 days, and in some cases several years after the conclusion of a case. Substantial reasons should be given regarding the lapse of time in making the application; commonly these would be that the victim of trafficking was unaware of the proceedings and was convicted in their absence as a result of being trafficked or re-trafficked, or has only been identified as a victim of trafficking post-conviction, or was advised to plead guilty by trial representative and was not advised of any defence available to them at the time and has since been advised by new representatives.

---

6 [1997] 2 Cr App Rep 411.
7 The Director of Public Prosecutions applied for a judicial review.
8 [2012] EWHC 1444 (Admin), [2012] 2 Cr App Rep 24.
9 Ibid.

9.11

The application may be made orally or in writing to the convicting magistrates' court. It is likely that a written application will be required before the court will agree to list it for an oral hearing, particularly where the application is delayed. It is advisable that written applications are addressed to the legal advisor at the magistrates' court.

9.12

If new representatives are instructed, then where there were any failures by trial representatives to advise on relevant human trafficking law, this should be set out in the application. The courts are generally reluctant to re-open cases where a defendant was represented, so an explanation as to failure to advise on a defence under the MSA 2015, s 45, or failure to advance an abuse of process argument should be clearly set out to the court. Cases where a defendant was convicted in his absence are likely to be re-opened, as it is usually in the interests of justice for a defendant to be able to defend himself. A re-hearing will usually be the normal course[10].

Effect of re-opening

9.13

If the matter is re-opened successfully the conviction will be set aside, as will any sentence or ancillary orders and the matter will be treated as an adjourned trial. The justices who sat on the original hearing or application to re-open the hearing cannot sit on the trial. It is then that steps should be taken to ask the CPS to review the prosecution in light of its trafficking guidance[11]. The prosecution has the power to offer no evidence after a case has been re-opened (see Chapters 5 and 7 regarding CPS guidance, non-prosecution principles and abuse of process).

Appeals to the Court of Appeal

Preparation of appeals and disclosure – defence investigation

9.14

Defence investigations play a vital part in the success of an appeal. In cases involving victims of slavery and human trafficking a significant amount of preliminary work must be conducted by the defence. The objective is to obtain

---

10 See *R (on the application of Morsby) v Tower Bridge Magistrates' Court* [2007] EWHC 2766 (Admin).
11 An abuse of process argument should also be considered, see Chapters 7 and 5.

material that can be used as fresh evidence in support of a prospective applicant's human trafficking and modern slavery claim. Victims may not be able to recall many details about the previous proceedings, or who their trial representatives were. The first step is to contact the convicting court to try to obtain as much information as possible. It is not necessary to ask for a certificate of conviction, although this document may contain useful information. The court may be asked to provide basic information needed for an applicant's representative, such as:

(i)   details of trial representatives;

(ii)   date of conviction;

(iii)   date of sentence;

(iv)   sentence received;

(v)   number of days spent on remand;

(vi)   details of court transcribers;

(vii)   case number;

(viii) confirmation of whether a pre-sentence report was ordered.

9.15

When contacting previous trial lawyers for their files, it important to obtain a complete set of papers, including the following:

(i)   case papers;

(ii)   all witness statements and exhibits;

(iii)   any expert reports;

(iv)   interview tape;

(v)   correspondences and working file;

(vi)   police station notes;

(vii)   defence statement;

(viii) any basis of plea;

(ix)   pre-sentence report, if one was prepared;

(x)   instructions;

(xi)   all attendance notes;

(xii)   counsel's notebooks and notes;

(xiii) unused material;

(xiv)   any previous advice on appeal.

9.16

Subject access requests will also be necessary in cases where an applicant was either unrepresented or, in older cases, where the trial lawyers are no longer in possession of their file: the obligation is only to keep a file for six years[12]. In cases where previous representatives confirm they have destroyed the file, it is advisable to ask if they hold anything electronically by way of emails or on their digital case management system.

9.17

Subject access requests under the Data Protection Act 1998 can be made to the police, Ministry of Justice, CPS and Home Office. Material which contains personal information about a client can be obtained through making an application under the Data Protection Act 1998, s 7. If making these requests on behalf of a client, signed authority is needed: it is likely that certified copies of an identity document and proof of address of the client will be required when making such an application. Most bodies will have specific subject access request forms that will need to be completed. There may also be a small fee attached to the request. Applications for data held by police authorities that do not fall under the Data Protection Act 1998, s 7 can be made under the Freedom of Information Act 2000, s 1.

9.18

If any other litigation or proceedings are ongoing, such as immigration proceedings, claims against public authorities or judicial review proceedings, any witness statement taken or served in those proceedings should be obtained, and discussion with the other legal teams should take place to determine what material they hold which may be served as fresh evidence. It may be that a multi-professionals' meeting will be beneficial, where there is ongoing litigation to discuss fresh evidence, witness statements, legally privileged material and timetables.

9.19

Representatives should also consider obtaining the following documents from other legal representatives or via subject access requests to the relevant bodies:

(i)   the competent authority file, including NRM referral form, minutes, all material relied upon in making its determination, interview notes, a full copy of the reasonable and conclusive grounds determinations and full reasoning;

(ii)   prison and probation files;

(iii)   immigration file;

---

12 See *R v Ealing Magistrates' Court, ex p Sahota* (1997) 162 JP 73, [1997] 45 LS Gaz R 29, QBD.

(iv)   medical notes;

(v)   Home Office file;

(vi)   Upper Tribunal judgments;

(vii)   First-tier Tribunal judgments;

(viii)   judicial review material;

(ix)   asylum interview;

(x)   all witness statements and accounts given in related proceedings;

(xi)   screening interview.

9.20

A statement from the applicant should be taken, and a decision should be made as to whether this is served as fresh evidence. The statement should cover background trafficking, life in the UK and personal circumstances, details of the offending, any nexus between the offence and the exploitation, and instructions on what advice the applicant was given during the original proceedings. It should also be considered best practice to work from any pre-existing witness statement, already recently taken regarding the trafficking background and exploitation in other live proceedings such as an asylum claim or judicial review claim. It is common that during the process of preparing a criminal appeal an applicant will be engaging with numerous lawyers such as immigration, public law and community care. By taking a joint statement, the risk of unnecessary trauma and possible mistaken inconsistencies and inaccuracies can be avoided or minimised.

9.21

A transcript of the summing up, sentencing remarks and mitigation should be obtained. Each court will have a specified transcription company. The requests for transcripts will need to be made through the approved company. Permission to obtain the transcript from the court is now generally needed via the submission of a form EX107.

Appeal against sentence

9.22

In *R v L*[13] the Lord Chief Justice recognised the spectrum of culpability or criminality of victims of trafficking that applied. The court emphasised, at para 14, that offences committed which were unconnected with the status of an individual as a victim of trafficking could still amount to mitigation:

---

13 [2013] EWCA Crim 991, [2014] 1 All ER 113.

'These defendants are not safeguarded from prosecution or punishment for offences which were unconnected with the fact that they were being or have been trafficked, although we do not overlook that the fact that they have been trafficked may sometimes provide substantial mitigation.'

This spectrum of culpability was again highlighted at para 33, where the court said that 'due allowance [was] to be made in the sentencing decision for their diminished culpability.'

9.23

It is possible that victims will not be recognised as victims of human trafficking during the sentencing exercise, they may not have been referred into the NRM at that stage, and therefore no mitigation evidence concerning trafficking would have been placed before the sentencing court. It is possible for the Court of Appeal to consider material to which the sentencing judge did not have access, or which was not in existence at the time.

9.24

Even in cases where the criminality is not directly linked to exploitation, or in cases where an MSA 2015, s 45 defence would not apply, it may be possible to appeal against a sentence where fresh evidence regarding the defendant's victim status has come to light.

9.25

In general, the court does not regard itself bound by the fresh evidence rules[14], although an explanation must still be given as to why the evidence was not placed before the Crown Court. The court may also order probation reports where they feel they would be assisted by one, even in cases where no previous report was prepared in the Crown Court.

9.26

Under the Criminal Appeal Act 1968, s 9, a defendant may appeal to the Court of Appeal against a sentence imposed by the Crown Court on indictment[15]:

'(3) On an appeal against sentence the Court of Appeal, if they consider that the appellant should be sentenced differently for the offence for which he was dealt with by the court below may—

(a)   quash any sentence or order which is the subject of the appeal; and

---

14 *R v Roberts* [2016] EWCA Crim 2915.

15 In certain circumstances a defendant may appeal against sentence imposed by the Crown Court following conviction in the magistrates' court, including summary offences sent to the Crown Court under the Criminal Justice Act 1988, s 41.

(b) in place of it pass such a sentence or make such an order as they think appropriate for the case and as the court below had the power to pass or make when dealing with him for the offence;

but the Court shall so exercise their powers under this subsection that, taking the case as a whole, the appellant is not more severely dealt with on appeal than he was dealt with by the court below'[16].

Grounds of appeal against sentence

9.27

When making an application for leave to appeal against sentence, an applicant should include the ground on which the sentence is being challenged, eg 'manifestly excessive' or 'wrong in principle'. It is likely in relation to victims of trafficking that the ground of appeal will be confined to an assertion that the sentence was manifestly excessive because of the failure to advance mitigation that attaches to a person's status as a victim of trafficking. While the court will not interfere with sentences which are said to be too long unless they are *manifestly* excessive, it may be argued that a sentence is manifestly excessive by months and in some instances weeks. It is important to note when dealing with victims of trafficking applicants that any reduction in sentence is likely to have a direct impact on various elements of ongoing proceedings, such as automatic deportation proceedings. In cases where victims of trafficking have been recommended for deportation this is a component of the sentence and maybe the subject of an appeal[17].

Common grounds of challenge on appeal against conviction

9.28

Common scenarios where an appeal is brought by a defendant are:

(i) the defendant did not disclose that he was or self-identify as a victim of trafficking at the time of the defendant's criminal proceedings (first instance) and there were no or few indicators present of trafficking during the criminal proceedings. After conviction the defendant is identified either through experts, supporting organisations or by the competent authority, other statutory agencies or in other legal proceedings (ie immigration appeal hearings) as a victim of trafficking. The defendant's conviction is then challenged as unsafe on the premise that: (1) ECAT, Art 26 or the EU Trafficking Directive, Art 8 was engaged; (2) the CPS was unaware at

---

16 Criminal Appeal Act 1968, s 11(3).
17 Criminal Appeal Act 1968, s 50.

the time when the prosecution was brought against the defendant that the defendant was: (i) a victim of trafficking; and (ii) the offence for which the defendant was being tried was connected to their trafficking status; and (3) had the CPS been made aware of the defendant's status as a victim of trafficking, it would or 'might well' have concluded that it was not in the public interest to prosecute the defendant[18];

(ii) the defendant did present with trafficking indicators during the course of the criminal proceedings but the legal representatives of the defendant did not advise at all or adequately on ECAT, Art 26 or the EU Trafficking Directive, Art 8 and did not make either public interest representations to the Crown or advance an abuse of process application (see Chapter 7). The Court of Appeal requires that applications are only made to the court after due diligence[19]. It is therefore necessary that any new legal appellate team apprises itself fully of what happened in the course of the criminal proceedings that might be relevant to the grounds of challenge, and ensures the facts are correct[20]. In pleading this ground, either actual or implied allegations of incompetence by previous legal representatives will be made. It is therefore necessary that enquiries are made of the previous lawyers concerning the particulars of implied or actual incompetence and that they are made aware of the allegation[21]. Further, it is important to secure other objective and independent evidence to substantiate the allegations made. Any grounds which will go to the conduct of the trial are likely to require a waiver of privilege from the defendant. A formal waiver should be lodged with the grounds, or the court should be informed if the defendant is unwilling to give a waiver;

(iii) the CPS failed to adequately or at all to review whether the prosecution of the defendant was in the public interest; see para **7.28** on abuse of process submissions.

Fresh evidence

9.29

Section 23 of the Criminal Appeal Act 1968 addresses the receipt of fresh evidence by the Court of Appeal Criminal Division. The admission of evidence under this section is at the court's discretion and evidence will be admitted if it is necessary or expedient in the interests of justice (s 23(1)). Section 23(2) provides factors to be taken into account when deciding whether the evidence

---

18 See *R v O* [2011] EWCA Crim 2226 and *R v LZ* [2012] EWCA Crim 1867.
19 *R v A* [2014] EWCA Crim 567.
20 *R v McCook* [2014] EWCA Crim 734, [2016] 2 Cr App Rep 388; see further *R v Grant-Murray* [2017] EWCA Crim 1228, [2017] All ER (D) 62 (Aug), para 131.
21 Send draft grounds to former representatives inviting their comments, particularly on the facts. On receipt, reconsider draft grounds and include confirmation that trial counsel has seen them. If there is no response, then this should be recorded.

should be admitted. With an application to admit fresh evidence the court will consider whether it is capable of belief, whether the evidence may afford a ground for allowing the appeal, whether the evidence would have been admissible in the court below and whether there was a reasonable explanation for the failure to adduce the evidence in criminal proceedings below. Chapters 5 and 6 set out the types of expert evidence relevant to appeals brought by victims of trafficking. A large portion of fresh evidence in trafficking cases will be the competent authority trafficking determination, findings made by immigration tribunals and any witness statements served in those proceedings. All fresh evidence needs to be accompanied by a Form W with a supporting '*Gogana* statement'[22] setting out how this new evidence was obtained and why it was not deployed in the original Crown Court proceedings. Applications to adduce fresh evidence will now usually require inquiries by the court as to whether privilege has been waived. If not, then an explanation should be provided as to why it is not necessary. Recommendations to the single judge as to the steps to be followed in deciding whether to grant leave in out of time cases where 'fresh evidence' is said to apply, are set out in *R v Singh*[23]:

> '50. First, single judges faced with an application for leave to appeal based on fresh evidence, before making any decision, should inquire whether privilege has been waived and, if not, an explanation should be provided as to why it is not necessary.

> '51. Second, if an application reaches the single judge without a Respondent's Notice and the single judge would be assisted by one, the single judge should direct the Respondent to consider the application and submit a response.

> 52. Third, the single judge should not simply refer an application based on fresh evidence to the full court without any consideration. Once the single judge has ascertained the position from trial representatives and the Respondent, he or she may well be in a position to determine whether the application is potentially arguable. If it is not, the application can be rejected at that stage. If it is potentially arguable, the single judge should normally not grant applications for leave or an extension of time but should refer them to the full court.

> 53. Fourth, if the single judge decides to refer an application to the full court, he or she should follow the course adopted by the single judge in this case and refer it for directions. The parties should then seek to agree those directions and submit them to the Registrar for approval by the court. Only if agreement cannot be reached should it be necessary for there to be an oral hearing in relation to them.'

---

22 *R v Gogana* (1999) Times, 12 July.
23 [2017] EWCA Crim 466.

Extensions of time

9.30

An application for leave to appeal must be lodged no later than 28 days after the decision which is being appealed[24]. The court has the power to grant an extension of time if it decides there is merit to the application for leave. A significant number of appeals brought by victims of trafficking against their convictions are brought out of time and therefore an application for an extension of time must be set out in the body of the grounds. In most instances there will be new lawyers instructed to advise on appeal, and the preparation and defence's investigation stage will usually take considerable time; however there is always a need to show expedition. It is important to set out either within the body of the grounds the steps taken to prepare the application for leave to appeal, or for solicitors to set out a chronology in Criminal Justice Act 1967, s 9 format to serve with the application. In short, there is no coherent test for granting leave to appeal out of time, but substantial grounds should be considered necessary. In cases concerning trafficked victims it has historically been possible to overcome the hurdle of showing that exceptional leave should be granted. However, there are parallels between cases involving the prosecution of human trafficking victims and the prosecution of refugees who failed to avail themselves of the refugee defence under the Immigration and Asylum Act 1999, s 31. In *R v Ordu*[25] the Court of Appeal said that, in change of law cases (appeals brought on the ground that the law was not generally understood at the time of the case or has changed or developed), following *R v Jogee*[26] (the well-known joint enterprise authority) and *R v Johnson*[27], even where a clear injustice could be shown in relation to an applicant who had pleaded guilty to a document offence before the law changed, if a 'substantial injustice' could not be shown, then exceptional leave to appeal out of time should not be granted. This approach to the grant of leave to appeal out of time should be contrasted with similar cases where advice was deficient, but not because of a change in law; see *R v K(P)*[28] in which it was said obiter that all that was necessary for the grant of leave to appeal out of time was for an applicant to show that there would be a clear injustice. This was approved in *R v H* as part of the ratio decidendi of the decision[29]. Thus in a case involving an application for leave to appeal which did not concern a guilty plea and did not involve a change in law, while some exceptionality should be shown, in fact, it seems that it would merely be necessary to show that the conviction was unsafe: it would not be necessary to show a substantial injustice.

---

24 CAA 1968, s 18(2).
25 [2017] EWCA Crim 4, [2017] 1 Cr App Rep 391.
26 [2017] AC 387, [2016] 1 Cr App Rep 31.
27 [2016] EWCA Crim 1613, [2017] 1 Cr App Rep 12.
28 [2017] EWCA Crim 486.
29 20 October 2017 (CAO Reference 201604765B5).

9.31

The direction of travel in the regional trafficking instruments and domestic policy guidance is that victims of trafficking should be identified and safeguarded. The observations of the Lord Chief Justice in *R v L*[30] are helpful in steering a submission on exceptional leave:

> 'It is surely elementary that every court, whether a Crown Court or magistrates' court, understands the abhorrence with which trafficking in human beings of any age is regarded both in the United Kingdom and throughout the civilised world. It has not, however, and could not have been argued that if and when victims of trafficking participate or become involved in criminal activities, a trafficked individual should be given some kind of immunity from prosecution, just because he or she was or has been trafficked, nor for that reason alone, that a substantive defence to a criminal charge is available to a victim of trafficking. What, however, is clearly established, and numerous different papers, reports and decided cases have demonstrated, is that when there is evidence that victims of trafficking have been involved in criminal activities, the investigation and the decision whether there should be a prosecution, and, if so, any subsequent proceedings require to be approached with the greatest sensitivity. The reasoning is not always spelled out, and perhaps we should do so now. The criminality, or putting it another way, the culpability, of any victim of trafficking may be significantly diminished, and in some cases effectively extinguished, not merely because of age (always a relevant factor in the case of a child defendant) but because no realistic alternative was available to the exploited victim but to comply with the dominant force of another individual, or group of individuals.'

Appeal following a guilty plea in the Crown Court

9.32

Most of the notable cases which have been brought before the Court of Appeal Criminal Division to date concerning non-punishment of victims of human trafficking have been cases where the applicants entered guilty pleas. A guilty plea does not preclude an appeal against conviction. The court has allowed appeals against conviction following guilty pleas following flawed advice. Significantly, where the appeal relates to the public interest limb of the CPS Full Code not being applied, the fact that a guilty plea was unequivocal will not necessarily prevent a successful appeal[31].

---

30 [2013] EWCA Crim 991, [2014] 1 All ER 113 at para [13].
31 *R v O* [2011] EWCA Crim 2226 and *R v LZ* [2012] EWCA Crim 1867.

Further applications that may be made with an application for leave to appeal

Applications for bail

9.33

Whilst the single judge cannot grant bail pending an appeal, the court can grant bail pending an appeal in exceptional circumstances, where it is necessary in order to do justice in the case[32]. The application should be made at the same time as the application for leave or prior to leave being determined.

9.34

The application should be made with a Form B. In exceptional cases, where the applicant's sentence is short or he is in very ill health, then a note should be sent to the Registrars, highlighting the immediate issues, particularly if the victim of trafficking has any mental health issues. If bail is being applied for, practitioners should liaise with the relevant first responder and support organisation to ensure a suitable bail address can be put forward (see Chapters 7 and 11 for further considerations regarding bail).

Anonymity for applicants in the Court of Appeal Criminal Division

9.35

Requests for anonymity should always be considered when making an application for leave to appeal where the applicant is a victim of trafficking. In *R v GL and R v N*[33] on 23 November 2017 the Court of Appeal reviewed the principles that govern anonymity in criminal appeals brought by victims of trafficking who have been convicted following criminal proceedings, without purporting to give general guidance.

9.36

A practice has developed in cases involving trafficking victims and refugees of withholding the names of appellants during the hearing of appeals where human rights (in particular the European Convention on Human Rights and Fundamental Freedoms, Arts 2, 3 or 8) might be violated through the risk created by publishing details of the case. Then, if the risk is ruled to outweigh ECHR, Art 10 and open justice, an order will be made under the Contempt of

---

32 *R v Watton* (1979) 68 Cr App Rep 293.
33 [2017] EWCA Crim 2129.

Court Act 1981, s 11 prohibiting the publication of that name in connection with the proceedings. This has been expressly endorsed in *GL and N*.

9.37

Anonymity orders and other regulation of the court's procedures, pursuant to inherent or Human Rights Act ('HRA') 1998 powers, concern restrictions that a court can impose on what may be said in open court, whilst reporting restrictions concern what the media can report about what has already been aired in open court. As was recognised in *Khuja (formerly known as PNM) v Times Newspapers Ltd*[34], 'The distinction between these two aspects [of open justice] is not always recognised in the case law'.

9.38

Recognising that open justice has never been absolute, the Supreme Court in *Khuja* set out examples of the historic exceptions to open justice, in the context of the court regulating its procedures, in particular the inherent power to sit in private. The court stated that:

> 'The inherent power of the courts extends to making orders for the conduct of the proceedings in a way which will prevent the disclosure in open court of the names of parties or witnesses or of other matters, and it is well established that this may be a preferable alternative to the more drastic course of sitting in private: see *R v Socialist Worker Printers and Publishers Ltd, ex p Attorney General* [1975] QB 637, 652; *Attorney General v Leveller Magazine Ltd* [1979] AC 440, 451–452 (Lord Diplock), 458 (Viscount Dilhorne), 464 (Lord Edmund-Davies)'[35].

9.39

As far as the criminal courts are concerned, the Supreme Court confirms later in that same paragraph that:

> '...the court retains the power which it has always possessed to allow evidence to be given in such a way that the identity of a witness or other matters is not more widely disclosed in open court, if the interests of justice require it. Where a court directs that proceedings before it are to be conducted in such a way as to withhold any matter, the Contempt of Court Act 1981, s 11 allows it to make ancillary orders preventing their disclosure out of court. Measures of this kind have consistently been treated by the European Court of Human Rights as consistent with article 6 of the Convention if they are necessary to protect the interests of the proper administration of justice: *Doorson v The Netherlands* (1996) 22 EHRR 330, para 71; *V v United Kingdom* (1999) 30 EHRR 121,

---

34 [2017] UKSC 49, [2017] 3 WLR 351 at [16].
35 At para [14].

para 87; cf *A v British Broadcasting Corpn* [2015] AC 588, paras 44–45 (Lord Reed).'

9.40

Importantly, the Supreme Court confirmed 'that necessity remains the touchstone of this jurisdiction'[36]. The court stated (at [15]) that two factors have combined to broaden the scope of the exceptions to the open justice principle, namely civil and criminal litigation raising issues of national security and the recognition of rights derived from the ECHR, which by the HRA 1998, s 6, bind the courts as public authorities. In relation to the latter, the Supreme Court said:

> 'The Convention right most often engaged in such cases is the right under article 8 to respect for private and family life. Article 8 rights are heavily qualified by the Convention itself, and even when they are made good they must be balanced in a publication case against the right to freedom of expression protected by Article 10. But other Convention rights may occasionally be engaged which are practically unqualified, such as the right to life under article 2 and to protection against serious ill-treatment under Article 3: *A v British Broadcasting Corpn* [2015] AC 588. These countervailing interests have become significant, not just because they have come to be recognised as legal rights, but because the resonance of what used to be reported only in the press and the broadcasting media has been greatly magnified in the age of the internet and social media'.

9.41

Thus an anonymity order can usually only be justified where it is strictly necessary. As Lord Roger indicated in *Re Guardian News and Media Ltd*[37]:

> '… in an appropriate case, where threats to life or safety are involved, the right of the press to freedom of expression obviously has to yield: a newspaper does not have the right to publish information at the known potential cost of an individual being killed or maimed. In such a situation the court may make an anonymity order to protect the individual'.

9.42

R v Z[38] (which is now largely superseded by the fuller exegesis of the law in *GL and N*) was an appeal (a CCRC reference) which was allowed on the ground that the appellant had not been given adequate advice in the context

---

36 At para [14].
37 [2010] UKSC 1, [2010] 2 AC 697 at para 26.
38 [2016] EWCA Crim 1083.

of an identity document offence concerning the application of the refugee defence under the Immigration and Asylum Act 1999, s 31. In advance of the appeal, the Vice-President asked the appellant's counsel for assistance in relation to the principles which apply when reporting restrictions/anonymity might be appropriate in appeals:

> 'Mr Thomas was asked by the Registrar to provide a note on this court's powers to impose reporting restrictions. He has done so and he has set out the powers of the Crown Court and the powers of the Court of Appeal, Criminal Division, which are, perhaps surprisingly, different. But it is quite plain that we do have the power to impose reporting restrictions, particularly where it is necessary to protect the rights of an appellant as protected by Articles 2, 3 or 8 of the European Convention. We cannot go into the details of why it is necessary in this case to protect those rights because to do so may well lead to the inevitable identification of the appellant. Suffice it to say that we consider it appropriate on the facts of this case to follow, as the Civil Division of this court have done, the universal practice of anonymising judgments in cases involving asylum seekers. We are satisfied that the publication of the name of the appellant would create an avoidable and serious risk for her and or for other people'[39].

9.43

Insofar as the HRA 1998 is concerned, Lord Roger in his judgment in *Re Guardian News and Media Ltd*[40] addressed anonymity orders giving effect to ECHR rights as follows:

> 'States are, of course, obliged by Articles 2 and 3 to have a structure of laws in place which will help to protect people from attacks on their lives or assaults, not only by officers of the state but by other individuals. Therefore, the power of a court to make an anonymity order can be seen as part of that structure'.

See also *Re Trinity Mirror plc*[41] by way of example, in which the power was also said to arise from the HRA 1998, s 6.

9.44

Although *R v Marine A*[42] was not mentioned in *GL and N*, the court in *GL and N* was referred to it and the checklist in *Marine A* provides an essential tool for the application of anonymity principles (as reaffirmed in *Khuja* above).

---

39 At para 39.
40 [2010] UKSC 1, [2010] 2 AC 697 at para 26.
41 [2008] EWCA Crim 50, [2008] QB 770 at para 26.
42 [2013] EWCA Crim 2367, [2014] 1 WLR 3326.

9.45

In *Marine A* the Court Martial board found Marine A guilty of murder but acquitted Marines B and C. The judge advocate then lifted the prohibition on identification of the marines, on the ground that identification would not create or increase an immediate risk to their lives, although he stayed the order pending appeal. The marines applied for leave to appeal against the order lifting the prohibition on their identification and the media parties applied for leave to appeal against the rulings denying them access to the video clips and the stills which had not been made available. In a joint judgment to which Lord Thomas of Cwmgeidd CJ and Tugendhat J contributed, the court held:

> '84 … a defendant in a criminal trial must be named save in rare circumstances.
>
> 85 However, the court has a power to withhold the name and address of a defendant in cases where circumstances justify that …'.

9.46

The court went on to say under the heading 'A structured approach to restrictions on open justice in the reporting of criminal trials':

> '86 In our view, applications to restrict reporting of criminal proceedings should be approached in a structured way. For example, in considering whether reporting restrictions should be imposed, the Court of Appeal (Criminal Division) set out in *Ex p The Telegraph Group plc* [2001] 1 WLR 1983 , para 22 a three-stage test. That was approved in *Independent Publishing Co Ltd v Attorney General of Trinidad and Tobago* [2005] 1 AC 190, para 69 by the Privy Council:
>
> "in considering whether it was 'necessary' both in the sense under section 4(2) of the 1981 Act of avoiding a substantial risk of prejudice to the administration of justice and therefore of protecting the defendants' right to a free trial under article 6 of the Convention and in the different sense contemplated by article 10 of the Convention as being 'prescribed by law' and 'necessary in a democratic society' by reference to wider considerations of public policy, the factors to be taken into account could be expressed as a three-part test; that the first question was whether reporting would give rise to a not insubstantial risk of prejudice to the administration of justice in the relevant proceedings, and if not that would be the end of the matter; that, if such a risk was perceived to exist, then the second question was whether a section 4(2) order would eliminate the risk, and if not there could be no necessity to impose such a ban and again that would be the end of the matter; that, nevertheless, even if an order would achieve the objective, the court should still consider whether the risk could satisfactorily be overcome

by some less restrictive means, since otherwise it could not be said to be 'necessary' to take the more drastic approach; that, thirdly, even if there was indeed no other way of eliminating the perceived risk of prejudice, it still did not follow necessarily that an order had to be made and the court might still have to ask whether the degree of risk contemplated should be regarded as tolerable in the sense of being the lesser of two evils; and that at that stage value judgments might have to be made as to the priority between the competing public interests represented by articles 6 and 10 of the Convention …"

87 We consider that the court should approach the making of an order that a defendant be not identified in a similar way. The starting point is, in our judgment, the duty of the court, as a public authority, to ensure compliance with the principles (1) of open justice, and (2) that there be no interference with an individual's rights under articles 2 and 3, and (3) no unnecessary or disproportionate interference with (a) the rights of the public under article 10 (having regard to the position of the media under section 12 of the Human Rights Act 1998), and (b) of any relevant individuals under article 8 .

88 As open justice is so important a principle, an order that a defendant be not identified will not be necessary if some other measure is available to protect those rights of the individuals, and that other measure would be proportionate. In other cases alternative measures have been taken, most notably in *Venables v News Group Newspapers Ltd* [2001] Fam 430. No order was made at the trial of Venables and Thompson that they be not named (there was an order restricting reporting of their names, which was lifted at the end of the trial). Subsequently those defendants changed their names, and orders were made to prohibit the disclosure of their identities under their new names.'

9.47

Anonymity is achieved in the Court of Appeal Criminal Division through the interplay of the power under common law and/or the HRA 1998, s 6 to cause the name of the appellant not to be mentioned during the appeal hearing and the further power under the Contempt of Court Act 1981, s 11 prohibiting the publication of that name in connection with the proceedings[43].

9.48

In *GL and N*[44] the court considered whether the applicants' Art 2 and 3 rights were or were potentially engaged. On balance the court decided that anonymity should be afforded for these victims of trafficking. If their accounts were accepted, they may have a genuine or well-founded fear of reprisals on

---

43 See *Khuja* (above) at [14].
44 [2017] EWCA Crim 2129.

them or on their families at home. Additionally the court found that if it did not grant anonymity it would undermine the anonymity orders in the immigration tribunals and in related Administrative Court proceedings.

Requests to expedite the hearing

9.49

Victim of trafficking applicants are some of the most vulnerable. Practitioners should consider submitting a note attached to the application highlighting that the case concerns a victim of modern slavery/trafficking and asking that the Registrar consider expediting the hearing. He has the power to refer the case to the full court immediately for a hearing, where the application for leave and final appeal can be determined.

Applications for funding

9.50

When applying for leave to appeal, representatives must indicate on the form NG if they are applying for a funding certificate, which ordinarily will only be granted for counsel if leave is granted. See Chapter 13 on funding.

Request for transcripts

9.51

It is likely in most cases where slavery or human trafficking is put forward as a ground of appeal that a transcript will have been obtained in preparation for making the application, particularly where there are new representatives. However, the Registrar routinely obtains copies of the summing up, sentencing remarks and the prosecution opening of the facts where relevant. If the application seeks any other transcripts of part of the proceedings, representatives should indicate why they are being requested[45].

Request for an oral leave hearing

9.52

An application for an oral hearing to argue grounds of appeal is rarely made and, if made, rarely, granted, although historically in cases concerning victims of human trafficking the court will do so.

---

45 Criminal Procedure Rules 2015, r 5.5.

Absconding

9.53

It is important to appreciate that there are risks of a victim of trafficking applicant being re-trafficked. The Court of Appeal, Criminal Division, provided guidance as to the approach to be taken when defendants' representatives apply for leave to appeal or appeal against conviction and/or sentence in circumstances where the defendant has absconded during the appeal process. First, it allows legal representatives to lodge appeals even in the absence of their clients, providing that they have actual or implied authority or where, in any event, the court may wish to intervene in the public interest. It is, however, incumbent upon them to notify the Registrar of the position. In *R v Okedare*[46], the applicant went missing/absconded before the application for leave was lodged. The court considered that he 'may well have been re-trafficked or simply absconded.' It was viewed that because there had been written consent to the defence representatives as to a wish to appeal against the conviction, that this implied there was nothing to suggest that the applicant wished to withdraw his appeal. The court, in assessing the case, said that 'in any event there remains the possibility that his disappearance was not his fault'. On account of this, the Court of Appeal considered that it had no option but to stay the application for permission to appeal sine die[47], until the applicant was able to satisfy the evidential requirements as to whether or not he had in fact been trafficked and/or whether he had been compelled to commit the offence.

9.54

If leave has been granted and a waiver of legal privilege has been signed, it is possible to continue with the determination of the appeal. Representatives will, however, need to notify the court as to the applicant's status.[48] In circumstances where a victim of trafficking applicant has absented himself, representatives should ensure they obtain evidence to submit to the court regarding the circumstances of the applicant going missing. For those applicants who are minors, the local authority and police will be engaged and the applicant's legal team should obtain a crime reference number and information regarding the circumstances of the child going missing. Other evidence can be obtained from the support organisation or first responder involved in the care of the victim of trafficking.

9.55

If a missing victim of trafficking ,whose appeal has been stayed, subsequently comes into contact with the authorities, the Court of Appeal and defence representatives will not automatically be made aware of this and the stay may

---

46 [2014] EWCA Crim 228, [2014] 1 WLR 4071.
47 See also *R v Joseph* [2017] EWCA Crim 36, [2017] 1 WLR 3153.
48 *R v L* [2013] EWCA Crim 991, [2014] 1 All ER 113.

be left in place for many years, even if the applicant is again known to the authorises. Many who have been re-trafficked will continue in a cycle of further criminalisation and prosecution. In cases that are stayed sine die, the court may direct that police put an intelligent marker against the applicant's details, so that in the event of the apprehension or arrest of the applicant the Court of Appeal Criminal Division and his representatives can be notified. The court in *R v Joseph*[49] in relation to the missing applicant held that 'should he still be in this country and he comes to the attention of the Police then this court is to be notified forthwith so that these applications may be then heard as speedily as possible'.

Applications to the Criminal Cases Review Commission

9.56

The CCRC is a body corporate created under the auspices of the Criminal Appeal Act 1995[50]. It should consist of at least 11 commissioners, at least two thirds of whom must appear to the prime minister to have knowledge of the criminal justice system.

9.57

Where a person has been: (1) convicted on indictment in England and Wales; (2) sentenced following conviction; (3) found not guilty by reason of insanity; or (4) found to be under a disability, and that he did the act or made the omission charged against him the CCRC may refer the case to the Court of Appeal[51]. A reference is then taken as an appeal to the Court of Appeal, ie leave to appeal is not necessary.

9.58

Where a person has been convicted of an offence by a magistrates' court in England and Wales the CCRC may at any stage refer the conviction to the Crown Court. It may also refer any sentence imposed following the conviction to the Crown Court[52]. The reference to the Crown Court is treated as an appeal under the Magistrates' Court Act 1980, s 108. The Crown Court cannot impose a more severe penalty than was originally imposed following the reference. It may grant bail pending the hearing.

9.59

The CCRC can only make a reference if:

---

49 [2017] EWCA Crim 36, [2017] 1 WLR 3153.
50 Criminal Appeal Act 1995, s 8.
51 Criminal Appeal Act 1995, s 9.
52 Criminal Appeal Act 1995, s 11.

(i) it '... considers that there is a real possibility that the conviction, verdict, finding or sentence would not be upheld were the reference to be made';

(ii) because of an argument, or evidence, not raised in the proceedings which led to the conviction, verdict, finding or sentence or in the case of a sentence, because of an argument on a point of law, or information, not raised; and

(iii) an appeal has been determined or leave to appeal refused[53]. The statute sets out that nothing '... shall prevent the making of a reference if it appears to the Commission that there are exceptional circumstances which justify making it'.

9.60

In R v Mateta[54] the Court of Appeal praised the CCRC for its work in identifying wrongful convictions in the context of refugees whose possible defences under the Immigration and Asylum Act 1999, s 31 had been overlooked. Four of the five cases in that combined appeal were first appeal-CCRC references where the exceptionality provision had been invoked[55]. However, in R v YY; R v Nori[56] the Court of Appeal invited the CCRC to consider a 'triage system' so that the exceptional procedure was not deployed as a matter of routine in cases where a defence had been overlooked in the Crown Court, where the Registrar could refer the consideration of leave to the Full Court. This was by way of an '... attempt to ensure that those cases in which there is no available means of redress other than through the CCRC are investigated and dealt with as expeditiously as possible'[57]. The court noted that the exceptional procedure should be available to defendants seeking a reference to the Crown Court following a guilty plea in the magistrates' court because of the '... constraints put on the Crown Court (sitting on appeal) in relation to unequivocal pleas of guilty'[58].

9.61

The CCRC must have regard to matters including '... any application or representations made to the Commission by or on behalf of the person to whom it relates'[59]. Those representing prospective appellants should consider whether to make an application for leave to appeal to the Court of Appeal or to make an application to the CCRC for a reference. Following *R v Nori and R v YY* it will almost invariably be appropriate for first appeals to be the subject of an application for leave to appeal to the Court of Appeal.

---

53 Criminal Appeal Act 1995, s 13.
54 [2013] EWCA Crim 1372, [2014] 1 WLR 1516.
55 See para 57.
56 [2016] EWCA Crim 18, [2016] 1 Cr App Rep 435.
57 See paras 38–45.
58 See para 42 and the Magistrates' Courts Act 1980, s 108.
59 Criminal Appeal Act 1995, s 14(2).

9.62

Examples ('illustrative categories'[60]) of what *may* amount to exceptional circumstances are set out in the CCRC's Formal Memorandum on Exceptional Circumstances[61]. They include:

(i)   sensitive information that should only be disclosed in a confidential annex to the Court of Appeal;

(ii) evidence of a compelling or compassionate need for the case to be considered quickly by an appellate court (such as terminal illness of the applicant);

(iii) where the applicant has a mental illness or disability placing him at a serious disadvantage in securing legal representation and/or pursuing an application for leave to appeal;

(iv) summary matters where the applicant pleaded guilty and there is a real possibility that the conviction would not be upheld;

(v)   conviction is referred to the Commission by a prosecuting authority with concerns about some aspect of the evidence on which the Crown has previously relied, in circumstances where relevant evidence/information cannot be disclosed due to its sensitivity or where the Commission's involvement is in the public interest;

(vi) the Commission's powers under the Criminal Appeal Act 1995, s 17 might secure relevant information which the applicant would be unable to obtain;

(vii) new scientific, medical or expert evidence that an applicant could not reasonably be expected to discover or present;

(viii) the applicant is linked with co-defendants whose cases have been or are to be referred by the Commission and, in all the circumstances, it would not be in the public interest to require the co-defendant to appeal directly;

(ix) the applicant's case is linked to other cases by a common nexus, such as a material witness, a criticised expert or a point of law and the Commission's involvement is in the public interest.

9.63

Where an application is made to the CCRC, there is a form to complete which provides for details of the application to be set out, but it will assist the commission and the prospective appellant if submissions akin to grounds of and an advice on appeal and a chronology are sent to the Commission,

---

60 See para 17 of the March 2017 updated version of the Formal Memorandum: Exceptional Circumstances, available on the CCRC website.
61 See para 18, ibid.

as this must (by the Criminal Appeal Act 1995, s 14(2)) inform the way the CCRC approaches the review of the case. From a practical perspective the case managers at the CCRC will provide advice on procedure. Sometimes it will be of assistance for the assigned Commissioner to meet with the applicant's legal representative. While there is no right to an 'oral hearing' before the CCRC, the Commission may decide that oral submissions to the Commission are appropriate[62].

9.64

Whether the CCRC sees fit to refer a case to the Court of Appeal (or Crown Court) or not, it will prepare a statement of reasons[63]. An applicant aggrieved by the decision of the CCRC not to refer a case (or in relation to an interim issue) may be able to rely on judicial review in the event that the decision is impeachable in a public law sense (ie *Wednesbury* unreasonable, perverse, etc). It will rarely be the case that such a challenge will be successful, as there is a very high threshold for such challenges[64].

9.65

In the context of the convictions of possible victims of modern slavery and human trafficking, practitioners should be alive to the power of the CCRC to conduct investigations for the Court of Appeal. The Court of Appeal may direct the CCRC to conduct inquiries into matters directed to it and report back to the Court of Appeal. Such investigations may have broad scope and are not restricted to cases where a reference is applied for[65]. Practitioners should also have in mind the fact that the CCRC has the power to obtain '... a document or other material which may assist the Commission in the exercise of any of their functions'[66]. Where it is 'reasonable to do so', the Commission may require the appropriate person in relation to a public body to produce the document or other material to the Commission or to give the Commission access to it and take away the material to copy or take away a copy of it. The Commission may also direct that person that the document or other material must not be destroyed, damaged or altered.

9.66

The documents and other material include, in particular, items obtained or created during an investigation or proceedings relating to the case being considered by the CCRC and any other case which may be in any way connected with that case (whether or not any function of the Commission

---

62 *R v Criminal Cases Review Commission, ex p Pearson* [1999] 3 All ER 498, [2000] 1 Cr App Rep 141.

63 Criminal Appeal Act 1995, s 14(4) in respect of a positive decision to refer and s 14(6) in respect of a decision not to refer.

64 *R (on the application of Cleeland) v Criminal Cases Review Commission* [2009] EWHC 474 (Admin) at 48.

65 Criminal Appeal Act 1995, s 15. See, eg, *Coles (unreported)* (960227313) 11 November 1997.

66 Criminal Appeal Act 1995, s 17.

could be exercised in relation to that other case)[67]. The duty to comply with a CCRC requirement is not affected by secrecy or any limitation on disclosure[68].

---

67 Criminal Appeal Act 1995, s 17(3).
68 Criminal Appeal Act 1995, s 17(4).

10 International protection claims brought by victims of human trafficking and modern slavery

Introduction

10.1

Victims of trafficking who have escaped or are rescued from their traffickers may fear serious harm, including being re-trafficked, by the individuals and/or criminal gangs that trafficked them, if they are returned to their country of origin. In addition, victims of trafficking may be more vulnerable to re-trafficking or further exploitation by other individuals or criminal gangs, as in many cases they would be returning to the same, similar or worse conditions that originally placed them at risk. Some victims of trafficking cannot face the prospect of return to their country of origin, or they would be at risk on return where they may be without a support network and/or due to their ongoing vulnerability. The trauma they have experienced can impact on their ability to function and survive, and in some cases may raise a real risk of suicide (see Chapter 8).

Refugee Convention

Introduction

10.2

The Palermo Protocol[1] and ECAT[2] both expressly provide that they do not affect individuals' and states' rights, obligations and responsibilities under international law and in particular, under the Refugee Convention and protocol. The EU Trafficking Directive is without prejudice to the principle of non-refoulement under the Refugee Convention[3].

---

1 Protocol to Prevent, Suppress and Punish Trafficking in Persons, especially Women and Children, supplementing the United Nations Convention against transnational organised Crime 2000, Art 14(1).
2 Council of Europe Convention on Action against Trafficking in Human Beings 2005, Art 40(4).
3 Directive 2011/36/EU of the European Parliament and of the Council of 5 April 2011 on preventing and combating trafficking in human beings and protecting its victims, and replacing Council Framework Decision 2002/629/JHA, preamble recital (10).

Definition

10.3

The legal definition of the term 'refugee' is set out at Art 1A(2) of the Refugee Convention, which defines a refugee as a person who:

> 'Owing to well-founded fear of being persecuted for reasons of race, religion, nationality, membership of a particular social group or political opinion is outside the country of his nationality and is unable or owing to such fear, is unwilling to avail himself of the protection of that country; or who, not having a nationality and being outside the country of his former habitual residence is unable or, owing to such fear, unwilling to return to it'.

Well-founded fear of persecution

10.4

There must be a genuine subjective fear of persecution. The fear of persecution by a victim of trafficking could be reprisals from traffickers or criminal networks and/or re-trafficking. It is also sometimes the case that victims of trafficking fear persecution from their family members or other non-state actors.

10.5

Many acts associated with trafficking such as 'abduction, incarceration, rape, enforced prostitution, forced labour, removal of organs, physical beatings, starvation, the deprivation of medical treatment … constitute serious violations of human rights which will generally amount to persecution'[4]. The experience of being trafficked should, in most instances, be regarded as persecution.

10.6

The EU Qualification Directive defines acts of persecution as those which are

> 'sufficiently serious by their nature or repetition as to constitute a severe violation of basic human rights, in particular, the rights from which derogation cannot be made under Art 15(2) of the European Convention for the Protection of Human Rights and Fundamental Freedoms'[5].

---

4   UNHCR 'Guidelines on International Protection: The application of Art 1(A)2 of the 1951 Convention and/or Protocol relating to the status of refugees to victims of trafficking and persons at risk of being trafficked' (2006) HCR/GIP/06/07, para 15.

5   Council Directive 2004/83/EU of 29 April 2004 on minimum standards for the qualification and status of third country nationals or stateless persons as refugee or as persons who otherwise need international protection and the content of the protection granted, Art 9(1)(a).

Trafficking commonly has those characteristics. It 'constitutes a violation of human rights and an offence to the dignity and integrity of the human being'[6]; it is 'a gross violation of fundamental rights and explicitly prohibited by the Charter of Fundamental Rights of the European Union'[7] and it falls within the scope of the ECHR, Art 4[8], which is one of the non-derogable rights identified in Art 15(2).

10.7

If the victim of trafficking consents to the trafficking, it may still constitute persecution given that the individual's consent is irrelevant if one of the 'means' contained in the trafficking definition is used[9]. See Chapters 1 and 2 for a fuller exploration of 'consent' in trafficking cases.

10.8

The fear of persecution is not sufficient in itself, but must also be well-founded. There is no requirement that persecution must have occurred in the past, but past persecution will always be of great significance because, as recognised by the immigration rules, it is 'a serious indication of the person's well-founded fear of persecution or real risk of suffering serious harm, unless there are good reasons to consider that such persecution or serious harm will not be repeated'[10].

Burden and standard of proof

10.9

The burden of establishing a well-founded fear is on the applicant. For a fear to be well-founded the question is whether there is a 'real and substantial risk' or a 'reasonable degree of likelihood' of persecution for a Refugee Convention reason[11]. It is a lesser standard than proving that persecution will occur on the balance of probabilities. The correct approach to the assessment of past events was authoritatively set out by the Court of Appeal in *Karanakaran v Secretary of State for the Home Department*[12], and would include any account of past persecution, including trafficking, as follows:

'There may be circumstances in which a decision-maker must take into account the possibility that alleged past events occurred even though it finds that these events probably did not occur. The reason for this is that the ultimate question is whether the applicant [in an asylum case] has a real substantial basis for his fear of future persecution. The decision-

---

6   ECAT, preamble.
7   EU Trafficking Directive, Recital (1).
8   *Rantsev v Cyprus and Russia* (2010) 51 EHRR 1, 28 BHRC 313, para 282.
9   ECAT, Art 4(b); *AM and BM (trafficked women) Albania CG* [2010] UKUT 80 (IAC).
10 Immigration Rules 339K.
11 *R v Secretary of State for the Home Department, ex p Sivakumaran* [1998] AC 958.
12 [2000] 3 All ER 449.

maker must not foreclose reasonable speculation about chances of the future hypothetical event occurring'.

Credibility and the role of NRM decisions in decision-making

10.10

Whether a victim of trafficking is able to discharge the burden of proof is clearly linked with his credibility. It is important to look at this in detail, because the Secretary of State frequently rejects asylum claims by rejecting an applicant's credibility[13].

10.11

The Home Office is a first responder, and can therefore refer a potential victim of modern slavery into the National Referral Mechanism ('NRM')[14]. For a detailed description of the NRM process see Chapter 2 on the determination of trafficking status.

10.12

There is detailed guidance for Home Office frontline staff on how to identify a victim of trafficking[15]. An applicant can be identified as a potential victim of trafficking and referred to the NRM at any stage of the asylum process. The Home Office would then defer the determination of the applicant's asylum/ human rights claim until the Competent Authority has determined whether the applicant is a victim of trafficking.

10.13

Cases will be referred to the Home Office to determine whether the applicant is a victim of trafficking where there is an immigration or asylum issue. The Home Office has a number of competent authorities, which currently includes:

- UK Visas and Immigration NRM HUB (Leeds (England cases));
- Cardiff (Wales cases);
- Glasgow (Scotland and Northern Ireland cases);
- Third Country Unit;
- Detained Asylum Casework;
- Criminal Casework (dealing with deportation cases relating to EEA and Non-EEA nationals)[16].

---

13 The House of Commons, Home Affairs Committee, Seventh Report of Session 2013–2014, paras 12–13.
14 Home Office, *Victims of modern slavery – Competent Authority guidance* (21 March 2016) p 22.
15 Home Office, *Victims of modern slavery – Frontline Staff guidance* (18 March 2016).
16 Home Office, *Victims of modern slavery – Competent Authority guidance* (21 March 2016) p 21.

10.14

Competent authorities are entitled to consider credibility as part of their decision-making process at both the reasonable grounds and conclusive grounds stages and are advised when assessing the credibility of an account to consider both the external and internal credibility of the material facts[17].

10.15

The competent authority guidance recognises that there may be 'mitigating reasons' why a potential victim of trafficking is 'incoherent, inconsistent or delays giving material facts' and directs that the competent authority *must* take those reasons into account when considering the credibility of a claim. In particular, the guidance states that such factors may include:

• trauma (mental, psychological, or emotional);

• inability to express themselves clearly;

• mistrust of authorities;

• feelings of shame;

• painful memories (including those of a sexual nature).

Children may be unable to disclose or give a consistent credible account due to additional factors such as:

• their age;

• the ongoing nature of abuse throughout childhood;

• fear of traffickers or modern slavery facilitators, violence, or witchcraft[18].

10.16

Whilst the guidance acknowledges the reasons why a victim of trafficking may be incoherent, inconsistent or delay in giving material facts, the guidance also directs that it is 'reasonable to assume that a potential victim who has experienced an event will be able to recount the central elements in a broadly consistent manner' and an ability to remain consistent throughout may lead the competent authority to disbelieve his claim[19].

10.17

The Home Office Asylum Policy Instruction, Assessing Credibility and Refugee Status states that Home Office competent authority caseworkers are responsible for deciding whether someone referred to the NRM is a victim of trafficking[20].

---

17 Home Office, *Victims of modern slavery – Competent Authority guidance* (21 March 2016) p 97.
18 Ibid p 99.
19 Ibid p 98.
20 Home Office, *Asylum Policy Instruction: Assessing Credibility and Refugee Status* (6 January 2015) p 7.

Accordingly, caseworkers determining an applicant's asylum/human rights claim usually adopt the decisions of the competent authority as to whether the applicant is a victim of trafficking unless an applicant has been accepted as a victim of trafficking and there is clear evidence to the contrary[21].

10.18

However, a finding that an applicant is a victim of trafficking does not necessarily lead to a grant of asylum or humanitarian protection. To qualify for protection an applicant needs to demonstrate that he is at risk of persecution and/or serious harm on return to his country of origin[22].

For reasons of race, religion, nationality, membership of a particular social group or political opinion

10.19

The definition of refugee requires the reasons for the persecution to be considered. The fact of facing persecution is not sufficient: it must be connected to one of the reasons assigned by the Refugee Convention:

> 'for reasons of race, religion, nationality, membership of a particular social group or political opinion'.

10.20

Victims of trafficking are most likely to face persecution for reason of their particular social group. The dictum of Sedley J in *R v Immigration Appeal Tribunal, ex p Shah*[23], as to the nature of the task involved in identifying a particular social group has been widely cited and approved:

> 'Its adjudication is not a conventional lawyer's exercise of applying a legal litmus test to ascertained facts; it is a global appraisal of an individual's past and prospective situation in a particular cultural, social, political and legal milieu, judged by a test which, though it has legal and linguistic limits, has a broad humanitarian purpose'.

10.21

By a majority, their Lordships held in the case of *Islam and Shah*[24] that women in Pakistan constituted a 'particular social group' because as members of a group

---

21 Home Office, *Asylum Policy Instruction: Assessing Credibility and Refugee Status* (6 January 2015) p 15.
22 Home Office, *Victims of modern slavery – Frontline Staff guidance* (18 March 2016) p 61.
23 *R v Immigration Appeal Tribunal ex p Shah* [1997] Imm AR 145 at 153.
24 *Islam v Secretary of State for the Home Department (United Nations High Comr for Refugees intervening); R v Immigration Appeal Tribunal, ex p Shah (United Nations High Comr for Refugees intervening)* [1999] 2 AC 629.

sharing innate characteristics of sex they were discriminated against because of their gender[25]. Women who have been victims of sexual violence in the past may also form a particular social group, because they are linked by an immutable characteristic, independent of, and the cause of, their ill-treatment[26].

10.22

The EU Qualification Directive deals with the 'particular social group' at Art 10(1)(d) and states:

'A group shall be considered to form a particular social group where in particular (i) members of that group share an innate characteristic or common background that cannot be changed, or share a characteristic or belief that is so fundamental to their identity or conscience that a person should not be forced to renounce it; and (ii) that group has a distinct identity in the relevant country, because it is perceived as being different by the surrounding society.'

10.23

Victims of trafficking share a common background that cannot be changed and in many countries will be perceived as being different. Former victims of trafficking have been found to be a particular social group in Moldova, Nigeria, Thailand, Albania and China[27].

Unable or ... unwilling to avail himself of the protection of that country

10.24

To qualify as a refugee an applicant must be unable or unwilling to avail themselves of the protection of his own country. In *Horvath v Secretary of State for the Home Department*[28] Lord Clyde found that sufficient protection would involve the following:

'There must be in place a system of domestic protection and machinery for the detection, prosecution and punishment of actions contrary to the purposes which the Convention requires to have protected. More importantly there must also be an ability and a readiness to operate that machinery'.

---

25 Lord Steyn at 644E, Lord Hoffmann at 652CF, Lord Hope at 658E.

26 *R v Special Adjudicator ex p Hoxha* [2005] 1 WLR 1063 at 37.

27 *SB (PSG – Protection Regulations – Reg 6)* Moldova CG [2008] UKAIT 00002; *PO (Trafficked Women)* Nigeria CG [2009] UKAIT 00046; *AZ (Trafficked women)* Thailand CG [2010] UKUT 118 (IAC); *AM and BM (Trafficked women)* Albania CG [2010] UKUT 80 (IAC); *HC & RC (Trafficked women)* China CG [2009] UKAIT 00027.

28 *Horvath v Secretary of State for the Home Department* [2001] 1 AC 489 at 510H.

10.25

The EU Qualification Directive provides that protection 'can be provided by a state or by parties or organisations, including international organisations, controlling the state or by parties or organisations, including international organisations, controlling the state or a substantial part of the territory of the state'[29].

10.26

In *R (on the application of Bagdanavicius) v Secretary of State for the Home Department*[30] the House of Lords left undisturbed the proposition set out by Auld LJ on real risk and sufficiency of protection in the Court of Appeal[31]:

> 'Summary of conclusions on real risk/sufficiency of state protection.
>
> *The common threshold of risk*
>
> 1) The threshold of risk is the same in both categories of claim; the main reason for introducing section 65 to the 1999 Act was not to provide an alternative, lower threshold of risk and/or a higher level of protection against such risk through the medium of human rights claims, but to widen the reach of protection regardless of the motive giving rise to the persecution.
>
> *Asylum claims*
>
> 2) An asylum seeker who claims to be in fear of persecution is entitled to asylum if he can show a well-founded fear of persecution for a Refugee Convention reason and that there would be insufficiency of state protection to meet it; *Horvath* [2001] 1 AC 489.
>
> 3) Fear of persecution is well-founded if there is a 'reasonable degree of likelihood' that it will materialise; *R v SSHD, ex p Sivakumaran* [1988] AC 956, per Lord Goff at 1000F–G.
>
> 4) Sufficiency of state protection, whether from state agents or non-state actors, means a willingness and ability on the part of the receiving state to provide through its legal system a reasonable level of protection from ill-treatment of which the claimant for asylum has a well-founded fear; *Osman v UK* [1999] 1 FLR 193,

---

29 Council Directive (2004/83/EU) of 29 April 2004 on minimum standards for the qualification and status of third country nationals or stateless persons as refugee or as persons who otherwise need international protection and the content of the protection granted, art 7(1)(a)(b).

30 *R (on the application of Bagdanavicius) v Secretary of State for the Home Department* [2005] UKHL 38, [2005] 2 AC 668.

31 *R (on the application of Bagdanavicius) v Secretary of State for the Home Department* [2003] EWCA Civ 1605, [2004] 1 WLR 1207.

Horvath, Dhima [2002] EWHC 80 (Admin), [2002] Immigration Judge AR 394].

5) The effectiveness of the system provided is to be judged normally by its systemic ability to deter and/or to prevent the form of persecution of which there is a risk, not just punishment of it after the event; *Horvath*; *Banomova* [2001] EWCA Civ 807; *McPherson* [2001] EWCA Civ 1955 and *Kinuthia* [2001] EWCA Civ 2100.

6) Notwithstanding systemic sufficiency of state protection in the receiving state a claimant may still have a well-founded fear of persecution if he can show that its authorities know or ought to know of circumstances particular to his case giving rise to his fear, but are unlikely to provide the additional protection his particular circumstances reasonably require; *Osman*.

Article 3 claims

7) The same principles apply to claims in removal cases of risk of exposure to Art 3 ill-treatment in the receiving state, and are, in general, unaffected by the approach of the Strasbourg Court in *Soering*; which, on its facts, was, not only a state-agency case at the highest institutional level, but also an unusual and exceptional case on its facts; *Dhima, Krepel* [2002] EWCA Civ 1265 and *Ullah* [2004] UKHL 26.

8) The basis of an article 3 entitlement in a removal case is that the claimant, if sent to the country in question, would be at risk there of Art 3 ill-treatment.

9) In most, if not all, Art 3 cases in this context the concept of risk has the same or closely similar meaning to that in the Refugee Convention of a 'well-founded fear of persecution', save that it is confined to a risk of Art 3 forms of ill-treatment and is not restricted to conduct with any particular motivation or by reference to the conduct of the claimant; *Dhima, Krepel, Chahal v UK* [1996] 23 EHRR 413.

10) The threshold of risk required to engage Art 3 depends on the circumstances of each case, including the magnitude of the risk, the nature and severity of the ill-treatment risked and whether the risk emanates from a state agency or non-state actor; *Horvath*.

11) In most, but not necessarily all, cases of ill-treatment which, but for state protection, would engage Art 3, a risk of such ill-treatment will be more readily established in state-agency cases than in non-state actor cases – there is a spectrum of circumstances giving rise to such risk spanning the two categories, ranging from breach of a duty by the state of a negative duty not to inflict Art 3 ill-

treatment to a breach of a duty to take positive protective action against such ill-treatment by non-state actors; *Svazas*.

12) An assessment to the threshold of risk appropriate in the circumstances to engage Art 3 necessarily involves an assessment of the sufficiency of state protection to meet the threat of which there is such a risk – one cannot be considered without the other whether or not the exercise is regarded as 'holistic' or to be conducted in two stages; *Dhima, Krepel, Svazas* [2002] EWCA Civ 74.

13) Sufficiency of state protection is not a guarantee of protection from Art 3 ill-treatment any more than it is a guarantee of protection from an otherwise well-founded fear of persecution in asylum cases – nor, if and to the extent that there is any difference, is it eradication or removal of risk of exposure to Art 3 ill-treatment'; *Dhima, McPherson; Krepel*.

14) Where the risk falls to be judged by the sufficiency of state protection, that sufficiency is judged, not according to whether it would eradicate the real risk of the relevant harm, but according to whether it is a reasonable provision in the circumstances; *Osman*.

15) Notwithstanding such systemic sufficiency of state protection in the receiving state, a claimant may still be able to establish an Art 3 claim if he can show that the authorities there know or ought to know of particular circumstances likely to expose him to risk of Art 3 ill-treatment; *Osman*.

16) The approach is the same whether the receiving country is or is not a party to the ECHR, but, in determining whether it would be contrary to Art 3 to remove a person to that country, our courts should decide the factual issue as to risk as if ECHR standards apply there – and the same applies to the certification process under section 115(1) and/or (2) of the 2002 Act'.

10.27

Points (6) and (15) are of particular relevance in cases involving victims of trafficking. A victim of trafficking may be able to demonstrate that whilst it could not be said that such a general insufficiency of state protection had been established, having regard to his particular circumstances (and in particular that he had already been subjected to persecution) the authorities in his country of origin would be unlikely to provide the additional protection which the circumstances particular to that applicant reasonably required[32].

---

32 See *AW (sufficiency of protection) Pakistan* [2011] UKUT 31(IAC) at 34–35, 39–40.

Internal relocation

10.28

As outlined above, the Refugee Convention provides international protection to those unable to receive protection in their own country. Accordingly, a purely localised risk will generally be insufficient to qualify for refugee status, because the victim could relocate to another area within his own country.

10.29

The correct approach to internal relocation was confirmed by the House of Lords in *AH (Sudan) v Secretary of State for the Home Department*[33]. Lord Bingham recalled what he had said in *Januzi v Secretary of State for the Home Department*[34] at [21]:

'The decision-maker, taking account of all relevant circumstances pertaining to the claimant and his country of origin, must decide whether it is reasonable to expect the claimant to relocate or whether it would be unduly harsh to expect him to do so'.

Lord Bingham continued in *AH (Sudan)* at para 5:

'It is, or should be, evident that the enquiry must be directed to the situation of the particular applicant, whose age, gender, experience, health, skills and family ties may all be very relevant. There is no warrant for excluding, or giving priority to, consideration of the applicant's way of life in the place of persecution. There is no warrant for excluding, or giving priority to, consideration of conditions generally prevailing in the home country'.

10.30

Lord Hope explained at para 47:

'The words "unduly harsh" set the standard that must be met for this to be regarded as unreasonable. If the claimant can live a relatively normal life there judged by the standards that prevail in his country of nationality generally, and if he can reach the less hostile part without undue hardship or undue difficulty, it will not be unreasonable to expect him to move there.'

10.31

In *AB (Jamaica) v Secretary of State for the Home Department*[35] Lloyd LJ held:

---

33 *AH (Sudan) v Secretary of State for the Home Department* [2007] UKHL 49, [2008] 1 AC 678.
34 *Januzi v Secretary of State for the Home Department* [2006] UKHL 5, [2006] 2 AC 426.
35 *AB (Jamaica) v Secretary of State for the Home Department* [2008] EWCA Civ 784.

'31. It is plain from what Lord Bingham said that the test that he enunciated ... which has in itself made reference to "a relatively normal life", is one which needs to be addressed by decision makers in relation to the facts of a particular case and, accordingly, by reference to those aspects of the facts which are said to ... be relevant to the question of unreasonableness or undue harshness ...'

'35 ... to say that "destitution is the test" is oversimplified and could lead into error a reader who did not pursue the cross-reference to *Januzi*'.

10.32

Particular considerations are likely to arise when considering removing a victim of trafficking to their country of origin. In *AA (Uganda) v Secretary of State for the Home Department*[36] in applying the factors identified by Lord Bingham in *AH (Sudan)* to the female appellant, the Court of Appeal highlighted that she was 'faced not merely with poverty and lack of any sort of accommodation, but with being driven to prostitution'. Buxton LJ concluded that enforced prostitution in the place of relocation would be unacceptable to the extent that it would be unduly harsh[37].

European Convention on Human Rights

Introduction

10.33

Where a victim of trafficking is not a refugee, he may be entitled to humanitarian protection if there are substantial grounds for believing that he will face a real risk of 'serious harm' under the Immigration Rules[38] or to human rights protection if there is a real risk that his removal would engage a breach of the ECHR.

Article 3

10.34

Article 3 of the ECHR states that 'no one shall be subjected to torture or to inhuman or degrading treatment'. The right not to be tortured or subjected to inhuman or degrading treatment is an unqualified right and can never be balanced or given way to other competing considerations[39].

---

36 *AA (Uganda) v Secretary of State for the Home Department* [2008] EWCA Civ 579, [2008] INLR 307.
37 *AA (Uganda) v Secretary of State for the Home Department* [2008] INLR 307 at 17.
38 Immigration Rule 339C.
39 See *MSS v Belgium and Greece* (2011) 53 EHRR 28.

10.34A

The ECtHR has repeatedly held that the benchmark for the necessary level of severity required to prove torture or inhuman and degrading treatment is relative, and depends on factors including the duration of the treatment, its physical or mental effects, and the age, sex, vulnerability and state of health of the victim[40]. It could include the risk of reprisals or re-trafficking from the victim of trafficking's former traffickers and/or other forms of exploitation from others.

10.35

The assessment of the risk is carried out by reference to the applicant's personal history and to the human rights conditions in the country of origin in much the same way as the Refugee Convention assessment. However, there is no requirement that the torture or inhuman or degrading treatment be for reason of a Convention reason (ie for reasons of race, religion, nationality, membership of a particular social group or political opinion).

10.36

In addition, on account of the trauma victims of trafficking have experienced, some cases may raise a real risk of suicide. Article 3 may be breached if there is a real risk of committing suicide as a foreseeable consequence of the decision to remove, whether on being informed of the removal direction, in the course of removal or after arrival in the country of origin[41]. The court drew a distinction between 'domestic cases' and 'foreign cases'[42]. The risk of suicide on being informed of an adverse immigration decision and in the course of being removed from the UK (both of which are 'domestic cases'), the tribunal would be entitled to assume that the UK authorities would take all reasonable steps in accordance with its obligations under the Human Rights Act 1998 to protect the individual from self-harm, including by the practice of arranging escorts to accompany the person on removal[43]. A real risk that the person would commit suicide after arrival in the receiving State might not be sufficient to establish an Art 3 breach, because what happens to the person on and after arrival is treated as a 'foreign case' (ie one in which the alleged violation takes place outside of the jurisdiction of the sending State), making the Art 3 threshold particularly high[44]. An issue of considerable relevance in this context is whether the removing and the receiving states have effective mechanisms for reducing the suicide risk and whether those mechanisms are accessible to the particular individual[45].

---

40 For example see *Soering v UK* (1989) 11 EHRR 439 at 100.
41 *J v Secretary of State for the Home Department* [2005] Imm AR 409.
42 Ibid at 16–17.
43 Ibid at 57, 61–62.
44 Ibid at 28.
45 *AJ (Liberia) v Secretary of State for the Home Department* [2006] All ER (D) 230 at 27–31.

10.37

Although suicide risk cases are rarely successful, in *Y v Secretary of State for the Home Department*[46] the Court of Appeal found that the removal of a brother and sister to Sri Lanka, where they had both been tortured and the sister raped, where they subjectively feared similar treatment if returned, notwithstanding that their fear was not objectively well-founded, and where they would have no family or other social support, created such a likelihood that they would commit suicide in order to escape isolation and fear, that their removal would breach Art 3.

Article 4

10.38

Article 4 of the ECHR states that:

'1   No one shall be held in slavery or servitude.

2   No one shall be required to perform forced or compulsory labour.

For the purposes of this Article the term 'forced or compulsory labour' shall not include:

(a)   any work required to be done in the ordinary course of detention imposed according to the provisions of Article 5 of this Convention or during conditional release from such detention;

(b)   any service of a military character or, in the case of conscientious objectors in countries where they are recognised, service exacted instead of compulsory military service;

(c)   any service exacted in case of an emergency or calamity threatening the life or well-being of the community;

(d)   any work or service which forms part of normal civic obligations.'

10.39

Article 4(1) absolutely prohibits slavery and servitude. The prohibition of slavery, servitude and forced labour is unqualified and enshrines one of the fundamental values of democratic society.

---

46 *Y v Secretary of State for the Home Department* [2010] INLR 178.

Slavery

10.40

The ECtHR refers to the definition of slavery contained in the 1926 Slavery Convention, which is that slavery is 'the status or condition of a person over whom any or all of the powers attaching to the rights of ownership are exercised'[47]. The Supplementary Convention on the Abolition of Slavery, the Slave Trade and Practices similar to Slavery 1956, Art 1, defined 'institutions and practices similar to slavery' as including the following: debt bondage[48]; serfdom[49]; forced and servile forms of marriage[50] and the delivery of a child by his or her parents or guardians for the exploitation of the child's labour.

Servitude

10.41

'Servitude' is an obligation to provide one's services that is imposed by the use of coercion and is linked with the concept of slavery[51]. The ECtHR understanding of servitude and forced labour has been informed by the findings of the Parliamentary Assembly of the Council of Europe that 'today's slaves are predominantly female and usually work in private households, starting out as migrant domestic workers'[52]. Domestic servitude involves a complex set of dynamics, involving both overt and more subtle forms of coercion to force compliance, investigation of which requires an understanding of the

---

47 *Siliadin v France* App No 73316/01 (2005) 43 EHRR 287, 20 BHRC 654.

48 '[T]hat is to say, the status or condition arising from a pledge by a debtor of his personal services or of those of a person under his control as security for a debt, if the value of those services as reasonably assessed is not applied towards the liquidation of the debt or the length and nature of those services are not respectively limited and defined'.

49 That is to say, the condition or status of a tenant who is by law, custom or agreement bound to live and labour on land belonging to another person and to render some determinate service to such other person, whether for reward or not, and is not free to change his status.

50 Any institution or practice whereby: (i) a woman without the right to refuse, is promised or given in marriage on payment of a consideration in money or in kind to her parents, guardian, family or any other person or group; or (ii) the husband of a woman, his family, or his clan has the right to transfer her to another person for value received or otherwise; or (iii) a woman on the death of her husband is liable to be inherited by another person. See also OSCE, *Unprotected Work, Invisible Exploitation: Trafficking for the Purposes of Domestic Servitude* (June 2010) p 44. Payment of money to a woman's parents in respect of a marriage would not necessarily be 'considered to amount to a price attached to the transfer of ownership, which would bring into play the concept of slavery. The court reiterates that marriage has deep-rooted social and cultural connotations which may differ largely from one society to another. According to the court, this payment can reasonably be accepted as representing a gift from one family to another, a tradition common to many different cultures in today's society': *M v Italy* (2013) 57 EHRR 29, para 161.

51 *Siliadin v France* (Application 73316/01) (2005) 43 EHRR 287, 20 BHRC 654.

52 *Siliadin v France* [2005] ECHR 545, para 88, noting the Parliamentary Assembly's Recommendation 1663 (2004), adopted on 22 June 2004 cited in para 49.

many subtle ways an individual can fall under the control of another[53]. The International Labour Organization's ('ILO') Domestic Workers Convention[54] recognises that domestic work is 'mainly carried out by women and girls, many of whom are migrants or members of disadvantaged communities and who are particularly vulnerable to discrimination in respect of conditions of employment and of work, and to other abuses of human rights'. It aims to protect them by regulating relations between domestic workers and their employers, eg by requiring specified terms and conditions of employment[55]; a contract of employment for a worker recruited in one country to be employed in another[56]; the worker to retain possession of his passport and identity card[57] and regular payment of wages[58]. An employer's non-compliance with such requirements may support an inference that there is a situation of servitude or forced labour.

10.42

A number of decisions by the ECtHR have concerned such workers. In *Siliadin v France* the court found a young woman to have been held in servitude given the circumstances: that she was brought to France as a child by a relative; her relatives transferred her to her employers; her employers manipulated her fear of being arrested owing to her unlawful immigration status; she was made to work long hours, seven days each week without remuneration; she was not permitted to leave the house in which she worked, save to take the children to school; she had no freedom of movement and no free time; the promise that she would be sent to school was broken and she had no hope of her situation improving[59]. In a subsequent case the court found the applicant's claimed circumstances to be 'remarkably similar' and to give rise to a credible suspicion that she had been held in domestic servitude[60].

---

53 *CN v UK* 4239/08 [2012] ECHR 1911, para 80. See OSCE, *Unprotected Work, Invisible Exploitation: Trafficking for the Purposes of Domestic Servitude* (June 2010), noting as features of domestic servitude subjugation to place the worker in a situation of vulnerability and dependence, low or no salary, no days off, food and sleep deprivation, no access to medical treatment, psychological, sexual and/or physical violence, limited or restricted freedom of movement, threats of denunciation, and the impossibility of a private life. See also OSCE Resource, *Police Training Guide: Trafficking in Human Beings* (July 2013) p 71, noting that the following are established indicators of domestic servitude: living with the family, not eating with the rest of the family, having separate sleeping quarters to the rest of the family, never or rarely leaving the house for social reasons, never or rarely leaving the house without the employer, only being given leftover food to eat, subjected to insults, abuse, threats or violence.

54 C189 – Domestic Workers Convention 2011 (No 189); Convention concerning decent work for domestic workers.

55 Ibid, Art 7.

56 Ibid, Art 8.

57 Ibid, Art 9.

58 Ibid, Art 12.

59 *Siliadin v France* [2005] ECHR 545, para 129.

60 *CN v UK* App No 4239/08 [2012] ECHR 1911.

Forced or compulsory labour

10.43

The drafters of the ECHR relied on the definition of 'forced or compulsory labour' contained in the ILO's Forced Labour Convention[61] and the ECtHR has relied on the ILO Conventions which are binding on almost all of the Council of Europe Member States for the purpose of interpreting Art 4[62]. The Forced Labour Convention defines 'forced or compulsory labour' as meaning 'all work or service which is exacted from any person under the menace of any penalty and for which the said person has not offered himself voluntarily'[63]. The ECtHR treats that definition as 'a starting point' for interpreting Art 4, whilst bearing in mind that the ECHR is a living instrument to be read in the light of currently prevailing notions[64]. It is noteworthy that the ILO definition refers to 'all work or services' and so encompasses all types of work, employment or occupation, irrespective of the nature of the activity performed, its legality or illegality under national law or its recognition as an 'economic activity'; thus it can apply as much to factory work as to prostitution or begging[65].

10.44

The ILO has developed indicators of forced labour, described by the ECtHR in *CN v United Kingdom* as 'a valuable benchmark in the identification of forced labour'[66]. As listed by the court they were:

'1   threats or actual physical harm to the worker;

2   restriction of movement and confinement to the work place or to a limited area;

3   debt bondage: where the worker works to pay off a debt or loan, and is not paid for his or her services. The employer may provide food and accommodation at such inflated prices that the worker cannot escape the debt;

4   withholding of wages or excessive wage reductions that violate previously made agreements;

5   retention of passports and identity documents, so that the worker cannot leave, or prove his/her identity and status;

6   threat of denunciation to the authorities, where the worker is in an irregular immigration status'[67].

---

61   *Van der Mussele v Belgium* App No 8919/80 (1983) 6 EHRR 163, [1983] ECHR 8919/80, at 32.

62   *Siliadin v France* [2005] ECHR 545 at 115.

63   Forced Labour Convention 1930 (No 29), Art 2(1).

64   *Van der Mussele v Belgium* App No 8919/80 (1983) 6 EHRR 163, [1983] ECHR 8919/80, at 32.

65   *Joint UN Commentary on the EU Directive – A Human Rights-Based Approach* (2011) p 102, citing ILO, *The Cost of Coercion* (2009).

66   *CN v UK* App No 4239/08 [2012] ECHR 1911 at 35.

67   Ibid at 35. An ILO publication, *ILO Indicators of Forced Labour* lists 11 indicators that are 'derived from the theoretical and practical experience of the ILO's Special Action Programme to Combat Forced Labour'.

In *Chowdury v Greece*[68] the ECtHR held that freedom of movement is not determinative of whether there is forced labour or trafficking.

10.45

In *CN v United Kingdom* the ECtHR held the UK's investigation of an allegation of trafficking to have been inadequate because it failed to give any weight to features of the applicant's situation that were among the ILO's indicators of forced labour[69]. The Supreme Court in *Hounga v Allen* applied the ILO's indicators of forced labour to hold that the appellant was (at least for the purposes of that case) a victim of trafficking on the basis that there had been physical harm or threats of physical harm from her employers; there had been withholding of wages and there had been threats of denunciation to the authorities in circumstances where she had irregular immigration status[70]. In *Siliadin* the ECtHR held that the applicant domestic worker was in a situation of forced labour. Whilst not threatened by a 'penalty' she was nevertheless in an equivalent position: 'she was an adolescent girl in a foreign land, unlawfully present on French territory and in fear of arrest by the police. Indeed, [her employers] nurtured that fear and led her to believe that her status would be regularised'[71].

10.46

Giving prior consent to undertaking the labour does not by itself establish that the individual offered himself voluntarily: account has to be taken of all the circumstances of the case, including whether it imposed a burden which was so excessive or disproportionate to the anticipated rewards or advantages that resulted in the consent being given[72].

Child labour

10.47

The employment of children may constitute servitude or forced labour. Employment of children is prohibited by the Charter of Fundamental Rights of the EU[73]. ILO Conventions reiterate the need for states to set a minimum age for children to work and to prohibit those under 18 from engaging in work likely to jeopardise the health, safety or morals of young persons. Child domestic servitude is an increasingly prevalent form of exploitation, often facilitated by

---

68 App No 21884/15, at para 123.
69 *CN v UK* App No 4239/08 [2012] ECHR 1911, para 80. Those features were 'the applicant's allegations that her passport had been taken from her, that [her employer] had not kept her wages for her as agreed and that she was explicitly and implicitly threatened with denunciation to the authorities'.
70 *Hounga v Allen* [2014] UKSC 47, [2014] 1 WLR 2889, [2014] IRLR 811 at 49.
71 *Siliadin v France* [2005] ECHR 545 at 118.
72 *Van der Mussele v Belgium* App No 8919/80 (1983) 6 EHRR 163, [1983] ECHR 8919/80 at 37.
73 Art 32.

socially and culturally-accepted practices of placing a child with a wealthier family or household in the belief that doing so will improve the child's access to education and life chances[74]. These practices, rooted in misplaced trust, are prohibited by the Supplementary Convention on the Abolition of Slavery, the Slave Trade and Practices similar to Slavery 1956[75]. Members States of the ILO are obliged to eliminate 'the worst forms of child labour'[76]. ILO Convention 182 also proscribes the use, procuring or offering of a child for illicit activities, in particular for the production and trafficking of drugs as defined in the relevant international treaties, this is echoed in Art 33 of the UN Convention on the Rights of the Child 1989. There is increasing prevalence that children are targeted by organised criminal networks or gangs for drug production and movement of drugs (see Chapter 15 for further information).

Trafficking and Art 4

10.48

In *Rantsev v Cyprus and Russia*[77] the ECtHR considered on the one hand, evidence about the increasing scale of trafficking in human beings as a global phenomenon, and on the other the proliferation of measures taken to combat it. Whilst noting that the ECHR, Art 4 makes no reference to trafficking,

---

74 OSCE, *Unprotected Work, Invisible Exploitation: Trafficking for the Purposes of Domestic Servitude* (June 2010) p 24. Arrangements are often made as a purported 'private fostering' whereby a child may enter the UK on another child's passport to live with a 'relative' or to join someone claiming asylum or may be left behind in the UK when the parents leave. Although a regulatory system is in place for social services to assess and monitor bone fide private fostering arrangements of which they are notified, those involving trafficked children exploited for domestic servitude or benefit fraud remain hidden: see www.ecpat.org. uk/sites/default/files/understanding_papers/understanding_private_fostering.pdf.

75 Art 1(d) prohibiting 'any institution or practice whereby a child or young person under the age of 18 years, is delivered by either or both of his natural parents or by his guardian to another person, whether for reward or not, with a view to the exploitation of the child or young person or of his labour.'

76 ILO Convention concerning the prohibition and immediate action for the elimination of the worst forms of child labour No 182 (1999), Art 6(1). The 'worst forms of child labour' are identified in Art 3 as: 'a. all forms of slavery or practices similar to slavery, such as the sale and trafficking of children, debt bondage and serfdom and forced or compulsory labour, including forced of compulsory recruitment of children for use in armed conflict; b. the use, procuring or offering of a child for prostitution, for the production of pornography or pornographic performances; c. the use, procuring or offering of a child for illicit activities, in particular for the production and trafficking of drugs as defined in the relevant international treaties; d. work which, by its nature or the circumstances in which it is carried out, is likely to harm the health, safety or morals of children". Hazardous work may include: work which exposes children to physical, psychological or sexual abuse; work underground, under water, at dangerous heights or in confined spaces; work with dangerous machinery, equipment or tools; work in an unhealthy environment exposing children to hazardous substances, agents or processes; work under particularly difficult conditions such as work for long hours or during the night or whether the child is unreasonably confined to the premises of the employer: 'ILO Worst Forms of Child Labour, Recommendation No 190, paragraph 3 (1999); ILO Convention concerning decent work for domestic workers No 189 Art 4 – setting a minimum age for domestic workers that is consistent with the Minimum Age Convention No 138 and the Worst Forms of Child Labour Convention No 182. ILO Domestic Worker Recommendation No 201. The ILO Declaration on Fundamental Principles and Rights at Work, 1998, declares that the effective abolition of child labour is an obligation arising from membership of the ILO.

77 *Rantsev v Cyprus and Russia* (2010) 51 EHRR 1.

it reminded itself that the Convention is 'a living instrument which must be interpreted in the light of present-day conditions. The increasingly high standards required in the area of protection of human rights and fundamental liberties correspondingly and inevitably require greater firmness in assessing breaches of the fundamental values of democratic societies'[78]. It also reminded itself of the obligation to interpret the ECHR in harmony with other rules of international law[79] and cited in particular the definitional provisions in the Palermo Protocol and ECAT[80]. Having done so, it held[81]:

> 'In view of its obligation to interpret the Convention in light of present-day conditions, the Court considers it unnecessary to identify whether the treatment about which the applicant complains constitutes "slavery", "servitude" or "forced and compulsory labour". Instead, the Court concludes that trafficking itself, within the meaning of Article 3(a) of the Palermo Protocol and Article 4 of [ECAT], falls within the scope of Article 4 of the Convention.'

Positive obligations under ECHR, Art 4

10.49

Article 4 of the ECHR imposes a range of positive obligations on signatory states. National legislation must contain a spectrum of safeguards 'adequate to ensure the practical and effective protection of victims or potential victims of trafficking'[82].

10.50

The state's potential obligations under ECHR, Art 4 are to:

(1)   make specific provisions in their criminal law (see Chapter 4);

(2)   identify victims of trafficking (see Chapter 2);

(3)   investigate/identify situations of potential trafficking (see Chapters 2 and 6); and

(4)   compensate victims of trafficking (see Chapter 12).

This chapter is limited to reviewing how the state's obligations may impact on a victim of trafficking's proposed removal.

---

78 Ibid at 277.
79 Ibid at 274.
80 Palermo Protocol, Art 3 and ECAT, Art 4.
81 *Rantsev v Cyprus and Russia* at 282.
82 *Rantsev v Cyprus and Russia* (2010) 51 EHRR 1 at 283.

10.51

The Upper Tribunal has found that a decision by the Secretary of State to remove a victim of trafficking was not in accordance with the law because it was made without taking account of: (i) the link between the appellant's precarious state of health and the breach of the respondent's protective obligations, in terms of her policy regarding foreign domestic workers and the ECHR, Art 4; and (ii) the duties engaged under ECAT, Arts 12, 14 and 16[83]. Any attempt to remove a trafficking victim from the UK in circumstances where the said procedural obligations have not been discharged will normally be unlawful[84].

Article 8

10.52

Article 8 of the ECHR provides a right to respect for one's 'private and family life, his home and his correspondence', subject to certain restrictions that are 'in accordance with law' and 'necessary in a democratic society'. Accordingly, the victim of trafficking's private life will need to be balanced against the interests of immigration control in considering whether his removal would breach his Art 8 rights.

10.53

On 13 June 2012, the Secretary of State laid amendments to the immigration rules, which came into force on 9 July 2012. These were intended to define the ambit of ECHR, Art 8. Paragraph 276ADE of the Immigration Rules sets out the circumstances in which the Secretary of State will grant leave to remain in the UK on the ground of private life. With effect from 28 July 2014, para 276ADE(1)(vi) reads as follows:

'is aged 18 years or above, has lived continuously in the UK for less than 20 years (discounting any period of imprisonment) but there would be very significant obstacles to the applicant's integration into the country to which he would have to go if required to leave the UK'.

10.54

The Secretary of State's Immigration Directorate Instruction on Family Migration[85] provides guidance on this. It states:

'The decision maker must consider all the reasons put forward by the applicant as to why there would be obstacles to their integration in

---

83 *EK (Article 4 ECHR: Anti-Trafficking Convention) Tanzania* [2013] UKUT 00313 (IAC).
84 *MS (Trafficking – Tribunal's Powers – Art 4 ECHR) Pakistan* [2016] UKUT 00226 (IAC).
85 Home Office, *Immigration Directorate Instruction on Family Migration*, Appendix FM Section 1.0b Family Life (as a Partner or Parent) and Private Life: 10-Year Routes (August 2015).

the country of return. These reasons must be considered individually and cumulatively to assess whether there are very significant obstacles to integration. In considering whether there are very significant obstacles to integration, the decision maker should consider whether the applicant has the ability to form an adequate private life by the standards of the country of return – not by UK standards. The decision maker will need to consider whether the applicant will be able to establish a private life in respect of all its essential elements, even if, for example, their job, or their ability to find work, or their network of friends and relationships may be differently constituted in the country of return.'

10.55

There are clear reasons why there may be very significant obstacles to a victim of trafficking integrating into the country of origin, even if he was not at risk. These include, but are not limited to, his physical or mental health, the stigma and discrimination he may suffer from his family members, community or wider society.

10.56

In any event, it is now clear that whilst the Immigration Rules are a 'relevant and important' consideration which decision-makers are required to take into account in assessing proportionality, they are not a complete code that defines the ambit of the ECHR, Art 8[86]. The Immigration Rules and ECHR, Art 8 are not coterminous. Cases can succeed under Art 8 even when they fail under the Immigration Rules[87].

10.57

The Secretary of State introduced the Art 8 public interest considerations, which apply in all cases where a court or tribunal is required to determine whether a decision made under the Immigration Acts breaches a person's rights under Art 8[88]. This includes a provision that:

'(5) Little weight should be given to a private life established by a person at a time when the person's immigration status is precarious'.

10.58

This provision can have an impact on victims of trafficking. However, the public interest considerations detailed in the Nationality, Immigration and Asylum Act

---

86 *Hesham Ali v Secretary of State for the Home Department* [2016] UKSC 60.
87 *MM v Secretary of State for the Home Department* [2017] UKSC 10.
88 Nationality, Immigration and Asylum Act 2002, ss 117A and 117B, which are found in Part 5A, headed 'Article 8 ECHR: Public Interest Considerations'.

2002 are not exhaustive[89]. It is arguable that this should not apply to victims of trafficking, in light of the government's (and in particular the Home Office's) apparent sympathy with victims of trafficking[90].

Expert evidence in asylum and immigration proceedings

10.59

A trafficking expert can be instructed to comment on whether a victim's account meets the trafficking definition and/or chimes with his knowledge of trafficking cases from that particular region. A country expert can be instructed to comment on whether the victim of trafficking's account is plausible in light of his knowledge of that particular country and risks on return for that victim.

10.60

In addition, expert evidence can be used to comment on issues that the victim of trafficking is unable or unwilling to comment on. For example,

(i)   the power and reach of the traffickers[91];

(ii)   whether the victim of trafficking may still be under the control of the traffickers and therefore reluctant to provide full disclosure and/or be at risk of returning to them willingly;

(iii)   the ability and/or willingness of the authorities in the country of origin to provide protection;

(iv)   what support there is, if any, for victims of trafficking in the country of origin and the nature of that support;

(v)   whether the victim of trafficking would be able to access accommodation, employment, healthcare, etc in his country of origin[92].

This is not intended to be an exhaustive list, merely an indicator of the sort of matters an expert may be instructed to comment on.

10.61

All experts will need to demonstrate that they have the requisite expertise to comment on the matter that they are being instructed on. There are no set

---

89 *Forman (ss 117A-C considerations)* [2015] UKUT 00412 (IAC).

90 In *Hounga v Allen* [2014] UKSC 47 Lord Wilson (with whom the majority agreed) found that the Court of Appeal's decision to uphold a defence of illegality to a complaint by an employee that an employer had discrimination against her ran *'counter to the prominent strain of current public policy against trafficking and in favour of its victims'* and allowed the employee's appeal at 52.

91 An expert may be able to comment on whether the traffickers' modus operandi indicates that they are likely to have been operated as an organised crime network.

92 This is relevant in assessing whether they would be at risk of destitution/further exploitation in the country of origin. See Internal Relocation at para 34.

criteria to judge whether a person is qualified to be an expert witness. He should have particular expertise on the matters upon which he is being asked to comment, but that can have been obtained through study and qualifications or work experience. A trafficking expert may have gained expertise on trafficking through his work in specialist NGOs or the police force.

10.62

In *AA (unattended children) Afghanistan CG*[93], the Upper Tribunal rejected the Home Office's objection that an archaeologist did not qualify as a country expert 'as his professional expertise is as an archaeologist'. The Tribunal responded that 'We accept that he is not one who has conventionally come to be described as a "country expert"; but his considerable personal and recent experience of Afghanistan, and of the political situation within that country, together with the objectivity that is implicit in his professional qualifications and experience, give the authority to his evidence'.

10.63

More recently in *AAW (expert evidence – weight) Somalia*[94] the Upper Tribunal found that it was able to attach little weight to the expert evidence of a journalist as an expert witness because it lacked objectivity. However, the Upper Tribunal acknowledged that the expert's evidence was not to be disregarded as it stood as 'the view of an experienced journalist with personal experience of the city from her regular visits.'

10.64

Expert evidence is regulated by guidance provided in case law, practice directions and procedure rules. In *MS (Trafficking – Tribunal's Powers – Art 4 ECHR) Pakistan*[95] the President of the Upper Tribunal considered that there was 'some force in the criticisms levelled' at the expert evidence in that case and highlighted the detailed treatment of the duties of expert witnesses in the decision of the Tribunal in *MOJ (Return to Mogadishu) Somalia*[96] (set out in detail below). The President directed that:

> 'those engaging expert witnesses should, in every case, ensure that the expert is provided with a copy of this section of the *MOJ* decision, as a matter of course, at the initial stage of receiving instructions. Each expert's report should, in turn, make clear that these passages have been received and read by the mechanism of a simple declaration to this effect'.

---

93 *AA (unattended children) Afghanistan CG* [2012] UKUT 00016 (IAC) at 116.
94 *AAW (expert evidence – weight) Somalia* [2015] UKUT 00673 (IAC) at 46.
95 *MS (Trafficking – Tribunal's Powers – Art. 4 ECHR) Pakistan* [2016] UKUT 00226 (IAC) at 69.
96 *MOJ (Return to Mogadishu) Somalia CG* [2014] UKUT 00442 (IAC).

10.65

The relevant passages of *MOJ (Return to Mogadishu) Somalia*[97] are as follows:

'23 We consider it appropriate to draw attention to this subject, given the prevalence and importance of expert evidence in Country Guidance cases. Mindful that substantial quantities of judicial ink have been spilled on this subject, we confine ourselves to highlighting and emphasising what appear to us to be amongst the most important considerations. The general principles are of some vintage. In *National Justice CIA Naviera SA v Prudential Assurance Company Ltd* [1993] 2 Lloyds Reports 68, Cresswell J stated, at pp 81–82:

"The duties and responsibilities of expert witnesses in civil cases include the following:

1   Expert evidence presented to the court should be, and should be seen to be, the independent product of the expert uninfluenced as to form or content by the exigencies of litigation ....

2   An expert witness should provide independent assistance to the Court by way of objective unbiased opinion in relation to matters within his expertise .... An expert witness in the High Court should never assume the role of an advocate ...

3   An expert witness should state the facts or assumption upon which his opinion is based. He should not omit to consider material facts which could detract from his concluded opinion. ....

4   An expert witness should make it clear when a particular question or issue falls outside his expertise.

5   If an expert's opinion is not properly researched because he considers that insufficient data is available, then this must be stated with an indication that the opinion is no more than a provisional one. In cases where an expert witness who has prepared a report could not assert that the report contained the truth, the whole truth and nothing but the truth without some qualification, that qualification should be stated in the report ....

6   If, after exchange of reports, an expert witness changes his view on a material matter having read the other side's expert's report, or for any other reason, such change of view should

---

97 [2014] UKUT 00442 (IAC), paras [23]–[27].

> be communicated (through legal representatives) to the other
> side without delay and when appropriate to the Court."

This code was duly approved by the Court of Appeal: see [1995] 1
Lloyds Reports 455, at p 496. It has been considered in a series of
subsequent report cases: see, for example, *Vernon v Bosley (No 2)* [1997]
1 All ER 577, at page 601. In the latter case, Evans LJ stated, at page 603:

> "… Expert witnesses are armed with the court's readiness to
> receive the expert evidence which it needs in order to reach a fully
> informed decision, whatever the nature of the topic may be. But
> their evidence ceases to be useful, and it may become counter-
> productive, when it is not marshalled by reference to the issues in
> the particular case and kept within the limits so fixed."

Judicial condemnation of an expert who does not appreciate his
responsibilities is far from uncommon: see, for example, *Stevens v Gullis*
[2000] 1 All ER 527, where Lord Woolf MR at pp 532–533 stated that
the expert in question had:

> "… demonstrated by his conduct that he had no conception of
> the requirements placed upon an expert under the CPR … 19 It
> is now clear from the rules that, in addition to the duty which an
> expert owes to a party, he is also under a duty to the court."

24. The requirements of CPR 31 also featured in *Lucas v Barking
Hospitals NHS Trust* [2003] EWCA Civ 1102, where the emphasis was
on CPR 31 and CPR 35. These provide (inter alia) that:

(i)   a party may apply for an order for inspection of any document
        mentioned in an expert's report which has not already been
        disclosed,

(ii)   every expert's report must state the substance of all material
        instructions, whether written or oral, on the basis of which the
        report was written, and

(iii)   such instructions are not privileged against disclosure.

Laws LJ made the following noteworthy observation:

> "[42] As it seems to me the key to this case …. is the imperative
> of transparency, a general theme of the CPR but here specifically
> applied to the deployment of experts' reports. Thus the aim of rule
> 35.10(3) and (4) is broadly to ensure that the factual basis on which
> the expert has prepared his report is patent."

25. Thus in the contemporary era the subject of expert evidence and experts' reports is heavily regulated. The principles, rules and criteria highlighted above are of general application. They apply to experts giving evidence at every tier of the legal system. In the specific sphere of the Upper Tribunal (Immigration and Asylum Chamber), these standards apply fully, without any qualification. They are reflected in the Senior President's Practice Direction No 10 (2010) which, in paragraph 10, lays particular emphasis on a series of duties. We summarise these duties thus:

(i)   to provide information and express opinions independently, uninfluenced by the litigation;

(ii)   to consider all material facts, including those which might detract from the expert witness' opinion;

(iii) to be objective and unbiased;

(iv)   to avoid trespass into the prohibited territory of advocacy;

(v)   to be fully informed;

(vi)   to act within the confines of the witness's area of expertise; and

(vii) to modify, or abandon one's view, where appropriate.

26. In the realm of expert testimony, important duties are also imposed on legal practitioners. These too feature in the aforementioned Practice Direction. These duties may be summarised thus:

(i)   to ensure that the expert is equipped with all relevant information and materials, which will include information and materials adverse to the client's case;

(ii)   to vouchsafe that the expert is fully versed in the duties rehearsed above;

(iii) to communicate, promptly, any alterations in the expert's opinion to the other parties and the Tribunal, and

(v)   to ensure full compliance with the aforementioned Practice Statement, any other relevant Practice Statement, any relevant Guidance Note, all material requirements of the Rules and all case management directions and orders of the Tribunal.

These duties, also unqualified in nature, are a reflection of the bond between Bench and Representatives which features throughout the common law world.

27. The interface between the role of the expert witness and the duty of the Court or Tribunal features in the following passage in

the judgment of Wilson J in *Mibanga v Secretary of State for the Home Department* [2005] EWHC 367:

> "[24] It seems to me to be axiomatic that a fact finder must not reach his or her conclusion before surveying all the evidence relevant thereto ...
>
> The Secretary of State argues that decisions as to the credibility of an account are to be taken by the judicial fact finder and that, in their reports, experts, whether in relation to medical matters or in relation to in-country circumstances, cannot usurp the fact finder's function in assessing credibility. I agree. What, however, they can offer is a factual context in which it may be necessary for the fact finder to survey the allegations placed before him; and such context may prove a crucial aid to the decision whether or not to accept the truth of them. ...
>
> It seems to me that a proper fact finding enquiry involves explanation as to the reason for which an expert view is rejected and indeed placed beyond the spectrum of views which could reasonably be held."

To this we would add that, as the hearing of the present appeals demonstrated, this Tribunal will always pay close attention to the expert's research; the availability of empirical data or other information bearing on the expert's views; the quality and reliability of such material; whether the expert has taken such material into account; the expert's willingness to modify or withdraw certain views or conclusions where other evidence, or expert opinion, suggests that this is appropriate; and the attitude of the expert, which will include his willingness to engage with the Tribunal. This is not designed to be an exhaustive list.'

11 Safeguarding child and adult victims of trafficking and immigration detention

Safeguarding and immigration detention: children

Introduction

11.1

In order to effectively advise and prepare a case involving a victim of trafficking it is essential to understand the particular safeguarding needs of victims.

Policy and guidance

11.2

An assessment of whether a child is being exploited or is at risk of exploitation, including where there is reason to believe a child has been trafficked, is a child protection decision. Where vulnerable children are detained in immigration or criminal proceedings it is essential that all responsible persons engage with the correct policy, procedures and guidance.

11.3

In 2011 the Department for Education and the Home Office jointly published the practice guidance, *Safeguarding children who may have been trafficked*[1]. This followed an update of earlier guidance and it sits under the primary multi-agency policy framework for safeguarding children in England and Wales, referred to as *Working together to safeguard children*[2]. The practice guidance covers the broader responsibilities of all authorities who may have first contact with children suspected to be trafficked or exploited. Similar multi-agency guidance exists in Scotland and Northern Ireland. The 2011 practice guidance is now supplemented by *Care of unaccompanied and trafficked children: Statutory guidance*

---

1 Available at www.gov.uk/government/publications/safeguarding-children-who-may-have-been-trafficked-practice-guidance, last accessed 16 December 2017.
2 Last updated in Feb 2017, available at www.gov.uk/government/publications/working-together-to-safeguard-children--2, last accessed 16 December 2017.

for local authorities on the care of unaccompanied asylum seeking and trafficked children, issued under the Local Authority Social Services Act 1970, s 7, which requires local authorities in exercising their social services functions to act under the general guidance of the Secretary of State[3]. Although the statutory guidance is addressed to Chief Executives, Directors of Children's Services and Lead Members for Children's Services it is also relevant to police and Home Office due to the joint responsibility to cooperate with the local authority in safeguarding the child.

11.4

The Children Act 2004, s 13 requires each local authority to establish a Local Safeguarding Children Board ('LSCB') for its area. LSCBs are responsible for developing multi-agency policy and guidelines for safeguarding children in their areas, and should have integrated the statutory guidance into their own localised policy documents. Local police forces must be represented on the LSCB. The localised version of the trafficked children policy and guidance should be publicly available and is often accessible via the LSCB website.

Assessment of vulnerability

11.5

All children and young people are vulnerable because of their age and lack of maturity, but the assessment of vulnerability requires professionals to look beyond what children say and to understand, observe and record emotional, behavioural and presentational indicators of risk and to act quickly to put in place the appropriate protection measures even if the child has not disclosed. Guidance on trafficked children provided by the Association of Directors of Children's Services ('ADCS') states:

> '… Aside from the physical, sexual or emotional abuse they may have suffered, many trafficked children have been forced by their traffickers to learn a story to tell if they are questioned. Many children and young people are under threat directly themselves, or may have family members elsewhere who are under threat, or perceived threat. Children and young people may not know who they can trust. As a result, they may give information that is later contradictory to information provided initially. This is not necessarily an indication that a child or young person is trying to deceive social workers, and should not be considered as such…'[4].

---

3 (November 2017), available at www.gov.uk/government/uploads/system/uploads/attachment_data/file/330787/Care_of_unaccompanied_and_trafficked_children.pdf, last accessed 16 December 2017.

4 ADCS, *Age Assessment Guidance* (October 2015), available at http://adcs.org.uk/assets/documentation/Age_Assessment_Guidance_2015_Final.pdf, last accessed 16 December 2017.

11.6

Home Office guidance for National Referral Mechanism Competent Authorities acknowledges that trafficking victims may be reluctant to come forward with information; may not recognise themselves as having been trafficked or enslaved and may tell their stories with obvious errors[5]. In addition, Home Office guidance for frontline staff advises that:

'You must not expect a person to feel or behave as a "victim" (in the sense of being totally dependent on help and protection from someone else). Many victims do not recognise themselves as such, but as migrants who happen to be in a "difficult" situation. If they will not identify themselves as a victim, you must consider if there are any objective signs. Such indicators help you identify potential victims of modern slavery It is important you do not rely on victims to identify themselves, but instead know how to recognise and identify the signs of modern slavery'[6].

11.7

Similarly, the College of Policing guidance on modern slavery directs that:

'Child victims of modern slavery are amongst the most vulnerable, the easiest to control and the least likely to admit to their situation. They may not show obvious signs of distress, as they may not realise that they have been enslaved or see themselves as being at risk of harm and in danger. Parents and relatives may also be involved in the exploitation of the child. Children are likely to be extremely loyal to their parents or carers so it is not likely that they will, of their own initiative, seek protection against such people. It is also possible that a child's experiences of modern slavery perpetrated by adults, and experience of corruption and abuse by police, officials and/or authorities in their home countries, may make them wary of all adults, including police officers. They may, therefore, be reluctant to disclose any information in an interview until they have built a trusting relationship with those interviewing. Interviews should take place in a child-friendly environment. During the interview, the child should be asked what measures would make them feel safe, how they perceive authority figures and people in uniform, and the police should clearly explain their role to the child. The child should be provided with emergency contact numbers, including 999, and know that these are free of charge.

---

5 Home Office, *Victims of modern slavery – Competent Authority guidance* (21 March 2016) p 48, available at www.gov.uk/government/uploads/system/uploads/attachment_data/file/521763/Victims_of_modern_slavery_-_Competent_Authority_guidance_v3_0.pdf, last accessed 16 December 2017.

6 Home Office, *Victims of modern slavery – Frontline Staff guidance* (18 March 2016) p 22, available at www.gov.uk/government/uploads/system/uploads/attachment_data/file/509326/victims-of-modern-slavery-frontline-staff-guidance-v3.pdf, last accessed 16 December 2017.

If a child is housed and goes missing before or after the interview, and is suspected of being enslaved or exploited, they should be treated as a missing person. A suitably trained person should conduct a debrief'[7].

Children detained in immigration or criminal proceedings

11.8

When the first 24–48 hours of contact focuses only on addressing the child as an offender, the result is that the specific statutory safeguarding and identification procedures for children who may be trafficked are less likely to be triggered. Early indicators of trafficking and exploitation, including behavioural and psychological indicators, are thus not observed or recorded, and this has implications for subsequent immigration, criminal or care proceedings. If a child is subsequently released on bail into the community or into local authority care without a robust risk assessment, then special protection measures will not be put into place and the risk of harm to the child escalates. The policy framework for safeguarding children and the Modern Slavery Act ('MSA') 2015 should prevent this from happening, but there are still significant gaps in training and management practices across the country.

11.9

The College of Policing accepts that all potential victims are vulnerable and should, therefore, be interviewed in compliance with Ministry of Justice guidance[8].

11.10

In circumstances where a victim of trafficking is involved in criminality and has been charged with offences linked to his exploitation, protective bail conditions should be a consideration when making an application for bail. Bail is a key issue to consider in the context of trafficking. As a minimum, an NRM conclusive grounds decision will not be made for at least 45 days (the recovery and reflection period). In practice it can be significantly longer.

11.11

When preparing and presenting any bail application on behalf of a victim, consideration should be given to protective conditions such as no unsupervised

---

7   First response and the national referral mechanism, available at www.app.college.police.uk/app-content/major-investigation-and-public-protection/modern-slavery/national-referral-mechanism/, last accessed 16 December 2017.

8   Achieving Best Evidence in Criminal Proceedings: Guidance on interviewing victims and witnesses, and guidance on using special measures, available at www.app.college.police.uk/app-content/major-investigation-and-public-protection/modern-slavery/risk-and-identification/, last ˙ accessed 10 January 2018.

use of phones or electronic equipment. It is common for victims who are being controlled by their traffickers or in debt bondage to make contact with either traffickers or those who are involved in the organised criminal network. For other safeguarding measures and considerations see Chapters 7 and 8. It should be highlighted that proposed bail addresses should be suitable and not in an area where the victim's exploitation has taken place and where the traffickers operate.

The duty to identify

11.12

From 1 November 2015, specified public authorities have a duty to notify the Secretary of State of any person encountered in England and Wales whom they believe may be a victim of slavery or human trafficking. Under the MSA 2015, s 52, UK Visas and Immigration, Border Force and Immigration Enforcement must also comply with the duty as a matter of Home Office policy[9].

11.13

In addition the MSA 2015, s 52 places a duty on a local police force to begin an investigation as soon as it believes that a modern slavery crime may have been committed, regardless of whether a victim makes an allegation, whether a report is made, whether consent to be entered into the NRM is provided or refused, or whether the NRM decision is negative or positive. Once the scale of the investigation is known, the ownership of it can be reassessed[10].

Missing children

11.14

Vulnerable children at risk of going missing should not be detained as a de facto way to stop them absconding. In November 2016 the organisations ECPAT UK and Missing People published a report into unaccompanied and trafficked children who went missing from care, which found that more than a quarter of all trafficked children and over 500 unaccompanied asylum-seeking children went missing at least once in the year to September 2015, while 207 have not been found[11].

---

9 Home Office, *Victims of modern slavery – Frontline Staff guidance* (18 March 2016); Modern Slavery Act 2015, s 52.
10 See   www.app.college.police.uk/app-content/major-investigation-and-public-protection/modern-slavery/reporting-and-first-contact/, last accessed 17 December 2017.
11 *Heading back to Harm*, available at www.ecpat.org.uk/heading-back-to-harm-a-study-on-trafficked-and-unaccompanied-children-going-missing-from-care-in-the-uk, last accessed 17 December 2017.

11.15

Some groups of children are at very high risk of going missing because they are under instructions from traffickers, have been groomed or given instructions, feel unable to trust anyone in authority or are very frightened of what will happen to them or their family if they do not return to the trafficker. For example children held under debt bondage or who owe a debt for their journey are particularly vulnerable to returning to the trafficker. Children arrested for criminal offences may also be highly vulnerable, as witnesses to organised crime, and frightened about retribution from those who control them. Acknowledging the risk of going missing and then putting in place robust multi-agency planning to mitigate it is central to safeguarding children procedures. Measures such as placing children in specialist foster care out of the area, temporarily removing mobile phone and internet access and having the child escorted outside the home should be considered as part of wider safeguarding procedures on release from detention along with a safety plan shared with the child and with police.

11.16

The statutory guidance on children who run away or go missing from home or care and the addendum flowchart, showing roles and responsibilities when a child goes missing from care, were issued in 2014 and contain information on procedures for children who have gone missing, suspected trafficked[12]. Paragraphs 73–79 of the guidance reinforce the joint responsibility between local authorities, police, the Home Office and others in collecting, recording and sharing data to monitor and assess on-going risk. Risk is not static, and can rapidly increase when the child is under stress if, for example, the child receives a phone call or is due to attend court. A child fitting the profile of a victim of trafficking and who has gone missing but is not yet referred into the NRM should still be treated as a high-risk missing person by police. High-risk is where:

- the risk posed is immediate and there are substantial grounds for believing that the child is in danger through his own vulnerability;

- the child may have been the victim of a serious crime; or

- the risk posed is immediate and there are substantial grounds for believing that the public is in danger.

Child trafficking advocates

11.17

Section 48 of the MSA 2015 legislates for Independent Child Trafficking Advocates, a model of guardianship for children who may be trafficked. The

---

12 Available at www.gov.uk/government/publications/children-who-run-away-or-go-missing-from-home-or-care, last accessed 17 December 2017. (It should be noted that new guidance is due to be published imminently.)

government has rolled out a small pilot and has published *Interim Guidance for the three Independent Child Trafficking Advocates Early Adopter Sites – Greater Manchester, Wales and Hampshire*[13]. It is a matter of Home Office policy, and Immigration Enforcement, Border Force, and UK Visas and Immigration must follow this guidance. Independent Child Trafficking Advocates will be required to work alongside existing provision and to advocate in the best interests of the child and, where necessary and appropriate, provide effective challenges to statutory services on how to best support the children they represent.

Policy versus practice

11.18

The precautionary measures for keeping child victims safe go beyond the core statutory safeguards, should be triggered as soon as possible and in most circumstances prior to an NRM decision being made. This is why earlier guidance was published as 'Safeguarding children who *may be* trafficked', in recognition that special protection measures must apply from the moment of first contact in order to keep the child safe while investigations are ongoing. The policy framework recognises that even when a child has been taken into local authority care, or is in detention or in custody, the child could still be under the control of the trafficker. This has implications for the immediate safety of the child. This is why recommended practice that may seem overly intrusive in other circumstances is considered to be in the child's best interest, as long as it is used in the correct way: for example, monitoring children's contact with others, monitoring phone calls, identifying and tracing phone numbers found in their clothes or possessions, removing sim card for examination, tracking internet use and so on. Due to the high risk of trafficked children going missing and being re-trafficked, it is recommended that the child is photographed immediately and notes taken of what they are wearing when first placed in care. Where children are in immigration detention or in police custody with co-defendants extra precautions must be exercised because the child may be under threat of harm and have been coached in what to say by someone being held in the same facility. An assessment of current and future risk should be recorded and shared with the local authority to enable the social work team to make decisions about safe accommodation arrangements and the level of security needed for the child's protection[14].

Safeguarding children who may be affected by immigration control

11.19

In September 2008, the UK announced that it would lift reservations on the UN Convention on the Rights of the Child in respect of immigration matters

---

13 (January 2017), available at www.gov.uk/government/uploads/system/uploads/attachment_data/file/586796/trafficking_Interim_guidance.pdf, last accessed 17 December 2017.

14 'Child victims shall not be returned to a State, if there is indication, following a risk and security assessment, that such return would not be in the best interests of the child' ECAT, Art 16[7].

concerning children. That announcement marked a significant step toward bringing the Home Office's obligations to safeguard and promote children's welfare closer in line with the established framework for safeguarding and promoting children's welfare that had applied to other public authorities (including the police, youth offending team, social services, schools, hospitals)[15], since the Children Act 2004 came into force. In 2009, the Borders Citizenship and Immigration Act 2009, s 55 was enacted, providing that the Secretary of State for the Home Department must make arrangements for ensuring that in the discharge of his functions relating to immigration, asylum, nationality, he must have regard to the need to safeguard and promote the welfare of children who are in the United Kingdom.

The s 55 safeguarding duty

11.20

Under the Borders Citizenship and Immigration Act 2009, s 55(2)(b), immigration officers making decisions on behalf of the Home Secretary under the powers of the Immigration Acts must have regard to the safeguarding welfare duty, and further must have regard to any statutory guidance given by the Secretary of State under s 55(3).

11.21

Although the statute itself does not define 'welfare', the statutory guidance does provide the following at para 1.4:

- protecting children from maltreatment;

- preventing impairment of children's health and development (where health means 'physical or mental health' and development means 'physical, intellectual, emotional, social or behavioural development');

- ensuring that children are growing up in circumstances consistent with the provision of safe and effective care;

- undertaking that role so as to enable those children to have optimum life chances and to enter adulthood successfully.

11.22

This is not dissimilar to the description of welfare set out in the mirror provision of the Children Act 2004, s 11. The jurisprudence around both provisions makes clear that the duty to safeguard welfare must in terms comply with the spirit, if not the language, of the obligations under the UN Convention on the Rights of the Child and in particular Art 3(1), which requires that 'in all actions concerning children... the best interests of the child shall be a

---

15 See the Children Act 2004, s 11(1) for the full list.

primary consideration'[16].Whilst the best interests of the child is not the supreme consideration or trump card, the Supreme Court's judgment in *ZH (Tanzania) v Secretary of State for the Home Department* made clear that the child's best interests is a factor of the highest rank which should only be displaced or rendered of less importance if there are very strong countervailing factors[17].

11.23

Statutory guidance issued under the Borders Citizenship and Immigration Act 2009, s 55(3) provides expanded guidance governed by the following principles:

- the Home Office must maintain 'clear arrangements' and 'operation and policy instructions' to ensure the effectiveness of arrangements for safeguarding and promoting the child's welfare: paras 2.12 and 2.13;

- the duty is not limited to a requirement by the Home Office to put in place policies and a system for safeguarding children. It applies to individual decision-making across all areas of immigration law and is underpinned by a recognition that 'children cannot put on hold their growth or personal development until a potentially lengthy application process is resolved': para 2.20. See also *AAM v Secretary of State for the Home Department*[18];

- work with the child should be child-centred, take account of the child's views, informed by evidence, and have regard to the professional views and information available from other agencies involved with the child: paras 1.16 and 2.27;

- the onus is on the Home Office to demonstrate how a decision was made in compliance with the Borders Citizenship and Immigration Act 2009, s 55 both by the implementation of an operational policy and/or on an individual basis. In *Nzolameso v Westminster City Council*[19], the Supreme Court held (at [24]–[27]) that the analogous Children Act 2004, s 11 applies not only to the formulation of general policies and practices, but also to their application in an individual case.This entails identifying 'the principal needs of the children, both individually and collectively, and having regard to the need to safeguard and promote them when making the decision': per Baroness Hale at [27].

Detention and safeguarding of children

11.24

The obligation to safeguard children arises in two principal ways in the context of immigration detention: firstly, when children (including those whose age

---

16 *ZH (Tanzania) v Secretary of State for the Home Department* [2011] UKSC 4, [2011] 2 AC 166 per Lady Hale at [23].
17 See Lady Hale at [25]–[27] and [33], Lord Hope at [44], and Lord Kerr at [46].
18 [2012] EWHC 2567 (QB) at [119].
19 [2015] UKSC 22, [2015] 2 All ER 942.

may be disputed) are detained, and secondly, when dependent children are separated from parents and primary carers who are detained.

Safeguarding unaccompanied children

11.25

In respect of unaccompanied children, as a general principle, even where one of the statutory powers to detain is available in a particular case, the Home Office's policy, *Chapter 55 of the Enforcement Instructions and Guidance* (EIG 55) states that they must 'not be detained other than in very exceptional circumstances' and if they are detained it should be for the 'shortest possible time, with appropriate care'. This approach is consistent with the UN Convention on the Rights of the Child, Art 37, which provides that detention of a child shall be used 'only as a measure of last resort and for the shortest appropriate period of time'. Under EIG 55.9.3A an exceptional circumstance may be where it is necessary to deal with unexpected situations for example in order to await collection by a parent or relative or local authority children's services. Detaining to interview a newly-arrived unaccompanied child at port would *not* fall within the ambit of 'very exceptional circumstances'. The Court of Appeal held in *R (AN and FA) v Secretary of State for the Home Department*[20] that once basic information has been obtained at port of entry from a newly-arrived unaccompanied child, the Home Office must immediately refer the child to a relevant local authority children's services. At this early stage, the Home Office should not be asking the child questions relating to why he has come to the UK. That is a question that should be asked in the presence of an appropriate adult. The priority, consistent with the duty under the Borders Citizenship and Immigration Act 2009, s 55, is to safeguard and promote the child's immediate welfare and to refer the child for safe accommodation and support from a local authority children's services department.

11.26

The same approach is adopted in most cases where a dispute is raised in respect of the child's age. The Home Office's policy is to treat an age disputed child as a child until verification, unless the child's physical appearance and demeanour very strongly suggests that they are significantly over 19 years of age and no other credible evidence exists to the contrary. This is clearly a high threshold and requires an individualised consideration. It also operates in a precautionary way to ensure that the presumption of minority applies with a benefit of doubt afforded to the child[21]. Whilst documentary evidence may sometimes be available, the Home Office's guidance on assessing age recognises that documents may frequently be obtained by traffickers and smugglers under

---

20 [2012] EWCA Civ 1636.
21 EIG 55.9.3.1 and the Home Office's asylum policy instruction *Assessing Age*.

false pretence to make the child appear older than they actually are in order to evade the attention of the authorities. Similarly, the mere existence of a visa application in the child's name (or with the child's photograph), with a date of birth used that is older than claimed, should not be deemed to be determinative documentary evidence of a claimed child being over 18. The precautionary approach applies even where a putative child previously gave a date of birth that would make them an adult. Even in those cases, the Home Office's policy makes clear that if the putative child has yet to have a *Merton* compliant age assessment or a court finding indicating he is not a child, the benefit of doubt as to minority should still be afforded to him unless his physical appearance and demeanour very strongly suggests that he is significantly over 18: see EIG 55.9.3.1 and Detention Services Order 14/2012[22].

11.27

As for putative children who had previously been sentenced by the criminal courts as adults, the Home Office's policy states that they will be treated as being over 18 years of age (irrespective of any late disclosure of their minority) unless new documentary evidence has come to light[23]. This approach illustrates why it is so important in the context of criminal proceedings for the fact of age to be resolved properly and correctly as if the criminal courts make a factually wrong finding as to age, it can have significant repercussions for a putative child who is subject to immigration control. See also Chapter 3 on age disputes.

Safeguarding child victims of trafficking

11.28

The arrangements for safeguarding child victims of trafficking should, in principle, fit within the overall framework of child safeguarding under the Borders Citizenship and Immigration Act 2009, s 55, the UN Convention on the Rights of the Child and ECHR, Art 8. The Home Office acknowledges the specific vulnerabilities of separated children. However it would be naïve not to recognise the particular needs of the subset of separated children who have been subject to trafficking and modern slavery.

11.29

There is currently a significant gap in arrangements available to ensure specific measures are implemented to safeguard child victims of trafficking who are identified in detention. If an NRM referral has been made in respect of the child whilst in detention, the local authority should be contacted to make care arrangements in the community. However, there is currently no joined-up work done by the Home Office and local authority children's services to conduct

---

22 DSO 14/2012 Care and management of age dispute cases.
23 DSO 14/2012, section 10.

risk assessments and convene safeguarding meetings prior to the release of a child victim of trafficking (including an age-disputed one) from immigration detention, particularly to ensure that any risks of re-trafficking are mitigated to the extent possible. In *R (TDT) v Secretary of State for the Home Department*[24] the failure to put measures in place to safeguard against the risk of re-trafficking led to the claimant going missing on release. The court held, in that case, that the Home Office had implemented proper systems for ensuring compliance with the duty to protect a potential child victim of trafficking and thus the failure did not breach ECHR, Art 4. However, this decision is currently under appeal.

Detention of families

11.30

Detaining families with children has been controversial. The Home Office operates a policy whereby families with children can be detained for the purposes of ensured return of families to their country of origin by the use of pre-departure accommodation. There are restrictions on when this can be used, stays being limited to a maximum of 72 hours save in the exceptional circumstances where ministerial authority is given for a total of seven days. In criminal casework cases, mothers with infant children may be detained in a prison mother and baby unit at end of sentence and pending deportation. Decision-making in this respect can only be done with the Home Office having properly applied the Borders Citizenship and Immigration Act 2009, s 55 and ECHR, Art 8 considerations to the best interests of the child as a primary consideration.[25]

11.31

The same Borders Citizenship and Immigration Act 2009, s 55/ECHR, Art 8 approach ought to be applied in the context of detention of parents or primary carers where the consequence is separation of children from their carers. This happens most frequently in the context of cases where the primary carer or parent is subject to deportation.

11.32

The ECtHR has interpreted the ECHR, Art 8 to encompass a positive obligation to protect an individual's right to 'physical and psychological integrity,' an aspect of the right to private life[26]. In *Beoku-Betts v Secretary of State for the Home Department*[27] the House of Lords held that where a breach of a claimant's right to respect for his family life was alleged the public authority must consider

---

24 [2016] EWHC 1912 (Admin).
25 See EIG 55.9.4.
26 *Botta v Italy* (1998) 26 EHRR 241, para 39.
27 [2008] UKHL 39, [2009] 1 AC 115.

the complaint with reference to the family unit as a whole. The assessment of proportionality under Art 8(2) must be carried out in the context where each affected family member was to be regarded as a victim in his own right.

11.33

In *ZH (Tanzania) v Secretary of State for the Home Department*[28] the Supreme Court had to grapple with the respective Art 8 rights of a mother, whom the defendant proposed to deport, and her children, who would be left behind in the UK as British citizens. The Supreme Court (per Lady Hale at [23]) held that the jurisprudence in the Strasbourg Court expects national authorities to apply the UN Convention on the Rights of the Child, Art 3(1) and treat the child's best interests as a primary consideration. Article 3(2) provides that:

'States Parties undertake to ensure the child such protection and care as is necessary for his or her wellbeing, taking into account the rights and duties of his or her parents, legal guardians, or other individuals legally responsible for him or her, and to this end, shall take all appropriate legislative and administrative measures.'

11.34

Article 9(1) deals with the separation of parent and child, providing that:

'States Parties shall ensure that a child shall not be separated from his or her parents against their will, except when competent authorities subject to judicial review determine, in accordance with applicable law and procedures, that such separation is necessary for the best interests of the child. Such determination may be necessary in a particular case such as one involving abuse or neglect of the child by the parents, or one where the parents are living separately and a decision must be made as to the child's place of residence.'

Arguably this would apply to primary carers, even if they are not the child's parents.

11.35

Article 12 is also relevant. It provides:

'1   States Parties shall assure to the child who is capable of forming his or her own views the right to express those views freely in all matters affecting the child, the views of the child being given due weight in accordance with the age and maturity of the child.

2   For this purpose, the child shall in particular be afforded the opportunity to be heard in any judicial and administrative

---

28 [2011] UKSC 4, [2011] 2 AC 166.

proceedings affecting the child, either directly, or through a representative or an appropriate body, in a manner consistent with the procedural rules of national law.'

11.36

Thus, whilst the Home Office may consider a parent or carer to pose risks of absconding, harm and re-offending, these considerations are distinct considerations from the welfare of the children, which is equally relevant in the context of considering the decision to detain[29]. The onus is on the Home Office to make reasonable inquiries to gather the facts necessary to inform a proper consideration of the child's welfare in this context, bearing in mind that the child's best interests is a primary consideration (per Lord Kerr at [46] in *ZH (Tanzania)*) and the starting point.

Safeguarding and immigration detention: adults

11.37

The various statutory powers of immigration detention[30] have in common that, provided the broad statutory conditions for detention are met (liability to removal or deportation, plus in some cases service of a decision to remove), there are no *express* statutory limits on the exercise of the power by the defendant. The width of the statutory provisions to detain, however, has been limited by policies published by the Home Office, secondary legislation, in the form of the Detention Centre Rules 2001 and the obligations under the Human Rights Act 1998.

11.38

For over 20 years, until September 2016, the Home Office adopted a policy[31] of not detaining certain vulnerable persons, save in very exceptional circumstances. This included not detaining children, the elderly, pregnant women, those suffering from serious medical conditions, the mentally ill, people with serious disabilities and those who had independent evidence that they may have been victims of torture. The inclusion of those who have been tortured as a separate category was in explicit recognition of the particular vulnerability of torture victims and the harm that detention could

---

29 *R (on the application of NXT) v Secretary of State for the Home Department* [2011] EWHC 969 (Admin).

30 Most notably, the Immigration Act 1971, Sch 2, para 16(2), used to detain pending administrative removal, and various powers to detain pending deportation in Sch 3, para 2 to that Act and (for automatic deportation cases) the UK Borders Act 2007, s 35.

31 The policy regarding detention of vulnerable persons first appeared in Chapter 38 of the Operational Enforcement Manual ('OEM'), and then under EIG 55.10. It had not been altered since its introduction in 2000 until 12 September 2016, when the statutory guidance, *Immigration Act 2016: Adults at Risk Guidance* came into force.

do to them[32]. Once it appeared that the individual fell within a category of vulnerable persons, the burden shifted to the Home Office to demonstrate that there were 'very exceptional circumstances' to justify detention of the person. This has been judged to be a high threshold by the courts[33]. Thus, the mere fact of removal within a reasonable period of time or a criminal conviction in and of itself does not suffice to meet the high threshold. Under the Enforcement Instructions and Guidance, section 55.10, there was also no additional requirement for a detainee with independent evidence of a history of torture to demonstrate that detention was likely to be injurious or harmful. The policy proceeded on a precautionary basis, accepting that detention *per se* will be harmful for victims of torture.

11.39

A framework of rules and further policy was put in place to ensure compliance with this overarching policy relating to the detention of vulnerable adults and children. For adults, this included the Detention Centre Rules 2001, EIG 55, the Detention Rule 35 Process Guidance, and the Detention Service Order 17/2012.

11.40

The Detention Centre Rules 2001[34], introduced under the Immigration and Asylum Act 1999, s 153, provide as follows:

'Rule 33 Medical practitioner and health care team

(1) Every detention centre shall have a medical practitioner, who shall be vocationally trained as a general practitioner and a fully registered person within the meaning of the Medical Act 1983.'

'Rule 34 Medical examination upon admission and thereafter

(1) Every detained person shall be given a physical and mental examination by the medical practitioner (or another registered medical practitioner in accordance with rules 33(7) or (10)) within 24 hours of his admission to the detention centre.

(2) Nothing in paragraph (1) shall allow an examination to be given in any case where the detained person does not consent to it.

(3) If a detained person does not consent to an examination under paragraph (1), he shall be entitled to the examination at any subsequent time upon request.'

---

32 Paras 12.3–12.4 of the White Paper *Fairer, Faster and Firmer*.
33 *R (on the application of Das) v Secretary of State for the Home Department* [2014] EWCA Civ 45.
34 SI 2001/238.

'Rule 35 Special illnesses and conditions (including torture claims)

(1) The medical practitioner shall report to the manager on the case of any detained person whose health is likely to be injuriously affected by continued detention or any conditions of detention.

(2) The medical practitioner shall report to the manager on the case of any detained person he suspects of having suicidal intentions, and the detained person shall be placed under special observation for so long as those suspicions remain, and a record of his treatment and condition shall be kept throughout that time in a manner to be determined by the Secretary of State.

(3) The medical practitioner shall report to the manager on the case of any detained person who he is concerned may have been the victim of torture.

(4) The manager shall send a copy of any report under paragraphs (1), (2) or (3) to the Secretary of State without delay.

(5) The medical practitioner shall pay special attention to any detained person whose mental condition appears to require it, and make any special arrangements (including counselling arrangements) which appear necessary for his supervision or care.'

11.41

The Detention Centre Rules 2001, r 35 is the statutory mechanism for bringing those detainees who may be vulnerable and whose detention may be unsuitable to the attention of those officers responsible for deciding whether to maintain detention, as well as those responsible for considering the individual's asylum application, if any. It operates with r 34 to displace any notion that the burden is on the detainee to demonstrate a vulnerability within the three limbs[35]. The obligation is on the Home Office, as a detaining authority, to ensure that detainees can access the r 35 safeguard by arranging medical appointments and identifying those who require consideration for a report.

11.42

Rule 35(3) is the most used of the three limbs of r 35. As to the meaning of the word 'torture' under r 35(3), it was held in *R (on the application of EO) v Secretary of State for the Home Department*[36] to mean:

---

35 *R (on the application of D and K) v Secretary of State for the Home Department* [2006] EWHC 980 (Admin).
36 [2013] EWHC 1236 (Admin) (at [82] and [98]).

'any act by which severe pain or suffering, whether physical or mental, is intentionally inflicted on a person for such purposes as obtaining from him or a third person has committed, or intimidating or coercing him or a third person, or for any reason based on discrimination of any kind'.

In coming to this conclusion, Burnett J explicitly rejected the defendant's contention for a definition of torture by reference to the UN Convention against Torture, Art 1, finding that 'the word "torture" in the 2001 Rules and policy documents governing this detention has a broader meaning than that found in [the UN Convention].' Burnett J expressed particular concerns about the difficulty a caseworker or a doctor may have if a technical definition of torture such as that in the UN Convention against Torture were to be applied because 'unravelling state involvement or complicity … might be difficult at the best of times, but virtually impossible at a short medical examination in a detention centre or necessarily fairly brief review by a case worker'[37]. Following judgment in *EO*, the Home Office decided not to implement a new policy that would introduce a narrower UN Convention against Torture definition (that is, until September 2016: discussed below).

11.43

The Home Office's compliance with her detention policy and the efficacy of the r 35 statutory mechanism has been the subject of criticisms from statutory and non-governmental organisations, such as the HM Chief Inspector of Prisons[38], and HM Chief Inspector of Borders and Immigration[39]. There have been a number of successful individual challenges to the failures in the implementation of r 35 resulting in unlawful detention of individuals who should not normally be detained[40], as well as findings by the Court of general evidence of failure in the system[41]. There had also been two audits of the operation of the detention policy relating to vulnerable persons (see further below).

---

37 At [98] of *R (on the application of EO) v Secretary of State for the Home Department* [2013] EWHC 1236 (Admin).

38 Report on Harmondsworth IRC (November 2011), which found that r 35 reports and responses were often insufficient and formulaic; the quality of r 35 reports were often poor, often providing no clinical judgment; none of the healthcare staff had received training. Since the case of *EO*, HM Chief Inspector of Prisons has made criticisms of r 35 reports and/or their consideration by the defendant in all but one of the ten inspections of immigration removal centres it has conducted. These included reports of inspections on Yarl's Wood, The Verne, Dungavel, Tinsley House, Campsfield, Haslar, Dover and Harmondsworth.

39 Joint Report of HMCIP and HMCIBI, *The effectiveness and impact of immigration detention casework* (December 2012).

40 *R (Detention Action) v Secretary of State for the Home Department* [2014] EWHC 2245 (Admin) per Ouseley J at [133]; *R (on the application of JM) v Secretary of State for the Home Department* [2015] EWHC 2331 (Admin).

41 See *EO* per Burnett J observing (at [3]) that the evidence of the operation of r 35 to be 'disturbing'. See also *R (Detention Action) v Secretary of State for the Home Department* [2014] EWHC 2245 (Admin) per Ouseley J at [133] and *R (on the application of JM) v Secretary of State for the Home Department* [2015] EWHC 2331 (Admin) per Blake J reading into the court record the defendant's concession that 'the safeguards in the DFT including screening and r 35 of the Detention Centre Rules 2001 did not operate sufficiently effectively to prevent an unacceptable risk of vulnerable or potentially vulnerable individuals, whose claims required further investigation, being processed in the DFT'.

11.44

In January 2016, the Home Office published Stephen Shaw's *Review into the Welfare in detention of Vulnerable Persons*. This independent inquiry was commissioned in February 2015 by then Home Secretary, Theresa May MP, following criticisms relating to the welfare of vulnerable detainees. The Shaw Review made a wide range of findings and recommendations, particularly in respect of the identification and handling of detainees with vulnerabilities. It made recommendations for the improvements to the existing policy framework toward vulnerable persons under EIG 55.10. Amongst the findings were that:

- r 35 'does not do what it was intended to do – that is, to protect vulnerable people who find themselves in detention'. Then 'the Home Office immediately consider an alternative to the current rule 35 mechanism'[42];

- on a literature review of the effects of detention on the mental health, that detention has a negative impact per se on detainees' mental health, that impact increasing the longer detention continues and enduring after release. Asylum seekers, victims of torture, children and women are particularly vulnerable to adverse mental health outcomes in detention[43];

- there should be an expanded list of vulnerable persons who would have the protective benefit of the presumption against detention including: victims of sexual or gender-based violence, transsexuals, those with a diagnosis of post-traumatic stress disorder, and/or learning difficulties[44]. A further category of vulnerability generally should also be added 'to reflect the dynamic nature of vulnerability, and thus encompass 'persons otherwise identified as being sufficiently vulnerable that their continued detention would be injurious to their welfare'[45];

- as for the approach to the mentally ill, it should be accepted that those with serious mental illness should be removed because it is difficult to see how their treatment and care in detention can equate to good psychiatric practice (whether or not it is satisfactorily managed) and their detention would be 'an affront to civilised values'[46].

11.45

The government, in a Written Statement dated 14 January 2016, accepted 'the broad thrust of [Mr Shaw's] recommendations', in particular the recommendation 'to adopt a wider definition of those at risk ... and to recognise the dynamic

---

42 Section 4.118. He observed that 'The Home Office's approach has been to focus on whether forms can be clearer or more user-friendly, and on better training for medical staff. Both of these might help, but they will not fundamentally change the issue at hand, which is – and I put this bluntly – that the Home Office does not trust the mechanisms it has created to support its own policy.

43 Shaw Review, section 8.9.

44 Shaw Review, sections 4.24, 4.40, 4.42, 4.44.

45 Shaw Review, section 4.51.

46 Shaw Review, section 4.36.

nature of vulnerabilities'[47]. In a note published in March 2016, the government further announced the introduction of a new 'adults at risk' concept into decision-making on immigration detention with a clear presumption that people who are at risk should not be detained. The purpose is directed at fewer vulnerable people being detained, and even where detention is necessary, for the period to be shorter than at present[48].

Adults at risk: Immigration Act 2016 and statutory guidance

11.46

Following the Shaw Review, the government introduced into the Immigration Act 2016 a new s 59, entitled 'Guidance for adults at risk' which required the Home Secretary to issue guidance specifying matters to be taken into account by a Home Office detaining officer in determining:

> 'whether a person ('P') would be particularly vulnerable to harm if detained or if P were to remain in detention, and if P is identified as being particularly vulnerable to harm in those circumstances, whether P should be detained or remain in detention'.

The guidance must be approved by Parliament pursuant to s 59(4) before it is issued. It was said by the government that the Adults at Risk statutory guidance would build on EIG 55.10 and improve the protections from detention for particularly vulnerable individuals[49].

11.47

The Adults at Risk Statutory Guidance was laid before Parliament on 21 July 2016 (and was implemented from 12 September 2016 together with a new Detention Service Order 9/2016 Detention Centre Rule 35). Casework guidance in Chapter 55b of the EIG was also issued, which gave more detail than the statutory guidance on the implementation of the Immigration Act 2016, s 59. By the implementation of this new Adults at Risk framework, the previous iteration of the policy relating to detaining vulnerable adults, namely EIG 55.10, was withdrawn.

11.48

The new Adults at Risk framework has already been subject to criticism for its adoption of the definition of torture to the UN Convention against Torture

---

47 604 HC Official Report (6th series) HCWS470 by James Brokenshire.
48 See *Annex B: Detaining individuals for the purposes of Immigration Control – Consideration of Risk Issues* (1 March 2016).
49 Lord Keen, at 768 HL Official Report (5th series) col 1693, 1 February 2016; Immigration Minister James Brokenshire MP, at 608 HC Official Report (6th series) col 1190, 25 April 2016, Lord Keen, at 771 HL Official Report (5th series) col 1652, 10 May 2016.

definition, a definition that had previously been subject to litigation and found to be inappropriate in this context[50]. The use of the UN Convention against Torture definition of torture has been declared to be unlawful by Ouseley J in a recent judgment handed down on 10 October 2017[51]. Ouseley J held that the UN Convention against Torture definition was overly restrictive, in limiting torture to that which has been perpetrated by or with the acquiescence of the state. This definition did not align with the statutory purpose of the Immigration Act 2016, s 59, which was to afford a strong protective presumption against immigration detention for a wide cohort of vulnerable persons. In this context, the definition of torture ought, as held by the judge, to be construed widely.

Adults at risk: statutory guidance and practice

11.49

The Adults at Risk statutory guidance is not intended to alter the strong presumption in favour of liberty in respect of vulnerable detainees. There remains a clear presumption that detention will not be appropriate if a person is considered to be 'at risk'. The intention is that fewer people with a confirmed vulnerability will be detained in fewer instances and that where detention becomes necessary, it will be for the shortest period necessary. However, the determination of who is at risk, and what weight to be placed on the evidence of 'at risk' is more prescriptive under the new Adults at Risk framework. At section 7, the Adults at Risk statutory guidance regards an individual as an adult at risk if:

- he declares that he is suffering from a condition, or has experienced a traumatic event (such as trafficking, torture or sexual violence), that would be likely to render him particularly vulnerable to harm if he is placed in detention or remains in detention

- those considering or reviewing detention are aware of medical or other professional evidence, or observational evidence, which indicates that an individual is suffering from a condition, or has experienced a traumatic event (such as trafficking, torture or sexual violence), that would be likely to render him particularly vulnerable to harm if he is placed in detention or remains in detention – whether or not the individual has highlighted this himself.

11.50

Indicators that a person may be at risk include those identified at section 11, such as a person[52]:

---

50 See *R (on the application of EO) v Secretary of State for the Home Department* [2006] EWHC 980 (Admin).
51 *Medical Justice v Secretary of State for the Home Department* [2017] EWHC 2461 (Admin).
52 This is not an exhaustive list.

- suffering from a mental health condition or impairment (this may include more serious learning difficulties, psychiatric illness or clinical depression, depending on the nature and seriousness of the condition);

- having been a victim of torture (individuals with a completed Medico Legal Report from reputable providers will be regarded as meeting level 3 evidence, provided the report meets the required standards);

- having been a victim of sexual or gender based violence, including female genital mutilation;

- having been a victim of human trafficking or modern slavery;

- suffering from post-traumatic stress disorder (which may or may not be related to one of the above experiences);

- being pregnant (pregnant women will automatically be regarded as meeting level 3 evidence);

- suffering from a serious physical disability;

- suffering from other serious physical health conditions or illnesses;

- being aged 70 or over;

- being a transsexual or intersex person.

11.51

The Adults at Risk statutory guidance, section 9, considers the weight to be placed on indicators that a person is an adult at risk:

- self-declaration of being at risk should be afforded limited weight and be regarded as 'Level 1 evidence';

- professional evidence (eg from a social worker, medical practitioner or NGO), or official documentary evidence, which indicates that the individual is an adult at risk, should be afforded greater weight. Individuals in these circumstances will be regarded as being at evidence level 2;

- professional evidence (eg from a social worker, medical practitioner or NGO) stating that the individual is at risk and that a period of detention would be likely to cause harm – for example, increase the severity of the symptoms or condition that have led to the individual being regarded as an adult at risk – should be afforded significant weight. Individuals in these circumstances will be regarded as being at evidence level 3.

11.52

Casework Guidance EIG 55b supplements the statutory guidance by setting out further details of how to assess the balance of evidence of risk (as an adult at risk) against immigration factors which may justify the exercise of the power to detain or continue detention. The more weighty the evidence of risk, the more grave the immigration factors would need to be to displace the strong presumption in favour of liberty. For example, if a person is treated as an adult at risk with level 3 evidence (the highest level), then EIG 55b recognises that this is a person for whom detention is 'likely to lead to a risk of significant harm', thus detention should only be considered in a limited set of circumstances, such as when a removal date has been set for a date in the immediate future, there are no barriers to removal and escorts and other appropriate arrangements have been made to ensure safe management of the individual's return. Or, detention may be considered in a Level 3 adult at risk's case if the person poses significant public protection concerns or poses a serious relevant national security concern. The variety of factors under EIG 55b that need to be considered is set out in detail in the policy.

Adults at risk and trafficking

11.53

In respect of victims of trafficking and potential victims of trafficking, the Adults at Risk framework needs to be read with the *Victims of Modern Slavery: Competent Authority Guidance*. This states that pending identification of a potential victim of trafficking or modern slavery (ie from the point of NRM referral), no removal action should be taken until a conclusive grounds decision has been made. The policy goes on to state that for those potential victims who have had a positive reasonable grounds decision, they will not be detained save in 'limited circumstances ie where their detention is necessary on grounds of public order.' As for those potential victims who are awaiting a reasonable grounds decision, the policy is silent on whether they can be detained. Chapter 9 of the EIG (which was in force until 12 September 2016) was highly suggestive that these potential victims also should not be detained because they are generally considered to be vulnerable. However in *R (XYL) v Secretary of State for the Home Department*[53] the High Court found that there was no bar to detention of a potential victim pending a reasonable grounds decision. Whilst that may be so[54], any decision to detain would still be subject to the strong presumption of liberty, as potential victims of trafficking will inevitably be considered adults at risk. Arguably, where a potential victim has been referred by a first responder to the NRM, this will be considered professional evidence and thus at least level 2 evidence of being an adult at risk.

---

53 [2017] EWHC 773 (Admin).
54 *XYL v Secretary of State for the Home Department* is pending consideration of an application for permission to appeal to the Court of Appeal.

Safeguarding and release

11.54

By Detention Service Order 8/2016 (published in February 2017), there is now a clearer pathway for release of vulnerable adults at risk from immigration detention. In cases where IRC or healthcare staff have significant concerns about releasing a detainee considered to be at risk, a multi-disciplinary meeting (or teleconference if a physical meeting is not possible due to time constraints), should be held to agree a plan to safely release the individual. This should be expedited to avoid any impact on release timings as the Home Office will use the outcome of the meeting to inform implementation of the release decision. In cases where the detainee requires support or accommodation from the local authority, a referral should be made for a needs assessment prior to release.

11.55

Part 1 of the Care Act 2014 set out the framework within which local authority adult social care services should act where there appears to be a vulnerable adult in its area. By the Care Act 2014, s 9(1), the local authority is required to undertake an assessment where it appears there is an adult who may have needs for care and support. The threshold for a request for an assessment is low. Questions about whether a person will require services at the end of the assessment process should form a part of the assessment process rather than be used as a barrier to the assessment process commencing.

11.56

The Care Act assessment is for the purposes of determining what needs, if any, the adult has; what impact the needs have on the adult's well-being; and what support is required. Regulation 3 of the Care and Support (Assessment) Regulations 2014[55] set down further requirements of the needs assessment, importantly including the requirement that the adult is able to participate in the process as effectively as possible and the assessment is conducted in a proportionate way. It is important for the local authority to have regard to the wishes and preferences of the adult, the outcome the adult seeks from assessment and the severity and overall extent of the adult's needs. By reg 5, the local authority is obliged to ensure that anyone carrying out an assessment has the relevant skills, knowledge and competence and is appropriately trained. The local authority must also consult a person who has 'expertise in relation to the condition or other circumstances of the individual whose needs are being assessed in any case where it considers that the needs of the individual concerned require it to do so'. This should be done before or during the assessment process. The need to draw on appropriate expertise, particularly

---

55 SI 2014/2827.

where there are complex needs and specific clinical conditions, is reiterated by the statutory guidance to the Care Act 2014 at paras 6.7, 6.86 and 6.88.

11.57

Where an assessment identifies needs, the local authority must decide if any of the needs are sufficient to meet the eligibility criteria[56] and, if so, consider with the individual how to meet those needs[57]. To be eligible, they must satisfy three requirements under the Care Act (Eligibility Criteria) Regulations 2015[58], reg 2. In essence, the test is:

- their needs must be the result of a physical or mental impairment or illness;

- as a result they must be unable to achieve two or more specified outcomes (under reg 2(2));

- as a consequence there is (or there is likely to be) a significant impact on their well-being.

11.58

'Significant impact' carries its 'everyday meaning' and includes 'whether the adult's needs and their consequent inability to achieve the relevant outcomes will have an important consequential effect on their daily lives, their independence and their wellbeing'[59]. 'Outcomes' is specified in the Care Act (Eligibility Criteria) Regulations 2015, reg 2(2). These are broadly drawn and cover managing and maintaining nutrition; maintaining personal hygiene; managing toilet needs; being appropriately clothed; being able to make use of the home safely; maintaining a habitable home environment; developing and maintaining family or other personal relationships; accessing and engaging in work, training, education or volunteering; making use of necessary facilities or services in the local community including public transport, and recreational facilities or services.

11.59

Paragraph 6.106 of the statutory guidance elaborates on what is meant by 'unable to achieve' an outcome under reg 2(3) and includes the following circumstances, where the adult:

- *is unable to achieve the outcome without assistance*: including where the adult may need prompting: for example, some adults may be physically able to wash but need reminding of the importance of personal hygiene;

---

56 Care Act 2014, s 13(1).
57 Care Act 2014, s 13(3).
58 SI 2015/313.
59 Statutory guidance, para 6.110.

- *is able to achieve the outcome without assistance but doing so causes the adult significant pain, distress or anxiety*: for example, an adult may be able to prepare a meal, but this would leave him in pain and unable to eat the meal;

- *is able to achieve the outcome without assistance, but doing so endangers or is likely to endanger the health or safety of the adult, or of others*: for example, if the health or safety of others could be endangered when an adult attempts to complete a task or an activity without relevant support;

- *is able to achieve the outcome without assistance but takes significantly longer than would normally be expected*: for example, an adult with a physical disability is able to dress himself in the morning, but it takes him a long time to do this, leaves him exhausted and prevents him from achieving other outcomes.

11.60

Eligible needs can, in principle, be met by the provision of accommodation, particularly if the care and support would be rendered ineffective if accommodation is not provided[60]. However the Care Act 2014 is not directed at meeting a bare need for accommodation because of destitution[61]. Access to Care Act support may also depend on a person's immigration status. The starting point is that if someone has no leave to remain in the UK, is a failed asylum seeker or an overstayer, the individual is not normally eligible for support under the Care Act 2014[62]. However, if withholding (or withdrawing) support from someone who is otherwise ineligible would cause a breach of his rights under the ECHR or under EU law, then he will become eligible for the support if it is necessary to avoid such a breach[63].

11.61

Pending an assessment, the local authority has a power to provide interim care and support under the Care Act 2014, s 19. This would apply to vulnerable adults referred by the Home Office for assessment and who can be released into the community pending assessment. There is no reason in law for there to be delay in release simply because the assessment has not been completed, particularly where the criteria for detention are no longer met.

---

60 Care Act 2014, ss 8 and 18.
61 Care Act 2014, s 21(1).
62 Nationality Immigration and Asylum Act 2002, Sch 3, paras 4–7A.
63 *R (on the application of Limbuela) v Secretary of State for the Home Department* [2004] EWCA Civ 540 and *R (on the application of Clue) v Birmingham City Council* [2010] EWCA Civ 460.

12 Compensation for victims of trafficking

Introduction

12.1

As recognised by professionals working in the field of human trafficking and modern slavery, effective compensation has an important role to play in the recovery process of survivors. Focus on Labour Exploitation (FLEX) put it this way in its working paper *Access to Compensation for Victims of Human Trafficking*:

> 'Compensation awards can provide economic empowerment, facilitating reintegration into society and reducing individual victims' vulnerability to re-trafficking. Obtaining fair compensation can contribute to a sense of justice and closure, and can play an important role in a survivor's psychological recovery'[1].

12.2

The difficulty is that the available routes to compensation present very specific challenges to victims of trafficking, in particular where there has been no, or no successful, criminal prosecution of the alleged traffickers. Where there are successful criminal prosecutions, there is the possibility of the court making a compensation order for the benefit of the victim(s) or a Slavery and Trafficking Reparation Order pursuant to the Modern Slavery Act ('MSA') 2015, s 8. The very small number of such convictions annually means that practitioners have to find alternative, creative solutions to obtain compensation for the majority of trafficked victims.

12.3

This chapter will examine the following potential routes to compensation:

- compensation available in criminal proceedings;
- the Criminal Injuries Compensation Scheme;
- statutory claims for miscarriages of justice;
- Human Rights Act 1998 claims against public bodies;
- claims against traffickers.

---

1   FLEX (July 2016).

Compensatory obligations

12.4

The UK does have compensatory obligations to trafficked victims, as set out in the two key regional instruments in this area (see Chapter 1 for a full discussion as to their legal effect). The relevant parts are set out below:

Article 15 of ECAT[2]

'Compensation and legal redress

1   ...

2   ...

3   Each Party shall provide, in its internal law, for the right of victims to compensation from the perpetrators.

4   Each Party shall adopt such legislative or other measures as may be necessary to guarantee compensation for victims in accordance with the conditions under its internal law, for instance through the establishment of a fund for victim compensation or measures or programmes aimed at social assistance and social integration of victims, which could be funded by the assets resulting from the application of measures provided in Article 23'[3].

Article 17 of the EU Trafficking Directive[4]

'Compensation to victims

Member States shall ensure that victims of trafficking in human beings have access to existing schemes of compensation to victims of violent crimes of intent'.

12.5

The UK seeks to satisfy ECAT, Art 15(4) and the EU Trafficking Directive, Art 17 through the Criminal Injuries Compensation Scheme. Article 15(3) is broadly framed, and whilst there are various avenue for redress, explored below, often the right is more illusory than real.

---

2   The Council of Europe Convention on Action against Trafficking in Human Beings ('ECAT').

3   ECAT, Art 23 deals with the provision of sanctions and measures, both criminal and non-criminal, including confiscation, for those who are criminally liable for trafficking in human beings.

4   Directive 2011/36/EU of the European Parliament and of the Council of 5 April 2011 on preventing and combating trafficking in human beings and protecting its victims, and replacing Council Framework Decision 2002/629/ JHA ('the EU Trafficking Directive').

Compensation in criminal proceedings

Compensation orders

12.6

Compensation orders are governed by the Powers of Criminal Courts (Sentencing) Act 2000, ss 130–133, as amended by the Legal Aid, Sentencing and Punishment of Offenders Act 2012. The power to make an order arises upon conviction of *any* offence. It does not require a victim to apply to the court for an order to be made[5]. Section 130(2A) of the Powers of Criminal Courts (Sentencing) Act 2000 provides that 'A court must consider making a compensation order in any case where this section empowers it to do so. Section 130(3) requires the court to 'give reasons … if it does not make a compensation order …'.

12.7

The order is for compensation 'for any personal injury, loss or damage resulting from that offence or any other offence which is taken into consideration by the court when determining sentence…' (s 130(1)(a)). Courts will order compensation for such amount as the court considers appropriate, taking into account any evidence and representations made by or on behalf of the accused or the prosecutor (s 130(4)). The maximum amount a magistrates' court can order in relation to a young offender is £5,000 per charge (s 131)[6]. Otherwise, the court has unlimited powers, but should have regard to the means of the offender (s 130(11)).

12.8

In order to maximise a compensation application, prosecutors (via the police) should seek evidence in support. Distress and anxiety are recoverable losses[7] but evidence is necessary[8].

12.9

Historically the criminal courts have only made compensation orders in a 'simple, straightforward case where the amount of compensation can be readily and easily ascertained'[9], avoiding the technicalities of claims for loss in the civil courts. In some cases a more modern approach has been adopted, given the criminal courts' familiarity with more complex financial assessment in

---

5   *Holt v DPP* [1996] 2 Cr App Rep (S) 314, [1996] Crim LR 524.
6   Which also sets out the position in relation to offences taken into consideration.
7   *R v Godfrey* (1994) 15 Cr App Rep (S) 536.
8   *R v Vaughan* (1990) 12 Cr App Rep (S) 46.
9   *R v Donovan* (1981) 3 Cr App Rep (S) 192.

confiscation proceedings[10]. However, in *R v Bewick*[11] the Court of Appeal held that since the sentencer can only hear submissions from the prosecution and the defence, not third parties (including victims), policy demands that complex issues should not be dealt with in the criminal courts.

12.10

Victims of offences will not receive the compensation ordered until there is no further possibility of an appeal in which the compensation order could be varied or set aside (s 132(1)). Further, the offender can apply to the magistrates' court, any time before the whole amount has been paid, to vary or discharge the amount ordered on a number of grounds (see s 133). Double recovery in subsequent civil proceedings is not possible (see s 134). Enforcement of a compensation order is the function of the magistrates' courts, which can impose a period of imprisonment in default of payment.

12.11

As the above demonstrates, this is very unlikely to be a fruitful source of compensation for the majority of victims of trafficking not just because it requires a successful prosecution of a trafficker as well as full co-operation with the police by victims, but also because it requires revelation of the details of loss to the trafficker himself, with only a remote prospect of receiving the money within any reasonable period of time, if at all.

Slavery and trafficking reparation orders

12.12

Section 8 of the MSA 2015 introduces slavery and trafficking reparation orders ('STROs') against defendants convicted of an offence under ss 1, 2 or 4 of the Act (as to which see Chapter 4) *and* where a confiscation order is made. A reparation order requires the defendant to pay compensation to the victim for *any* harm resulting from the offence (s 9(1)), but must not be made if a compensation order has been made under the Powers of Criminal Courts (Sentencing) Act 2000, s 130 (see para **12.6** above) (s 10(1)). In any case in which the court has power to make a STRO, it must consider making one, whether or not the prosecutor applies for one to be made, and it must give reasons if it does not make one (s 8(7)).

12.13

Like compensation orders, courts will order compensation for such amount as the court considers appropriate, having regard to any evidence and representations

---

10 See for example *R v Pola* [2009] EWCA Crim 655, [2010] 1 Cr App Rep (S) 32.
11 [2007] EWCA Crim 3297, [2008] 2 Cr App Rep (S) 184.

made by or on behalf of the accused or the prosecutor (s 9(3)). The maximum amount cannot exceed the amount the convicted person is required to pay under the confiscation order (s 9(4)) and the court must have regard to the person's means (s 9(5)). Section 10(3) imports the same powers to appeal, review etc a compensation order available under the Powers of Criminal Courts (Sentencing) Act 2000, ss 132–134. Section 10 of the MSA 2015 demonstrates that the confiscation order and STRO are to be dealt with in tandem: if the confiscation order is varied, discharged or quashed, so can the STRO be dealt with in the same way.

12.14

Given the low number of successful prosecutions under the MSA 2015 to date and the difficulties already identified in relation to compensation orders (which apply equally), this is also highly unlikely to be a fruitful source of compensation for the majority of victims of trafficking.

The Criminal Injuries Compensation Scheme

12.15

The first Criminal Injuries Compensation Scheme was introduced in 1964. It was non-statutory and provided for *ex gratia* payments. The Criminal Injuries Compensation Act 1995 was enacted and schemes from that time have been statutory, pursuant to the Act. The schemes are government funded and designed to compensate 'blameless' victims of violent crime. The current scheme is the Criminal Injuries Compensation Scheme 2012, which came into force in September 2012[12]. It is administered by the Criminal Injuries Compensation Authority ('CICA'). There is a right of appeal to the First-tier Tribunal.

12.16

The Scheme specifically contemplates victims of trafficking and on the face of it meets the requirements of ECAT and the EU Trafficking Directive set out at para **12.4** above. Whilst it does not require a criminal conviction of an assailant as a condition precedent, the Scheme poses other significant difficulties for victims of trafficking.

12.17

Firstly, it compensates violent crimes only and those have to have been committed in Scotland, England and Wales[13]. The definition includes threats and causing fear of immediate violence, but does not cover, for example, deception or forced

---

12 *Criminal injuries compensation: a guide* (March 2014) is available at www.gov.uk/guidance/criminal-injuries-compensation-a-guide, last accessed 17 December 2017.
13 Northern Ireland has its own scheme.

labour or other exploitation. Secondly, it requires reporting of the crime to the police and co-operation in bringing the assailant to justice, otherwise the award will be withheld. Many victims of trafficking are extremely reluctant to report crimes or assist in prosecutions for fear of reprisals from traffickers and for fear of being prosecuted themselves (for example, those who have been trafficked for sexual exploitation or forced criminality). Thirdly, awards can be withheld or reduced if victims have unspent previous convictions, even if they were committed in the context of being trafficked (see Chapter 9 for guidance on appealing criminal convictions of victims of trafficking). Fourthly, if a decision to award a claim is initially refused or reduced (which is common), the appeal to the First-tier Tribunal will usually require a victim of trafficking to give evidence and be subject to cross-examination by CICA and/or questioning from the tribunal itself. Those who are traumatised and/or suffering with significant psychiatric conditions as a result of their trafficking experience may not wish to be pressed about their injuries and the details of how they were sustained. Fifthly, there is a two-year time limit to apply from the date of the incident. Further, there are practical difficulties: there is no public funding available to get assistance in completing the application form (see Chapter 13 for guidance on public funding) and CICA decision-making is very slow.

Eligibility

12.18

Paragraph 4 of the 2012 Scheme provides that:

> 'A person may be eligible for an award under this Scheme if they sustain a criminal injury which is directly attributable to their being a direct victim of a crime of violence committed... The meaning of 'crime of violence' is explained in Annex B ...'

12.19

'Criminal injury' means an injury which appears in Part A or B of the tariff in Annex E:

- Part A: physical and psychological injuries;
- Part B: physical and sexual abuse.

12.20

The accompanying note states that 'mental injury' must be disabling and does not include temporary mental anxiety and similar temporary conditions. A mental injury is disabling if it has a substantial adverse effect on a person's ability to carry out normal day-to-day activities for the time specified (eg impaired work or school performance or effects on social relationships or sexual dysfunction).

12.21

The definition of 'crime of violence' includes a physical attack and sexual assault without consent[14] but also 'a threat against a person, causing fear of immediate violence in circumstances which would cause a person of reasonable firmness to be put in such fear'. However, any criminal injury sustained has to be directly attributable to that threat.

12.22

In relation to those who are not ordinarily resident in the UK, para 10(c) of the Scheme provides that:

'A person is eligible for an award under this Scheme only if: …One of the conditions in paragraph 13 is satisfied in relation to them on the date of their application under this Scheme'.

12.23

Paragraphs 13–16 provide:

'13.The conditions referred to in paragraph 10(c) are that the person has:

(a) been referred to a competent authority as a potential victim of trafficking in human beings; or

(b) made an application for asylum under Immigration Rules made under section 3(2) of the Immigration Act 1971.

14. A person who has made an application under this Scheme and satisfies a condition in paragraph 13 may request that their application under this Scheme is deferred until a final decision has been taken in relation to the referral or application mentioned in that paragraph.

15.Where a person is eligible for an award under this Scheme by virtue of paragraph 10 only because a condition in paragraph 13 is satisfied in relation to them, that person will not be eligible for an award unless, as a result of the referral or application mentioned in paragraph 13, they have been:

(a) conclusively identified by a competent authority as a victim of trafficking in human beings; or

(b) granted temporary protection, asylum or humanitarian protection.

16. In paragraphs 13 and 15:

---

14 See the discussion on consent and sex trafficking in G Hutt, H Dykes and H Lovells, 'Compensation Claims by Victims of Trafficking under the Criminal Injuries Compensation Scheme' in P Chandran (ed), *Human Trafficking Handbook* (LexisNexis, 2011).

(a)   a person is conclusively identified as a victim of trafficking in human beings when, on completion of the identification process required by Article 10 of the Council of Europe Convention against Trafficking in Human Beings (CETS No.197, 2005), a competent authority concludes that the person is such a victim;

(b)   "competent authority" means a person who is a competent authority of the United Kingdom for the purpose of that Convention; and

(c)   "victim of trafficking in human beings" has the same meaning as under that Convention.'

Time limits

12.24

If the applicant is an adult at the time of the incident, he must apply as soon as reasonably practicable and no later than two years after it occurred. If the applicant was under 18 at the time of the incident, later applications may be considered (particularly in historic child sexual abuse case). Paragraph 89 of the Scheme states that time may be extended where the claims officer is satisfied that:

'(a)   due to exceptional circumstances the applicant could not have applied earlier; and

(b)   the evidence presented in support of the application means that it can be determined without further extensive enquiries by a claims officer.'

12.25

In *MJ v FTT (No 3)*[15], a case decided under the old test for extension in the 2008 Scheme, the Upper Tribunal held that (a) and (b) were conditions precedent for the exercise of a discretion to waive the time limit, not exceptions to it. Where a decision-maker accepted that (a) and (b) were both satisfied, then there would have to be good reasons to justify not exercising discretion in the applicant's favour. The Upper Tribunal said that where a claim was made in respect of historic sexual abuse of a child, it was not enough simply to decide that the application was out of time. That would be to ignore the very real reasons such an individual would have for not disclosing either the abuse itself, or the full extent of such abuse, and the time that it takes to begin to come to terms with such traumatic experiences, citing *JM, petitioner*[16]. There may well be parallels in relation to delay in making claims by victims of trafficking, particularly those who have been sexually assaulted.

---

15   [2014] UKUT 279 (AAC).
16   [2013] CSOH 169, 2014 SLT 475.

Level of awards

12.26

Section 2(1) of the Criminal Injuries Compensation Act 1995 provides 'The amount of compensation payable under an award shall be determined in accordance with the provisions of the Scheme'. The value of the payments made is calculated by reference to a Parliament-set tariff of injuries (Annex E to the S scheme). The size of the award will be altered to reflect the seriousness of the injury.

12.27

Types of payment which can be made include:

- injury payments;

- loss of earnings payments: where the applicant has no/limited capacity to work as a direct result of a criminal injury (Annex F sets out the multiplier tables);

- special expenses payments.

12.28

The maximum award which can be made, before any reductions, is £500,000. The amount of any injury payment will be determined according to the tariff. Where an application concerns two separate injuries, the award will be for the full tariff amount for the injury with the highest payment, and 30 per cent of the tariff for the second injury. Where there are three or more criminal injuries, it will be 15 per cent of the tariff amount for the criminal injury with an equal or third highest payment. Where a person has sustained a mental injury as a result of a sexual assault, the victim will be entitled to an injury payment for whichever of the sexual assault or the mental injury would give rise to the highest payment under the tariff. If an injury does not fall within the tariff, the claims officer may refer it to the Secretary of State for inclusion if considered of equivalent seriousness.

Grounds for withholding or reducing an award

12.29

Paragraph 86 of the Scheme provides that 'An application for an award will be determined by a Claims Officer in the authority in accordance with this Scheme.' Paragraphs 22–29 set out grounds for withholding or reducing an award from those who would otherwise have been entitled to one pursuant to paras 4–21. Paragraphs 22–29 reflect the requirements of s 3(1) of the Act, which provides

'The Scheme may, in particular, include provision –

a.   As to the circumstances in which an award may be withheld or the amount of compensation reduced …'

12.30

The grounds for withholding an award are:

- a failure to report the incident to the police as soon as reasonably practicable (in deciding whether this requirement is met, particular account will be taken of: (a) the age and capacity of the applicant at the date of the incident; and (b) whether the effect of the incident on the applicant was such that it could not reasonably have been reported earlier)[17];

- a failure to co-operate as far as reasonably practicable in bringing the assailant to justice.

12.31

Where victims have been referred into the National Referral Mechanism ('NRM'), it may be arguable that they reported and/or co-operated sufficiently.

12.32

The grounds for withholding or reducing an award include:

- where the applicant fails to take all reasonable steps to assist a claims officer or other body or person in relation to consideration of his application. Such failure includes repeated failure to respond to communications sent to the address given by the applicant;

- where the conduct of the applicant before, during or after the incident giving rise to the criminal injury makes it inappropriate to make an award or a full award. For this purpose, conduct does not include intoxication through alcohol or drugs to the extent that such intoxication made the applicant more vulnerable to becoming a victim of a crime of violence;

- where the applicant to whom an award would otherwise be made has unspent convictions. The award will be withheld entirely if the applicant received a sentence listed in paragraph 3 of Annex D, including a community order, and reduced if a different sentence.

---

17 The Anti Trafficking and Labour Exploitation website contains details of a decision in which it is said that the First-tier Tribunal found that withholding an award on this basis was contrary to the EU Trafficking Directive, Art 17: see http://atleu.org.uk/cases/2015/12/11/c-v-criminal-injuries-compensation-authority, last accessed 17 December 2017. A transcript of the judgment is not available.

12.33

In *R (on the application of McNiece) v Criminal Injuries Compensation Authority*[18], the claimants argued that the provisions of the Scheme impose an unlawful 'blanket ban' on awards being made under the Scheme to those with an unspent conviction which led to a custodial or a community sentence. The grounds supporting the argument that the 'blanket ban' was unlawful included the following:

(i)   that the ban constitutes a disproportionate interference in the claimant's rights under ECHR, Art 1 of Protocol 1;

(ii)   it is unjustifiably discriminatory contrary to Art 1 of Protocol 1, read together with ECHR, Art 14;

(iii) it is ultra vires the statutory powers pursuant to which the Scheme was made, and

(iv)   it is in breach of the EU Trafficking Directive, Art 17; and

(v)   Art 1 of Protocol 1, read together with ECHR, Art 4.

12.34

Wilkie J found that the extent of the obligations of a State under Art 17 is clear. Those obligations are to ensure that victims of trafficking have access to the existing national scheme in the sense of being entitled to have their claim considered substantively. That is achieved under the Scheme by virtue of paras 10–15. He found that Art 17 does not impose an obligation on the State to compensate victims of crimes of trafficking beyond the terms of the existing national scheme. It does not require a State to change the terms of its existing scheme to comply with Art 17, save by providing access to it, which it does[19].

The Miscarriage of Justice Application Scheme

12.35

The Miscarriage of Justice Application Scheme is a discretionary compensation scheme administered by the Secretary of State for Justice. It provides compensation for those who have been wrongfully convicted and punished, pursuant to the Criminal Justice Act 1988, s 133[20].

---

18 [2017] EWHC 2 (Admin).
19 The judge did, however, grant leave to appeal to the Court of Appeal. At the time of writing, the appeal is still outstanding.
20 Guidance on how the Scheme operates is available at https://hmctsformfinder.s3.amazonaws.com/forms/guidance/index.htm, last accessed 17 December 2017.

12.36

Section 133 was enacted to give effect to the UK's international obligations under Art 14(6) of the International Covenant on Civil and Political Rights 1966, which was ratified by the UK in May 1976. There is an almost identical provision in Art 3 of the Seventh Protocol of the ECHR. Section 133 of the Criminal Justice Act 1988 was very significantly amended by the Anti-social Behaviour, Crime and Policing Act 2014, so as to require an applicant to effectively prove innocence (as opposed to show that his conviction has been set aside because fresh evidence so undermined the case against him such that no conviction could possibly be based upon it[21]).

12.37

Section 133(1) of the Criminal Justice Act 1988 provides that:

> '... when a person has been convicted of a criminal offence and when subsequently his conviction has been reversed or he has been pardoned on the ground that a new or newly discovered fact shows beyond reasonable doubt that there has been a miscarriage of justice, the Secretary of State shall pay compensation for the miscarriage of justice to the person who has suffered punishment as a result of such conviction or, if he is dead, to his personal representatives, unless the non-disclosure of the unknown fact was wholly or partly attributable to the person convicted.'

12.38

Section 133(1ZA), as inserted by the Anti-social Behaviour, Crime and Policing Act 2014, s 175, provides there will have been a miscarriage of justice 'if and only if the new or newly discovered fact shows beyond reasonable doubt that the person *did not commit the offence*' (emphasis added).

12.39

Following that amendment, in *R (on the application of Nealon) v Secretary of State for Justice*[22] the appellants contended that s 133 (as amended) was incompatible with the presumption of innocence enshrined in ECHR, Art 6(2). The Court of Appeal accepted that Art 6(2) was engaged, but not that the amended s 133 is incompatible with it. The court said that s 133 does not require the applicant to prove his innocence generally, but focuses on 'the effect of the new or newly discovered fact and nothing else' (para 50). Any denial of compensation does not undermine his acquittal or the presumption of innocence. On 12 April 2017, the Supreme Court granted permission to appeal[23].

---

21 See *R (on the application of Adams) v Secretary of State for Justice* [2011] UKSC 18, [2012] 1 AC 48.

22 [2015] EWHC 1565 (Admin), 165 NLJ 7657.

23 See www.supremecourt.uk/news/permission-to-appeal-decision-13-april-2017.html, last accessed 17 December 2017.

12.40

The test as currently enunciated is a high threshold to cross, given the very narrow definition of miscarriage of justice. However, if the test is satisfied (as to which see para **12.41** below), there are many advantages for those victims of trafficking who have been wrongly prosecuted, convicted and incarcerated to apply under this scheme rather than trying to bring a civil claim against a public authority that failed to protect him. This is because a similar approach is used by the Independent Assessor to quantify damages as in tortious claims, and as the assessment is made on written evidence, the victim of trafficking will not have to go through the trauma and stress of giving evidence in court where tortious claims do not settle. Also, Legal Help is available to assist in making the initial application, and if accepted on the Scheme, legal costs are recoverable, including counsel's fees (see Chapter 13 on funding).

Are victims of trafficking who have had their convictions set aside eligible under the Scheme?

12.41

An applicant will be eligible if the two conditions of s 133 are met:

- the applicant's conviction has been reversed, or he has been granted a free pardon; and

- the conviction must have been reversed, or the pardon granted, on the ground that a new or newly-discovered fact shows beyond reasonable doubt that the person did not commit the offence.

12.42

The criminal convictions of victims of trafficking (obtained before the coming into force of the MSA 2015) are usually set aside by the Court of Appeal Criminal Division not because no offence was committed but because, under ECAT, Art 26, as amplified by the EU Trafficking Directive, Art 8, criminal proceedings should or would not have been brought at all if the prosecuting authorities had known at the time that the defendant was a victim of trafficking whose offending was inextricably linked with his trafficked status (see Chapters 5 and 9).

12.43

Thus, for the purposes of the Scheme, the newly-discovered fact is the fact that he was a trafficked victim (for sexual exploitation or servitude) who was *compelled* to commit the offence he did (these are most commonly cannabis cultivation and identity fraud) and thus the criminality of the defendant was extinguished[24]. Whilst the Art 26 protection is about prosecutorial discretion, the victim of trafficking was innocent (or not guilty) in that the newly-discovered fact shows that he would have had a common law defence of duress available to him at trial. The words 'did not commit the offence' in s 133(1ZA) must, by definition, include those who are not guilty of the offence by reason of having a common law or statutory defence. By analogy, in the MSA 2015, s 45(1), an adult[25] is not guilty if the compulsion is attributable to slavery or relevant exploitation.

12.44

There is no case law on this point to date but the author is aware of (and acted in) one case where a victim of trafficking was accepted onto the Scheme and awarded compensation on this basis[26].

Procedure

12.45

The applicant must submit a written application to the Miscarriages of Justice Team, along with copies of the NG form 2, Court of Appeal judgment, perfected grounds of appeal and any CCRC Statement of Reasons. The application form (which is available online) requires a clear exposition of the applicant's personal details, case details, appeal details, and reasons for applying.

12.46

There is two-year time limit for all Criminal Justice Act 1988, s 133 applications, beginning with the date on which the applicant has been pardoned, or their conviction reversed. Out of time applications may exceptionally be allowed. However, ignorance of the scheme does not constitute 'exceptional' circumstances.

12.47

Following a decision of eligibility (which falls solely to the Secretary of State under s 133(3)), the Independent Assessor[27] will determine the amount of the award. The applicant must put in his submissions to the Miscarriages of Justice Team within six months from the date of the notice of eligibility. Funding for a barrister to draft these can be approved by the assessor.

---

24 See *R v L* [2013] EWCA Crim 991, [2014] 1 All ER 113 at [13].
25 The elements of the defence are different in relation to child victims of trafficking: see Chapter 5.
26 The successful applicant's conviction was set aside because she should have had the protection of Art 26: *R v Y* [2015] EWCA Crim 123.
27 See   www.gov.uk/government/news/new-independent-assessor-of-compensation-for-miscarriages-of-justice, last accessed 17 December 2017.

12.48

The onus is on the applicant to quantify all relevant losses flowing from the miscarriage of justice, and to support it with documentary evidence (including loss of earnings and medical and expert reports). Funding for such reports can be approved by the assessor in advance. The applicant must provide signed and dated statement of evidence, including a brief personal history, account of their time in prison and any resultant difficulties, and an account of his life since release. The assessor will then aim to make final assessment of the applicant's case within three months.

The award

12.49

The total amount of compensation payable cannot exceed the overall compensation limit: £1 million for cases where applicant has been detained for at least ten years (s 133B) and £500,000 in any other case. Interim payment may be granted, depending on the information available to the assessor on the miscarriage of justice, and attendant consequences.

12.50

There are two parts to the award:

- non-pecuniary: loss of liberty, hardship, distress and injury to feelings, inconvenience, damage to reputation and possible psychiatric damage;

- pecuniary: loss of past/future earnings, expenses and legal costs related to the miscarriage of justice. Claims for loss of earnings for any one year limited to 1.5 times the median annual gross earnings at the time (s 133A(6)). The assessor may make a deduction from any pecuniary award for saved living expenses – the cost an applicant would have had to pay for essentials from his net income, had he not been wrongly imprisoned[28].

12.51

The overall objective of s 133, as described by Lord Bingham is 'that the State representing the public at large should make fair recompense to victims of miscarriages of justice'[29]. In assessing the amount payable to the applicant, the Independent Assessor will have particular regard to the seriousness of the offence of which the applicant was convicted, and the severity of the punishment suffered as a result, and the conduct of the investigation and prosecution of the offence (s 133A(2)). It is open to the assessor to reduce the award if he believes that the applicant has contributed towards his circumstances, or has a bad criminal record.

---

28 *R (on the application of O'Brien) v Independent Assessor* [2007] UKHL 10, [2007] 2 AC 312.
29 Ibid.

Non-pecuniary loss

12.52

In making an award, the assessor must have regard to the amounts awarded by the courts in personal injury cases, although no direct analogy can be drawn between physical injuries and the effect of a miscarriage of justice. The assessor also needs to be aware of the awards made in civil wrong cases, in particular malicious prosecution and false imprisonment[30].

12.53

In assessing an award for loss of liberty, the assessor will have regard to cases decided in the context of false imprisonment by the police and other detaining authorities, such as *Thompson v Metropolitan Police Comr*[31] and *Muuse v Secretary of State for the Home Department*[32]. An applicant can also be awarded a sum for any features that aggravated the loss of liberty.

12.54

In *Thompson* Lord Woolf MR recommended the following brackets for basic damages: £500 for the first hour of detention, £3,000 for the first day, with a progressively reducing rate thereafter. These figures, adjusted for inflation are currently approximately £800 and £4,900 respectively. The *Thompson* guidelines were approved in *R (on the application of Miller) v Independent Assessor* in relation to any s 133 assessment. The respondent submitted that *Thompson* did not indicate the scale of any tapering award, and that any extrapolation from a period of relatively short detention would presume an artificial tariff. However, it was held that the guidelines were an 'essential starting point', from which a longer period of detention had to be related proportionately, 'not by means of a simple arithmetical progression'[33]. Accordingly, an award for loss of liberty of £55,000 for a period of over four years' custodial detention was set aside.

12.55

In *Muuse*, an award of basic damages for £25,000 (uprated to £31,000) was made for a period of 128 days' (just over four months) unlawful detention. This award accounted for the fact that the claimant had been lawfully imprisoned for 147 days prior to this period, pursuant to criminal justice powers. The relevance of any preceding period of lawful detention was affirmed in *R v Governor of Brockhill Prison, ex p Evans (No 2)*[34], where the House of Lords upheld the Court of Appeal's award of £5,000 (uprated to £7,700) for a 59-day detention of a prisoner whose release date was miscalculated. One of several factors justifying

---

30 *R (on the application of Miller) v Independent Assessor* [2009] EWCA Civ 609.
31 [1998] QB 498, [1997] 2 All ER 762.
32 [2010] EWCA Civ 453.
33 At para 46.
34 [2001] 2 AC 19, [2000] 4 All ER 15.

this lower level of damages was the fact that the unlawful extension of detention occurred in the context of a custodial sentence of two years, of which ten months had been served following a proper conviction. As such, the appellant had 'already made the necessary adjustments to serving a prison sentence'[35].

12.56

In assessing an award for psychiatric damage, the assessor has no power to make an award for compensation for the effects of the trafficking, but rather must focus solely on the effect of the wrongful conviction and sentence. Where an applicant has suffered psychiatric damage as a result of his trafficking, any expert report must address to what extent the conviction and sentence exacerbated or caused any psychiatric condition.

12.57

Any final award is not to be negotiated, but can be challenged by way of judicial review. Of course if there is a civil claim made for a failure to investigate (see below), which in turn resulted in incarceration, there cannot be double recovery for the same loss.

Human Rights Act 1998 claims against public bodies

12.58

In deciding whether or not to bring such a claim, it is important to bear in mind, that HRA 1998 claims have a short limitation period of one year, subject to the court finding it equitable to extend the period. Section 7(5) of the HRA 1998 provides that:

'(5) Proceedings under subsection 1(a) must be brought before the end of—

(a) the period of one year beginning with the date on which the act complained of took place; or

(b) such longer period as the court considers equitable having regard to all the circumstances,

but that is subject to any rule imposing a stricter time limit in relation to the procedure in question.'

12.59

In addition, the civil legal aid process can take some time. Although the decided cases on extensions under the HRA 1998 are generally unhelpful, in *R (on the application of D) v Metropolitan Police Comr*[36], Eady J overturned Master Leslie's

---

35 [1999] QB 1043 at 1060D.
36 [2012] EWHC 309 (QB).

refusal to exercise his discretion under s 7(5)(b) to extend time to allow a claim to be brought under the ECHR, Art 3. D claimed that the police had infringed her Art 3 rights by failing to properly investigate her complaint of rape. The man whom D had accused had been arrested, tried and acquitted in 2006. The trial judge criticised the police for serious failings in their evidence gathering.

12.60

The essence of D's complaint was that the unit responsible for investigating rape and other serious sexual offences was under-resourced and inadequately staffed, and the trainee in charge of her case was inexperienced, untrained and overworked. She brought proceedings in February 2010, three years after the expiry of the one-year time limit. The Master in the QBD focused on the delay between March 2009 (when he found that D had become aware of the potential claim), and February 2010. D argued that during that period she had suffered from depression, domestic violence and struggled with drug-taking, as well as twice attempting suicide. In October 2009, D applied for legal aid, and issued proceedings when it was granted. The Master found that D need not have waited for the legal aid determination before issuing the claim – and expressly based his decision solely on that finding. However, Eady J found that, while it was a 'relatively simple matter' to issue a claim form, it was reasonable to wait to have legal representation before making an application for anonymity. D had, in addition, wished to avoid committing herself to any costs liability while awaiting the legal aid grant.

12.61

Furthermore, unless the claim settles, victims of trafficking will need to be advised that they will have to give evidence at trial and likely to be subject to robust cross-examination, notwithstanding their vulnerabilities.

The investigative duty

12.62

In *Rantsev v Cyprus and Russia*[37], the ECtHR held that '[l]ike Articles 2 and 3, Article 4 also entails a procedural obligation to investigate situations of potential trafficking'. That investigation must be effective, and, in that regard, the court held as follows[38]:

> '[…] For an investigation to be effective, it must be independent from those implicated in the events. It must also be capable of leading to the identification and punishment of individuals responsible, an obligation

---

37 (2010) 51 EHRR 1.
38 At 288–289.

not of result but of means. A requirement of promptness and reasonable expedition is implicit in all cases but where the possibility of removing the individual from the harmful situation is available, the investigation must be undertaken as a matter of urgency. The victim or the next-of-kin must be involved in the procedure to the extent necessary to safeguard their legitimate interests.

Finally, the Court reiterates that trafficking is a problem which is often not confined to the domestic arena. When a person is trafficked from one state to another, trafficking offences may occur in the state of origin, any state of transit and the state of destination. Relevant evidence and witnesses may be located in all states. Although the Palermo Protocol is silent on the question of jurisdiction, [ECAT] explicitly requires each Member State to establish jurisdiction over any trafficking offence committed in its territory. Such an approach is, in the Court's view, only logical in light of the general obligation, outlined above, incumbent on all states under Article 4 of the Convention to investigate alleged trafficking offences. In addition to the obligation to conduct a domestic investigation into events occurring on their own territories, Member States are also subject to a duty in cross-border trafficking cases to co-operate effectively with the relevant authorities of other states concerned in the investigation of events which occurred outside their territories. Such a duty is in keeping with the objectives of the Member States, as expressed in the preamble to the Palermo Protocol, to adopt a comprehensive international approach to trafficking in the countries of origin, transit and destination. It is also consistent with international agreements on mutual legal assistance in which the respondent states participate in the present case.'

12.63

In *OOO v Commissioner of Police for the Metropolis*[39] the claimants (young Nigerian women) claimed that the police had infringed their rights under the ECHR, Arts 3 and 4. Each of the claimants was trafficked into the UK from Nigeria when a girl, for the purpose of domestic servitude and each alleged that thereafter and over a number of years she was made to work for no pay in a household in and around London and subjected to physical and emotional abuse by the householders. They argued that their treatment over these years was such that they were subject to inhuman and degrading treatment and that they were held in slavery or servitude contrary to Arts 3 and 4 respectively of the ECHR. The claimants' complaints against the police were essentially that when officers of the Metropolitan Police were asked to investigate the treatment that had been meted out to them, they had failed to undertake any such investigation. It was the first time the domestic courts had to consider the scope of the *investigative* duty under Arts 3 and 4.

---

39 [2011] EWHC 1246 (QB).

12.64

The police contended that whilst the householders had breached the claimants' Art 3 and 4 rights, the scope of the investigative duty was such that it had not been breached. The High Court found that the view of the ECHR upon the scope of the investigative duty arising under Arts 3 and 4 of the Convention was sufficiently explained by reference to the decision in *Rantsev*, in that the police were under a duty to carry out an effective investigation of an allegation of a breach of Art 4 once a credible account of an alleged infringement had been brought to their attention. The trigger for the duty would not depend upon an actual complaint from a victim or near relative of a victim. The investigation, once triggered, would have to be undertaken promptly.

The scope of the investigative duty revisited

12.65

The scope of the investigative duty under the ECHR, Art 3 was revisited in the now leading case of *DSD v Commissioner of Police for the Metropolis*[40]. The claimants were victims of John Worboys, a serial sex offender known as the Black Cab Rapist and thought to be responsible for the drugging and sexual assault of over 100 women. Both NBV and DSD reported their assault to the police, and in NBV's case Worboys was quickly arrested as a suspect but released without charge. In DSD's case, he was never identified. Worboys was eventually charged with 23 offences relating to 14 victims and convicted of 19 counts (including the assault on NBV). Both women brought damages proceedings against the police, alleging failure to carry out effective investigations into their complaints that amounted to inhuman or degrading treatment contrary to Art 3. Green J found that there had been a series of systemic and operational errors, which included the following:

(i)   a substantial failure to train relevant officers in the intricacies of sexual assaults and, in particular, drug-facilitated sexual assaults;

(ii)   serious failures by senior officers properly to supervise investigations by more junior officers and to ensure that investigations were being conducted in accordance with standard procedure;

(iii)   serious failures in the collection and use of intelligence sources to cross-check complaints to see if there were linkages between them;

(iv)   failures to allocate proper resources to sexual assaults including pressure from borough management to focus resources on other allegations; and

(v)   a failure to maintain the confidence of victims in the integrity of the investigative process.

---

40 [2014] EWHC 436 (QB).

12.66

The police argued that insofar as a duty to investigate arose at all it was a limited duty which arose only where the State was in some way *itself* complicit in a breach of Art 3. Green J rejected this argument and found that the claimants' Art 3 rights had been breached. In a separate judgment (as to which see below), he also awarded damages. The Court of Appeal dismissed the police's appeal[41]. However the Supreme Court granted leave to appeal in relation to the following important issues (which will also impact on the Art 4 duty)[42]:

(i)   whether there is an obligation under the HRA 1998, s 6, read with ECHR, Art 3, to investigate ill-treatment which has been perpetrated by a private individual without any complicity of a public authority; and/or

(ii)   whether in the case of such ill-treatment any positive obligation is confined to a requirement to put in place the necessary structure to enable such investigation to be conducted but does not extend to the conduct of an individual investigation into a particular alleged crime.

12.67

It is hoped that the argument that the investigative duty does not apply in the absence of state complicity is rejected by the Supreme Court, although there remains the possibility of a 'sliding scale' approach. The Court of Appeal noted at [45] that:

'There is perhaps a sliding scale: from deliberate torture by State officials to the consequences of negligence by non-State agents. The energy required of the State to combat or redress these ills is no doubt variable, but the same protective principle is always at the root of it. The margin of appreciation enjoyed by the State as to the means of compliance with Article 3 widens at the bottom of the scale but narrows at the top. At what may, without belittling the victim, be called the lower end of the scale where injury happens through the negligence of non-State agents, the State's provision of a judicial system of civil remedies will often suffice: the individual State's legal traditions will govern the means of compliance in the particular case. Serious violent crime by non-State agents is of a different order: higher up the scale. In these cases, which certainly include *DSD/NBV*, a proper criminal investigation by the State is required'[43].

---

41   *DSD v Metropolitan Police Commissioner* [2015] EWCA Civ 646, [2016] QB 161.
42   The case was heard in March 2017 (Lord Neuberger, Lady Hale, Lord Mance, Lord Kerr and Lord Hughes), and at the time of writing, judgment is awaited.
43   [2015] EWCA Civ 646.

Just satisfaction

12.68

In *OOO v Commissioner of Police for the Metropolis*, Wyn Williams J awarded £5,000 to each of the claimants for the significant frustration and distress (none had psychiatric conditions), over and above a declaration that Art 4 had been breached.

12.69

In the quantum decision of *DSD v Commissioner of Police for the Metropolis*[44] (which was not challenged on appeal), the essential question for the court was whether it was 'necessary' to award damages in order to 'afford just satisfaction' to DSD and NBV within the meaning of the HRA 1998, s 8. Green J reviewed the relevant Strasbourg authorities in this area, and awarded both women damages. He said at [118]:

> 'The main factors that I take into account are: the nature of the harm suffered and treatment costs; the duration of the breach by the Defendant; the nature of the failings and whether they were operational and/or systemic; the overall context to the violations; whether there was bad faith on the part of the Defendant or whether there is any other reason why an enhanced award should be made; where the award sits on the range of awards made by Strasbourg and in similar domestic cases; other payments; totality and "modesty"'.

12.70

He awarded to DSD the sum of £22,250 comprising a sum (£20,000) for (more general) non-pecuniary harm which was calculated to cover the period to the date of judgment and a small incremental component (£2,500) for *future* treatment. He awarded NBV the sum of £19,000. This comprised £17,000 for the fact of the rape and the post-rape psychological harm to the date of judgment, and £2,000 as a contribution to future treatment costs.

12.71

Whilst the damages in *DSD* were primarily about the psychiatric harm caused by the investigative failure (which was separate from the harm caused by the sexual violence itself), in victims of trafficking cases, there may be the additional element of a prosecution and incarceration of a victim of trafficking who commits an offence and should have had the non-prosecution/ non-penalty protection (see Chapter 5). If the loss of liberty can be shown to flow directly from the failure to investigate, then damages for that loss can be included. The approach to loss of liberty damages is dealt with at para **12.52** above. There cannot, of course, be double recovery if there has been a successful CICA claim for the psychiatric damage or a successful miscarriage claim for the detention.

---

44 [2014] EWHC 2493 (QB).

Claims against traffickers

Tortious claims against individual traffickers

12.72

Whilst civil claims against traffickers for a host of torts (for example, false imprisonment, harassment, assault, battery) are available in theory, such claims are rare, not least because victims of trafficking are usually terrified of their traffickers and the reprisals that would follow if a civil claim was initiated, and even if they were successful, enforcing any judgment would be problematic. The recent decision of *R (on the application of Tirkey) v Director of Legal Aid Casework*[45] is a chilling demonstration of how the statutory charge can wipe out even a large award for damages. The claimant was an Indian national who was trafficked into the UK by an Indian couple, for whom she was forced to work in conditions of servitude. She brought proceedings against them in the employment tribunal for which she was granted exceptional case funding by the Legal Aid Agency. The claim was successful and resulted in a substantial award of damages (£266,536.14) but, owing to delays by Central London County Court in dealing with an application by the claimant's solicitor for an interim charging order, the couple dissipated their assets before a charge could be obtained over them. The total sum ultimately recovered by the claimant was £35,702.80, and once the Legal Aid Agency had exercised its statutory charge under s 25 of the Legal Aid, Sentencing and Punishment of Offenders Act 2012 to recover the cost of the legal aid provided to the claimant, she was left with nothing. Her judicial review, relying on the EU Charter of Fundamental Rights, ECAT and the ECHR failed on all grounds.

12.73

In *AT v Dulghieru*[46], the only known civil claim of its kind, four Moldovan women in their twenties brought claims based on their allegation that they were victims of an unlawful conspiracy to traffic them into the UK from Moldova for the purposes of sexual exploitation and prostitution. The two defendants were significant players in that conspiracy and each of them has been convicted of criminal offences and sentenced to long terms of imprisonment. In this case, the claimants were granted anonymity and eventually judgment was entered in default of a proper defence. The judgment turns on the assessment of damages after hearing from each claimant (which fortuitously for them was in the absence of either defendant, who, although invited by the court to participate, did not). The total amount awarded to the claimants against the defendants, who were liable jointly and severally, was, in the case of AT £175,000, NT £162,000.00, in the case of ML £132,000 and in the case of AK £142,000. However, it is

---

45 [2017] EWHC 3403 (Admin).
46 [2009] EWHC 225 (QB).

unlikely that those damages were ever recovered from the defendants, given that they were incarcerated, and any assets would be difficult to trace[47].

Tortious and other claims against a company

12.74

In *Galdikas v DJ Houghton Catching Services Ltd*[48], the first civil case of its kind, the claimants, six individuals who alleged they were trafficked from Lithuania and subjected to severe labour exploitation, brought civil claims against a limited company engaged in the supply of labour to chicken farms in the UK. The claimants were recognised by the NRM as victims of trafficking. The claims encompassed claims in, inter alia, breach of contract, breach of the Agricultural Wages Act 1948, negligence, harassment and assault. The claimants alleged that they suffered loss and damage, including personal injury, distress and unpaid wages, as a result of the defendants' wrongful acts. They also joined the Gangmasters Licensing Authority[49] (a statutory regulatory body responsible for the licensing of gangmasters) as a defendant. The judgment deals with various preliminary applications for strike out/summary judgment by both the claimants and DJ Houghton (the latter failed). The claimants were granted summary judgment in relation to their claims for breaches of the Agricultural Wages Orders and the Gangmasters (Licensing Conditions) Rules 2009[50] relating, inter alia, to their inadequate wages and unlawful withholding of wages and inadequate working facilities. The case settled in December 2016, some four years after the claimants were exploited[51].

Employment tribunal claims

12.75

Claims against traffickers are more usually brought in the employment tribunal for employment-related abuses such as failure to pay the minimum wage, failure to pay holiday pay and race discrimination.

12.76

In *Hounga v Allen*[52], Miss Hounga knowingly illegally entered the UK from Nigeria in January 2007, when aged 14. For the following 18 months Miss

---

47 For a detailed analysis of this litigation see J Luqmani, 'Traffickers in the UK Courts for Harm Associated with Trafficking' in P Chandran (ed), *Human Trafficking Handbook* (LexisNexis, 2011).
48 [2016] EWHC 1376 (QB), [2016] IRLR 859.
49 Now the Gangmasters and Labour Abuse Authority: http://www.gla.gov.uk/, last accessed 17 December 2017.
50 SI 2009/307.
51 See www.leighday.co.uk/News/News-2016/December-2016/Joy-for-trafficked-workers-while-UKs-Worst-Gangma, last accessed 17 December 2017.
52 [2014] UKSC 47, [2014] 1 WLR 2889.

Hounga lived in the home of Mrs Allen and of her husband (who had facilitated her illegal entry). Although Miss Hounga had no right to work in the UK, and after July 2007 no right to remain in the UK, Mrs Allen employed her, unpaid, to look after her children in the home. There Mrs Allen inflicted serious physical abuse on Miss Hounga and threatened her if she reported the abuse. In July 2008, Mrs Allen forcibly evicted Miss Hounga from the home and thereby dismissed her from the employment. The appeal proceeded on the basis that, by dismissing her, Mrs Allen discriminated against Miss Hounga in that on racial grounds, namely on ground of nationality, she treated Miss Hounga less favourably than she would have treated others. The Court of Appeal held that the illegality of the contract of employment formed a material part of Miss Hounga's complaint and that to uphold it would be to condone the illegality. The Supreme Court unanimously allowed her appeal in relation to her claim for the statutory tort of discrimination, committed in the course of dismissal. The majority in the Supreme Court held that it would be an affront to current anti-trafficking public policy to allow an employer to evade liability to an employee by reference to the illegality of the contract of employment entered into between them, where the employer had trafficked the employee for domestic servitude. The UK authorities are striving in various ways to combat trafficking and to protect its victims. The public policy in support of the application of the defence of illegality, to the extent that it exists at all, should give way to the public policy to which its application is an affront.

12.77

It should be noted that in *Taiwo v Olaigbe*[53], the Supreme Court held that those who are exploited due to their vulnerable immigration status cannot bring a race discrimination claim, as immigration status (as distinct from nationality) is not a protected characteristic within the meaning of the Equality Act 2010. Ms Taiwo had entered the UK on a false basis, had her passport taken from her by her employer and she was expected to work during most of her waking hours for minimal wages. She was starved and subject to physical and mental abuse. She escaped and brought successful claims in the employment tribunal for the failure to pay her the minimum wage, for unlawful deductions from wages, for failure to provide rest periods and to give her written terms of employment. She was awarded compensation in respect of these claims but her claim for race discrimination, which would have entitled her to damages for the fear and distress she suffered, was dismissed. The tribunal found that her mistreatment was because she was a vulnerable migrant worker who was reliant on the respondents for her continued employment and residence in the UK, not because she was Nigerian. The Supreme Court dismissed her appeal (as well as that of another related appellant). Lady Hale noted that the present law does not offer redress for all the harm suffered by the appellants. She stated that Parliament might wish to consider extending the remedy available under the

---

53 [2016] UKSC 31, [2016] 1 WLR 2653.

MSA 2015 to give employment tribunals jurisdiction to grant compensation for ill-treatment meted out to workers.

12.78

Lastly, in *Reyes v Al-Malki*[54], a domestic worker who alleged that she was a victim of trafficking brought claims for direct and indirect discrimination, unlawful deductions from wages (failure to pay the national minimum wage), and breach of the Working Time Regulations, against a Saudi Arabian diplomatic agent and his wife. Mr and Mrs Al-Malki left the UK when Mr Al-Malki's posting came to an end. The Court of Appeal held that the Employment Tribunal had no jurisdiction because Mr Al-Malki was entitled to diplomatic immunity under Art 31 of the Vienna Convention on Diplomatic Relations, and Mrs Al-Malki was entitled to a derivative immunity under Art 37(1) as a member of his family. The Supreme Court unanimously allowed the appeal but on a narrow basis. In short, it held that once a diplomat's posting has come to an end, his immunity after leaving the receiving state is ordinarily limited to a 'residual immunity' under Art 39(2). That residual immunity applies only to acts performed in the exercise of 'official functions'. Acts performed in the exercise of a diplomat's official functions are limited to acts which are part of the diplomatic functions of the diplomatic mission, performed on behalf of the state which that diplomat represents. Mr and Mrs Al-Malki left the UK at the end of Mr Al-Malki's posting, so the only potentially relevant immunity is the 'residual immunity' in respect of official acts. The employment of Ms Reyes to carry out domestic tasks in the residence of Mr and Mrs Al-Malki was not an act in the exercise of the diplomatic functions of the mission. Nor was it done on behalf of Saudi Arabia, even though it assisted Mr Al-Malki in the performance of his official functions. It was not there the exercise of an official function. Consequently, neither Mr Al-Malki nor Mrs Al-Malki could rely on that residual immunity.

---

54 [2017] UKSC 61, [2017] 3 WLR 923.

13 Public funding for victims of trafficking

13.1

Victims of trafficking will generally require public funding if they are to be able to benefit from legal advice in relation to the various legal issues that they encounter. Public funding is administered by the Legal Aid Agency ('LAA') and is commonly referred to as 'legal aid'. The nature and extent of the funding available depends on the type of legal problem under consideration. Eligibility for the relevant public funding is not uniform across the various legal aid schemes.

Advice on arrest for a criminal offence

13.2

The Police Station Advice and Assistance Scheme provides for free and independent legal advice to be available to any person arrested for a criminal offence in England and Wales regardless of their nationality or means. Advice under the scheme can only be provided by a firm of solicitors which holds a Standard Crime Contract 2017 ('SCC 2017')[1] and must be provided by a solicitor or accredited police station representative.

13.3

If the individual arrested does not know a solicitor to contact on arrest, he is entitled to advice from the duty solicitor. Most firms holding the SCC 2017 will have solicitors who are qualified as duty solicitors and who are allocated slots on the rota for the specific police stations local to their office. The LAA has to ensure that a solicitor is available at every police station at all times, and does so through the duty solicitor scheme.

13.4

The scope of advice under the scheme can be limited and, in some circumstances, the advice will be provided not by the requested solicitor or the duty solicitor but by Criminal Defence Direct ('CDD'). The following matters fall within the scope of the CDD scheme[2]:

---

1   The SCC 2017 started on 1 April 2017. For police station attendances prior to that date the firm would have had to hold the SCC 2010.
2   SCC 2017 Specification A9.9.

(i)   an individual detained in relation to any non-imprisonable offence;

(ii)   someone arrested on a bench warrant for failing to appear and being held for production before the court, except where the individual's solicitor has clear documentary evidence available that would result in him being released from custody, in which case attendance may be allowed provided that the reason is recorded on the solicitors' file;

(iii)   anyone arrested on suspicion of:

- driving with excess alcohol, who is taken to the police station to give a specimen (Road Traffic Act 1988, s 5);

- failure to provide a specimen (Road Traffic Act 1988, ss 6, 7 and 7A); or

- driving whilst unfit/drunk in charge of a motor vehicle (Road Traffic Act 1988, s 4); or

(iv)   anyone detained in relation to breach of police or court bail conditions.

13.5

The matter is removed from the CDD scheme if[3]:

- an interview or an identification procedure is going to take place;

- the person arrested is eligible for assistance from an appropriate adult under the PACE codes of practice;

- the individual is unable to communicate over the telephone;

- the individual complains of serious maltreatment by the police;

- the investigation includes another alleged offence which does not fall within the above restrictions;

- the solicitor is already at the same Police Station, albeit that the fee payable is limited to the Police Station Telephone Advice Fixed Fee;

- the advice relates to an indictable offence; or

- the request is a Special Request[4].

13.6

When an individual is arrested, the custody officer at the police station will provide him with his rights and entitlements under the Police and Criminal

---

3   SCC 2017 Specification A9.10.
4   A 'Special Request' is a request identified to the solicitor as such by the DSCC. Special Requests may include, for example: requests where CDD considers that, because of a conflict of interest, the request should be handled by the solicitor (instead of by a CDD Telephone Adviser); or considers that Advocacy Assistance is required.

Evidence Act 1984. One such entitlement is to speak to a solicitor free of charge[5]. The custody officer will notify a central agency called the Defence Solicitor Call Centre ('DSCC'), who will allocate the case a reference number without which no claim for fees will be paid. It is possible to receive instructions for an attendance by agreement or via a third party but the DSCC has to be informed within 48 hours of the attendance and a number allocated to the case[6].

13.7

If the case falls within the CDD scheme, advice will initially be provided by CDD, an agency contracted directly by the LAA to provide such advice. If CDD considers that the circumstances take the matter outside of the CDD scheme, the nominated solicitors will be called.

13.8

Those arrested who may be victims of trafficking will not always have been identified as victims of trafficking at this very early point after initial arrest. It is therefore possible that a victim of trafficking will be directed to CDD instead of his own (or the duty) solicitor in circumstances where advice from his solicitor would be appropriate and remunerable under the Police Station Advice and Assistance Scheme (for example the entitlement to an appropriate adult). It is equally likely that unless specifically trained to identify the potential signs of a victim of trafficking, the CDD adviser will not pick up the issue of trafficking at this stage.

13.9

Funding for legal advice under the police station Legal Advice and Assistance scheme is not subject to a financial eligibility test. It is, however, subject to a form of merits test known as the Sufficient Benefit Test. For police station advice the Sufficient Benefit Test is deemed to be satisfied in circumstances where a person arrested has a right to legal advice, for example under PACE 1984 or the Terrorism Act 2000, at the police station and has requested such advice. The right to non-means tested legal advice arises where a suspect is to be interviewed either at a police station or another location and includes advice to a person detained under the Terrorism Act 2000, Sch 7 in accordance with Sch 8 thereof, either at a port or in a police station[7].

13.10

The SCC prescribes that the solicitor may provide further legal advice to the client immediately following charge. However, attendance upon the client thereafter, whilst fingerprints, photographs and swabs are taken, will not meet

---

5   PACE 1984, s 58.
6   SCC Specification A9.20.
7   SCC Specification A9.14.

the Sufficient Benefit Test except where the client requires further assistance owing to his particular circumstances, in which case the relevant factors must be noted on the solicitor's file. The solicitor may remain at the police station if required to make representations about bail, provided that this justification is noted on the file[8]. It is likely that the particular vulnerabilities of a victim of trafficking will enable the solicitor to remain at the police station until all post-charge procedures have been completed.

13.11

Once a police station matter has been accepted from the DSCC by the solicitors, a telephone call should be made to the police station to provide initial advice and make contact with the police. Unless there are exceptional circumstances, the following is mandatory: attendance at the police station, to attend all police interviews with the arrested person in connection with an offence, to attend any identification parade, group identification or confrontation, or in circumstances where there is a complaint of serious maltreatment by the police[9]. Attendance at video identification parades is discretionary[10].

13.12

Once instructed, the solicitors should conduct the matter throughout the investigation stage (ie up to the point where a charging decision is made). There are restrictions on another firm taking over the case at the investigation stage and being entitled to claim a fee under the scheme. This may cause problems with victims of trafficking who are released on bail by police or released under investigation and then latterly come into contact with solicitors who have an expertise in this area (ie trafficking expertise).

13.13

The solicitor must not make a claim under the SCC for Police Station Advice and Assistance given to a client who has received Police Station Advice and Assistance for the same matter from another firm within the six months except where:

- there is a gap in time and circumstances have changed materially between the first and second or subsequent occasions when the Police Station Advice and Assistance was sought;

- the individual has reasonable cause to transfer from the first solicitor; or

- the first solicitor has confirmed that no claim for payment for the Police Station Advice and Assistance will be made[11].

---

8   SCC Specification A9.16.
9   SCC Specification A9.38.
10 SCC Specification A9.40.
11 SCC Specification A9.67.

13.14

The second firm should not take on the case and claim for a fee where:

- the client simply disagrees with the first advice and wants a second opinion;
- there is only a short time between the first and second occasions when the Police Station Advice and Assistance is sought and no material change of circumstances has occurred;
- the change requested is from a second to a third solicitor (unless exceptionally it is reasonable for a further change); or
- there is no reasonable explanation for the client seeking further Police Station Advice and Assistance from a new solicitor[12].

13.15

The most likely provision to apply in cases concerning victims of trafficking will be the victim of trafficking having reasonable cause to transfer from one firm to another based on the second firm's specialist knowledge of trafficking issues, especially in circumstances where the first firm has not identified that the individual may be a victim of trafficking. The second firm takes the risk of non-payment in these circumstances and should justify the change with a detailed file note of the client's concerns and reasons for transfer. There is no formal transfer process at this stage and the second firm can merely request the papers from the first firm who will then close and bill the case.

13.16

Remuneration for police station advice is on a fixed fee structure subject to a threshold at which hourly rate claims become available. There is a fixed fee for telephone only advice. The fee for providing advice at the police station is also fixed and depends on the location of the police station. The telephone advice fee is not payable in addition, but forms part of the attendance fee.

13.17

If the 'escape fee' threshold is reached, a fixed fee is payable plus a fee based on hourly rates for work done beyond the threshold figure. The firm calculates the fee by reference to hourly rates and once that figure exceeds the stated threshold for the police station attended, further fees are paid – but only for the work done beyond the threshold.

13.18

In very general terms, the fixed fee is roughly one-third of the threshold figure, so the firm will be paid a fixed fee and then have to undertake further work unpaid until the threshold is reached. The unpaid portion is never recouped on

---

12 SCC Specification A9.70.

an escape fee claim, which is also assessed for reasonableness by the LAA using a CRM18 form.

13.19

Only one fee is payable for the whole of the investigation stage of a case. This means that where an individual is released on bail or under investigation and subsequently re-interviewed, there is no further payment available for that attendance (unless it takes the case beyond the escape threshold).

13.20

It is possible to undertake work during the bail period or where someone is released under investigation but only if they are financially eligible for advice under the freestanding Advice and Assistance scheme[13]. This work is included in the calculation as to whether the case passes the escape threshold but, unless it takes the case beyond that threshold, no further fee is payable beyond the Police Station fixed fee.

13.21

The Police Station Advice and Assistance scheme applies to those attending the police station voluntarily to be interviewed under caution about criminal offences. The individual does not need to be under arrest to qualify for the funding.

13.22

Advice and Assistance is also available under the Advocacy Assistance provisions[14], where there is an application for a warrant of further detention, to vary police bail conditions or to extend police bail.

13.23

Each individual case is billed using a CRM11 form but the submission of bills to the LAA for payment is via the monthly aggregated submission form on a CRM6 form. Files are audited and can be selected for review by the LAA at any time.

Work after release from police station but before charge

13.24

Once a client is released from the police station but where a decision on charge has not been made, legal advice is available under the Advice and Assistance

---

13 See details below at paras **13.24–13.28** and **13.94** (re appeals and reviews), and SCC 2017 Specification A9.113–9.140.
14 SCC 2017 Specification A9.141–9.187.

scheme if the client is financially eligible. The eligibility limits are very low, but most clients who are potential victims of trafficking would usually meet the criteria.

13.25

This funding requires the client to sign a CRM1 and CRM2 form and for the financial eligibility details to be provided and checked. The client will need to provide proof of his income even if he is being supported by a charity or friend. A letter from that person or organisation setting out what support they are providing will suffice, as long as it covers the date that the form was signed.

13.26

This funding will enable the solicitors to make representations to the Crown Prosecution Service against charging the client with criminal offences.

13.27

However, the reality of the situation for the solicitors is that this work will not add to the fee they are paid for representing the client at the investigation stage. The work done under this scheme will only be remunerated if it takes the work done in the investigation stage above the fixed fee threshold. If it does not, and in most cases it will not, no further fee is payable in addition to the fixed fee for attending the police station.

13.28

The financial limit on the Advice and Assistance Scheme (see below)[15] applies and can be extended by online request using the CRM5 format. Disbursements for interpreters, experts, translators or any other necessary disbursement expense can be funded, subject to approval by the LAA. The disbursements will be funded additionally to the fixed fee.

Witnesses at risk of self-incrimination

13.29

On occasion a victim of trafficking may be requested to provide an account to police as a witness in a case, in particular where there is an investigation into that person's trafficked status and into the person allegedly responsible for the trafficking. This may be contemporaneous to a criminal investigation of the victim of trafficking or independent of it. These interviews are normally carried out under the Achieving Best Evidence video procedure.

---

15 See para **13.101**.

13.30

In such interviews the victim of trafficking is likely to be in a position where he may potentially admit to having committed criminal offences, albeit under coercion. Consequently there is a risk of self-incrimination and therefore a 'complicating factor'[16].

13.31

Advice and Assistance is available to a victim of trafficking in such circumstances under the SCC 2017[17] subject to a means test and passing the Sufficient Benefit Test.

13.32

The details of the Advice and Assistance Scheme are set out below[18]. The scheme is very strictly means tested, but potential victims of trafficking would normally expect to qualify for the funding subject to proof of their income.

Advice during criminal court proceedings at first instance

13.33

If a victim of trafficking is charged with a criminal offence, legal aid from a firm of solicitors with an SCC 2017 may be available, subject to means and passing a merits test. An application is made online and the defendant has to sign a hard copy of a declaration form confirming that the information provided is correct.

13.34

The online application requires details of the defendant's income, outgoings and capital as well as details about the nature of the case being prosecuted against them. Most victims of trafficking will qualify for legal aid if the offence passes the merits test. The forms to be used online are the CRM14 and CRM15 forms.

13.35

As a rough guide, anyone earning under £20,000 per annum is likely to qualify for legal aid for summary proceedings. For proceedings on indictment the financial limit is an annual disposable household income of £37,500. It should be noted that this is the disposable income after mortgage, rent and other expenses are deducted.

---

16 SCC 2017 Specification A9.3.
17 SCC 2017 Specification A9.3, 9.4, 9.113–9.140.
18 See para **13.91** ff.

13.36

Legal aid is assessed on income initially but it may be that a contribution from capital is ordered at the end of the case if the defendant is convicted and has assets in excess of £30,000. At this stage the LAA may request a contribution from capital.

13.37

If legal aid is granted, a representation order will be issued. This will cover the work indicated on the order.

Magistrates' court proceedings

13.38

If legal aid is granted for the magistrates' court in summary proceedings it will allow the solicitor to obtain experts' reports, interpreters and translations as necessary during the course of the case, as long as the work undertaken is reasonable.

13.39

It is advisable to make an application for prior authority from the LAA for any disbursement in excess of £100 using the CRM4 process on the LAA online portal. An estimate of the fees from three providers should be sought, although the LAA may not insist on this if the rates are within legal aid guidelines and the amount of time is reasonable. In cases of unusual expertise, it may be that higher rates might be agreed by the LAA and only one estimate may be possible in any event.

13.40

In most summary proceedings, the representation order will provide for representation by solicitors. Counsel can be instructed but would be paid by the solicitors rather than by the LAA. In these circumstances counsel is 'unassigned' and becomes an overhead of the firm. A fee will be agreed between the firm and chambers and the times worked by the advocate would be included in the solicitors' bill as if it were work undertaken by the firm.

13.41

In exceptional cases heard before the magistrates' court an advocate may be 'assigned' if the proceedings relate to an extradition hearing under the Extradition Act 2003 or an indictable (including either way) offence and the relevant court determines that because there are circumstances which make the proceedings unusually grave or difficult, representation by an advocate would be desirable[19]. An advocate cannot be assigned on summary only offences.

---

19 Criminal Legal Aid (Determinations by a Court and Choice of Representative) Regulations 2013, 2013/614, reg 16(2).

13.42

Assigned counsel is paid directly by the LAA but the bill is submitted by the solicitors' firm on a CRM8 form to accompany the firm's CRM7 claim form (which is submitted online).

13.43

The fees for magistrates' court cases are calculated on a fixed fee matrix but using underlying hourly rates excluding travel and waiting (except in certain (usually) rural areas). If the work done does not reach the 'lower limit', the lower fixed fee is payable. If the work done exceeds the lower limit but not the 'higher limit', the higher standard fee is claimed. If the work done exceeds the higher limit a non-standard fee is claimed whereby the work is claimed entirely at hourly rates and assessed for reasonableness by the LAA. There is a different fixed fee depending on whether the case is a trial, cracked trial or a guilty plea (or equivalent).

13.44

Standard fees are claimed by using a CRM11 to calculate the bill and then submitted as one line on the monthly CRM6 to the LAA. All bills are potentially subject to audit by the LAA on request.

13.45

Non-standard fees are submitted online using the CRM7 form. These are assessed on a case-by-case basis.

13.46

It is possible to claim enhanced hourly rates for all or part of the work undertaken and if such rates are claimed, the bill is submitted as a CRM7 for assessment. Enhanced rates should be claimed where it is considered, taking into account all the relevant circumstances of the case and compared to the generality of proceedings, that:

- the work was done with exceptional competence, skill or expertise; or

- the work was done with exceptional dispatch; or

- the case involved exceptional circumstances or complexity[20].

13.47

If the work or part of it attracts an uplift, the LAA will decide what rate to apply up to a maximum of 100% and having regard to the degree of responsibility accepted by the firm; the care, speed and economy with which the case was

---

20 SCC 2017 Specification A10.99.

prepared; and the novelty, weight and complexity of the case[21]. Any assessment can be appealed to an Independent Funding Adjudicator (sometimes known as an Independent Costs Assessor).

Crown Court proceedings

13.48

In the Crown Court, solicitors are paid via the Litigator Graduated Fee Scheme and advocates by the Advocates Graduated Fee Scheme. In both schemes the fees for the work undertaken are fixed by a series of proxies, namely the nature of the charge (which will fall into one of eleven categories), whether it is a guilty plea, cracked trial or trial (or equivalent outcome), number of pages of prosecution evidence, the trial length and – for advocates – the number of prosecution witnesses.

13.49

The fee payable is not related to the amount of work undertaken. Disbursements are paid in addition to the lawyers' fees via the solicitors who include them in their fee submission.

13.50

The number of pages of prosecution evidence is capped[22] and any work above that is paid on an hourly rate (not subject to enhancement) and assessed on submission of the bill for reasonableness. This is known as special preparation.

13.51

Work on unused material is not specifically remunerated but is deemed to be included in the fixed rates paid.

Prior authority for disbursements

13.52

As stated above, if a disbursement expense is to be incurred, an application for prior authority should be made to the LAA if the amount involved exceeds £100. This application is made online using the CRM4 form. The LAA may require three estimates from experts but this is not always essential. There are prescribed rates for experts of different types and it is occasionally possible to

---

21 SCC 2017 Specification A10.101–10.102.
22 For legal aid representation orders granted before 1 December 2017 this is at 10,000 pages but for orders granted on or after 1 December 2017 the cap is at 6,000 pages.

exceed those rates if no suitable expert can be found for the usual legal aid rate, or if the case requires a specific expert who will not undertake the work at those rates. Refusals to grant the prior authority requested can be appealed to an Independent Costs Assessor.

13.53

Once prior authority has been granted and the work undertaken, an interim claim can be made for the disbursement if the case is in the Crown Court under the Litigator Graduated Fee Scheme. No such claim can be made in magistrates' court cases.

13.54

Any work in excess of the prior authorised figure cannot be guaranteed payment and would have to be justified to the LAA at the conclusion of the case. Experts must therefore know that their fees are fixed by their estimates and the solicitor will not make up any shortfall if the final bill exceeds the estimate and is not reimbursed by the LAA. A provision to this effect should be put into the solicitors' letter of instruction to the expert.

Defendant intermediaries

13.55

An intermediary acts as a facilitator for a witness or defendant to ensure complete, accurate and coherent communication between the vulnerable individual and the legal professionals concerned. The core concept is to ensure the individual's general understanding of the process and an ability to provide coherent instructions to his legal team.

13.56

If the solicitor or advocate instructed considers that the individual client requires the assistance of an intermediary, the court must be notified so that the issues can be further explored and a timetable set to accommodate assessments.

13.57

A psychologist (with specific experience of adults or children) will have to be instructed in order to carry out specific communication assessments. Funding for this assessment is obtained via the LAA by making an online CRM4 application to cover the assessment and report fee.

13.58

Should the psychologist conclude that an intermediary ought to be appointed, a specific intermediary report should be obtained. This will require a further assessment of the individual by an intermediary to determine the individual's difficulties, specific needs and proposed requirements. The intermediary should be provided with information about the case prior to assessment, in addition to any medical records and reports previously obtained. Again, funding can be obtained via the CRM4 procedure.

13.59

The intermediary report once prepared shall provide specific recommendations as to language, breaks and general approach which must be adopted to ensure the most effective participation and understanding of the vulnerable individual in the case. Such issues shall be considered by the court in determining the application.

13.60

Once an intermediary report has been prepared, it must be sent to the relevant court. There is no statutory power to appoint an intermediary for a defendant and the court must be expressly invited to exercise its inherent power to appoint an intermediary.

13.61

The application shall be determined by the allocated judge and if the criteria is met, an intermediary shall be appointed by the court. The fees are then met by the court and do not come from the defendant's legal aid.

Extension of legal aid to Queen's Counsel or two advocates

13.62

Legal aid in the Crown Court automatically includes representation by solicitors and an advocate. It can be extended to include representation by Queen's Counsel, either alone or with a junior advocate by application to the Crown Court[23]. Very exceptionally Queen's Counsel can be instructed in the magistrates' court in extradition proceedings[24].

13.63

In Crown Court proceedings legal aid can be extended to include Queen's Counsel alone if the case involves substantial novel or complex issues of law or fact which could not be adequately presented except by a Queen's Counsel, and either the 'exceptional condition' is met or the 'counsel condition' is met.

---

23 Criminal Legal Aid (Determinations by a Court and Choice of Representative) Regulations 2013, SI 2013/614, reg 18.
24 Criminal Legal Aid (Determinations by a Court and Choice of Representative) Regulations 2013, reg 17.

13.64

The 'counsel condition' means that a Queen's Counsel or senior Treasury Counsel has been instructed on behalf of the prosecution. The 'exceptional condition' means that the case is exceptional compared with the generality of cases involving similar offences.

13.65

Legal aid can be extended to two junior advocates if the case involves substantial novel or complex issues of law or fact which could not be adequately presented by a single advocate, including a Queen's Counsel alone, and either the 'exceptional condition' is met or the 'prosecution condition' is met.

13.66

The 'prosecution condition' means either two or more advocates have been instructed on behalf of the prosecution and the relevant court is satisfied that the individual will be, or will be likely to be, prejudiced if they too are not represented by two or more advocates; or the number of prosecution witnesses exceeds 80; or the number of pages of prosecution evidence exceeds 1,000.

13.67

Legal aid can be extended to include a Queen's Counsel and a junior advocate if the case involves substantial novel or complex issues of law or fact which could not be adequately presented except by a Queen's Counsel assisted by a junior advocate, and either the exceptional condition is met, or the counsel condition and the prosecution condition are met.

Transfers of legal aid

13.68

If a defendant is not happy with his solicitors, he may apply to the court to transfer the legal aid to another firm. This is not always a straightforward process and courts are often unwilling to transfer representation orders where they fear that the system is being manipulated by the defendant or where large extra costs will be incurred. In fact, in most cases the extra costs incurred to the legal aid fund are not large, especially if the application is made at an early stage in proceedings and before any papers have been served or prior to the Plea and Trial Preparation Hearing.

13.69

The application is made by the defendant completing a form (available on the Justice website)[25] setting out his reasons for requiring a transfer of representation.

---

25 See www.justice.gov.uk/courts/procedure-rules/criminal/docs/october-2015/rep001-eng.pdf, last accessed 5 January 2018.

This is then sent to the proposed new solicitor to complete and then to the currently-instructed solicitor. The form is then submitted to the court for a decision by a judge at the Crown Court.

13.70

The transfer application is more likely to succeed if the incumbent firm does not object. In seeking a transfer, clients may be critical of their current solicitors. In trafficking cases, it may be justified by the client being a potential victim of trafficking, and this has not been identified by the solicitor, or they have failed to make representations about the case continuing as a result of the State's non prosecution obligations or they have not considered an abuse of process application or the defence under MSA 2015, s 45. Even in these circumstances, firms may object to the transfer request.

13.71

In order for legal aid to be transferred, the defendant has to demonstrate that[26]:

- there has been a breakdown in the relationship between the individual and the original solicitor such that effective representation can no longer be provided by the original solicitor; or

- there is some other compelling reason why effective representation can no longer be provided by the original solicitor.

13.72

Alternatively legal aid may be transferred if the original solicitor considers there to be a duty to withdraw from the case in accordance with his professional rules of conduct or is no longer able to represent the individual through circumstances outside the solicitor's control. In such circumstances the original solicitor has to supply the relevant court with details as to the nature of any such duty to withdraw from the case or the particular circumstances that renders him unable to represent the individual.

13.73

There will be issues of privilege involved and the form contains a box to tick if privilege is to be waived for the purposes of considering this application. In effect where there are criticisms of the current solicitor, privilege will have to be waived so that the solicitors can deal with the issue.

13.74

It is helpful for the proposed new solicitors to set out a reasoned argument as to why legal aid should be transferred, bringing the client's own reasons within

---

26 Criminal Legal Aid (Determinations by a Court and Choice of Representative) Regulations 2013, reg 14.

the regulation. Where solicitors object to transfer requests and the court refuses to grant the application, this leaves a vulnerable defendant with a firm that he does not want to be represented by, and this firm is aware that he has made complaints about their conduct of the case. This does not make for effective representation, particularly given the importance of building the trust of a potential victim of trafficking.

13.75

If the defendant chooses to revoke legal aid, he cannot be guaranteed that a fresh application will be granted and there is a significant risk that he will be unrepresented. In a potential victim of trafficking case, that situation could give rise to significant injustice.

13.76

It may be that the incumbent firm, while not accepting any overt criticism, would nonetheless agree that the transfer should take place in order that the defendant has a functional working relationship with his solicitors to prepare the case for trial. Even not objecting in principle on the basis that the client should be able to trust his legal representative implicitly, especially when the defendant is particularly vulnerable, will not guarantee a transfer of legal aid.

Billing time limits

13.77

Bills should be submitted within three months of the conclusion of the part of the case to which they relate.

Advice on appeal against conviction and/or sentence where the solicitors acted at trial

Appeals from the magistrates' court to the Crown Court

13.78

Legal aid granted for the magistrates' court includes advice on appeal to the Crown Court. If the advice is positive and an appeal is lodged, a new legal aid application has to be made to the LAA via the online portal.

13.79

Appeals against conviction and sentence in the Crown Court attract a fixed fee for advocates and litigators regardless of the nature of the case or its complexity.

The fee payable is generally considered to be derisory, not providing adequate remuneration.

13.80

The Law Society has recently provided guidance to solicitors that they are not obliged to take on legal aid cases if the fee is not economic. This guidance is particularly apt for appeals to the Crown Court.

Appeals from the Crown Court to the Court of Appeal

13.81

Legal aid in the Crown Court includes advice on appeal to the Court of Appeal (Criminal Division). If the advice to appeal from the Crown Court is negative, there is no additional fee to the litigator's or advocate's graduated fee.

13.82

If the advice is positive, a claim for the work done on an hourly rate can be made to the Court of Appeal once the decision on leave has been made.

Funding in the Court of Appeal (Criminal Division)

13.83

If leave is granted, legal aid will also be granted but this would normally be for the advocate only as long as the box indicating that legal aid was required was ticked on the form NG. Legal aid is not means tested at this stage and there are no forms to complete or submit to the court or the LAA. The Court may in due course require a means form to be completed, as costs may be an issue should the appeal fail.

13.84

Legal aid can be extended to include representation by solicitors as well as counsel and/or for two counsel. If the advocate considers that the assistance of a solicitor in preparing and presenting the appeal is required or that the case is suitable for representation by two advocates, a written application should be sent to the Registrar for an extension of the representation order. There is no prescribed form for such an application.

13.85

The Court of Appeal frequently limits representation orders granted to solicitors to include only specific work. This may not include all of the work that the solicitor might wish to undertake to prepare a case for the appeal. Any work outside of the limitations will not be remunerated.

13.86

It should be noted that the Advice and Assistance Scheme cannot be used to bridge any gap in funding.

13.87

If the Single Judge refuses leave, any advice and representation thereafter is on a pro bono basis unless the client is willing and able to pay privately. The client is entitled to advice as to whether to renew the application for leave to the full court and the potential consequences if such an application is unsuccessfully made. This would normally be by way of an advice from the advocate or letter from the solicitor and should be included in the bill to the court. It would not cover a meeting with the client unless specifically agreed with the court in advance.

13.88

For litigators it is possible to claim enhanced rates on the work undertaken up to 100% on the same basis as for work in the magistrates' court (see para **13.46**).

13.89

It is also possible to instruct experts if the representation order allows for their instruction. There are no prior authority provisions at this stage, but the court will sometimes pay in advance on specific request. Such payment will be subject to recoupment at the final assessment of the bill at the end of the case. Given that no agreement on rates or hours is given, the solicitors remain at risk if payment is made in this way.

13.90

Bills should be submitted within three months of the conclusion of the case to the Costs Department at the Court of Appeal.

Applications to the Court of Appeal out of time and CCRC applications: Advice and Assistance Scheme

13.91

In many cases the individual may not be identified as a victim of trafficking until after their conviction. In such circumstances it may be possible to appeal to the Court of Appeal or indeed the Crown Court out of time. Usually this will mean the instruction of a firm that did not represent the victim of trafficking at trial, there being at least an implication that the trial firm should have identified the issue earlier.

13.92

Public funding is available under the Advice and Assistance Scheme for work within the Appeals and Reviews class. The client will need to sign and complete a CRM1 and CRM2 form.

Sufficient Benefit Test

13.93

In order to receive Advice and Assistance under the scheme the case must meet the Sufficient Benefit Test:

> 'Advice and Assistance may only be provided on legal issues concerning English (or Welsh) law and where there is sufficient benefit to the Client, having regard to the circumstances of the matter, including the personal circumstances of the Client, to justify work or further work being carried out'[27].

This is an ongoing test throughout the life of the case, and must be considered at all times. As soon as it ceases to apply, no more work should be done on the case.

Financial test

13.94

In order to obtain advice under this scheme the potential client also has to meet the financial criteria. There is both an income and a capital limit so on occasions even people in prison will not qualify for advice under the scheme if they have too much capital. The limits are very low, currently set at £99 per week disposable income (only deducting tax and not items such as rent). There is a fixed deduction to take into account for dependants of £33.65 for a partner and £47.45 for each child.

13.95

As far as capital is concerned the limits depend on whether the client has any dependants. The limit is £1,000 if there are no dependants, £1,335 if one, £1,535 if two and an extra £100 is added for each extra dependant. The income and capital of any partner of the victim of trafficking is included, even

---

27 SCC 2017 Specification A3.10.

if the victim of trafficking is in prison, if they had been living as a couple prior to the incarceration.

13.96

Victims of trafficking, who are foreign nationals, are often in the position whereby they cannot work legitimately or claim benefits. They are often supported by friends or by a charity. It will be essential for the solicitor to obtain documentary proof of the support that the victim of trafficking is getting to ensure that they are below the threshold.

13.97

A letter from the person providing the support setting out how much they provide will be sufficient and it must cover the time at which the legal advice and assistance forms (CRM1 and CRM2) are signed by the victim of trafficking.

13.98

If the client does not pass both parts of the financial assessment, advice under the scheme is not available to them. There is no contribution-based system and no other public funding for this advice.

Previous advice

13.99

If the victim of trafficking has received an adverse opinion on appeal and wishes to obtain a further opinion, the scheme is not automatically available as the solicitor must consider how long it was since the first opinion was given. If it was recent and it appears that all issues have been considered, no further work should normally be undertaken[28].

13.100

However, where there is further evidence or the solicitor believes there may be some defect in the opinion or the proceedings, then further work may be justified for a further opinion, regardless of when the first opinion was obtained[29]. In relation to victim of trafficking cases, it is often the case that the fact that the defendant was a victim of trafficking was not identified at trial and therefore any advice given will automatically be flawed. This is rarely a bar to advice on these cases.

---

28 SCC 2017 Specification A11.5.
29 SCC 2017 Specification A11.6.

Financial limits and applications to extend

13.101

The scheme has an initial financial limit of £273.75 (approximately 6 hours' work) for out of time appeals and £456.25 for CCRC applications (approximately 10 hours' work). Up to the point that the limit of work has been reached, an application can be made to the LAA to extend it. If the limit is exceeded before an extension application is made, the work undertaken above the limit will not be funded.

13.102

An application for authority to exceed the upper limit must be made to the LAA online on a CRM5 form which should explain what work has been done, what needs to be done and the amount of any disbursements required or already incurred within the limit.

13.103

Advice and Assistance includes the solicitors' fees at the contracted hourly rate (not subject to any uplift) and any disbursements, including an advocate's fees which are properly incurred by the solicitor in connection with the giving of Advice and Assistance (VAT is not included). Disbursements will include experts, interpreters, transcripts, and translation of documents.

13.104

Once a limit has been granted it can be further extended, but at no point will work be remunerated if it exceeds the limit as then granted. It is important to note that extensions cannot be granted retrospectively and do not operate retrospectively.

13.105

If the LAA refuses to grant an extension to the upper limit, a right of review arises to the Independent Funding Adjudicator.

CCRC applications

13.106

Applications to the Criminal Cases Review Commission are funded under this scheme and come about where the victim of trafficking has already unsuccessfully appealed their conviction but something new has materialised since the time of the appeal which was not known about at the time of trial or appeal. It may be that a victim of trafficking is identified as such after an appeal has been lodged.

13.107

In addition, in cases where there has been a conviction in the magistrates' court on a guilty plea but it then transpires that the person is a victim of trafficking, the only recourse is to the CCRC under exceptional circumstances and this funding is available for such applications.

Postal application

13.108

In terms of the practical aspects of this funding, it may be more cost effective to send application forms for signature in the post. This is allowed 'where there is good reason to do so'[30] and the reason must be noted on the file[31].

13.109

In appellate work, the client may be in custody. It would be reasonable in those circumstances to send the client the CRM1 and CRM2 forms in the post, as this will be much cheaper to the fund than a visit, especially when the case is at such an early stage that a visit may not be necessary.

Telephone advice

13.110

Although unusual with victims of trafficking, the solicitor may claim payment for advice given to a client over the telephone before that client has signed the application form where the client cannot for good reason attend the office and the client meets the qualifying criteria and has subsequently signed the application form[32]. The solicitor would have to consider that in all the circumstances it was appropriate to provide the advice in this way and the reasons relied upon should always be noted and kept on the file[33].

13.111

The client does not have to attend the office to sign the application form after having been given the telephone advice. Instead, the solicitor may send the form to the client, after having given the advice, for signature and return.

---

30 SCC 2017 Specification A11.11.
31 SCC 2017 Specification A11.12.
32 SCC 2017 Specification A11.13.
33 SCC 2017 Specification A11.14 and 11.15.

Outward travel

13.112

The solicitor may claim for the mileage or cost of public transport for outward travel (but not travelling time) to visit a client away from the office before the application form is signed where the visit is justified for good reason (and noted on file) and the client meets the qualifying criteria and has subsequently signed the application form[34].

13.113

It is sometimes advisable to see victims of trafficking away from the solicitor's office, even if the individual is not in custody, where he is particularly vulnerable or needs the assistance of other parties to communicate effectively.

13.114

If the individual is in detention, prison or hospital a claim may also be made for the travelling time at the appropriate rate[35]. Costs must be reasonably incurred taking account of all the circumstances[36] including, for example, the distances involved as against the availability of advice from a more local firm and the justification for travelling to attend on the client at all, bearing in mind that telephone advice can be given and applications accepted by post.

13.115

With victims of trafficking it may not be possible for them to find firms more local to their place of detention with sufficient expertise to advise in trafficking-related matters, and travel may be more justifiable over a longer distance. The use of interpreters will mean that telephone advice will be of limited use and indeed even the use of video links to the prison can be problematic with extremely vulnerable individuals who do not speak English.

Previous advice under the Legal Advice and Assistance Scheme

13.116

In some cases the victim of trafficking may have received previous advice under this scheme. The solicitor must not claim for Advice and Assistance provided to a client who has received Advice and Assistance for the same matter from another solicitor within the six months preceding the application, except where:

---

34 SCC 2017 Specification A11.16.
35 SCC 2017 Specification A11.17.
36 SCC 2017 Specification A11.18.

- there is a gap in time and circumstances have changed materially between the first and second occasions when the Advice and Assistance was sought; or

- the client has reasonable cause to transfer from the first solicitor; or

- the first solicitor has confirmed to the new solicitor that they will not be making a claim for payment for the Advice and Assistance[37].

If the solicitor provides Advice and Assistance in these circumstances, he must record the justification for so doing on the file.

13.117

Where a client is requesting a further advice from a new firm under the Advice and Assistance scheme, there should be no claim under that scheme by the second solicitor where:

- the client simply disagrees with the first advice and wants a second opinion;

- there is only a short time between the first and second occasions when the Advice and Assistance is sought and no material change of circumstances has occurred;

- the change requested is from a second to a third solicitor (unless exceptionally it is reasonable for a further change); or

- there is no reasonable explanation for the client seeking further Advice and Assistance from a new solicitor[38].

13.118

Where the work is nonetheless justifiable, the solicitor must make a note on the file to confirm that Advice and Assistance has been given previously by another solicitor and the client must complete a fresh application form and must meet the qualifying criteria.

Counsel's fees

13.119

There is no fixed rate for counsel in the Contract. The LAA therefore relies on its own Guidance[39] to fix an appropriate rate. The Guidance applies to all Advice and Assistance matters (not just appellate work) and states that counsel

---

37 SCC 2017 Specification A11.26.
38 SCC 2017 Specification A11.29.
39 Last version is from 2010.

often provides advice for a fixed fee of £200–£400. Where higher sums are requested a full breakdown of times should be submitted.

13.120

However, it would be an extremely rare appeal case upon which counsel could advise for a fixed fee as low as those set out in the Guidance. It may be possible on other Advice and Assistance matters but is extremely unlikely on appeal cases. The Guidance recognises this, as it states that 'it should be noted that in Appeals cases, as the issues are likely to be more complex, it is more likely that the fixed fee will not be appropriate and that hourly rates and a full breakdown will be required'.

13.121

The Guidance seeks to fix an hourly rate for counsel, which it says should not exceed £80 per hour (unless a reasonable fixed fee is charged). However, if solicitors provide sufficient and detailed justification as to why a case may be considered to be exceptional, a higher rate can be authorised. A rate of £100 per hour may be agreed in exceptional cases and certainly has been in the past. Cases involving victims of trafficking may well be considered complex or involving novel or complex points of law.

Applications to re-open the case in the magistrates' court

13.122

In some cases where a client has pleaded guilty in the magistrates' court and it transpires they should not have been prosecuted, it may be possible to apply to the magistrates' court to re-open the case[40] instead of applying to the CCRC to refer the case to the Crown Court by way of appeal.

13.123

In such circumstances, initial work on the case to establish how the case should be dealt with and to gather the evidence that the client is a victim of trafficking and should not have been prosecuted should be undertaken under the Advice and Assistance Scheme.

13.124

However, if the application is to be made to reconsider the case at the magistrates' court, a fresh application for legal aid should be made by the LAA online portal using the CRM14 and CRM15 forms as if the matter were a new case in the magistrates' court.

---

40 Magistrates Court Act 1980, s 142.

13.125

If the LAA refuses to grant a representation order on the basis that one already exists for that case, an application for a transfer of legal aid will have to be made.

Applications for compensation under s 133

13.126

Applications for compensation for being the victim of a miscarriage of justice are made to the Ministry of Justice. The initial work involved in preparing representations to the Ministry of Justice as to whether the applicant qualifies for compensation can be funded by way of Legal Help. It is submitted that those firms holding an SCC 2017 but not a Civil Contract should be able to undertake this work as Associated Civil Work, although the SCC is not clear on the point. Before embarking on such work, the position should be checked with the firm's contract manager at the LAA.

13.127

If the claim is accepted, the work is undertaken effectively as a privately-funded case and the legal fees are part of the claimant's damages. The firm will have to obtain permission from the Ministry of Justice to incur any disbursement such as experts or to instruct counsel.

13.128

The rates payable are legal aid rates unless the firm can justify higher rates due to the circumstances of the case. In fact, the Ministry of Justice is likely to allow rates at the equivalent of private rates as this work is unusual and specialised.

13.129

The firm will also have to agree with its client how to deal with the situation where legal fees are requested but not paid in full as part of the compensation by the Ministry of Justice. The shortfall may come from the balance of the compensation, the firm could write it off or a compromise could be reached. Such agreement should be set out in writing in advance with the client.

The availability of legal aid for potential victims of trafficking on immigration matters

13.130

The Legal Aid, Sentencing and Punishment of Offenders Act (LASPO) 2012 removed many categories of immigration law from the scope of legal aid. Providers should refer to LASPO 2012, Sch 1 for the full list of matters which remain in scope, as there are some discrete categories which –although not commonly relevant to potential victim of trafficking claims – may be relevant to a case, such as representation for victims of domestic violence. However, subject to the individual satisfying the financial means and merits test, the immigration civil legal aid categories which remain in scope and that are most relevant to such cases are as follows:

(i) **Legal Help**

- rights to enter or remain in the UK arising from the Refugee Convention 1951 or ECHR, Arts 2 and 3 (asylum/international protection claims)[41];

- representation on any immigration claim where an individual has been granted a positive reasonable grounds decision or conclusive grounds decision[42];

- if a potential victim of trafficking is detained in an Immigration Removal Centre (IRC), they can receive Legal Help for advice and assistance on detention, temporary admission and bail[43]; and

- restrictions on residence, such as a challenge to a requirement for a potential victim of trafficking to report to the Home Office or police on a regular basis, or a curfew, of asylum seekers or pending deportation[44];

(ii) **Controlled Legal Representation (Help at Court; CLR)**

- representation at a First-tier Tribunal or Upper Tribunal statutory appeal in relation to rights to enter or remain in the UK arising from the Refugee Convention 1951 or ECHR, Arts 2 and 3 (asylum/international protection claims[45];

- representation at a First-tier Tribunal or Upper Tribunal statutory appeal to appeal a refusal of any type of immigration claim where an individual has been granted a positive reasonable grounds decision or conclusive grounds decision[46]; and

- if a potential victim of trafficking is detained, representation at a tribunal to represent him at a bail hearing[47];

(iii) **Civil Legal Aid**

- civil legal services provided in relation to judicial review of an enactment, decision, act or omission, subject to the exclusions set out in LASPO 2012 (discussed below)[48].

---

41 LASPO 2012, Sch 1, Part 1, para 30(1).
42 LASPO 2012, Sch 1, Part 1, para 32(1).
43 LASPO 2012, Sch 1, Part 1, paras 25–26.
44 LASPO 2012, Sch 1, Part 1, para 27.
45 LASPO 2012, Sch 1, Part 1, para 30(1).
46 LASPO 2012, Sch 1, Part 1, para 32(1).
47 LASPO 2012, Sch 1, Part 1, paras 25–26.
48 LASPO 2012, Sch 1, Part 1, para 19.

13.131

It should be noted that where an individual has a positive reasonable grounds or conclusive grounds decision, this opens up the possibility of legal aid representation for that individual in immigration matters which are normally out of scope for legal aid. The most common relevant claims for (potential) victims of trafficking are claims based on ECHR, Art 8 (family and private life), claims based on the free movement rights of EEA nationals and/or their family members (relying on the EU Directives and Regulations which flow from their 'Treaty rights' under Art 45 of the Treaty on the Functioning of the European Union) and representations made to request a grant of discretionary leave to remain as a victim of trafficking in the UK. Further, whilst many areas of immigration law are out of scope for Legal Help and CLR, an individual can potentially later secure legal aid to fund a judicial review challenge of a decision, act or omission of a public body taken in respect of an out of scope area of law.

The gap in legal aid provision for victims of trafficking

13.132

Notwithstanding this advantage for potential victims of trafficking, LASPO 2012 created a gap in the legal aid available for such persons who have not received a positive reasonable grounds decision or who have a negative reasonable/conclusive grounds decision (in Legal Help/CLR matters). This lacuna is concerning, particularly given that potential victims of trafficking can be at their most vulnerable before receiving a positive reasonable grounds decision or after receiving a negative reasonable or conclusive grounds decision. Legal intervention is often critical at these stages.

13.133

There are some practical solutions available to the legal aid practitioner in these circumstances. Firstly, it is possible to provide advice and assistance to a potential victim of trafficking if the trafficking claim is inextricably linked to a matter that is within scope under LASPO 2012. A common example is a potential victim of trafficking who also has an international protection claim. For example, if a potential victim of trafficking fears return to his country of origin because he fears his traffickers, or if he is at risk of re-trafficking on return and faces conditions of destitution, this is likely to be so intertwined with his protection claim that the provider is justified in advising and making representations in relation to the trafficking claim, as the asylum claim cannot be properly determined without first considering the trafficking claim. Secondly, another common scenario arises where an advice on a potential/refused trafficking claim is linked to advice and assistance on detention and temporary admission (which is within scope). The Home Office guidance provides that if someone is a potential victim of trafficking, it is an indication that he may be vulnerable within detention, and progressing that person's trafficking claim can be essential to securing his release from immigration detention and/or challenging the legality of his detention[49]. It is advisable to set out in a detailed attendance note justification for providing advice and representation specific to the trafficking claim by detailing how the trafficking claim is linked to the 'in scope' aspects of the case.

13.134

An alternative approach is to open a Legal Help for pre-action work only. This may be suitable if the potential victim of trafficking already has a negative reasonable grounds or conclusive grounds decision at the point of instruction, or there is an issue in a pre-reasonable grounds case which may be challenged by way of judicial review. A pre-action Legal Help is funded as an hourly-rates matter with a limit of £500 for profit costs and £400 for disbursements[50].

Exceptional case funding

13.135

When LASPO 2012 removed large swathes of legal aid assistance for the general population, provision for legal aid funding to be granted in exceptional cases on any out of scope matter was provided for through the possibility of a grant of Exceptional Case Funding ('ECF'). The aim of ECF is to provide a mechanism by which to avoid a breach of ECHR, or a breach of Art 47 of the Charter of Fundamental Rights of the European Union.

13.136

If funding is granted under ECF the individual can access legal aid representation. An ECF team within LAA deals with such applications and cases. To qualify for ECF, the person must meet the ECF criteria as set out in LASPO 2012 and described in the Lord Chancellor's funding guidance;[51] they must be financially eligible for legal aid and their case must meet the merits criteria. Form CIV ECF1 should be completed and signed by the potential victim of trafficking. The application should be sent with a copy of the CW1 (Legal Help form) or CW2 (controlled legal representation) (depending on the type of matter), along with the relevant evidence to meet the ECF criteria and sent by post to Legal Aid Agency: Post Point 8.51, Eighth Floor, 102 Petty France London SW1H 9AJ or Legal Aid Agency, DX 161440 Westminster 8. Applications may

---

49 Home Office, *Immigration Act 2016, Adults at Risk in Immigration Detention* (August 2016); Home Office, *Victims of modern slavery – Competent Authority guidance* (21 March 2016) p 57.
50 2013 Standard Civil Contract Specification: Immigration and Asylum, Part D, section 8 (amended July 2015).
51 Legal Aid: Exceptional Case Funding Form and Guidance, 1 June 2014, available at www.gov.uk/government/publications/legal-aid-exceptional-case-funding-form-and-guidance, last accessed 5 January 2018.

also be scanned and submitted by e-mail to the ECF team e-mail address at contactECC@legalaid.gsi.gov.uk. At present the LAA aim to process claims within 20 working days and if funding is granted, it will be back-dated to the date the CIV ECF1 was signed. If a decision is required urgently, this should be flagged up with the ECF team. If a provider is applying for a civil legal aid in a non-judicial review matter which is out of scope, exceptional case funding can be applied for online via the Client and Cost Management System (see para **13.164** below).

13.137

An ECF grant of funding can apply to part of a case, if only part of the case is in scope for legal aid funding. For example, the provider may be providing Legal Help advice on a protection claim and a trafficking claim, however there may be an additional element of the case, such as a claim under Art 8 ECHR, which will require a grant of exceptional case funding. If the potential victim of trafficking is then granted a positive reasonable or conclusive grounds decision, all immigration legal work is then in scope. Conversely, providers may also need to be alert to potentially having to apply for exceptional case funding part way through a case. For example, if Legal Help was initially provided on the basis of a positive reasonable grounds decision, but subsequently the potential victim of trafficking is given a negative conclusive grounds decision and there is no other way of justifying representation.

Legal aid for potential victims of trafficking in immigration detention

13.138

It is common to encounter potential victims of trafficking who are detained in an Immigration Removal Centre. All detainees are able to sign up to receive 30 minutes free legal advice from the duty solicitor at advice surgeries that are held regularly (normally a few times per week) at all the detention centres around the UK. The detainees should put their name on the list for legal advice at the library or the welfare office within the detention centre. The 30 minutes advice can be in relation to any immigration/detention matter, even if it is out of scope. However, if the detainee is signed up for legal aid, it must be a matter that is within scope under LASPO 2012, otherwise ECF must be applied for.

13.139

At present only specific legal aid providers who have an exclusive schedule agreement with the LAA can attend the duty advice surgeries. The exclusive schedule agreement providers are contractually obliged to take on all cases which meet the financial means and merits eligibility requirements. These providers are also allocated the cases of detainees whose asylum claims are being processed in the detained asylum casework process through a rota. Only exclusive schedule agreement providers can take on cases for Legal Help and Controlled Legal Representation through the rota or the detention advice surgeries[52]. Other than via the detention advice surgeries, detainees can only be represented by a legal aid provider without an exclusive schedule agreement if: (i) the provider has already carried out at least five hours of work on the case; (ii) they already represent a close family member and it is in the detainee's best interests to continue to be represented by that legal aid provider instead of an exclusive schedule agreement provider; or (iii) where there are no exclusive schedule agreements where the person is detained[53].

What practical steps are needed to represent a potential victim of trafficking under legal aid in immigration matters?

Legal help

13.140

In order for an immigration legal representative to begin assisting a potential victim of trafficking, the common starting point is by opening a Legal Help matter so that the legal representative can take initial instructions and give initial advice. The legal aid provider will complete a CW1 form[54] with the client, and once the declaration has been fully understood and signed by the client, the practitioner can open a file and begin work.

Evidence of means

13.141

Detailed guidance as to what evidence of means (evidence of a client's income and savings showing their financial eligibility for legal aid) is required is set out in the LAA Guidance. All practitioners should comply with this guidance[55].

---

52 2013 Standard Civil Contract Specification: Immigration and Asylum, section 8, para 8.5 (amended July 2015), available at www.gov.uk/government/uploads/system/uploads/attachment_data/file/441393/category-specific-rules-immigration-and-asylum.pdf, last accessed 5 January 2018.
53 2013 Standard Civil Contract Specification: Immigration and Asylum, section 8, para 8.5 (amended July 2015).
54 CW1 form, available at www.gov.uk/government/uploads/system/uploads/attachment_data/file/346196/legal-aid-controlled-work-1.pdf, last accessed 5 January 2018.
55 Legal Aid Agency, *Guide to Determining Financial Eligibility for Controlled Work and Family Mediation* (April 2015), available at www.gov.uk/government/uploads/system/uploads/attachment_data/file/420970/laa-determine-controlled-work-mediation.pdf, last accessed 5 January 2018.

13.142

Certain individuals are 'passported' and do not require evidence of means other than evidence that they are in receipt of the passported benefit. The relevant benefits are Income Support, Income-based Jobseeker's Allowance, Income-related Employment and Support Allowance or Guarantee Credit or asylum support provided by the Home Office[56]. In all other cases, evidence of the potential victim of trafficking's income (and their partner's income if necessary) which was received during the exact month prior to the client signing the form (the computation period) is required. For example, bank statements, pay slips and a tenancy agreement. If a potential victim of trafficking has no income and is supported by friends or a third party, a letter of support from the person/third party supporting them should be provided, confirming what support is provided and since when.

13.143

In practice many potential victims of trafficking are destitute or have a very low income, and are likely to be eligible for legal aid. In order to be eligible, after deducting income needed for outgoings for dependants, housing costs and other specified expenses, the individual qualifies if they have £733 per calendar month or less in disposable income and £8,000 or less in savings. In some cases a potential victim of trafficking may state that he has no access to any income or capital, and he has no documentary evidence showing this. It would be for the provider to decide and make a detailed note on the file whether such a statement was credible and whether or not it was therefore impracticable to obtain evidence of means. A common scenario is for a potential victim of trafficking to instruct his legal representative whilst in prison or detention where he has been detained for the computation period, and the only income received by the client is a small amount of pocket money provided to all those detained/incarcerated. It is not necessary to provide evidence of the income from this pocket money in such cases and an explanation should be provided on the file/legal aid form. A further common scenario is where a potential victim of trafficking has recently escaped a trafficking situation and it is not practical or safe for him to obtain evidence of any past income. Again, a detailed explanation should be provided on file.

Merits

13.144

To open a Legal Help file the provider should be satisfied that there is likely to be sufficient benefit to the individual, having regard to all the circumstances of the case, including the circumstances of the individual, to justify the cost of provision of Legal Help. The test for sufficient benefit is whether a reasonable private paying individual of moderate means would pay for the legal advice and

---

56 Support provided under the Immigration and Asylum Act 1999, s 4 and s 95.

assistance[57]. The guidance recognises that even in a matter with poor prospects of success, it may well be considered worthwhile for an individual to pay for initial advice, including the advice that the case is not worth pursuing further. The low threshold of the Sufficient Benefit test allows practitioners to open a Legal Help file in most cases in the first instance. However, the Sufficient Benefit test should be continually reviewed as the case continues, as the more Legal Help is provided, the more that the benefits deriving from the costs incurred will need to be taken into account[58].

Controlled Legal Representation

13.145

Controlled Legal Representation ('CLR' or 'Help at Court') may be granted by a legal aid provider to represent a client at the First Tier Tribunal or Upper Tribunal where there is a statutory right of appeal, and the matter is either in scope for legal aid or ECF funding has been granted. There is no statutory right of appeal in the event of negative reasonable grounds or conclusive grounds decision. However, as explained above, the potential victim of trafficking may also have an international protection claim which is inextricably linked to his trafficking claim, and therefore it is common for providers to grant CLR to represent clients at the Tribunal in relation to their protection claim and trafficking claim on this basis. Further, although an NRM decision is not an immigration decision, in *MS (Trafficking – Tribunal's Powers – Art 4 ECHR) Pakistan*[59], the Upper Tribunal held that although bringing judicial review proceedings provides the appropriate mechanism for a direct challenge of a negative NRM decision, the Tribunal does have jurisdiction to make its own decision on whether an appellant was a victim of trafficking or whether the respondent failed to follow its published policy in making an NRM decision.

13.146

The Civil Legal Aid (Remuneration) Regulations 2013[60] and the LAA guidance provide detailed information as to which matters are funded by hourly rates for the work carried out, and which cases are paid by the graduated fixed fee scheme, in addition to how much is payable for profit costs and disbursements. However, the profit costs and disbursements limits for CLR are higher than for Legal Help[61]. For graduated fixed fee matters in CLR matters, payment is divided into stage 2A (where CLR is granted to prepare an appeal but matter concludes

---

57 Lord Chancellor's Guidance, para 4.2.13, available at www.gov.uk/government/uploads/system/ uploads/attachment_data/file/330878/legal-aid-LAA-lord-chancellors-guidance.pdf, last accessed 5 January 2018.
58 Lord Chancellor's Guidance, para 4.2.14, see fn 57.
59 [2016] UKUT 00226 (IAC).
60 SI 2013/422.
61 Civil Legal Aid (Remuneration) Regulations 2013, Sch 1; 2013 Standard Civil Contract Specification: Immigration and Asylum, Part D (amended July 2015).

prior to the substantive hearing) and stage 2B (where a substantive hearing takes place)[62]. CLR can also be granted to represent a detainee at a First-tier Tribunal bail hearing, which is an hourly rates matter with a limit of £500, including disbursements. The legal aid provider will complete a CW2 IMM form[63] with the potential victim of trafficking, and once the declaration is fully understood and signed by the client, the practitioner can open a file and begin work.

Evidence of means

13.147

The evidence of means required is the same as set out for Legal Help (see paras **13.141–13.143**). Note, however, that for a grant of CLR, the capital savings limit is £3,000, rather than £8,000. The computation period is also one exact month prior to signing the CW2 IMM form.

Merits

13.148

CLR can only be granted where there is likely to be sufficient benefit to the individual, having regard to all the circumstances of the case, including the circumstances of the individual, to justify the cost of provision of help at court. The nature and circumstances of: (i) the proceedings; (ii) the particular hearing; and (iii) the individual, must be such that advocacy is appropriate and will be of real benefit to that individual[64]. The provider should be satisfied that there is more than a 50-50 chance of success. If a provider deems there is insufficient merit, he must advise the client of a right of review to the LAA of the provider's decision and assist him in completing a CW4 form[65].

Legal Help and CLR: extensions, costs limits and experts

13.149

The Civil Legal Aid (Remuneration) Regulations 2013 and the LAA guidance provide detailed information as to which matters are funded by hourly rates for the work carried out and which cases are paid by the graduated fixed fee scheme, in addition to how much is payable for profit costs and disbursements[66].

---

62 2013 Standard Civil Contract Specification: Immigration and Asylum, section 8, paras 8.64 and 8.65 (amended July 2015) 8.64 and 8.65.
63 Available at www.gov.uk/government/uploads/system/uploads/attachment_data/file/346246/legal-aid-controlled-work-2-immigration.pdf, last accessed 5 January 2018.
64 Civil Legal Aid (Merits Criteria) Regulations 2013, reg 33.
65 Available at www.gov.uk/government/uploads/system/uploads/attachment_data/file/346249/laa-cw4-version-10-8-2014.pdf, last accessed 5 January 2018.
66 Civil Legal Aid (Remuneration) Regulations 2013, Sch 1; 2013 Standard Civil Contract Specification: Immigration and Asylum, section 8, Part D (amended July 2015).

A provider will only be paid the fixed fee for a case, even if he has carried out more work than the fixed fee value, unless the work carried out has reached three times the value of the fixed fee, when it will then become payable by hourly rates, subject to being assessed and accepted as the same by the LAA as an 'Escape Fee Case' before payment is approved. In practice, given that many trafficking cases are complex, the clients are vulnerable and it may be necessary to instruct experts, it is common to reach the escape fee threshold.

13.150

Instructing experts to assess potential victims of trafficking and produce expert reports can be crucial to the prospects of success of a case and case planning should always consider whether an expert should be instructed to address any material issue. When representing victims of trafficking, experts that are commonly instructed include psychologists, psychiatrists, scarring experts and trafficking experts. Providers should refer to the detailed LAA guidance on requesting funding for experts before applying for funding for experts on Legal Help and CLR cases[67]. Funding for expert reports in a pre-decision Legal Help case can be difficult to secure, therefore it may be preferable to consider whether funding can be obtained for expert reports after the grant of a legal aid certificate or for a CLR appeal matter.

13.151

Extensions for disbursements in graduated fixed fee cases are applied for via form CW3C, and hourly rates cases via form CW3B. A paper form can be completed and scanned, however it is envisaged that eventually extensions will only be submitted via the electronic online form. At present, both can be submitted via email to cw3@legalaid.gsi.gov.uk.

Civil legal aid for judicial review

13.152

As there is no right of appeal against a negative reasonable or conclusive grounds decision, providers have to apply for a civil legal aid certificate to fund potential judicial review proceedings to challenge such negative decisions.

Evidence of means

13.153

The evidence of means required for an application for a civil legal aid certificate is similar to controlled representation, although providers should refer to the

---

67 Legal Aid Agency, *Escape Cases Electronic Handbook, Controlled Work* (updated 21 April 2017), available at www.gov.uk/government/uploads/system/uploads/attachment_data/file/610132/escape-cases-electronic-handbook-v.1.6.pdf, last accessed 5 January 2018.

guidance specific to certificated legal aid[68]. Evidence of income and savings for the three months prior to instruction is required, rather than one month. In practice many potential victims of trafficking are destitute or have a very low income, and are likely to be eligible for legal aid. The maximum income threshold per calendar month is still £733, however if a client earns between £316 and £733 per calendar month, or has capital savings over £3,000, a monthly contribution is payable[69]. The maximum capital savings limit is £8,000.

Merits

13.154

The provider must firstly be satisfied of the standard criteria for determinations of legal representation: that the client could not pay for their legal case by any other means, that the client has exhausted other remedies and that there is a need for legal representation, considering the complexity, the interests of the parties and existence of other proceedings[70]. As many potential victims of trafficking have limited resources, there is no statutory right of appeal against a negative trafficking decision and a judicial review challenge is likely to be complex, the standard criteria for civil legal aid is likely to be met in most cases. Additionally, for immigration judicial reviews, LASPO 2012 excludes potential victims of trafficking from civil legal representation where a previous judicial review or appeal to a court or tribunal about the same/substantially the same issue was refused, and that the new legal aid is applied for before the end of the period of one year beginning with the day of that refused determination[71]. However, this exclusion does not apply where the potential judicial review relates to removal directions where the directions were given not more than one year after the latest of: (i) the decision to remove the individual by way of removal directions; (ii) the refusal of leave to appeal against that decision; and (iii) the determination or withdrawal of an appeal against that decision[72].

13.155

When the representative has considered the merits of the case, he must then decide whether to apply for investigative representation or full representation.

Investigative representation

13.156

Investigative representation is defined as:

---

68 Legal Aid Agency, *Means Assessment Guidance* (2 April 2015), available at www.gov.uk/government/uploads/system/uploads/attachment_data/file/420973/means-assessment-guidance.pdf, last accessed 5 January 2018.
69 Ibid, App 11.
70 Civil Legal Aid (Merits Criteria) Regulations 2013, reg 39.
71 LASPO 2012, Sch 1, para 19(5).
72 LASPO 2012, Sch 1, para 19(6).

'legal representation which is limited to the investigation of the strength of the contemplated proceedings and includes the issuing and conducting of proceedings but only so far as necessary: (a) to obtain disclosure of information relevant to the prospects of success of the proceedings; (b) to protect the position of the individual or legal person applying for investigative representation in relation to an urgent hearing; or (c) to protect the position of the individual or legal person applying for investigative representation in relation to the time limit for the issue of the proceedings'[73].

13.157

A legal aid certificate for investigative representation is appropriate in cases where: (i) the prospects of success of the case are 'unclear' and substantial investigative work is required before those prospects can be determined; and (ii) there are reasonable grounds for believing that, once the investigative work is completed, the case will satisfy the criteria for full representation (discussed below)[74]. For a potential judicial review, funding under investigative help would only be granted if the LAA accepts that: (a) the act, omission or other matter complained of in the proposed proceedings appears to be susceptible to challenge; and (b) the individual exhausted all administrative appeals and other alternative procedures which are available to challenge the act, omission or other matter before bringing a public law claim[75].

13.158

Before applying for investigative representation, the representative has to notify the proposed defendant of the individual's potential challenge, which can be done by way of a simple letter to the Home Office caseworker and litigation team. If this is not done, the representative must provide the LAA with evidence as to why doing so would be impracticable[76].

Full representation

13.159

Although it is possible to issue judicial review proceedings on an investigative representation certificate, it is more commonly done with a full representation legal aid certificate. To meet the merits test for full representation the prospects of success at a final hearing should be:

- 'very good' (80% or more chance of obtaining a successful outcome);

---

73 Civil Legal Aid (Merits Criteria) Regulations 2013, reg 18.
74 Ibid reg 40.
75 Ibid reg 53.
76 Ibid reg 54.

- 'good' (60% or more chance, but less than 80%); or

- 'moderate' (at least 50%, but less than 60%)[77].

13.160

If the prospects of success are:

- 'borderline' (not possible, by reason of disputed law, fact or expert evidence to decide whether the case is 'moderate' or 'poor'); or

- 'poor' (20% or more chance, but less than a 50% chance),

the test is only met if it is necessary to represent the client to prevent a breach of: (i) the individual's Convention rights; or (ii) any rights of the individual to the provision of legal services that are enforceable EU rights[78].

13.161

If the prospects of success are 'very poor' (less than 20% chance of obtaining a successful outcome), funding would not be granted. However, if the prospects of success become very poor and services have been provided on the basis that a case has significant wider public interest, and the case is close to trial it may be appropriate to fund the case to a conclusion if there may be a public benefit in having a legal issue resolved one way or the other[79].

13.162

Note the distinction between 'unclear' merits as opposed to 'borderline' or 'poor' merits. In 'unclear' prospect cases, there must be identifiable preliminary investigations that can be undertaken, after which it should be possible to assess prospects as within one of the other categories. By contrast, the prospects of success of a case assessed as borderline may remain uncertain up to a final hearing itself[80].

13.163

The cost benefit criteria must also be met. In many cases, challenging a negative trafficking decision where the claim is not primarily for damages is likely to meet the test of 'overwhelming importance to the individual', and accordingly, the cost benefit criteria is met if the Director of Legal Aid Casework is satisfied that a reasonably private paying individual would pay for the legal services[81]. For damages claims, the specific cost benefit ratio should be satisfied, which is set out in the regulations[82].

---

77 Ibid reg 60(3)(a), amended by the Civil Legal Aid (Merits Criteria) (Amendment No 2) Regulations 2015.
78 Ibid reg 60(3), (5), amended by the Civil Legal Aid (Merits Criteria) (Amendment No 2) Regulations 2015.
79 Lord Chancellor's Guidance, para 8.49, see fn 57.
80 Lord Chancellor's Guidance, para 4.1.3, see fn 57.
81 Civil Legal Aid (Merits Criteria) Regulations 2013, reg 42(3).
82 Ibid reg 42(2).

Application process

13.164

An application for investigative or full civil legal aid representation is now done online via the LAA online portal, Client and Cost Management System ('CCMS')[83]. To complete the application, the client (and his partner, if relevant) would need to attend the representative's office with his evidence relating to his financial eligibility and the merits of his case. At the appointment, the legal representative then uploads all the relevant information and evidence to CCMS with the client, the declarations relating to means and merits must be read to the client and, if he agrees, the application is submitted, printed and signed by the client (and his partner, if relevant) at the same appointment.

Emergency certificate

13.165

It is frequently necessary to apply for an emergency legal aid certificate. For example, if a client is detained, if a client has received a notice of a scheduled removal/deportation from the UK (with or without notice), or the limitation period is due to expire or has already expired. In such circumstances an emergency certificate can be applied for. The LAA aim to process emergency certificates within 48 hours, therefore the representative must factor in the time required to wait for the certificate to be considered and processed by the LAA when advising clients on whether it is feasible to issue judicial review proceedings on an emergency basis. For example, if an advisor encountered a potential victim of trafficking at a detention surgery with a viable judicial review challenge and a flight to remove that person from the UK had been scheduled, the representative would usually need to factor in four clear working days in order to prevent a removal by issuing judicial review proceedings: 24 hours to send pre-action correspondence (if a truncated timescale for a response is required owing to the urgency) and wait for a response, 48 hours to apply for emergency legal aid and wait for a response, 24 hours for counsel to draft grounds and issue proceedings. If the emergency certificate is granted, it will be to cover all steps up to the decision on permission on the papers, to the value of £1,350. The emergency certificate expires eight weeks after the grant and the representative must ensure that he applies to amend the emergency certificate to a substantive certificate within seven calendar days of the grant of the emergency certificate.

---

83 See https://portal.legalservices.gov.uk.

Substantive certificate

13.166

A substantive certificate can be applied for either by amending an emergency certificate within seven calendar days of the grant of the emergency certificate, or by applying for a substantive certificate in the first instance. At present it takes between one week and three weeks to wait for a grant of a substantive certificate. If granted, funding is granted for all steps and all costs (including counsel's fees, disbursements and expert's fees) until a decision on permission on the papers to a value of £2,250.

Declaration against instructions

13.167

As above, a legal aid practitioner representing a potential victim of trafficking should be ready for a potential judicial review from the point of instruction, and to potentially do so on an emergency basis. For this reason, in addition to completing the relevant legal aid forms with the client at the first interview – to enable the representative to assist the client under Legal Help or controlled legal representation, it is also prudent to take the necessary instructions/evidence needed to complete and sign the 'declaration against instructions' form[84]. This is in case it is necessary to apply for investigative or full representation on an emergency or substantive application and the client (or his partner, if relevant) is unable to attend the office for a good reason (for example, if he is hospitalised, imprisoned or detained).

13.168

Before the client (and his partner, if necessary) signs the declaration against instructions, the representative should either have first completed the paper means and merits forms (CIV APP1 and correct CIV MEANS form)[85] or have drafted his own attendance note to record the client's information about his means and the merits of his case. This information will be inputted onto CCMS once instructions have been obtained. The signed declaration against instructions will then replace the signature that would usually be obtained on the Application Summary screen on CCMS. In order to ensure the client retains the protection awarded by the existing process, the Application Summary must be sent by the provider to the client, and the client is given 14 days to advise if any of the information is incorrect. If any of the information is incorrect a further signed declaration should be obtained. The provider should

---

84 See http://ccmstraining.justice.gov.uk/__data/assets/pdf_file/0010/7975/CCMS_Client-Declaration-Against-Instructions.pdf, last visited 5 January 2018.
85 Available at www.gov.uk/topic/legal-aid-for-providers/forms, last visited 5 January 2018.

give the required warnings and information as stated in the means and merits declarations to the client. Providers must comply with the full process as set out by the LAA in its guidance[86].

The permission decision, amending scope

13.169

After proceedings are issued and a permission decision on the papers is received, if permission is granted, the provider must pay the continuation fee to the court and also apply to amend the scope of the legal aid certificate to cover all steps up to and including the full trial. If permission is refused, if the provider is instructed to apply for permission to be heard at an oral renewal hearing, the provider must seek counsel's opinion on prospects of success at an oral renewal hearing. If there are sufficient merits, the provider must apply to amend the scope of the certificate to cover the costs of an oral renewal hearing. Amendments to the scope and costs limit are done on CCMS.

Experts and extensions of cost limits

13.170

Instructing experts to assess potential victims of trafficking and produce expert reports can be crucial to the prospects of success of a case and case planning should always consider whether an expert should be instructed to address any material issue in the case. It is advisable to seek counsel's opinion as to whether experts should be instructed. The LAA Guidance on the Remuneration of Expert Witnesses[87] introduced new rates for most types of expert, instructed since 2 December 2013. The rates are set out in Annex 1 of the Guidance. The LAA cannot pay fees or rates in excess of those listed in the guidance or the Civil Legal Aid (Remuneration) (Amendment) Regulations 2013 unless the LAA has granted prior authority to exceed the fees or rates. If an expert can be instructed within the existing costs limit on the certificate, it should be within the codified rates at Annex 1 in the guidance and there should be clear justification on the file as to why an expert is needed. If the type of expert is not listed in Annex 1 and/or there are insufficient funds to pay for the expert within the existing cost limit, prior authority should be applied for before instructing the expert. The application to request prior authority or increase the cost limit should be done on CCMS.

---

86 See http://ccmstraining.justice.gov.uk/__data/assets/pdf_file/0010/7966/Client-Declaration-Against-Instructions-v2-0.pdf, last visited 5 January 2018.

87 Legal Aid Agency, *Guidance on the Remuneration of Expert Witnesses* (reviewed September 2014), available at www.gov.uk/government/uploads/system/uploads/attachment_data/file/420106/expert-witnesses-fees-guidance.pdf, last visited 5 January 2018.

Civil legal aid: financial risks

13.171

Unfortunately the legal aid provider bears a disproportionate financial risk in terms of payment for judicial review cases and all providers should be fully alive to the financial risks they are undertaking by applying for certificated legal aid on behalf of the client. The Civil Legal Aid (Remuneration) Regulations 2013[88] provide that the representative is only paid for the work carried out if:

- the court gives permission to bring judicial review proceedings;

- the court neither gives nor refuses permission, and the LAA considers payment is reasonable in the circumstances: a 'discretionary payment';

- the defendant withdraws the decision to which the application for judicial review relates and the withdrawal results in the court (a) refusing permission to bring judicial review proceedings, or (b) neither refusing nor giving permission;

- the court orders an oral hearing to consider whether to give permission to bring judicial review proceedings;

- the court orders a rolled-up hearing.

13.172

The financial risk to providers is particularly acute in this area of law where the representative may have to deal with unforeseen circumstances such as a potential victim of trafficking who goes missing/is potentially re-trafficked before judicial review proceedings are concluded. Whether a case is granted permission or not, particularly on a decision made on the papers, is not necessarily an indication of the merits of the case. In cases where a potential victim of trafficking has gone missing, it may be advisable to seek a stay in proceedings to protect the client's position. However, this is also a difficult financial burden for the representative who has a refusal of permission on papers and was awaiting an oral permission hearing. In such circumstances, the provider cannot expect payment unless the client is encountered, his claim is continued and thereafter a positive permission decision is made. However, if no decision has been made on the papers, it is possible to apply for a discretionary payment (as above). It should also be noted that the provider will be paid for work carried out in relation to applications for interim relief and some disbursements, even if the rest of the work is not paid for under the Civil Legal Aid (Remuneration) Regulations 2013[89].

---

88 Regulation 5A, as inserted by the Civil Legal Aid (Remuneration) (Amendment) Regulations 2015, SI 2015/898. The position now generally reflects the previous position, as set out by the Civil Legal Aid (Remuneration) (Amendment) (No 3) Regulations 2014, SI 2014/607, while additionally taking into account the findings of the High Court in *R (on the application of Ben Hoare Bell Solicitors) v The Lord Chancellor* [2015] EWHC 523 (Admin).

89 As amended by the Civil Legal Aid (Remuneration) (Amendment) Regulations 2015, regs 2(2) and (3).

14 Extradition

Introduction

14.1

Extradition proceedings are a sub-set of general crime, but follow their own timetable and do not involve a finding of guilt or innocence. Whether an individual who is subject to extradition proceedings ('the requested person') has been, is, or might also be a victim of trafficking is likely to be an important issue, both procedurally and substantively.

14.2

The National Crime Agency ('NCA') record of European Arrest Warrant ('EAW') numbers and consequent UK arrests gives a flavour of the significant growth in extradition proceedings, suggesting that this area deserves to be considered in its own right[1]:

Fiscal year	2007–08	2008–09	2009–10	2010–11	2013–14	2014–15	2015–16
EAWs certified	2,483	3,526	3,870	5,770	7,881	12,134	14,279
UK EAW arrests	546	683	1,057	1,295	1,660	1,586	2,102

14.3

With the commitment towards increased UK trafficking prosecutions, better awareness, and hopefully an increasingly effective National Referral Mechanism ('NRM'), more extradition cases involving a victim or potential trafficking victim seem likely.

14.4

Guidance as to how trafficking issues should be dealt with within extradition proceedings is conspicuous by its absence. The House of Lords Select Committee on Extradition Law briefly referred to three issues:

---

1 NCA statistics per fiscal year are available at www.nationalcrimeagency.gov.uk/publications/european-arrest-warrant-statistics/historical-eaw-statistics/693-historical-european-arrest-warrants-statistics-calendar-and-financial-year-totals-2004-may-2016 and www.nationalcrimeagency.gov.uk/publications/european-arrest-warrant-statistics/wanted-from-the-uk-european-arrest-warrant-statistics/830-eaw-part-1-master-fiscal-year-v1-0-final-2009-2017, last accessed 8 January 2018.

- 'how extradition hearings should interact with the obligations that the ECHR places on a state where a person has been the victim of trafficking;

- how the courts can make a proper evaluation of whether the claim is true; and

- what assessment the courts can make of what potential there might be for being re-trafficked if extradited'[2].

14.5

The Committee concluded 'further investigation [of this area] is necessary' so recommended 'the government commission a review into these matters'[3]. The government reply promised to 'give further consideration to how extradition law ought to interact with ... people trafficking law'[4], but to date the only developments have been through the courts, mostly via cases limited to their own facts[5].

14.6

In terms of procedure, extradition cases are supposed to be fast, so they do not sit well with the time required for an NRM assessment (see Chapter 2).

14.7

If a person is identified as a victim of trafficking then that *might* explain the commission of the extradition offence. However, scenarios where there is a causal link between the requested person's extradition offence (whether convicted or merely accused) and trafficking are comparatively rare, as opposed to discrete criminal proceedings prompting an extradition request which focus on entirely distinct offending and have no nexus to the trafficking of the individual. Attempts to raise trafficking as an issue in the latter category of unrelated offending have attracted harsh commentary from the Divisional Court, even endorsing an assessment by the District Judge in place of a conclusive NRM decision[6]. It remains to be seen whether this will continue to be the approach of the extradition courts in the light of the Lord Chief Justice's judgment in *R v Joseph*[7], endorsing the former Lord Chief Justice's judgment in *R v L*[8], viz the weight to be placed on identification decisions by the competent authority. In any event, the court in *Ministry of Justice of Lithuania v AI*[9] did consider and place

---

2 House of Lords Select Committee, *Extradition: UK Law and Practice* p 58 (Recommendation 8; para 199) (10 March 2015).
3 Ibid.
4 Government response to the second report from the Select Committee on Extradition Law, p 5 (July 2015).
5 Eg *Ministry of Justice of Lithuania v AI* [2010] EWHC 2299 (Admin) and *Z v Poland* [2014] EWHC 1242 (Admin).
6 *Polish Judicial Authorities v Celinski* [2015] EWHC 1274 (Admin), [2016] 1 WLR 551, paras 42–53. However, this must be read in the light of *R v Joseph* [2017] EWCA Crim 36, [2017] 1 WLR 3153.
7 [2017] EWCA Crim 36, [2017] 1 WLR 3153. See para 20 of the judgment.
8 [2013] EWCA Crim 991, [2014] 1 All ER 113.
9 [2010] EWHC 2299 (Admin) 2010 WL 3515648.

significant weight upon the evidence of AI's trafficking and the psychological harm that had been caused to AI as a consequence of her trafficking. The court concluded in the face of this evidence that there would be a real risk that AI's rights under the ECHR, Art 3 would be breached if extradited to Lithuania. In *AI* the trafficking had no nexus to the offending which was the subject of the extradition and had post-dated the offending.

14.8

In the event that there is a link between the extradition offence and the trafficking of the individual, arguably the non-punishment provisions (see Chapter 5) should be considered by the requesting judicial authority or state before proceeding with the request. How this would work in practice is uncharted territory[10]. In *Polish Judicial Authorities v Celinski*[11], the court observed that factors that mitigate the gravity of the offence or culpability will ordinarily be matters that the court in the requesting state will take into account. However, where there is a nexus between the offending and the trafficking, consideration should be given as to how the requesting state implements the identification of victims and non-punishment provisions of ECAT and the EU Trafficking Directive. As identified by the Group of Experts on Action against Trafficking in Human Beings ('GRETA')[12] in their country reports, there are countries that have not effectively (or at all) implemented either identification mechanisms or the non-punishment provisions.

14.9

Nevertheless, if trafficking status is confirmed, there will normally be obvious consequences for substantive issues that are in any event routinely raised within extradition proceedings (eg the passage of time, ECHR, Art 4 and Art 8).

Extradition proceedings

Generally

14.10

Extradition is the legal transfer of an individual in custody for the purpose of criminal prosecution, sentencing, or the implementation of a custodial sentence previously imposed[13].

---

10 But referred to by Mitting J in *Z v Poland* [2014] EWHC 1242 (Admin), para 17 (obiter dicta).
11 [2015] EWHC 1274 (Admin), [2016] 1 WLR 551.
12 ECAT set up a mechanism to monitor compliance with the obligations contained in it. This monitoring mechanism is composed of GRETA, a multidisciplinary panel of 15 independent experts, and the Committee of the Parties to the Convention.
13 J Jones and R Davidson, *Extradition and Mutual Legal Assistance Handbook* (Oxford University Press, 2010) p 3.

14.11

The majority of extradition proceedings concern individuals arrested in this jurisdiction, wanted for prosecution or custodial punishment elsewhere, so-called 'export' extradition. 'Import' extradition requests issued from this jurisdiction, justifying arrest elsewhere and requesting extradition to our courts do not involve proceedings in open court, so will only become public during consequent criminal proceedings. In those circumstances the interaction of the trafficking issue with extradition proceedings is likely to be subordinate to any trafficking issue which could be raised during the criminal trial in any event.

14.12

In 'export' extradition cases, proceedings will either fall under the Extradition Act 2003 ('EA 2003'), Part 1 or 2, which codify a broad range of pre-existing schemes and police powers. Following arrest in this jurisdiction, the EA 2003 requires production in custody at Westminster Magistrates' Court[14] for a first appearance, or 'initial hearing' (eg EA 2003, ss 7–8 in Part 1 cases)[15]. Therefore there will not have been a police interview prior to the first court appearance.

14.13

The vast majority of 'export' extradition cases before Westminster Magistrates' Court are based on EAWs, pursuant to the EA 2003, Part 1[16]. The object of the EAW system is to remove the complexity and potential for delay inherent within extradition proceedings, by introducing a simplified system of surrender based on mutual respect for each state within the EAW framework[17]. Each Member State is supposed to have confidence in other Member States honouring their pre-existing obligations under the ECHR. This is, of course, subject to a person's pre-existing fundamental human rights[18]. In short, surrender is the rule and refusal is the exception, in Part 1 cases at least.

Time limits

14.14

The statutory framework emphasises expedition[19], but provides some flexibility where an adjournment is required in the interests of justice[20]. Where a person

---

14 Excluding Scotland, where it must be a sheriff at the sheriff's court.
15 To date, ongoing discussions about devolving extradition to equivalent first instance courts in regional centres such as Birmingham, Cardiff, Leeds and Manchester do not suggest any imminent change to this arrangement.
16 The EA 2003, giving effect to the Council Framework Decision on the European arrest warrant and the surrender procedures between Member States of 13 June 2012 (2002/584/JHA) ('EAW Framework Decision'), the duty of consistent interpretation noted in *Assange v Swedish Prosecution Authority (Nos 1 and 2)* [2012] UKSC 22, [2012] 2 AC 471, and arguably more robustly since 1 December 2014, after the UK's opt-back into the Framework Decision under Protocol No 36 to the Treaty of Lisbon and Case C-105/03 *Criminal Proceedings against Pupino* [2006] QB 83.
17 EAW Framework Decision, Recitals (1)–(11).
18 EAW Framework Decision, (12).
19 Eg Criminal Procedure Rules, 50.2 and Criminal Practice Directions 50A(1).
20 EA 2003, ss 8(5) and 75(3) and 76(4).

is facing an undetermined charge in this jurisdiction, the EA 2003 requires an adjournment [21].

14.15

In theory, an EAW extradition hearing should occur within 21 days of a person's arrest. In a Part 2 case the period will vary, but is usually two months from either the date of arrest[22], or when the full extradition request is supplied[23].

14.16

The EAW Framework Decision requires that an EAW 'shall be dealt with and executed as a matter of urgency'[24] and that 'the final decision' on surrender, so including any appeal, should be taken within 60 days of arrest[25]. An additional 30-day delay is allowed 'in specific cases'[26], but any more must be communicated to Eurojust with a full explanation[27].

14.17

As in any litigation, common causes of delays include legal aid, obtaining evidence on behalf of the requested person, particularly expert evidence, the CPS seeking evidence in reply from the requesting judicial authority, and the preparation of first instance judgments.

14.18

In reality, an extradition case including a statutory appeal (now protracted by a permission stage) will be far in excess of the 60-day time limit. Nevertheless, following concerted attempts by Westminster Magistrates' Court over several years, anecdotally first instance proceedings are often concluded within two months, which constitutes an improvement.

The Crown Prosecution Service and the NCA

14.19

The Crown Prosecution Service ('CPS') and NCA have key roles in any EAW case. The CPS act as an agent for the requesting judicial authority, making representations in favour of extradition. In this role, the CPS will not 'take a

---

21 Eg the mandatory provisions of the EA 2003, ss 8A and 22; there is a discretion to adjourn in the event of an incomplete UK custodial penalty via EA 2003, ss 8B and 23; and related ss 97–98 that apply to the Secretary of State's decision in Part 2 cases.
22 EA 2003, s 75(2).
23 EA 2003, s 76(3).
24 EAW Framework Decision, Art 17(1).
25 EAW Framework Decision, Art 17(3).
26 EAW Framework Decision, Art 17(4).
27 EAW Framework Decision, Art 17(7).

view' about whether to pursue a prosecution, as it might in routine criminal proceedings.

14.20

The NCA is the UK's designated 'central authority'[28] for the receipt and certification of EAWs. The NCA has a power to refuse to certify an EAW in very limited circumstances, particularly following the introduction of a proportionality test. The NCA also facilitates communication between the CPS and the requesting judicial authority throughout the extradition process, for example notifying the judicial authority of the date of arrest, transmitting requests for further evidence and details of remand time, and liaising regarding practical removal arrangements.

14.21

There are also cases where Eurojust has played a role in providing information about common practice across EAW Member States to our Supreme Court, or assisted in drafting EAWs arising from Joint Investigation Team projects that concern international crime. Eurojust's role appears somewhat opaque to the average extradition practitioner, as it seems focused on judicial liaison, out of the public sphere.

Common challenges

14.22

Representatives should be prepared to identify issues early and to substantiate them quickly with evidence[29].

14.23

The EA 2003 sets out specific 'bars' to extradition[30] and requires a specific finding that extradition would be compatible with the requested person's rights under the ECHR[31]. Technical arguments aside, common challenges to surrender include, but are not limited to:

(i)   injustice and/or oppression due to the passage of time;

(ii)   injustice and/or oppression due to the requested person's mental condition[32]; and

(iii) incompatibility with ECHR, Arts 2, 3, 6 and 8.

---

28 EAW Framework Decision, Art 7.
29 Criminal Procedure Rules, Pt 50.
30 EA 2003, ss 11, 79(1) and 93(2).
31 EA 2003, ss 21 and 87.
32 EA 2003, ss 25 and 91.

14.24

Whether a requested person is a fugitive from the requesting judicial authority is often in dispute during extradition proceedings. It is not just relevant to any bail decision, but also, if proved to the criminal standard, it can block a requested person from relying on the passage of time[33]. A finding that an individual has been using the UK as a safe-haven will also enhance the already weighty public interest in favour of extradition[34]. In the context of trafficking there should be consideration of whether the requested person had been trafficked out of the requesting state and/or was at risk of trafficking in the requested state and/or had been trafficked within the requested state. These factors could and should reduce the public interest in favour of extradition[35]. Similarly, if a person is convicted in his absence, whether or not that was deliberate can be key[36].

14.25

Particularly in an EAW or Council of Europe case such as Norway, there is a rebuttable, but nevertheless strong, presumption of compliance with fundamental rights[37].

Procedural issues

Evidence

14.26

If a requested person instructs that he has been trafficked, the first stage will be to obtain evidence and reasons for any NRM determination, or perhaps from a foreign NRM. There is no strict duty of disclosure within extradition proceedings, so although the NCA are by definition involved in any EAW case, there is no guarantee that any trafficking identification decision will be automatically disclosed, unless specifically requested of the CPS and NCA (who oversee the Modern Slavery Human Trafficking Unit ('MSHTU').

---

33 *Gomes v Government of Trinidad and Tobago* [2009] UKHL 21, [2009] 1 WLR 1038, para 26, but note the narrow exception preserved at para 29.

34 *Polish Judicial Authorities v Celinski* [2015] EWHC 1274 (Admin), [2016] 1 WLR 551, paras 6 and 9.

35 An analogy can be drawn to *Hounga v Allen* [2014] UKSC 47, [2014] 1 WLR 2889, where the illegal entry and employment in the UK was deemed irrelevant where that individual had been trafficked to the UK and then subjected to forced labour in the UK.

36 EA 2003, ss 20 and 86.

37 *Krolik v Regional Court in Czestochowa, Poland* [2012] EWHC 2357 (Admin), [2013] 1 WLR 490, para 4 ('clear, cogent and compelling evidence to the contrary') and para 7 ('something approaching international consensus is required'); but now see the CJEU on the need to examine specific facts when looking at the risk of breach in Cases C-404/14 and C-659/15/PPU *Criminal Proceedings against Aranyosi and Caldararu* [2016] QC 921, paras 88–103.

14.27

The absence of mutual recognition of trafficking victim status across jurisdictions and the prevalence of re-trafficking, means that despite a previous conclusive decision in another country, it may still be necessary to refer into the NRM in this jurisdiction. The reverse also applies: a requested person designated as a victim in the UK may have to go through the arduous process of 'victim identification' all over again if extradited. It is essential to determine whether the victim identification process in the requesting state is human-rights compliant, and/or whether the process would of itself further traumatise the requested person and thus breach their Art 3 rights (see the fact-specific example of *The Government of Lithuania v AP*[38]).

14.28

It is a standard direction for a requested person to provide a signed proof of evidence early on during extradition proceedings (allowing the CPS to seek instructions from the judicial authority) but this may be a difficult exercise for obvious reasons, particularly without access to relevant MSHTU material. Representatives must tread a delicate line between providing a full account, yet endeavouring to submit evidence which will be consistent with previous and subsequent statements made to the MSHTU. It is helpful to be aware of the nuances of the different means of trafficking, so the position does not change during proceedings and undermine credibility. Regrettably, given fear of retaliation, a client may be simply unwilling to provide information that will enter the public domain via the open nature of the proceedings and be transmitted to the requesting jurisdiction. The possibility of closed extradition proceedings exists, but is extremely rare[39].

14.29

Depending on the facts, it may be necessary to obtain expert psychiatric and/or psychological assessments of the impact of trafficking and the risk of further abuse. In the more extreme case, such as a client with very low IQ, an intermediary may be required, or at least a ground rules hearing prior to any substantive extradition hearing[40]. The use of expert evidence in cases concerning trafficking victims is set out in Chapters 2 (identification), Chapters 5 and 7 (criminal proceedings) and Chapter 10 (immigration/international protection/asylum proceedings).

---

38 [2010] EWHC 2299 (Admin), 2010 WL 3515648.

39 Eg *VB v Westminster Magistrates' Court* [2014] UKSC 59, [2015] AC 1195 (SC) and *Antonov v Prosecutor General's Office Lithuania* [2015] EWHC 1243 (Admin), [2015] All ER (D) 58 (May).

40 Although the court will rarely use its inherent powers to appoint intermediaries for vulnerable defendants, a ground rules hearing is good practice in any event (Criminal PD 3E(3)).

14.30

As in the immigration context, open source material will of course be relevant to demonstrate what anti-trafficking framework exists in theory and practice in the requesting jurisdiction[41].

Victim identification

14.31

There is no clear competent authority designed to assess trafficking allegations in the extradition context. In practice, and contrary to well-established principles, victim establishment *does* appear to depend on a complaint by the victim in extradition proceedings.

14.32

The arrest precipitating the extradition case may well be the first contact between a person and UK authorities, so it cannot be assumed the issue will have been raised previously. Even if raised, there is no guarantee that a historic or current NRM referral[42] will be relayed to the requested person's representative, usually the duty solicitor.

14.33

Historically, the CPS and the court have been reluctant to become involved in referring a requested person into the NRM as a potential victim, so the burden has fallen to the defence to facilitate a referral (see Chapter 2). This is despite the extradition District Judges often adopting a more inquisitorial role, in the absence of strict rules of criminal evidence applying to extradition proceedings[43].

14.34

The need for more training about trafficking in general crime is clear[44] and extradition cases are no exception. Advice regarding a self-referral into the NRM may not be a top priority at an initial hearing, but it should be encouraged. It can be particularly difficult, given that the legal representative is already likely to be overloaded with forms to fill and instructions to take from an understandably unforthcoming client.

---

41 Eg US Department of State Trafficking in Persons Reports; GRETA reports; UN commentary; regional human rights decisions; independent local experts etc.

42 See Chapter 2, which sets out in full the NRM process.

43 The District Judge 'has the same powers (as nearly as may be) as a magistrates' court would have if the proceedings were the summary trial of an information against the person', EA 2003, s 7(6).

44 Eg *R v L* [2013] EWCA Crim 991, [2014] 1 All ER 113.

14.35

If the issue is not identified early, it may be treated with increasing scepticism and there may not be time to gather the necessary evidence.

Undermining the NRM

14.36

The need for speed in extradition cases is compounded where there are concerns about a requested person's mental health condition, which is highly likely in this context[45]. Expedition grates against the imperative of a victim-based approach towards trafficking and the structure dictated by the NRM, requiring five days for a reasonable grounds decision and incorporating a 45-day recovery and reflection period.

14.37

Extensive litigation has proven that the NRM is not without its difficulties, but there have been extradition cases where it has been set aside completely. Instead, some District Judges have simply made their own trafficking decisions, although it should be noted that others have agreed to adjourn extradition proceedings in the interests of justice to allow for the NRM decision. The justification for deciding whether trafficking occurred in the course of the extradition case has not been merely expedition, but also assumptions about the NRM not being provided with all the evidence from the extradition case (the MSHTU possessing evidence that was not before the extradition court has not been mentioned) and not having had the 'benefit' of seeing the requested person 'perform' in the witness box.

14.38

A case in point[46] is Mr Pavol Cambal's ultimately unsuccessful extradition challenge, considered within *Celinski*[47]. The extradition case began on 1 May 2014 and the District Judge decided to discharge Mr Cambal on 11 December 2014 (on an ECHR, Art 8 ground), despite a finding of a concocted trafficking account and that Mr Cambal was a fugitive from Slovakia. It had taken until November 2014 for Mr Cambal to self-refer to the UK Human Trafficking Centre[48] and the District Judge made clear he would make no referral because he was satisfied there were not reasonable grounds to believe Mr Cambal was trafficked. The Slovakian judicial authority appealed the discharge decision,

45 *Wolkowicz v Regional Court of Bialystock, Poland* [2013] EWHC 102 (Admin), [2013] 1 WLR 2402, paras 14–15.
46 Although for a different set of facts, but a broadly similar approach, see *Igbinovia v President of The Criminal Division* [2014] EWHC 4512 (Admin).
47 [2015] EWHC 1274 (Admin), [2016] 1 WLR 551, paras 42–53.
48 Being the predecessor to the MSHTU.

which was joined as one of several Art 8 test cases before a specially convened Divisional Court[49]. By the time the appeal was heard, the UK Human Trafficking Centre had conclusively determined that Mr Cambal was a victim of trafficking, contrary to the District Judge's finding.

14.39

The focus of the decision was on the Art 8 determination, which was overturned and remitted for reconsideration, but the court also chose to comment on the trafficking issue. It was held that trafficking per se creates no bar to extradition and that a UK Human Trafficking Centre decision 'is in no way binding on a District Judge'. Further the court found[50]:

> '52. A district judge, having heard the evidence, must therefore himself determine the issue as to whether the requested person has been trafficked, having been assisted by the Crown Prosecution Service and the UKHTC by provision of the relevant evidence in their possession, subject to principles of public interest immunity from disclosure. Judges should not normally adjourn hearings for a referral to the UK competent authority, nor defer the effect of their extradition decisions pending a decision on a referral by the UK competent authority.
>
> 53. In the present case, therefore, the fact that the UKHTC has made the determination to which we have referred can make no difference. The judge has heard the evidence of Cambal and rejected it. Although the issue of his fugitive status was a factor considered in the appeal, the findings of fact below must be respected.'

14.40

The *Celinski* judgment did not refer to the Criminal Court of Appeal decision in *R v L*[51]. The Lord Chief Justice held at para 28:

> 'Neither the appellants nor the interveners accept that the conclusive decision of UKBA (or whichever department becomes a competent authority for these purposes) is determinative of the question whether or not an individual has been trafficked. They, of course, are concerned with the impact of a decision adverse to the individual. We are asked to note that the number of concluded decisions in favour of victims of trafficking is relatively low, and it seems unlikely that a prosecutor will challenge or seem to disregard a concluded decision that an individual has been trafficked, but that possibility may arise. Whether the concluded decision of the competent authority is favourable or

---

49 Lord Thomas of Cwmgiedd CJ (as he then was), Ryder LJ, Ouseley J.
50 *Celinski* [2015] EWHC 1274 (Admin), [2016] 1 WLR 551, paras 52–53.
51 [2013] EWCA Crim 991, [2014] 1 All ER 113.

adverse to the individual it will have been made by an authority vested with the responsibility for investigating these issues, and although the court is not bound by the decision, unless there is evidence to contradict it, or significant evidence that was not considered, it is likely that the criminal courts will abide by it.'

A subsequent application to certify a point of law of public importance was refused.

14.41

The decision obviously fetters, but does not prevent, applications to adjourn first instance hearings in order to obtain relevant evidence and a conclusive grounds decision.

14.42

The consequences of this decision are obviously out of kilter with the anti-trafficking framework[52] and the positive obligations owed to potential victims of trafficking. Although concerning, this approach has not been the subject of any more general judicial comment[53]. It is hoped that greater awareness will eventually prompt a different analysis, more likely perhaps in the immigration context where trafficking issues are less scarce.

Substantive issues

14.43

As noted in *Celinski*, a finding that a requested person is or was a trafficking victim is not a trump card to prevent extradition[54]. In a particularly compelling case, it is possible that an abuse of process argument could be raised, but on the law as it stands it would be extremely difficult to succeed in this. An abuse argument could reason from distinct scenarios where the CPS accept that extradition would be an abuse of process, as it would be for no real purpose (for example a requested person had already completed the full custodial penalty whilst awaiting extradition), or antithetical to principles of non-refoulement if a person had claimed asylum in this jurisdiction from the requesting country[55]. However, abuse of process is a residual jurisdiction, to be considered after the mandatory issues have been determined by the court.

---

52 Arguably including the status to be given to NRM decisions within criminal proceedings noted in *R v L* [2013] EWCA Crim 991, [2014] 1 All ER 113.

53 Subsequent decisions concerning scenarios where it is common ground that the requested person was trafficked, eg. *Cakule v Prosecutor General's Office of the Republic of Latvia* [2016] EWHC 2211 (Admin) and *Vilionis v Vilnius County Court* [2017] EWHC 336 (Admin).

54 Contrast, for example, a scenario where a requested person's surrender is sought from a jurisdiction that he has previously been granted asylum from.

55 Eg *District Court in Ostroleka, Poland v Dytlow* [2009] EWHC 1009 (Admin) at paras 11–31.

14.44

More straightforwardly, a trafficking finding will be relevant to the more commonplace extradition challenges[56]. The extent of the impact on standard challenges will depend on whether or not it is possible to show that the trafficking was linked to the index extradition offence, or perhaps the reason behind breach of bail abroad, or breach of a suspended sentence[57].

14.45

As a person's fugitive status is to be decided on each set of facts, demonstrating trafficking may not automatically settle that issue in the requested person's favour.

14.46

Recent decisions of the ECtHR regarding ECHR, Art 4 are undoubtedly useful in rebutting presumptions of ECHR compliance in Member States. In *LE v Greece*[58] the emphasis is on a global approach, incorporating indirect action by public bodies and affirming the prospective scope such that Art 4 includes prevention, protection and combatting of trafficking. Despite the best intentions it appears that the anti-trafficking provisions in many jurisdictions are still in their infancy, even within the Council of Europe, and that the whole system is only as effective as its weakest link. By a combination of these points and the procedural points above, ample room for argument remains.

---

56 Supra, para 23.
57 Although that argument did not find favour in *Vilionis*, ibid.
58 App No 71545/12, final 21 April 2016, paras 64–68 (general principles of Art 4).

15 Trafficking operations and modus operandi

Introduction

15.1

Human trafficking is one of the most lucrative illicit businesses globally, with criminal gangs and individuals making an estimated $3 billion from it per year. It is estimated that 45.8 million people are in some form of modern slavery in 167 countries.

15.2

There have been relatively low convictions of human trafficking related offences, both pre- and post-enactment of the Modern Slavery Act ('MSA') 2015[1]. This crime is known by a number of labels in the English language: modern slavery, trafficking in human beings, trafficking in persons, and human trafficking. They are all directly linked to the text of the national legislation that guides the state's response in its prevention, investigation, prosecution and victim support.

15.3

Regardless of how it is described, and regardless of how it manifests itself in society, the common denominator in trafficking cases is exploitation and the criminal profit that is generated by an individual's exploitation. It is the reason why people are trafficked and it is a global, multi-billion pound criminal industry. That is not to say trafficking cannot occur on a smaller scale – it does. This type of trafficking is often seen in the overseas domestic workers cases, where workers, often with visas tied to their employers, have to work for little or no economic benefit, or in the trafficking of children for domestic labour or other small-scale labour exploitation.

15.4

The UK is a source, transit, and destination country for men, women, and children subjected to sex trafficking, forced criminality and forced labour, including domestic servitude. The government estimates there may be up to 13,000 persons subject to trafficking, with about one-fourth to one-third of these victims being children. Most identified victims are subject to labour

---

1   Her Majesty's Inspectorate of Constabulary and Fire & Rescue Services Report, 'Stolen Freedom: the policing response to modern slavery and human trafficking', October 2017.

trafficking. Most foreign trafficking victims come from Africa, Asia, and Eastern Europe. Albania, Vietnam, Nigeria, Romania, and Poland were the top countries of origin during the past year[2].

15.5

In the UK, human trafficking has existed in its 'modern' form for longer than it has been routinely investigated. Currently, the agencies with responsibility for investigating and collecting intelligence on human trafficking and modern slavery are the National Crime Agency ('NCA'), which has primacy on national investigations, all UK Police Forces, the UK Border Force and the Gangmasters and Labour Abuse Authority.

15.6

All identified victims are reported to the National Referral Mechanism (NRM), which 'sits' within the United Kingdom Human Trafficking Centre ('UKHTC') itself a part of the NCA (see Chapter 2 for NRM victim identification). This model is likely to undergo significant revision in the coming months. If one were to combine the law enforcement response with the support provided by international organisations, NGOs, charities and other civil society actors working in the field of preventing and combating human trafficking within and into the UK, the national response looks substantial.

Exploitation typologies and common control methods

15.7

Victims of modern slavery are preyed upon due to a backdrop of complex issues. It is not possible to document all forms of exploitation in a short format, and there is no definitive list. Common forms of exploitation in the UK are forced criminality, sexual exploitation, forced labour and domestic servitude. Traffickers are often professional criminals and will seek to exploit vulnerable people wherever they can. Just as exploitation can come in many forms, so does vulnerability. In this respect, and in all cases, an open mind is vital. Every jurisdiction has varying trafficking typologies; this can be seen both internationally and domestically. The Polaris Project[3] recently recorded 25 typologies of trafficking throughout the USA. Each has its own business model, trafficker profiles, recruitment strategies, victim profiles and methods of control that facilitate human trafficking. The NCA 2016 statistics[4] only records domestic servitude, labour exploitation, sexual exploitation and unknown exploitation type as forms of exploitation in the UK. The Crown Prosecution

---

2   US Department of State Trafficking in Persons (TIP) Report 2017.

3   See https://polarisproject.org/typology, last accessed 17 December 2017.

4   Available at www.nationalcrimeagency.gov.uk/publications/national-referral-mechanism-statistics/2016-nrm-statistics/765-human-trafficking-national-referral-mechanism-statistics-april-to-june-2016-v2/file, last accessed 17 December 2017.

Service (CPS) guidance on human trafficking acknowledges that exploitation typologies, particularly involving children, are often varied and can include:

- domestic servitude;

- labour exploitation;

- criminal activity (eg cannabis cultivation, petty street crime, illegal street trade, drug mules etc);

- sexual exploitation (brothels, closed community, for child abuse images);

- application of residence;

- benefit fraud;

- forced begging;

- illegal adoption; and

- sham marriages.

15.8

Perpetrators use a variety of control methods to engage or coerce vulnerable individuals[5]. The Home Office Guidance for Competent Authorities stipulates that an adult victim of human trafficking must have been subject to a 'means' – the threat or use of force or other form of coercion to achieve the consent of a person having control over another person. It is not necessary for there to have been 'means' for a child to be a victim, because children cannot give informed consent. Any child who is recruited, transported, or transferred for the purposes of human trafficking is considered to be a potential victim, whether or not he has been forced or deceived[6].

15.9

Adults and children can be controlled through subtle, sometimes invisible, forces that even the victims themselves might not be able to fully understand or be able to articulate. Understanding how perpetrators abuse and exploit a position of vulnerability is fundamental in the investigation of trafficking but the less obvious signs often get overlooked. Common control methods are discussed in the following paragraphs.

Physical and sexual violence

15.10

When physical abuse is used as a means of control, it can be single or repeated violent episodes of abuse. Alternatively, it can be manipulation of the victims

---

5   College   of   Policing,   www.app.college.police.uk/app-content/major-investigation-and-public-protection/modern-slavery/risk-and-identification/#control-methods, last accessed 17 December 2017.

6   Home Office, *Victims of modern slavery – Competent Authority guidance* (21 March 2016) pp 31–32.

by making them witness beatings given to someone else, combined with the threat that it will happen to them if they do not do what they are told. Sexual violence, including rape, is a form of control that often goes undetected and unreported in situations of labour exploitation, domestic servitude and criminal exploitation. Traffickers will sexually abuse for their own gratification, but also as a means to control, to intimidate and silence the victim. Sexual abuse can affect children, women and men but embarrassment, shame and stigma can prevent immediate disclosure. Non-consensual sex is exploitation even if there is no monetary gain[7].

Deception

15.11

The promise of a better life is a common form of deception adopted. This is the point at which a web of deception traps victims into believing that the first steps they are taking will lead to a life better than the one they have now. This could be the promise of a job, or education, or to reunite with family or other promises that never materialise. The deception can be quite sophisticated, for example by using a fake job agency, advertising online, using family members as facilitators, or using other victims as recruiters. In other cases the ongoing deception and manipulation associated with withholding of wages or illegitimate wage deductions acts as a further means of control.

Debt

15.12

A close partner to deception is debt. Traffickers and their agents routinely use the accrual of debt and usury, where the rates of interest on loans are exorbitantly high, as a means to control victims. For example, what might appear as a genuine loan by an agent to finance travel arrangements traps the victim into a contract with the trafficker to pay back that debt. Debt bondage is a term often considered in situations where a victim is tied to one person for an unspecified amount of time and often for an unspecified amount. However, in human trafficking debt accrual as the means of control does not always have to conform to the strict notion of debt bondage. Victims can be sold or exchanged between traffickers and the debt rolls over. In some cultures the stigma of not being able to pay back debt or the deep shame of asking family members to sell their assets to pay back the debt, is enough to hold victims bonded to the trafficker or their agents. The threat of being exposed for non-payment of debt is a common tactic when the abuser and abused come from within the same

---

7   NCA, *Types of modern slavery crime*, available at www.nationalcrimeagency.gov.uk/crime-threats/human-trafficking/types-of-human-trafficking, last accessed 17 December 2017.

culture, family or kinship group. The use of debt as a means to control can manifest in different ways. It can be used to control both adults and children and is a significant contributor to why some victims go missing and are later found to have been re-trafficked.

Isolation

15.13

Keeping victims housed together, locking rooms and monitoring or removing any means of communication to the outside world are ways that traffickers keep control through isolating vulnerable people. Moving frequently from place to place reduces the likelihood of victims being identified by the public or police, and it also means that it is less likely the victim will be able to build trusting relationships with anyone or ask for help. Isolation can be both physical and emotional in nature. The circumstances can be just as controlling where the victim is not physically locked inside, because the terror of not knowing who to trust, whether the person with you is in similar circumstances or is an agent, can be debilitating. Isolation of a victim is often easy to achieve where the victim does not speak the language well, or at all, in the destination country and en route, and where a victim has irregular immigration status in these countries.

Dependency

15.14

Perpetrators knowingly and deliberately create a situation of dependency that increases the vulnerability of the victim and strengthens the control over them. Providing the only source of food and accommodation and taking away identification papers are common ways in which dependency is created. However, it can also involve the perpetrator deceiving, coercing or forcing the victim to take on a new identity by providing a different name on arrival, or the use of false documents and then subsequently threatening to report the victim to immigration officials. In other instances it can involve the supply and withholding of drugs or alcohol or always being with the victim and speaking on their behalf, for example when presenting at Accident and Emergency. In the case of children a situation of dependency can be created quickly and with little effort due to their young age and immaturity. It is well known that a common ploy in respect of child victims of domestic servitude is that they are brought through British airports with a visa. The children are not detected because the accompanying adult, often masquerading as a family member, presents a passport and speaks to the Immigration Officer on the child's behalf. The child only later finds out the implications of entering the country on false documents and the trafficker threatens him with being handed over to immigration and police, something the child fears through his own knowledge of corrupt authorities in his home country.

Emotional control

15.15

Emotional control can take many different forms, and some of this is already covered in other parts of this chapter. Inducing fear by threatening to harm the victim's family is a corrosive means of controlling the victim. Even after the victim has been removed from the situation of exploitation, the paralysing fear of threats to family has long-term consequences, including refusal to disclose and the high risk of re-trafficking. Making victims collude in crimes and then threatening to expose them to police unless they acquiesce is another pernicious form of control that has consequences for safeguarding and in later immigration and legal proceedings. Threats or action taken to expose the victim's sexual history, including taking sexually explicit photographs or distributing images online, has a devastating impact on women and girls, but it can also affect boys and men in the same way, particularly, but not only, in cultures or in faiths where homosexuality is considered taboo. Less obvious, but just as important, are signs of emotional control seen in situations described as 'Stockholm Syndrome', where through calculated manipulation by the perpetrator the victim forms a bond or strong emotional tie even though he may have suffered abuse. This is sometimes known as the 'Loverboy' model. Stockholm Syndrome can also be seen in cases of domestic servitude, where the victim has spent years living with the family in appalling conditions but has been responsible for every aspect of caring for the children and by developing a bond with them the thought of being responsible for the father and mother being arrested and taken away from the children could be entirely unthinkable.

Culture and faith

15.16

There are a number of ceremonial practices linked to spirit possession that are used by human trafficking networks to control victims. It would be wrong to group all of them together as 'juju', as this is not the case. There are a number of quite different belief systems across the continent of Africa and around the world that traffickers have exploited. Many of them are simply incomprehensible if you are not familiar with them; this can lead to victims not being believed or in some instances being derided for lacking credibility. Very subtle references to the oath or the packet means nothing if you are unaware, but can change everything within the context of spirit possession.

15.17

Juju, according to Andy Desmond, a former Metropolitan police detective and trafficking consultant, is commonly used by human traffickers of Edo and Delta States of Nigeria. Traffickers have hijacked the cultural beliefs in juju to blackmail their victims. To satisfy the greed for money for those involved, including traditional priests paid to carry out the ceremonies, the strong belief in the spirits makes this a powerful weapon for modern day slave traders. Once a potential victim has been put through and sworn an oath of obedience, he is captured, snarled in the trap without the need for physical restraints. The bondage is in the beliefs: there is no requirement to lock up victims and have them watched. You have the spirits to do that for you. Juju has been used extensively to control Nigerian children trafficked to the UK and via the UK into other European countries for servitude and sexual exploitation. Practices such as Kindoki, from the Democratic Republic of the Congo, or Obi, Obeah, or Obia known in parts of Nigeria and the West Indies may also be methods of control and relate to spirit possession and mysticism.

15.18

A related area of abuse is the practice of denouncing children as witches and warlocks, and saying that this is the reason that bad luck has befallen the family, for illness or for poverty. It is these children who are singled out, isolated and highly vulnerable to trafficking. Traffickers exploit their vulnerability and knowingly use the community condemnation as a witch or warlock as a form of control. These children lose any sense of self-worth, feel rejected, blame themselves and are reluctant to speak out[8].

Family involvement

15.19

Human trafficking can happen with the knowledge and involvement of family members, husbands, boyfriends or close acquaintances. Even after victims recognise and understand that they have been trafficked, the bonds of loyalty to the family or fear of the consequences of breaking free can be overwhelming. In cases of forced marriage young females can be forced by families to enter an arrangement of marriage which is a cover for servitude in exchange for some form of benefit. Often these cases involve men who are significantly older, who have dependent children from past relationships or have caring needs – however that is not always the case.

---

8   More detail on this subject is available at www.starsfoundation.org.uk/awards/organisations/stepping-stones-nigeria-child-empowerment-foundation, last accessed 17 December 2017.

15.20

It would be naïve to think that some families do not know what will happen to their children when they send them away with local agents and facilitators even if the children themselves do not know all the arrangement details. Unaccompanied or separated children are especially vulnerable to re-trafficking, in part because of the potential for risk if the child is reunited with family. In some cases the family will have had complicit involvement, especially if a debt has to be repaid or where the stigma of sexual abuse makes the child an outcast. In other situations filial piety, the deeply-entrenched cultural bond of loyalty to elders that exists in the Confucian beliefs found in Chinese and Vietnamese society, is part of a much more complex landscape of why children do not disclose abusive and exploitative relationships.

Modus operandi of known modern slavery cases

15.21

The investigation into the deaths of 23 Chinese nationals who drowned in Morecambe Bay on 5 February 2004 is probably the best example of a crime that had not yet registered on the law enforcement 'radar' until it came under significant public attention and was then scrutinised by criminal justice authorities. 'Trafficking in human beings' was not part of the UK law enforcement lexicon in 2004, yet there were clear indications almost four years earlier that the UK was being targeted by people smugglers and human traffickers.

15.22

On 18 June 2000, 58 Chinese illegal migrants were found suffocated in the back of a lorry that had arrived in Dover from Rotterdam via a channel ferry, driven by Perry Wacker, a Dutch national. Sentencing the driver at Maidstone Crown Court the following year, Mr Justice Moses said that 'human trafficking of this kind added to the climate of hostility against asylum seekers and encouraged government to take ever more draconian measures'.

15.23

Two months before the fatal shipment, Leo Nijveen, a close friend of Wacker's, was arrested by Kent Police after arriving at Dover with 50 Chinese migrants in his lorry. They had almost suffocated en route and had been released by Nijveen on the crossing. Nijveen was released without charge by the UK authorities and returned to the Netherlands. Today, it is likely that he would have been investigated as a people smuggler and human trafficker.

15.24

It is highly likely that once the Chinese migrants had been smuggled into the UK they would have been trafficked within the UK to pay the costs of their facilitated illegal entry, the 'debt bondage' that is now so familiar in current human trafficking investigations. The Chinese nationals who died in Morecambe Bay four years later were victims of human trafficking. They were paying off the costs of their smuggling by collecting shellfish in hazardous conditions.

15.25

The Chinese migrants who died in Dover and in Morecambe Bay had been smuggled by Chinese 'Snakehead' gangs into the UK, and their internal trafficking would have been/was controlled by Chinese traffickers. The Gangmasters Licensing Authority (since replaced by the Gangmasters and Labour Abuse Authority) was established in 2005 as a direct result of this investigation and the facts established about the role of those persons managing the migrants as 'a workforce', so called gangmasters.

15.26

In January 1998, West Sussex Police set up 'Operation Newbridge' to gather intelligence on children of West African origin and ethnicity who, having arrived in the UK at Gatwick Airport as unaccompanied minors, were routinely going missing after being placed in care. The suspicion was that they were being trafficked into the UK for sexual exploitation.

15.27

In January 2000, the National Crime Squad (SOCA and now NCA) presented a case against a number of men suspected of trafficking these children for prostitution, but the CPS rejected it citing the then legislation 'which makes convictions virtually impossible' with the authorities regarding the few witnesses who might be prepared to come forward as 'unreliable because they change their stories'.

15.28

On 21 September 2001 the torso of a young African male was found washed up along the River Thames. The lengthy enquiries into what was dealt with as a murder resulted in a strong suspicion that the child, who was Nigerian, had been brought to the UK and murdered as part of a ritual practice.

15.29

In 2007 'Operation Troy' led in the UK by SOCA and the UKHTC, working with police counterparts in Sweden, Denmark and Norway, investigated the trafficking of British males to Scandinavia by a 'traveller family'. The men, all homeless and vulnerable, were trafficked and forced to work laying tarmac at residential properties.

15.30

These widely-publicised cases emphasise that human trafficking is not a recent phenomenon. However, even today investigations, prosecutions and convictions for human trafficking are not routine. So much so that they are routinely heralded and commented upon as 'breakthroughs' against organised crime.

15.31

The Council Framework Decision of 13 June 2002 provided the legal basis for EU Member States to operate in Joint Investigation Teams ('JITs'). It would take another six years before the first ever JIT against an organised human trafficking network was established.

15.32

In 2008, JIT Golf, led by the UK's Metropolitan Police Service in cooperation with the Romanian National Police, investigated an organised ethnic Roma child trafficking network operating across the EU. Romanian Roma children were trafficked to EU Member States and exploited for the purpose of 'street crime'. This coordinated two year international investigation led to the first conviction for child trafficking, some 10 years after West Sussex Police first investigated the phenomenon.

15.33

What the above-mentioned cases illustrate is that state authorities have been slow to respond effectively to an emerging criminal threat that was first recognised in the late 1990s.

15.34

Whilst in all of the above-mentioned investigations there was clear evidence or intelligence identifying the involvement of organised crime, it has not been the sophistication and ability of the criminals involved that prevented their identification, apprehension and prosecution. Rather, it has been the lack of awareness, knowledge, strategy, policy, capacity, appropriate legislation and motivation of the competent authorities to deal with an emerging serious crime.

15.35

There is a rising awareness of British victims of trafficking who are trafficked within the UK and also outside of the UK. Common forms of trafficking of British victims outside of the UK are for forced marriage and as drug mules. In respect of the latter, this is often trafficking within an organised criminal framework, with the organised criminal gangs operating over several jurisdictions.

Organised crime

15.36

Organised crime is involved in human trafficking, which is often referred to as 'an organised crime'. The following definition is helpful in explaining what that means:

> 'Organized criminal group' shall mean a structured group of three or more persons, existing for a period of time and acting in concert with the aim of committing one or more serious crimes or offences established in accordance with this Convention, in order to obtain, directly or indirectly, a financial or other material benefit'[9].

15.37

Most traffickers identified by state authorities, in the course of investigating trafficking activity, worked in a group with at least two others, so in almost all cases, they were part of an organised crime group (OCG). That said, the dynamic or profile of an OCG will vary from one case to the next and its activity or operation will be driven or influenced by a range of factors, ie the push and pull factors which are the cause of an individual's vulnerability and susceptibility, the socio economic and environmental conditions or market forces and the ability or capacity of the criminals involved.

15.38

For example, ethnic Roma trafficking networks operating across the EU solely engaged in the trafficking of ethnic Roma victims (eg JIT Golf). These trafficking networks are often successful because of the significant discrimination suffered by the Roma across Europe. The structure of these trafficking groups is clan- and extended family-based. These networks often come to notice with investigations into the activities of children who are involved in organised street crime, such as pickpocketing and begging.

15.39

In a significant number of investigations where Roma children are exploited as street criminals, the traffickers are their parents or immediate family members. These networks operate in the capital cities of the EU's most wealthy countries, moving routinely and when necessary, swiftly from one country to another, taking advantage of the Schengen Free Travel Zone. For obvious reasons, a

---

9   UN Convention against Trans National Organised Crime 2000, Art 2a.

major challenge in an investigation involving ethnic Roma victims is obtaining a statement or testimony from the victim. The traffickers are aware of the challenges a child victim will present to the authorities and the 'use' of children has become a modus operandi, with the child victim being 'recycled' after initial detection.

15.40

Different trafficking groups active in the UK are also involved in defrauding 'the benefits system' using adults and children trafficked to the UK. The adults and children will be presented to the local authority as a newly-arrived family, corroborated by good quality forged documents. Usually the fake family will be one parent and multiple children, and will be entitled to a full range of benefits. Bank account details provided to the local authority will be in favour of the traffickers and any payment or debit cards will be handed to the traffickers. The fake family will be presented in another area to repeat the process, or be returned to their country of origin. The traffickers will then maintain the pretence and receive all benefit payments.

15.41

The 'Loverboy' method is the term often used to describe the trafficking of a girl or young woman into forced prostitution where the recruitment involves a young, good looking man befriending the victim. The victim is in almost all cases a young woman who has no or limited experience of meeting or speaking with a boy or young man, who quickly becomes flattered by his attention, his conduct and often apparent good financial circumstances. Very quickly the girl or young woman will be convinced she is in a loving and sound relationship with her new boyfriend, which she will inevitably keep secret from her family due to cultural and customary practices surrounding arranged relationships and marriage.

15.42

Early in the relationship the boyfriend will suggest that 'they' go to meet his parents (or something similar) in another city or even country with the intention of getting the girl to leave her home environment. On arrival in the new location the girl will be forced into prostitution by her 'boyfriend' or be handed over to others to do the same. This methodology is often seen in the investigation of Albanian trafficking networks, where both traffickers and victims are ethnic Albanian and other Eastern European gangs.

15.43

The exploitation by traffickers of their own nationals is also a common occurrence within the UK, especially where an established or substantial diaspora exists. A common language, culture and knowledge of the environment provide leverage for an established migrant in the UK over the newly arrived. The vulnerability of the migrant new to his or her surroundings leads to exploitation, and this is often found in the labour market which in many regions of the UK is dependent on a migrant labour force.

Other prevalent organised crime networks in the UK include Vietnamese, Chinese and, more recently, gangs from Latin America.

Forced criminality

15.44

Forced criminality is often overlooked and misunderstood. Very little data has been recorded on the characterisation of forced criminality. The 2016 NRM statistics produced by the NCA group forced criminality into forced labour[10]. Data collection systems are currently inadequate for a complete picture of the scale of forced criminality.

15.45

Examples of forced criminality may not be immediately obvious, and range from minor non-recordable offences to indictable only and those of the most serious nature. Organised criminal networks, and individuals who use human beings as commodities in this manner, continually evolve and adapt their modus operandi in order to evade the attention of the authorities and to increase profitability.

15.46

Often those who have been criminalised and prosecuted remain in a cycle of exploitation and will go on to be re-trafficked and re-criminalised several times. Criminalising victims in this way significantly reduces the possibility of the victims providing evidence or intelligence against their traffickers, so it is unsurprising that the UK continues to have low conviction rates of trafficking related offences.

15.47

The Law Society Practice Note on criminal prosecutions of victims of trafficking[11] lists common indicators of trafficking. Further non-exhaustive lists are provided by UN Office on Drugs and Crime[12] (see further indicators at Chapter 2). Common trafficking indicators in the context of forced criminality are as follows:

---

10 See para **15.7** above.
11 Available at www.lawsociety.org.uk/support-services/advice/practice-notes/criminal-prosecutions-of-victims-of-trafficking/, last accessed 17 December 2017.
12 See www.unodc.org/pdf/HT_indicators_E_LOWRES.pdf, last accessed 17 December 2017.

- showing signs that their movement has been restricted or monitored;

- unable to recall facts about identity, location or situation;

- giving false accounts to authorities;

- giving the impression they are bonded by debt;

- being ashamed of having committed a criminal act;

- being fearful, anxious, withdrawn and/or apathetic;

- showing signs of physical, emotional or sexual abuse;

- living in undignified/cramped conditions/malnourishment;

- speaking as though they have been coached/instructed;

- not possessing their own passport and/or identity documents or having false documents;

- going missing from care or missing episodes;

- hiding phones or sim cards;

- showing fear for family in country of origin;

- exhibiting distrust of the authorities;

- fear of revealing immigration status;

- often receiving phone calls when at court;

- pressure to plead guilty to offences and sudden changes in plea;

- inconsistent about age;

- inconsistent account;

- physical signs of abuse such as scarring, malnourishment, migraines, tattoos and branding on the skin, drug and alcohol dependency;

- evidence of older or other individuals present during the commission of the offence.

15.48

Throughout England and Wales common offences committed by victims of modern slavery through forced criminality are as follows:

Sex offences[13]	
Rape	Sexual Offences Act 2003, s 1
Assault by penetration	Sexual Offences Act 2003, s 2
Sexual assault	Sexual Offences Act 2003, s 3
Causing a person to engage in sexual activity without consent	Sexual Offences Act 2003, s 4
Rape of a child under 13	Sexual Offences Act 2003, s 5
Assault of a child under 13 by penetration	Sexual Offences Act 2003, s 6
Sexual assault of a child under 13	Sexual Offences Act 2003, s 7
Causing or Inciting a child under 13 to engage in sexual activity	Sexual Offences Act 2003, s 8
Sexual activity with a child	Sexual Offences Act 2003, s 9
Causing or Inciting a child to engage in sexual activity	Sexual Offences Act 2003, s 10
Engaging in sexual activity in the presence of a child	Sexual Offences Act 2003, s 11
Causing a child to watch a sex act	Sexual Offences Act 2003, s 12
Arranging or facilitating commission of a child sex offence	Sexual Offences Act 2003, s 14
Meeting a child following sexual grooming	Sexual Offences Act 2003, s 15
Sexual communication with a child	Sexual Offences Act 2003, s 15A
Sexual activity with a child family member	Sexual Offences Act 2003, s 25
Inciting a child family member to engage in sexual activity	Sexual Offences Act 2003, s 26
Sexual exploitation of children	Sexual Offences Act 2003, s 47
Causing or inciting sexual exploitation of a child	Sexual Offences Act 2003, s 48
Controlling a child in relation to sexual exploitation	Sexual Offences Act 2003, s 49

---

13 It is common that those trafficked for the purpose of sexual exploitation will graduate into senior roles while still under the control of their trafficker. This is particularly common in females trafficked from countries such as Morocco, Nigeria and Eastern Europe. Many may incite sexual activity and have a role within a brothel, such as grooming others. Sex offences are also associated with other human trafficking and modern slavery offences, where victims will be forced into the trafficking of others. Such offences are excluded offences to an MSA 2015, s 45 defence (see Chapter 5 for full Sch 4 excluded offences).

Arranging or facilitating sexual exploitation of a child	Sexual Offences Act 2003, s 50
Causing or inciting prostitution for gain	Sexual Offences Act 2003, s 52
Controlling prostitution for gain	Sexual Offences Act 2003, s 53
Paying for sexual services of a prostitute subjected to exploitative conduct	Sexual Offences Act 2003, s 53A
Trafficking people for sexual exploitation	Sexual Offences Act 2003, s 59A
Keeping a brothel	Sexual Offences Act 1956, s 33, s 33A
Soliciting	Street Offences Act 1959, s 1 and Sexual Offences Act 2003, s 51A
Theft offences[14]	
Theft	Theft Act 1968, s 1
Robbery	Theft Act 1968, s 8
Burglary	Theft Act 1968, s 9
Burglary with intent	Theft Act 1968, s 9(1)(a)
Aggravated burglary	Theft Act 1968, s 10
Abstracting electricity[15]	Theft Act 1968, s 13
Going equipped	Theft Act 1968, s 25
Handling stolen goods	Theft Act 1968, s 22
Begging[16]	Vagrancy Act 1824, s 3
Fraud offences[17]	
Fraud by false representation	Fraud Act 2006, s 2
Fraud by failing to disclose information	Fraud Act 2006, s 3

---

14 Victims are used to commit theft offences, ranging from pick pocketing to robberies and burglaries. Commonly children of Roma descent will be used to pick-pocket for organised gangs and by elder family members. There is a significant discrepancy between the number of children identified by authorities as victims of trafficking and the number who have been charged with dishonesty offences such as theft, pick-pocketing. It is also common for Eastern European victims who are trafficked for forced labour to also be forced to collect and provide fraudulent charity bag and money collections, and be involved in the theft of metals from industrial sites.

15 Commonly associated with cannabis production.

16 Commonly Roma organised crime networks will use younger family members, often minors, to beg. Such cases are often unrecorded, as individuals are not arrested.

17 Victims will often be charged with possession of false passports or identity documents or because they have made an illegal entry. It is common that fraudulent identity documents will then be used to open bank accounts and commit various forms of fraud, including benefit fraud. Traffickers will apply for benefits or arrange for a victim to take up legitimate work under a false identity. The bank account that their official salary will go into from a legitimate employer is commonly only accessible to the trafficker and the victim will receive minimal or no money for their work.

Possession or control of articles for use in fraud	Fraud Act 2006, s 6
Making or supplying articles for use in fraud	Fraud Act 2006, s 7
Obtaining services dishonestly	Fraud Act 2006, s 11
Making a false instrument (forgery)	Forgery and Counterfeiting Act 1981, s 1
Copying a false instrument	Forgery and Counterfeiting Act 1981, s 2
Using a false instrument	Forgery and Counterfeiting Act 1981, s 3
Using a copy of a false instrument	Forgery and Counterfeiting Act 1981, s 4
Having custody or control of specified kinds of false instruments	Forgery and Counterfeiting Act 1981, s 5(1)
Making or having custody etc of machines, paper etc for making false instruments of that kind	Forgery and Counterfeiting Act 1981, s 5(3)
Possession of false ID document	Identity Documents Act 2010, s 4
Possession of false ID document with intent	Identity Documents Act 2010, s 6
Counterfeiting notes or coins	Forgery and Counterfeiting Act 1981, s 14
Passing, tendering or delivering counterfeit notes or coins	Forgery and Counterfeiting Act 1981, s 15
Custody or control of counterfeit notes or coins	Forgery and Counterfeiting Act 1981, s 16
Make or have materials and implements for counterfeiting[18]	Forgery and Counterfeiting Act 1981, s 17
Importation and exporting of counterfeit notes or coins	Forgery and Counterfeiting Act 1981, s 20, s 21
Obtaining services dishonestly	Fraud Act 2006, s 11
Dishonest representations to obtain benefits	Social Security Administration Act 1992, s 111A, s 112
Shoplifting	Magistrates' Court Act 1980, s 22A

---

18 Victims may be forced to produce and sell counterfeit goods, such as coins, DVDs, counterfeit cosmetics and designer products. Frequently this offence involves Eastern European, Vietnamese and Chinese national victims.

Criminal damage[19]	
Criminal damage	Criminal Damage Act 1971, s 1(1)
Aggravated criminal damage	Criminal Damage Act 1971, s 1(2)
Threats to destroy or damage property	Criminal Damage Act 1971, s 2
Possession with intent to destroy or damage property	Criminal Damage Act 1971, s 3
Offensive weapons[20]	
Possession of a firearm or ammunition without certificate	Firearms Act 1968, s 1(1)
Possessing shot gun without certificate	Firearms Act 1968, s 2(1)
Possessing prohibited weapons or ammunition	Firearms Act 1968, s 5(1)(a), (ab), (aba), (ac), (ad), (ae), (af), (c)
Possessing prohibited weapons designed for discharge of noxious liquid etc	Firearms Act 1968, s 5(1)(b)
Possessing firearm disguised as other object	Firearms Act 1968, s 4(1A)(a)
Possessing other prohibited weapons	Firearms Act 1968, s 5(1A)(b), (c), (d), (e), (f), (g)
Possessing firearm with intent to cause fear of violence	Firearms Act 1968, s 16A
Carrying firearm or imitation in public place	Firearms Act 1968, s 19
Possession of offensive weapon	Prevention of Crime Act 1953, s 1
Possession of a bladed article	Criminal Justice Act 1988, s 139(1)
Minding a dangerous weapon	Violent Crime Reduction Act 2006, ss 28, 29

---

19 It is not uncommon for victims who have been re-trafficked to be prosecuted for criminal damage as a result of breaking electronic monitoring tags off, which they may be subject to whilst on bail and licence. Victims may also be charged with damaging property while trying to escape a trafficking situation. Such offences are listed in Schedule 4 excluded offences to defence under the MSA 2015, s 45 (see the Annex to Chapter 5 for the full schedule).

20 It is common for victims, once they have arrived in the UK, to be used to transport weapons for their traffickers. This is commonly associated with running drugs and county lines cases, see fn 21.

Drugs offences[21]	
Possession of controlled drugs	Misuse of Drugs Act 1971, s 5
Produce or supply controlled drug	Misuse of Drugs Act 1971, s 4
Being Concerned in the Supply	Misuse of Drugs Act 1971, s 4(3) (b)
Possession with intent to supply	Misuse of Drugs Act 1971, s 5
Importing/exporting controlled drug	Misuse of Drugs Act 1971, s 3
Cultivation of cannabis	Misuse of Drugs Act 1971, s 6
Supplying articles for administering or preparing controlled drugs	Misuse of Drugs Act 1971, s 9A
Producing psychoactive substance	Psychoactive Substances Act 2016, s 4
Supplying or offering to supply psychoactive substance	Psychoactive Substances Act 2016, s 5
Possession of psychoactive substance with intent to supply	Psychoactive Substances Act 2016, s 7
Money laundering offences[22]	
Concealing etc criminal property	Proceeds of Crime Act 2002, s 327
Money laundering	Proceeds of Crime Act 2002, s 328
Acquires, uses or has possession of criminal property	Proceeds of Crime Act 2002, s 329

---

21 It is common that victims will be put to work in domestic houses adapted for the purpose of drug production, commonly cannabis cultivation. This involves extraction of electricity and use of hydraulics to cultivate and grow cannabis plants. It is common for Chinese and Vietnamese nationals to be trafficked for this purpose. Other common drugs offences include drug importation. Many victims will be trafficked from their country of origin for the purpose of couriering drugs into the UK or be used as a mule or courier throughout their destination country. Domestic national victims, often minors, are used in this way to transport drugs and weapons throughout one jurisdiction. The CPS guidance on Human Trafficking, Smuggling and Slavery guidance on running county lines cases gives the following guidance:

'Offending through "County Lines" is a national issue involving the exploitation of vulnerable children and adults by violent gang members in order to move and sell crack and heroin across the country, often associated with city-based organised crime gangs. The victims are often children, aged 14 to 17 years, who are groomed with money, gifts or through relationships and forced to carry out day to day dealing. Children as young as 11 years of age have been reported as being recruited. Violence is used against drug users to coerce them to become runners, enforce debts, and use their accommodation as an operating base.

Prosecutors are encouraged to consider all available charges when considering a prosecution in connection with County Lines offending, including the Modern Slavery Act in circumstances where there has been deliberate targeting, recruitment and significant exploitation of young and vulnerable people. Prosecutors should, however, be alert to the challenge of securing a conviction for a Modern Slavery Act offence.'

22 Commonly associated with those who have been forced into prostitution and charged with trafficking and controlling prostitution offences, victims are often involved in money laundering offences in these circumstances.

Immigration offences[23]	
Entry without leave	Immigration Act 1971, s 24
Obtaining leave by deception	Immigration Act 1971, s 24A
Facilitating unlawful immigration	Immigration Act 1971, s 25
Failure to produce immigration documents	Asylum and Immigration (Treatment of Claimants) Act 2004, s 2
Failure to comply with requirement to provide information required to obtain travel documents	Asylum and Immigration (Treatment of Claimants) Act 2004, s 35
Illegal working	Immigration Act 1971, s 24B
Offences of human trafficking, slavery and forced labour[24]	
Slavery	Modern Slavery Act 2015, s 1
Human trafficking	Modern Slavery Act 2015, s 2
Driving offences[25]	
Dangerous driving	Road Traffic Act 1988, s 2
Driving or being in charge when under the influence of drink or drugs	Road Traffic Act 1988, s 4
Using a vehicle in a dangerous condition	Road Traffic Act 1988, s 40A
Driving otherwise than in accordance with a licence	Road Traffic Act 1988, s 87
Driving while disqualified	Road Traffic Act 1988, s 103
Using vehicle without insurance	Road Traffic Act 1988, s 143
Forced and sham marriages[26]	
Forced marriage	Family Law Act 1996, s 63CA; Anti-Social Behaviour Crime and Policing Act 2014, s 121

---

23 Victims who are trafficked from outside the UK will frequently be charged with numerous immigration offences. If victims travel with an agent, they are likely to have possession of immigration documents for only a short period. Those who travel with legitimate documents commonly have their documents held by traffickers and then will over-stay visas or have their passports expire.

24 See fn 13.

25 European national victims are commonly trafficked to the UK for forced labour exploitation and frequently have car insurance policies and vehicles registered in their names and/or with fraudulent documents. They may also be forced to drive vehicles without proper driving licences or insurance, and will commit numerous road traffic offences as a result.

26 These offences commonly involve EU nationals trafficked to marry non-EU nationals in order for the latter to gain residency; traffickers usually obtain the payment for the marriage.

Sham marriages	Criminal Law Act 1977, s 1(1)
	Conspiracy to facilitate breach of immigration law.
	Immigration Act 1971, s 25(1)
	Assisting unlawful immigration (facilitation)

16 Ethics

16.1

Legal representatives acting for victims of modern slavery regularly encounter a plethora of professional ethics issues. Legal representatives have to act with considerable caution if they identify that their client is or may be a victim of human trafficking. At a minimum, the following factors need to be considered.

Whether to refer a client through the National Referral Mechanism

16.2

For a client accused of a criminal offence, exposing his traffickers may involve a significant risk, which will need a careful approach. Here the client's age is relevant, as consent will be required for the referral if the client is over 18 years old. Consent is not required for any client under the age of 18[1]. If the client's age is not clear, logically it must be appropriate to accept the client's instructions as to age, which may have to be re-visited with the client if an age assessment is undertaken and it is found that the client is an adult (see Chapter 3 for age assessments). A defence under the Modern Slavery Act ('MSA') 2015 does not require a National Referral Mechanism (NRM) referral, but the consequences of such a referral may provide evidence to support the defence and/or a review of any decision to prosecute[2]. Gathering such evidence may be particularly difficult for defence lawyers, particularly where it may exist by way of intelligence-based sources on the operation of a particular trafficking gang, so the balance will be in favour of referral[3].

How to advise a client in a police interview

16.3

Guidance issued by the National College of Policing after the implementation of the MSA 2015 is that

---

1 The NRM is a framework for identifying victims of human trafficking and ensuring they receive the appropriate protection and support. The NRM is also the mechanism through which the National Crime Agency (NCA) collects data about victims. This information aims to help build a clearer picture about the scope of human trafficking in the UK: see www.ecpat.org.uk/the-national-referral-mechanism, last accessed 17 December 2017.

2 See CPS guidance on human trafficking and people smuggling, available at www.cps.gov.uk/legal/h_ to_k/human_trafficking_and_smuggling/#a27, last accessed 17 December 2017.

3 See also Home Office, *Victims of modern slavery – Competent Authority guidance* (21 March 2016).

'if a person is arrested and so enters the criminal justice system as a perpetrator, and officers discover through the police interview under caution that the person committed a modern slavery offence through coercion and may also be a victim, the interview should continue and evidence should be obtained. On conclusion of the interview the person should be referred through the NRM if they consent'.

For further consideration of ethical issues at the police station stage, see Chapter 6.

16.4

The National College of Policing notes that the roles of victim, witness and suspect can be interchangeable in this context[4]. Legal representatives will also need to consider whether disclosure of coercion would affect the decision to charge, even if not an MSA 2015 allegation.

Privilege and confidentiality issues

16.5

It may be that the NRM referral and/or a defence statement made during the course of criminal proceedings[5] setting out details of the relevant trafficking will require the waiving of privilege[6]. This can be particularly complex where it involves a confession to a criminal offence, as the advice in relation to the referral or defence disclosure needs to be given in the context of advice on the criminal allegations and what evidence is available to prove the alleged offence or to raise a defence.

16.6

Victims of human trafficking and modern slavery do not always identify as such and do not make disclosures. They may often mistrust authorities and their legal representatives. It is also common that a client will have been coached by his traffickers to give a particular account. There may be circumstances where a client will display or make disclosures regarding exploitation. There are no specific

---

4   P Ahluwalia, 'Poacher Turned Gamekeeper' (2015) 3 *CBQ* 5.

5   For full details of the defence statement procedures see the Criminal Procedure and Investigations Act 1996, Pt 1 and Criminal Procedure Rules, r 22. In summary, in proceedings before the Crown Court, where the prosecutor has provided initial disclosure, or purported to, the accused *must* serve a defence statement on the prosecutor and the court. In the magistrates' court, the accused is not obliged to serve a defence statement but may choose to do so, in which case the Criminal Procedure and Investigations Act 1996 applies. In both, it is mandatory for the accused to provide the details of any witnesses to be relied on.

6   For a quick guide to privilege in English law, see Ashurst's overview of the principles governing the ability of a party to keep communications with its lawyer confidential under the English law of privilege. It reviews the main heads of privilege which can be claimed, how privilege can be lost, and how to ensure that communications that are privileged, stay privileged: www.ashurst.com/en/news-and-insights/legal-updates/privilege-quickguide/, last accessed 17 December 2017.

exceptions to the duty of confidentiality[7]. However, it is possible that where a child reveals information which indicates continuing sexual or other physical abuse, but refuses to allow such disclosure of information to an appropriate authority, a conflict may arise between the duty of confidentiality and the solicitor's ability to act with integrity (principle 2 of the SRA Handbook). Whether the solicitor's duties conflict will depend on how material the information in question is. It must be considered whether the threat to the child's life or health, both mental and physical, is sufficiently serious to justify a breach of the duty of confidentiality[8].

What to request by way of disclosure

16.7

Prosecution obligations on disclosure[9] go beyond the requirement to provide relevant unused material. They may intersect with issues surrounding public interest immunity and overlap in the context of financial investigations[10].

---

7   See Bar Standard Book CD2 and SRA Chs 4 and 3.

8   Law Society Practice Note, *Criminal prosecutions of victims of trafficking*, available at www.lawsociety.org.uk/support-services/advice/practice-notes/criminal-prosecutions-of-victims-of-trafficking/, last accessed 17 December 2017.

9   Attorney-General's Guidelines on Disclosure 2013, available at www.gov.uk/government/publications/attorney-generals-guidelines-on-disclosure-2013, last accessed 17 December 2017.

10 Disclosure Manual, available at www.cps.gov.uk/legal-guidance/disclosure-manual, last accessed 11 January 2018.

Index

N

Human Trafficking and Modern Slavery Law and Practice

The University of Law

The University of Law, Braboeuf Manor, Portsmouth Road, Guildford GU3 1HA
Telephone: 01483 216788   Email: library-guildford@law.ac.uk

Birmingham I Bristol I Chester I Guildford I Leeds I London I Manchester